W9-ADZ-971

Milton and the Grounds
of Contention

Medieval & Renaissance Literary Studies

Milton and the Grounds of Contention

edited by Mark R. **Kelley**
Michael **Lieb**
John T. **Shawcross**

Duquesne
University
Press
Pittsburgh, Pa.

Published in the United States of America by:

DUQUESNE UNIVERSITY PRESS
600 Forbes Avenue
Pittsburgh, Pennsylvania 15282

Library of Congress Cataloging-in-Publication Data

Milton and the grounds of contention / edited by Mark R. Kelley, Michael
Lieb, and John T. Shawcross.
    p. cm. — (Medieval & Renaissance literary studies)
Includes bibliographical references (p.) and index.
  ISBN 0-8207-0345-1 (alk. paper)
  1. Milton, John, 1608–1674—Criticism and interpretation. 2. Great
Britain—Intellectual life—17th century. I. Kelley, Mark R., 1961– II. Lieb,
Michael, 1940– III. Shawcross, John T. IV. Medieval and Renaissance
literary studies.
  PR3588.M476 2003
  821'.4—dc21

                                                            2003008561

∞ Printed on acid-free paper.

for Joseph Wittreich

Contents

Introduction

Mark R. Kelley, Michael Lieb and
John T. Shawcross

Critical approaches to literature in recent years have included
the significance of women writers and readers, and the
contemporary or near contemporary reception of an author
and her or his works. Implicit in such concerns is also an
awareness of an author's potential influence upon the thinking
and creative work of others. The literary world has finally
recognized that women writers contribute, and have contributed, as superior, meaningful and highly praiseworthy
poems, novels, dramas and belles lettres as their male counter-
parts. Gender may affect the creative result, but differences in
that result may be largely the differences that individuals
exhibit, regardless of gender. With the rise in the last few
decades of reader-response theory, it has also been finally
understood that women readers may experience responses to
a piece of literature that show differences from those of a male
audience. Most clearly people of varied life experiences —
racial, social, gendered, political, educational — will find in
the same literary work numerous varied reactions and readings.

The poem, the novel, the prose exposition is not self-contained, dominated by a view of its author writing. We have rejected the single interpretation of a literary work that former scholars have been more recently accused of proffering as well as the so-called "old historical" impingement on a literary work where delimitation to an event or issue only informs that work.

Nonetheless, we continue to encounter a ground of critical argument arising from the treatment and viability of women authors and feminine criticism. Joseph Wittreich is a major voice in recasting such issues concerning John Milton's works. His employment of the reception theory of Hans Robert Jauss has led us well beyond the simplistic epitomes of the past. It is incumbent upon a reader-critic to examine any literary work within its period of production, the political and social attitudes of its world and, in turn, its telling influence on any future looked at from that future's contemporaneity. Gender and contemporaneity (of the work and of its period of influence) set up a political climate for literature and its significance and for its reading at any specific point in time.

Grounds of contention for a readership of Milton's works abound in these statements. The issue of influence, its nature and importance, its relationship with and upon the political and social worlds that postdate a work's publication are all matters that admit of many interpretations, many "facts" (some conflicting), many evaluations. The issue of the place of women in the political and interpretive world seems not to have disappeared. The importance of this dimension in literature or of that pulse of the people upon the work itself, particularly in the frequent daily political, religious and social shiftings of the seventeenth century, has not been given the full and close attention it deserves.

The world out of which an author writes is of great significance, yet past criticism has often taken a path of either arguing for one interpretation on the basis of a historical element (at least this has been the accusation leveled by some more recent commentators) or ignoring that world, and particularly ignoring the author, to present an interpretation limited to an isolated, disembodied literary work. While so-called "new historical" approaches have at times left the literature itself behind, they have also made unavoidable the recognition that a literary work offers "power" in political, sociological and philosophical arenas. Such "power" is within the work and of the work in its effect upon its reading audience, contemporaneously and afterward. All of these avenues for reading and interpretation create a dynamic literature that can no longer be viewed as singular or only personal. To recognize that a piece of literature is not a fixed commodity with no ambiguities about it at all and with *only* an aesthetic experience is the welcome inheritance from the last half of the twentieth century. "Grounds of contention" arise clearly within these remarks, implying argument and counter-argument. These are pursued in the ten essays presented here which focus on John Milton, his poetry and his prose, his world and that which ensued and which reflects his continuing presence.

These issues — involving our reading of the works, Milton's position in the world of gender studies and politics, his artistic and ideational influence, and his own theological beliefs — have whirled around in recent literary criticism to yield both praise and scorn and much uncertainty. These issues and their relationships to Milton, and we say this approvingly, will not disappear, for they evoke additional knowledge, reinterpretation, revaluation. What we encounter are grounds of contention where these issues are interrogated by different, opposed critical positions. Such debate combats received critical commonplaces and leads to new awarenesses and interpretations, and perhaps shows the error or at least inadequacy of those commonplaces. *Paradise Lost, Samson Agonistes* and *De doctrina Christiana* have especially been sites of conflict. The chapters of this book, we trust, will contribute meaningfully to an understanding of these issues, and to changes in their substance. The discussions challenge any complacency in the state of Milton studies and aim at further interrogation of these contentions. Accordingly, this book's ten chapters fall into three divisions: four essays setting forth Milton's influence upon certain authors, particularly neglected women authors, in the late seventeenth century and the eighteenth century, with the political and ideational reverberations that arise from the later writers' work and, most importantly, from that of a specific later writer's preeminence as a political figure in England, America and the Continent; three essays offering readings of *Paradise Lost* and *Samson Agonistes* that get beyond the poetic surface by examining a philosophic context, the substruct of feminine concerns that direct us to reexamine these poems with some surprising results, and the significance of choice, not only within the poem but within the reader; and three essays dealing with issues of theology and belief, contributing to our understanding of some of the uncertainties of Milton's religious positions that commentators have raised in his writings. These chapters aim at setting up "grounds" which provide means of "exercise" of "triall by contrary" to deal with the "contentions" that have come to dominate Miltonic scholarship.

Numerous seventeenth and eighteenth century British and American women poets are brought into the Miltonic circle of influence by John Shawcross, David Norbrook and Sharon Achinstein. The eighteenth century seems to have been of two minds about Milton and his poetry, as one can easily observe in Samuel Johnson's praise and strictures in his "Life of John Milton." Shawcross looks at such questions as blank verse and the subgenre sonnet as points engaging the deleterious evaluations, and the counterstatements and emulating examples to suggest Milton's exaltation. The sublimity of *Paradise Lost* that perhaps is cited too often without delineation and too often as cliché is (usually at the same time) opposed by those who detect "faults" or "blemishes" in the language, in the structure and subject matter, in the breaking of "rules," in the intrusion of the author into his text. But one of the most unacceptable circumstances for us today is the ignoring of and the dismissal of women poets during the century as inferior. For Horace Walpole, a major figure in the advancement of Milton as author and influence, Ann Yearsley should quit blank verse because "Her expressions are more exalted than poetic," and he seems to place her among those who, either imitating or not imitating Milton, are "mere monkeys" or "flat and poor." Although one hopes that such unenlightened attitudes have disappeared, "feminist Milton" remains a point of contention in literary criticism.

Proposing the author of *Order and Disorder* (1664?, 1679) to be the republican and important writer Lucy Hutchinson, Norbrook examines this poem which clearly is indebted to *Paradise Lost* and analyzes its "striking convergence in theme and poetic strategy." The reassignment of the poem to a woman, rather than to her brother Sir Allen Apsley, whose candidacy was emboldened by the assumption that only a man would have written it, hits strongly at one of the key tenets that *Feminist Milton* aimed at upsetting. "On questions of gender, as in so many other areas, Milton and Hutchinson share a common ideological perspective," Norbrook writes, "though with important differences of emphasis." The poem itself, a hexaemeral epic with a mingling of biblical and classical conventions, deserves attention from readers, not only as a literary artifact and for its religious substance, but for its political tenor as Dissenters become "saints" and Charles II is identified with the "tyrant."

The devotional poet and prose writer, and friend and follower of Isaac Watts, Elizabeth Singer Rowe has generally been passed over and is little known except to those stressing her religious vehicles. Achinstein disagrees with those who have viewed Rowe's religious themes as a way out of women writers' disenfranchisement and a means of controlling "her unruly imagination." Quite on the contrary, Rowe is not only influenced by Milton's style in her poetry, she partakes of its "radical, dissenting literary tradition," singing "repeatedly of the liberty of the English people, the self-restraint and valor of their leaders," and praising "the violence of military success . . . in a moral and political campaign against the decadence and irreligion of the times." Rowe offers an empiricist poetics, Achinstein contends, that reveals theological truths: for her "Milton is the inspired poet, authorized by divine (not literary-traditional) authority." Rowe is not so much a "feminist" advocate as an important woman writer for whom Milton is an important influence and who should be acknowledged in her own right as a poet.

Edmund Burke, an admirer of Milton, has often been cited as a defender of the American Revolution but "inconsistently" an attacker of the French Revolution less than two decades later. The privileging of *Reflections on the Revolution in France* (1790) for an epitome of Burke's liberal and conservative thinking over *On Conciliation with the Colonies* (1774, 1775), the source of this view of Burke, is challenged by Annabel Patterson. The "myth" of the destruction of "beauty, order, and custom to no good purpose" should not obliterate the "myth" of "his emotionally powerful philosophy of empire" that is revealed in Burke's employment of allusions to *Paradise Lost* and *Paradise Regain'd,* perhaps most notably in the vision of the future which blends a satanic vision of "material wealth and nationalism conceived as expansionism" with an angelic vision of the hard life facing the inhabitants of the new world before them. The trajectory from Burke's ironic employment of Milton to suggest that the House of Commons was "in danger of assuming the posture of the fallen angels" to a rejection of the action of the people of France is detailed, with the upshot being a Burke of less heroic stance than some have seen. While much points toward the significance of Patterson's contention for a postcolonial reading of the last quarter of a century of American history, what she offers is a different reading of Burke's attitudes and thinking through an analysis of his employment of Milton in his arguments, not simply a statement of Milton's influence.

The second and third groupings of essays iterate two points that Wittreich has made: Milton's poetry does not eschew heterodox, esoteric and peripheral traditions and his scriptural interpretation demands acknowledgment of the difference between biblical and literary hermeneutics.[1] More than a poem of praise (as an epic is), *Paradise Lost* acknowledges God's originary power through the thematization of gratitude, a topic set forth arrestingly by Saint Thomas Aquinas. As Peter Medine manifests, gratitude and its unfortunate opposite inform the characterizations of Adam and Eve in their prelapsarian world and delineate the postlapsarian world they inaugurate. Ingratitude — we remember the Father's charge of "Ingrate" in book 3, line 97 — is fundamental to the depiction of the fallen state, whether angelic or human, and gratitude, to the unfallen state. As Medine writes, "Gratitude may well be the most difficult of the virtues," but it becomes, despite its inattention by former critics, a key to a fuller reading of this complex poem and its complex cast of personages. Likewise, a key to underlying issues in the poem is the legal concept of the *feme covert* that domestic life wrestled with (and still wrestles with despite some advances in gender issues) as Lynne Greenberg demonstrates in a study that involves contemporary legal opinions, particularly those concerning land ownership and transfer, and prejudice against the female. "The poem," she argues, "'rejects the Adam myth' as forcefully as it re-tells the myth, or, alternatively, it incorporates an 'Eve myth' alongside the 'Adam myth.'" Milton's position on gendered questions is not, Greenberg shows decisively, either the patriarchal one usually alleged (rather it "conflicts with patriarchy") or the frequent feminist denigration of Milton when Eve is discussed. The imagery and "message" of enclosure and boundary, in the poem and in "all that rests beyond its idyllic bounds," demand a new reading and understanding of Milton's epic. In discussing "choice" and "election," Susanne Woods inter-relates *A Mask* (*Comus*) and *Samson Agonistes* to establish the significance of Milton's "approach to enacting his own beliefs about human liberty and individual choice." While the Lady in the earlier poem lacks agency, Samson reasserts the ubiquitous question of knowledge and election, leading, because of agency, to choices and to freedom through choice. He learns that he can act freely and make the right choice when the call comes. The dramatic poem remains Milton's most indeterminate work, and in that offers "an invitation to the reader to make choices" about responsibility and freedom. The issues that Greenberg and Woods present and their "resolutions" will continue to create contentions in Milton scholarship as readers make choices.

The first of the last three chapters — each of which look at an issue that sets up opposed critical camps — John Rogers's examination of circumcision, provoked ostensibly by Milton's ode, views the poem as pivotal in Milton's theological develop-ment and as a kind of indicator of the origins of early liberal theology in England, specifically anti-Trinitarian movements. The acceptance of Atonement in the Passion and Crucifixion of Jesus, and the orthodox Trinitarian concept that underlies that acceptance, are challenged within the poem and, Rogers argues, in Milton's failure to pursue the subject of Jesus' final days. Thus Milton joins those opposed to substitutive corporal punishment and evidences in the poem an early rejection of an Abrahamic atonement. The incompatible connotations of the significance of circumcision that swirled around Western culture recall Paul's view of the "profit" of circumcision as "self-generated," not some "reward" conferred through Christ. "Even in the mature works of political philosophy," Rogers contends, "Milton would never fully disentangle his political sense of the individual's right to act from his theological sense of the individual's agency in his own salvation."

The ongoing debate over the authorship of *De doctrina Christiana* and thus its significance in reading and understanding Milton's theological precepts are the subjects of John Rumrich's contribution. He summarizes the basic stances of commentators and the basic issues, like the nature of Chaos, that fuel the discussions. A major issue is the Christology of the treatise and of *Paradise Lost*, and thus Rumrich turns his attention to the stylometric analysis that has been offered to help resolve the question of authorship. He faults that analysis because of the discrepancy in the epistemological conditions of the works involved, the lack of consideration of the respective goals set for the statistical methodology, and the vulnerability of its anachronistic premise. The inability of stylometrics to register contextual import or intentionality denies its meaningfulness in such a case as *De doctrina Christiana*, and the author's extraordinary dependence on and synthesis of Scripture cannot be dismissed, for the use of Scripture is distinctive though the words are obviously not the author's. The acceptance of Miltonic authorship for part of the treatise by those who have questioned its authorship and the nature of texts in the seventeenth century drawn from prior sources (such as Milton's *Artis Logicae Plenior Institutio*) lead Rumrich to conclude that "Milton may be confidently identified as the author of *De doctrina Christiana*."

Part of the difficulty in accepting Milton's authorship of the treatise and in interpreting *Paradise Lost* has been the assignment of the heresy of Arianism to those works and that of the linked heresy of Socinianism. Michael Lieb, in an extensive review of the latter belief — its origins, its further development in the seventeenth century, and its appearances in the eighteenth century — concludes that Milton was not a Socinian. The references to Milton as an adherent of this heresy appear before *De doctrina Christiana* was discovered in 1823 and emboldened by that work's appearance when Unitarianism was dominant. Though Milton may have "accepted 'this aspect,' as opposed to 'that aspect,' of Socinianism," what matters "is that the Socinian heresy was a crucial movement in his own time and that he responded to it at various points in his career."

All of the above issues that have been raised proffer strengths for the reading of Milton's works. While some commentators will offer interpretations as if closure of some ground of contention is possible, others will build on the radicalism of a tract like *Areopagitica* and demonstrate Wittreich's further analysis of "Milton's Transgressive Maneuvers" in *Milton and Heresy*. The dismissal of Milton's "liberalism," which has been cast aside by some with an accompanying statement of "closure," has been challenged by others who see critical differences and uncertainties in Milton's work and thought as vigorous and unexhausted. We dedicate this book to Joseph Wittreich in recognition of and in thankful appreciation for his penetrating studies of John Milton's life and works, and their afterlife. The "mental reverberations"[2] through which we recognize Milton's poetry and prose, his thinking and his achievements, in others' writing and beliefs, show the continuing consequence of Milton's life as the twenty-first century revaluates political and religious trends, discovers the worth of women writers and nonmainstream male writers, and revisits arguments for independence of thought and what should be humankind's advancement in social and civic worlds. Wittreich's critical studies pursue contentions that upset the inherited commonplaces of the past. His interrogation of the political world of *Paradise Lost* establishes it as a continuing site of conflict; his contention of a negative Samson, both biblically and contemporaneously, reverses the easy acceptance of a dramatic poem written by a disillusioned idealist in old age. A list of Wittreich's selected publications is appended. He, like Milton, has written much that "aftertimes" will "not willingly let die."

1 • The Deleterious and the Exalted

Milton's Poetry in the
Eighteenth Century

John T. Shawcross

Lying between the "Restoration" period of the last 40 years of the seventeenth century and the 1800 and 1802 pronouncements by William Wordsworth and Samuel Taylor Coleridge in *Lyrical Ballads*, the eighteenth century experienced a number of conflicting attitudes toward poetry and poets, reflecting the differences of opinion toward prosody and subject matter and treatment in the earlier years but also the "new" so-called Romantic principles of poetry. In our critical past a problem in describing and evaluating the literature of that period was the dominance of Samuel Johnson and his circle. His likes and dislikes, his ignoring of much literature of his day and particularly that of women writers, his strong political and religious beliefs color what was thought to be an adequate poetic history of the period.[1] Indeed, we still hear statements that the sonnet had to be reintroduced by the Romantics, that Milton's sonnets were at "best" "not bad" (for Johnson "only the eighth and the twenty-first are truly entitled to this slender commendation"), and that "The fabrick of a sonnet . . . has never succeeded in [our language]."[2] Toward the end of the century Henry White was to enunciate what "the sonnet should be," and classify four of Milton's 18 sonnets as "bad" (he does not say which and he apparently is not counting the Italian sonnets in the 18); he praises *Sonnet 8* and *Sonnet 20*, although some others are "not all free from certain hardnesses."[3] But we have made advances and even William Blake has now long been accepted by both eighteenth century scholars and Romantic specialists who used to exile him to the other group.

It should be needless to say today that there was much sonneteering during the period; that Milton's influence is easily observable in much of it; and that many, or perhaps most, of these eighteenth century sonnets are better than "not bad." Sir Richard Steele published "To Aristus, In Imitation of a Sonnet of Milton" (that is, *Sonnet 9*) in *Poetical Miscellanies*, dated December 1713, but the poem is not a sonnet; it is anonymous and other verse in this collection significantly enough includes poems by Alexander Pope, Thomas Parnell and Laurence Eusden. Alexander Pope's "Sonnet in a Glass at Chalfont in Bucks," ascribed to Milton, was a hoax (also allegedly with Lord Chesterfield's help) to fool Jonathan Richardson, who fell into the trap. (Its varying title replaces "glass" with "window," or, for a couple of examples, it is given as "Written upon occasion of the Plague, and found on a Glass-Window at Chalfont," "A Sonnet upon occasion of the plague in London, lately found on a glass window at Chalfont, where Milton resided during the continuance of that calamity.") Published by Thomas Birch in his *Complete Collection* (1738), the poem had been included in a letter from Pope to Richardson, dated July 18, 1737, and he communicated it to Birch.

A letter from George Vertue to Robert Harley, Earl of Oxford, dated February 24, 1737/38, records that Richardson was embarrassed and is awaiting another printing omitting the sonnet. It was often reprinted as Milton's even up to 1784 in an edition of Samuel Johnson's *The Works of the English Poets.*[4]

An anonymous "Sonnet. In Imitation of Milton's Sonnets," appearing in *London Magazine* in 1738, is only the first of many imitative sonnets.[5] Dustin Griffin's comment (257 n. 101) perhaps needs some reconsideration. He writes, "Indeed, his sonnets were relatively unavailable and unknown in the late seventeenth century. . . . the form was revived after 1750." Sonnets 1–10 were available in the 1645, 1673, 1695 and numerous 1705 and onward editions of the "Poems"; sonnets 11–23 (less four) were available in the 1673, 1695 and 1705 and onward editions; and numbers 15, 16, 17 and 22 entered Tonson's publications in 1713 onward. Thus, the sonnets were as available as the companion poems whose influence emerges frequently.[6] Likewise there was some sonneteering associated with Milton undertaken in addition to that noted above, prior to 1750: John Hoadly, "To Mrs. Bowes with y^e *force of Truth, an Oratorio. Sonnet in imitation of Milton,*" dated October 30, 1743; two sonnets by Charles Yorke, both entitled, "Sonnet in Imitation of Milton," dated March 4, 1743, and May 25, 1743; and anonymous, "Hope. A Sonnet. Written in the Stile of Milton" (1747) (see also Havens, *The Influence of Milton*, 685–86, 696). Even a collection of sonnets appears before 1750. Thomas Edwards's 14 sonnets, the thirteenth with an allusion (336), were printed by Robert Dodsley in *A Collection of Poems in Three Volumes*; these and more than 30 additional "Miltonic" sonnets were published in Edwards's *The Canons of Criticism, and Glossary* with allusions in Sonnets 17, 32, and 45.[7]

The point I make is that as we examine more literature of the period, without the narrowness that the past has exerted to ignore those who do not follow the "rules" or who do not

belong to some "desirable" social and intellectual stratifica-
tion, we find more examples of subgenres and Miltonic
influences than the past had observed.[8] Griffin especially
extends our knowledge of genres and themes during the period,
and George W. Sherburn demonstrated "The Early Popularity
of Milton's Minor Poems" in 1919–20, in contradiction of a
previous commonplace and thus implied that there might be
more popularity than even he had discovered.[9] Yet in 1922
Havens, noting at least ten editions of the complete poems
(plus the editions of 1645 and 1673),[10] commented, in his
important and groundbreaking work, "It is not strange, therefore, that in the period of approximately a century between
their publication and 1742 the total number of pieces thus far
discovered which show any influence from the various minor
poems [a footnote acknowledges 'To Aristus' and a sonnet by
Philip Yorke], except in borrowed phrases, is only forty-two,
and that of these only two, Parnell's *Hymn on Contentment*
and Dyer's *Grongar Hill*, were generally known or of much
importance" (420).[11] Havens went through a great number of
texts and collections and periodicals, yet my research just up
to 1701 has turned up 12 more not cited by Havens or Griffin,
and I have no doubt that more items will be discovered in
time (see appendix). (Six show influence from *Lycidas*, four
from *Comus*, two from the companion poems, and one from
the *Fifth Ode*; the Congreve poem shows double influence.)

Aside from the seventeenth century poems reprinted in the
eighteenth century, which are noted in the appendix, two other
early century poems should be mentioned (thus yielding 14
more poems). Havens lists James Ward's "Phoenix-Park" as one
of the "Loco-Descriptive Poems Not Known to be Miltonic"
(268), perhaps because it is in heroic couplets (see his note 1).
It is not an "imitation." However, the poem decidedly shows
influence from *L'Allegro*, *Il Penseroso* and *Comus*; it was first
published in *Miscellany of Poems* (1718). Havens cites it from
Matthew Concanen's collection *Miscellaneous Poems*, with

a remark that it was published before 1723. And, secondly, he infers that William Walsh ignored *Lycidas* from Walsh's letter to Alexander Pope in 1706, "I am sure there is nothing of this kind [the pastoral] in English worth mentioning."[12] He has misunderstood the reference. The letter from June 24, 1706, written in answer to an undiscovered letter from Pope, goes on to say, "and therefore you have that field open to yourself," the "field" being "Pastoral Comedy," "Pastoral Plays" as his letter makes clear and as is corroborated by Pope's answer on July 2, 1706 (1:18–20). (Continuing letters extend the pastoral genres.) As I have already indicated, three of his own pastoral eclogues are indebted to *Lycidas*, and he had read Pope's "Pastorals" with "great satisfaction" through the kindness of William Wycherley (see Walsh's letter of April 20 to Wycherley, 1:7). Further, as Wittreich has shown ("Under the Seal of Silence," 298–99), Walsh was strongly influenced by that poem in yet another pastoral eclogue, indeed, a *pastoral elegy*, "Delia: A Pastoral Eclogue; Lamenting the Death of Mrs. Tempest, Who dy'd upon the Day of the Late Storm." "Delia" is dated November 26, 1703, three years before Walsh's letter to Pope.[13] I assume that some of the foregoing poems would not be cast as very good poetry, and perhaps one reason would be chalked up to close Miltonic imitation (Mason's twin poems are so evaluated by Havens); I also assume that some of them — like Pomfret's "The Choice" or Dryden's ode on Purcell or Walsh's "Delia" — are deserving of a place in the literary history of the period and its readers.

"Influence," of course, can be variously interpreted, and Havens has not included poems with only allusions or borrowed phrases, although one might argue that in the background, at least, is the author and work cited. It is difficult to discount "influence," it seems to me, for such seventeenth century authors as Edward Benlowes or Andrew Marvell, even though their poems are not "imitations." In Benlowes's *Theophilia* there are appropriations from the Nativity ode, *L'Allegro*,

Il Penseroso, Comus and *Lycidas*, in at least six specific places. Marvell appropriates lines from the Nativity ode and *Lycidas* in *The First Anniversary of the Government* and from those poems and *Il Penseroso* at least in "The Garden," "Fleckno, an English Priest at Rome," "Upon Appleton House, to my Lord Fairfax" and "A Poem upon the Death of O. C."[14] Do we not have to include such authors and such poems in our appraisal of Milton's effect, and its deleteriousness or its positive worth?

With the revised critical attitudes that have created "canon-busting" and the discovery that there were praiseworthy women writers (although there has been a much less significant discovery of male writers as many of the "new" authors and poems that I have already cited evidence), those Johnsonesque evaluations that used to prevail have fallen away and a whole "new" group of writings and writers has emerged to yield a much more valid picture of the literary milieu of the century and a half. And rather than the old assumptions that all of a sudden a new vitality burst upon the scene in the 1790s and that whichever pre-Romantics had been acknowledged were rather few and infrequent, we have learned that much was going on in conflict with the "line of wit," as F. R. Leavis termed it, and in conflict with a coterie of aristocratic men. A "line of vision" and poets from the middle or even lower middle class and notably poetic women existed as well. Havens' work instructed us significantly in the wide extent of Milton's influence on the literature of the period, and Griffin has provided discussion of both influence and less influence than we might have thought (for example, in the pastoral as a form and subject). Yet I think there are more pieces of evidence that we must consider to grasp the literary milieu more fully, and they lie in the writing of some of the women poets and the "lesser" men who have generally been unknown.

In this essay I shall again look at blank verse and the eighteenth century's penchant for asserting "rules" over art and thus finding defects, and at Milton's sublimity, paying attention to some who were not part of the right "coterie."

Blank Verse

Thomas Rymer damned Milton's blank verse and promised an examination of it, which Thomas Shipman, in agreement with the deleteriousness of such lack of form, awaited, but the discussion never appeared.[15] Throughout the following years negative criticism emerged, but also positive reactions and much imitation (a good deal of it poor imitation). John Philips's "In Imitation of Milton," meaning that it is written in blank verse, made its first appearance twice in 1701.[16] Its reprinting is very frequent throughout the century, acquiring its more well-known title in *The Splendid Shilling. An Imitation of Milton. Now First Correctly Publish'd* (1705). For Addison it is "Milton's Stile Imitated"; by 1712 it is "Miltonic verse"; and by 1716 "Miltonian Verse."[17] Meaning blank verse, other phrases are used as in *The Last Judgment of Men and Angels. A Poem, in Twelve Books: After the Manner of Milton* (1723), by Thomas Newcomb, and in "Miltonick Numbers," probably by Aaron Hill.[18] It becomes a simple substantive in *Lucifer's Defeat; or, The Mantle-Chimney. A Miltonic*; in "A Miltonick on Life, Death, Judgment, Heaven, and Hell"; and in Samuel Wesley Jr.'s "The Dog. A Miltonick Fragment," "The Descriptive: A Miltonick. After the Manner of the Moderns," and "Epigram on the foregoing Miltonicks."[19]

A poem not cited before in Milton scholarship, to my knowledge, makes specific reference to its own prosody and is written in blank verse, which evinces Milton's influence even before the fourth edition of *Paradise Lost* in 1688. That edition, as generally stated in the eighteenth century and today, helped create an audience for the poem.[20] Nehemiah Walter's "An Elegiack Verse, On the Death Of the Pious and Profound Grammarian and Rhetorician Mr. Elijah Corlet, Schoolmaster

of Cambridge, Who Deceased Annot Ætatis 77. Feb. 24, 1687"
begins:

> On *Roman* Feet my stumbling *Muse* declines
> To walk unto his Grave, lest by her Fall
> She trespass, in accosting of his Head
> With undeserved breach. In jingling *Rythme*
> She thinks it not convenient to Dance
> Upon his Sacred Herse; but *mournful* Steps
> If Metrically order'd, she computes
> The most becoming of this Tragick Scene.[21]

Milton had written of "jingling sound of like endings" in "The
Verse" prefacing the epic (second 1668 issue, fourth issue of
poem), apparently in rebuttal of such reactions as that
expressed by Rymer a few years later and in argument with
John Dryden in *Essay of Dramatick Poesie* (1668), who
championed rhyme. But further — and this, if within Walter's
knowledge, is extremely significant — we should remember
the beginning of Milton's poem to Giovanni Salzilli, who,
when Milton wrote it in 1638, was gravely ill:

> O Musa gressum quæ volens trahis claudum,
> Vulcanioque tarda gaudes incessu,
> Nec sentis illud in loco minus gratum,
> Quàm cùm decentes flava Dëiope suras
> Alternat aureum ante Junonis lectum.[22]

Walter rejects Latin verse with the same punning on feet, hence
"steps" and "gait," which would stumble when he would want
it to dance. The elegy is written in blank verse with strong
enjambement, attesting to a reading of Milton, an imitation
of Milton and an approval of the verse form. This contrasts
sharply with Samuel Wesley Sr. in *The Life of Our Blessed
Lord & Saviour Jesus Christ. An Heroic Poem* (1693), who
disavows blank verse in the preface but who throughout the
poem and its notes appropriates from Milton's epic and

acknowledges his debt to Milton often (although not without omission). Not only is *Paradise Lost* in the background but also *Paradise Regain'd*, another blank verse poem, and *Il Penseroso*. Walter's serious poem, of course, predates Philips's well-known parody by some ten years, and Wesley's religious verses by six.[23]

Another author who seems to have been ignored by scholarship was William Bowman, whose *Poems on Several Occasions* (1727) includes "Night. An Imitation of Milton" as well as "Part of the 7th Chapter of Job Paraphrased. An Imitation of Milton's Stile." Both are in blank verse with numerous echoes in diction and language from *Paradise Lost*, and "Night" is likewise an imitation in content of *Il Penseroso*. In the same year appeared *The Altar of Love. Consisting of Poems, and Other Miscellanies. By the Most Eminent Hands*, which includes these two poems as well as "An Imitation of Mr. John Philips's Splendid Shilling" (53–59), which naturally is thus imitative of Milton's versification.[24] Here, then, is just one piece of evidence from a plethora of examples that Milton's blank verse was influential for comic poems, serious poems, and religious poems, including translations / paraphrases, among poets whose presence — whether we rate their work high or low — should be engaged in any attempt at describing the literary times.

But too often "blank verse" was only ten-foot unrhymed lines, and detractors of Milton made the ineptness of such writing clear. In *A Letter of Advice to a Young Poet*, Jonathan Swift (at least the work was printed as his) spoke of the deleterious effect Milton had on young poets.[25] The author reviews *Paradise Lost* and says much about blank verse and rhyme; he does not censure the epic or Milton's blank verse, but makes clear that the inexperienced harm their poetic endeavors by simply circumventing rhyme. Joseph Spence has a similar tale in his *Essay on Pope's Odyssey*.[26] Voltaire's opinion that Milton was unable to rhyme ("not that he would not, he could not") and therefore produced blank verse has been repeated by detractors and rebutters recognizing Voltaire's lack of knowledge of Milton's early verse.[27] On the other hand, William Coward tells his reader of the advantage of blank verse;[28] but Coward's "True Test of Poetry. Without which it is impossible to judge of, or compose, a correct English poem," as his title page has it, "To which are added, Critical Observations on the Principal, Ancient and Modern Poets, viz. Homer, Horace, Virgil, Milton, Waller, Cowley, Dryden, &c. as Frequently Liable to Just Censure," is typical of the eighteenth century doctrine of "correctness" and the critic's boast of superior ability to know what is good and what is bad. Perhaps an epitome of the situation for Milton is a comment on a different verse form and prosody: "Milton has left us a few songs, which would have appeared to possess more merit if they had fallen from an author of less dignity."[29]

A most distressing evaluation by Horace Walpole of Anne Yearsley blares out attitudes toward blank verse, concepts behind "faults" and thus "correctness," the snobbishness of the aristocratic and "learned," and, it would appear, the negative attitude toward women authors. In a letter to Hannah More, dated November 13, 1784, that has been cited often in recent "feminist" criticism, Walpole writes, "Her expressions are more exalted than poetic; and discover taste, as you say, rather than discover flights of fancy, and wild ideas, as one would expect."[30] The opaqueness of the comment and its lack of full poetic appreciation, it seems to me, epitomizes what is considered of lesser worth in poetry: while Walpole has some remarks that seem to offer positive reaction to Yearsley's work, he basically is saying that she is an inferior versifier. One problem, I think undoubtedly, is her writing the language of ordinary people, a hope of Wordsworth in something like "Michael": the "classical" and the "romantic" are already at loggerheads. He continues, "I should therefore advise her quitting blank verse, which wants the highest colouring to distinguish it from prose; whereas her taste, and probably good sense, might give sufficient beauty to her rhyme." There's a lot of prejudiced implication in that word "sufficient"! "I do not understand," he admits, quoting "Night" (95–96), "the Muse / Has bid me fix on plans *Where learning dies*," which immediately leads to, "Her not being learned, is another reason against her writing in blank verse. Milton employed all his reading, nay all his geographic knowledge, to enrich his language — and succeeded; they who have imitated him in that particular, have been mere monkeys; and they who neglect it, flat and poor." Certainly *mere* imitation, whether of Milton or of Pope or of Shakespeare, would not be evaluated highly, but some attention, he counsels, is commendatory. Yet perhaps he is being too easily led by Yearsley's being the "Bristol Milkmaid" and by her reported lack of extensive reading; her lines do not say she is not "learned." What her lines mean (W. S. Lewis in his edition of the letter notes that the lines were altered, perhaps because of Walpole's remark) is poetry like "Clifton Hill," which presents "incidents and situations from common life," not from "learning."

Walpole does recognize significance in her writing and so offers advice, but his frame of mind is appallingly clear by his original language: "Were I not persuaded by the samples you have sent me, Madam, that this good thing has real talents, I should not advise her encouraging her propensity lest it should divert her from the care of her family, and after the novelty is over, leave her worse than she was." "This good thing has real talents" is changed in manuscript to "this woman has talents" — but we can hardly respect such demeaning language. For Walpole she as woman should care for her family, and this poetry writing is merely a lark, merely an idle hope. She is a "Lactilla," not a "Pastora." That he goes on to offer Stephen Duck as another example underscores his stance: Duck, known as the "Thresher Poet" for his "The Thresher's Labour" (1736), was a farm laborer in his native Wiltshire, self-educated, and yet a follower of Milton as his translation of "Ad Salsillum" (apparently he learned Latin) and other poems indicate. That Walpole then offers More herself as example is rather shocking: "poetry is one of your least excellencies, Madam — your virtues will forgive me."

Milton's Blemishes

The deleteriousness in Milton's work appears not only in its verse form and genre. Joseph Addison enumerated Milton's "several Defects" and "blemishes" in *Paradise Lost* despite the praise alongside such comments. He accounts "The first Imperfection . . . that the Event of it is unhappy," and "this Kind of Fable ["the Implex Fable"], which is the most perfect in Tragedy, is not so proper for an Heroick Poem." Similar is a second imperfection, "the Hero . . . is unsuccessful, and by no Means a Match for his Enemies."[31] Other faults involve its fable, its authorial digressions (even though "there is so great a Beauty in these very Digressions that I would not wish them out of his Poem"), the puns, the "blemish" of allusion to *heathen* fables, the ostentation of learning and the labored language, a jingling in his lines (for example, "This *tempted* our *Attempt*") and technical words. Can one really answer such concepts of "correctness," or of religious antagonism, or just plain inadequate reading?

The case of Richard Bentley's revisions in his 1732 edition of the epic has been discussed often. Its most distressing aspect, I think, is the fact that a number of people for so long before had tried to deter Bentley, who was attempting to regain approval after the significance of his important textual work on Philaras, Horace and Manilius had waned, and after his administrative difficulties at Trinity College, Cambridge. There were immediate rebuttals of his arguments and readings (see Griffin, *passim*, for discussion and a number of examples). But it should be noted that a separate text of corrections and emendations (but not the annotations) was printed, seriatim, in two editions, as *Dr. Bentley's Corrections and Emendations on the Twelve Books of Milton's Paradise Lost. For the Benefit of those who are possess'd of the former Editions* (1732). The "learned" readers seem to have relished these kinds of deflations (and we have the fiasco of William Lauder's plagiarisms in the next decade to gasp at). In "Essay IV: On the Faults of Shakespeare," for instance, William Richardson contrasts those faults with the merits of Milton's companion poems.[32]

Other fault-finders (and Johnson was among them) are answered by Joseph Warton in a letter to Johnson's *The Adventurer* two decades before Johnson's negativities in his "Life of Milton."[33] Warton observes that "we cannot wonder at the multitude of commentaries and criticisms of which he has been the subject," but he also expresses some less than glowing evaluations. He finds "The glaring picture of Paradise . . . not, in my opinion, . . . strong . . . evidence of Milton's force of imagination"; "Against his battle of the angels I have the same objections as against his garden of Eden." However, the nub of his letter is, "I think the sublimity of his genius much more visible in the first appearance of the fallen angels; the debates of the infernal peers; the passage of Satan through the dominions of Chaos, and his adventure with Sin and Death," continuing with six further examples, and discussing some of those. He finds "Innumerable beauties in the *Paradise Lost* . . . yet Mr. Addison has passed it over [Satan's speech at the beginning of book 9], unpraised and unnoticed." He concludes his discussion "in the words of Longinus: 'Whoever was carefully to collect the blemishes of Homer, Demosthenes, Plato, and of other celebrated writers, of the same rank, would find they bore not the least proportion to the sublimities and excellences with which their works abound.'" But Shakespeare and Milton were not the only ones treated with scorn as a woman poet of the lower class, Janet Little, points out in a

poem published in 1792.[34] "Given to a Lady Who Asked Me
to Write a Poem" begins:

> Swift, Thomson, Addison, an' Young
> Made Pindus echo to their tongue,
> In hopes to please a learned age;
> But Doctor Johnston, in a rage,
> Unto posterity did shew
> Their blunders great, their beauties few.
> But now he's dead, we well may ken;
> For ilka dunce maun hae a pen,
> To write in hamely, uncouth rhymes;
> An' yet forsooth they please the times.

(We remark her deliberate dialectic Scots alongside the
"learned" reference to Pindus!) She continues with reference
to herself and her socially inferior status and with the
trepidation she *says* she fears for her attempts as poetic
expression:

> But then a rustic country quean
> To write — was e'er the like o't seen?
> A Milkmaid poem-books to print;
> Mair fit she wad her dairy tent; . . .
> Does she, poor silly thing, pretend
> The manners of our age to mend?
> Mad as we are, we're wise enough
> Still to despise sic paultry stuff.

The satire of the "country quean" drips unavoidably; while it
meant "a young woman," it also had the connotation of a
"loose" woman. And because a critic talked of "her dogg'rel
scrawls" she "slinks behind the shade." "So much I dread their
cruel spite, / My hand still trembles when I write." But we
observe that she indeed *does* write!

In 1758 someone, quite seriously, produced a touchstone of
what opinionated attitudes had created: "The Poetical Scale,"
a discussion of relative achievement of various English poets

mathematically given in a graphic scale, rating, individually, genius, judgment, learning and versification. Milton's rating is high, but not the highest in any category except learning where he is equaled by Johnson, Dryden and Addison. Out of 20, he rates 18 in Genius, 16 in Judgment, 17 in Learning, and 18 in Versification. The comparison with Shakespeare leaves him wanting and some negative matters are cited.[35]

Sublimity

Yet many critics of the century agreed with Walpole's assessment of Milton's "exalted" and still "poetic" writing. The discovery of Longinus toward the end of the seventeenth century strongly influenced criticism in the next, and "sublimity" became a cliché for Milton's work (usually in *Paradise Lost*, but not exclusively). We have already noticed Joseph Warton's reference to "sublimity" and to Longinus. As early as Daniel Defoe's *Reformation of Manners, a Satyr* (1702) Milton's sublimity was being discussed (58–59). Most often cited is *Milton's Sublimity Asserted: In a Poem. Occasion'd by a Late Celebrated Piece, entitled, Cyder, a Poem; In Blank Verse, by Philo-Milton* (1709). John Philips's *Cyder* was first published in 1708; a popular poem, it was often imitated (such as the anonymous *Wine*, sometimes assigned to John Gay, in 1708), and it was translated by Lorenzo Magalotti into Italian verse in 1749. But the definition of the term often proved uncertain and often was only suggested by a quotation or a reference to the epic. Early on, Anthony Ashley Cooper, earl of Shaftesbury, discussed *Paradise Lost* and sublimity in *Soliloquy* (1710) with a theological base. *Proposals for Printing by Subscription, In Two Volumes in Octavo, the Following Miscellaneous Tracts, Written by Mr. John Dennis* (dated October 25, 1721) included "On the Sublimity and the Original Character of the Paradise Lost of *Milton*," and this appeared the same year as *Original Letters, Familiar, Moral and Critical,* the preface examining the epic's sublimity in terms of heroic action as well as in various letters from the prior five or so years. Building upon Shaftesbury's principles and asserting ideas of moral good and evil, Francis Hutcheson in *An Inquiry into the Original of Our Ideas of Beauty and Virtue* (1725) established how beauty arose from one's sense of moral good and its opposite; he is particularly concerned with book 4, lines 55–57 and 756–57: "And understood not that a grateful mind / By owing owes not, but still pays, at once / Indebted and discharg'd"; "all the Charities / Of Father, Son, and Brother first were known."[36]

In the meantime translations and editions of "On the Sublime" emerged: *The Works of Dionysius Longinus, On the Sublime* (1712), by Leonard Welsted, asserted the poem's accord with Longinus's analysis (particularly through allusions and quotations). *Dionysius Longinus on the Sublime* (1739), by William Smith, explored the way in which Milton excelled Homer, paid much attention to Satan, Sin, and Death and their horror, the fight of the angels and the description of Messiah, the grandeur in decay, Milton's fine hyperbaton, the sedate grandeur of some of the images, and Adam and Eve's conjugal love. But it was Edmund Burke's *A Philosophical Enquiry into the Origin of Our Ideas of the Sublime and Beautiful* (1757) that most frequently was quoted, with its emphasis on the description of Death and Satan and the fall of the angels and terror, even though so much had been anticipated by Smith.[37]

For most, "the sublimest Son of the Muses, *John Milton*" was poetic exemplar, the "British Homer," "the Prince of our English Poets."[38] Milton and sublimity seem almost coterminous when the epic is being discussed, but note also Robert Potter's *An Inquiry into Some Passages in Dr. Johnson's Lives of the Poets* (1783), in which Milton's reference to Shakespeare in *L'Allegro* is related to his sublimity. Typical of many poems, allusions and discussions is a 1735 essay "On the Sublime" appearing in the *Grub-street Journal* with reference to *Paradise*

Lost.[39] The very important *Lectures on Rhetoric and Belles Lettres* (1783) of Hugh Blair elaborates upon the subject throughout.[40] Richard Stack read an essay to the Royal Irish Academy on February 13, 1787, on "the Sublimity of Writing," in which the Satan of book 4 and the Son's victory in book 6 become focal points. The judgment was ubiquitous but the examples almost always omitted the presentation of Adam and especially Eve.[41] It is thus understandable why in this same year Mary Wollstonecraft objects to the excessive reference to Milton's sublimity in her *Thoughts on the Education of Daughters* (1787). As Wittreich informs us, she was reacting to "those who 'could not enter into the spirit' of Milton or understand him and who fail to remember that Eve is represented by Raphael, in Adam's discourse with the angel, not as a physical object but as a lustrous mind."[42]

Some Women Poets

The full statement just referred to really comments upon the issue of the "deleterious" or the "exalted," for Wollstonecraft includes "the elegance and harmony of Pope, and the original untaught genius of Shakespeare" along with Milton's sublimity. She states she "would have every one try to form an opinion of an author themselves, though modesty may restrain them from mentioning it. Many are so anxious to have the reputation of taste that they only praise the authors whose merit is indisputable." Some who should be accorded some praise, I argue in agreement, are the "lesser" male authors and women authors ignored in this jockeying for acceptance as critic and practitioner. Wollstonecraft has been a rallying point for some feminist criticism of the last couple of decades, particularly for Milton in rereadings of *Paradise Lost* and *Samson Agonistes*. The extent of her knowledge and appreciation of Milton has not always been recognized, and a major point in Wittreich's *Feminist Milton* is that oft-quoted lines from *The Vindication of Women* (1792) have been inadequately understood, for her "alert, sensitive, and chiefly female response to Milton" "suggests that Milton is an advocate for women, not their adversary" (41). "She finds 'proofs of reason, as well as genius' against all those arguments contemptuous of 'the female understanding,'" Wittreich argues, quoting from her book (42).

While a number of women writers have been rediscovered in recent years and while many of them reflect a knowledge of Milton and his works, I want to mention a few more (out of a great number that could be cited). Charlotte McCarthy's *The Fair Moralist* (1745)[43] reflects Raphael's advice to Adam in *Paradise Lost*, book 4, lines 774–75: "if you'd be happy wish to know no more" (48); gives various echoes in "My Farewel to Newington" (81), for example, to *Paradise Lost*, book 11, line 269; and adds in the second edition (1746) "The Author's Observations; or, A Looking-Glass for the Fair Sex" in which she writes of some rich women who treat people like slaves, "I know no Description just enough for such Women, except that which *Milton* gives of Satan in his first rebellious State" (137). In 1755 George Colman and Bonnell Thornton compiled *Poems By Eminent Ladies* in two volumes; included is Lætitia Pilkington's "To the Reverend Dr. Hales" with an allusion in the poem.[44] *Memoirs of Mrs. Lætitia Pilkington* shows overwhelming evidence of Milton's importance to her.[45] Volume 1 records comment and quotation of *Il Penseroso*, lines 155–66 (1.63); quotation of *Paradise Lost*, book 2, lines 308–9 (1.72); allusions and comments on Milton's knowledge of Shakespeare and the debt of *Comus* to *A Midsummer Night's Dream* (1.140–41); quotation of *Comus*, line 782 (1.225); comment and quotation of *Paradise Lost*, book 4, line 192 (1.248–49), and "To Miss Betty Pl———kett" with an allusion in the poem (1.261). Aside from the poem to Dr. Hales (2.12–16), "To His Grace, the Lord Archbishop of York" (2.40–44) shows influence; there is an allusion in "A View of the Present State of Men and Things. A Satyric Dialogue Between the Poet and His Friend. In the Year 1739" referencing Abdiel (2.62–76); a paraphrase of *Paradise Lost*, book 4, line 830 (2.83); quotation of *Paradise Lost*, book 4, lines 763–65 (2.88); an adaptation of *Il Penseroso*, lines 68–72 (2.99); quoted lines with an allusion to Ithuriel's spear (2.139); an allusion (2.152); quotations of *Comus*, lines 768–69 (2.206–7) and 180–81 (2.233); further allusions (2.251, 310); an allusion to Pandaemonium and to Milton's being inspired by Satan (2.310–11); quotation from *Paradise Lost*, book 1, line 26 (2.316); allusion in lines quoted from Alexander Pope's "Of Taste" and paraphrase of *Comus*, 779–84 (2.353), and more allusions (2.361–62). Volume 3 has a quotation of *Paradise Lost*, book 4, lines 55–57 (3.8); allusions, discussion of Pope's indebtedness to Milton, and quotations from *Il Penseroso*, lines 159–60 and 161–63 (3.10–11); quotation of *Paradise Lost*, book 5, line 638, and an alleged two-line quotation (actually from Shakespeare's *The Merchant of Venice*, 5.1.64–65) (3.84, 85); quotations of *Comus*, lines 476 and 480, of *Paradise Lost*, book 1, line 63, and of *On Shakespeare*, line 14 (3.131, 132, 210). Yet Mrs. Pilkington is not noticed at all by Havens, Griffin or Wittreich.

But Colman and Thornton also included other "eminent ladies" in editions two (1757) and three (ca. 1780): Mary Chudleigh's "The Ladies Defence; or, A Dialogue Between Sir John Bute, Sir William Loveall, Melissa, and a Parson" (1:171–95), first published in 1701, and discussed by Wittreich (51–52) as including an allusion in its preface;[46] Anne Finch, Countess of Winchelsea's "The Spleen" (2:243–48), which evidences influence; "Soliloquy on an Empty Purse" (1:157–59), in octosyllabics; Miss Pennington's "The Copper Farthing" (2:65–69) a parody in blank verse, following Philips; and Miss Mary Whateley's (that is, Mrs. Darwell's) "The Pleasures of Contemplation" (2:189–92), in blank verse with echoes from *Paradise Lost*.[47] In their periodical *The Connoisseur*, Colman and Thornton discuss the collection and treat Milton as a character in referencing *L'Allegro* and *Il Penseroso*; they make a spoofing comment that the companion poems were indebted to the verses of the duchess of Newcastle (Margaret Cavendish), and give a paraphrase of *Paradise Lost*, book 9, lines 1038–39, in talking about Aphra Behn (see no. 69 [May 22, 1755]).

A few others: "Conjugal Affection" by Elizabeth Griffith is clearly indebted to Milton; the poem is in blank verse and employs *Paradise Lost*, book 4, line 750, as epigraph.[48] Griffith also comments upon and quotes *Paradise Lost*, book 8, lines 596–606, and book 4, line 660 (22–23), and adapts *Paradise Lost*, book 3, line 50 (97). Significant for the subject of Milton and women writers is Laetitia Hawkins's *Letters on the Female Mind, Its Powers and Pursuits*.[49] In volume 1 she presents an adaptation of *Paradise Lost*, book 8, line 550, to empower her discussion of the sons of Adam (Letter 6, p. 99). In volume 2 the sight "purg'd with Euphrasie and Rue" (*PL* 8.414) allows for clear understanding of issues women face (Letter 10, p. 80); and the image of Satan in the fourth book of the epic, with quotation of lines 997–1004, prophesies eventual success for women under God. Interesting when we recall Little's poem, quoted in part earlier, and the writings of Wollstonecraft and Hawkins, is "On a Young Lady's being censured for reading Milton, and accus'd of not being the Author of many Poetical Pieces under her Name. She had 2 Stanza's of her suspected Assistance, She was to answer," by Erasmus Darwin and Anna Seward. It is a poem in nine quatrains with numerous allusions to Milton.[50] Seward, of course, wrote a great deal of poetry, starting young, and much of it is influenced by and related by allusions and quotations to Milton and his works.[51] *Sonnet 67* might be mentioned here: "On Doctor Johnson's Unjust Criticisms in His Lives of the Poets," with specific reference to *Paradise Lost* and *Lycidas* (3.188–90).

As we close in on the end of the century the poetry of people like Anne Yearsley and William Parsons engage themes and approaches that are to be explored by Wordsworth in *Lyrical*

Ballads, and indeed these may have been some of the poetic volumes he read while at university — to offset, like any college student in any age, the ponderous assignments of classical Latin (or even Greek).[52] But we find similar effects in poetry of a number of women during the last few years of the century as well, even though they will not be so highly evaluated as Wordsworth's writing. There is Eliza Daye, for example, in *Poems, On Various Subjects* (Liverpool, 1798), who is influenced by and echoes various Milton poems, notably "The Birth of Genius" (150), which has an allusion. There is Elizabeth Moody in *Poetic Trifles* (London, 1798), offering a cultural comment for students of the period in "The Address of a Toad to Mr Opie, the Painter, While Sitting For His Picture" (also an allusion, 58). (Havens cites her "On Youth," which is influenced by the companion poems and printed in *Gentleman's Magazine* 58 [1788]: 636.) And very importantly, I think, there is Mrs. Anne [MacIver] Grant, whose *Poems on Various Subjects, by Mrs. Grant, Laggan* was published in Edinburgh in 1803 (Havens notes only her octosyllabic "Ode to Hygeia"). The poems showing Miltonic influence or reference or quotation, written before 1800, are very numerous. Included are such items as "The Highlanders; or, Sketches of Highland Scenery & Manners: With some Reflections on Emigration. Written During the Author's Recovery from a Long Illness, in Spring 1795. In Five Parts" and "Written in one of the Duke of Athole's Walks at Blair, After making a Clandestine Entrance Through the River Tilt, Then Very Low: Summer 1796."[53] Further, while some contemporary criticisms of Wollstonecraft's volume, such as that by Hannah More, have been noted, no one to my knowledge seems to be aware of Grant's very negative comments in a letter to a friend, Miss Ourry, on January 2, 1794. Her assessment is that

> It has produced no other conviction in my mind, but that of the author's possessing considerable abilities, and greatly misapplying them. To refute her arguments would be to write

> another and a larger book; for there is more pains and skill required to refute ill-founded assertions, than to make them. Nothing can be more specious and plausible, for nothing can delight Misses more than to tell them they are as wise as their masters. . . . We know too well that our imaginations are more awake, our senses more acute, our feelings more delicate, than those of our tyrants.[54]

The question of gender differences and sexual equality is certainly not an invention of the present day, and women advocating "the desired revolution" that Grant talks about in Wollstonecraft's treatise are countered by women like Grant who find "the great advantage that women, taken upon the whole, have over men, is, that they are more gentle, benevolent, and virtuous. Much of this superiority they owe to living secure and protected in the shade" (277). Milton offers both sides evidence, it seems, for their interpretations of the epic and the divorce tracts and gender issues.

Concluding Observation

As we see from Potter's *An Inquiry*, there were contemporary objections to Johnson's criticism and often to his criticism of Milton. Potter was bothered by Johnson's political and religious treatment of Milton in the "Life," but James Burnet, Lord Monbaddo, was one of his most virulent antagonists:

> It was no wonder, therefore, that such a critic as Dr. Johnson, who, in my opinion, was neither a scholar nor a man of taste, should pronounce, among the other oracles which he has uttered from his tripod, that Milton does not write English, (and I have heard some of the Doctor's admirers say the same), but a Babylonish dialect. . . . The commendation of the *Paradise Lost*, with which he concludes his life of Milton, is I think more absurd than his censures of him, and so ridiculous that, if I had had a better opinion of the Doctor's critical talents, I should have imagined that he said it by way of irony and ridicule of Milton.[55]

The periodicals also became a source of antagonism toward Johnson, for example, J. Boerhadem's "On Milton's Piety," which takes him to task for misrepresentations. James Thomson Callender hits at the *Deformities of Dr. Samuel Johnson*, including Milton's "fantastic foppery" and Milton's "perverse and pedantic principle."[56] Johnson's friend Hester Lynch Piozzi Thrale argued for Milton's republicanism in a letter to him, dated August 20, 1780; and Anna Seward, "The Swan of Lichfield" (Johnson's place of birth), comments upon Johnson's envy of Milton, recounts an anecdote about him and *Lycidas*, and offers a parody of the poem ("What needs a mind-illumin'd breast for those, / Heart-melting thoughts, or fancy like the sun?") in a letter to Frances Brooke, dated April 21, 1785. One of her letters that champion the sonnet (she wrote many herself) specifically questions Johnson's judgments (see a letter to T. S. Whalley, dated April 7, 1789).[57] But other critics are also challenged, not just Johnson, including Addison: for example, an article in the *Gentleman's Magazine* confronts the "inadequacies" of his criticism of *Paradise Lost* through an analysis of Milton's cosmology.[58]

The "deleteriousness" and the "exaltation" provided by a poet's work, according to the rule-bound and "correct," politically and religiously opinionated, and sometimes imperceptive critics of the eighteenth century, have always existed in some fashion — think of Shelley, of Pound, of Joyce or Woolf in the novel. But some of the judgments about Milton's presence and influence cannot be totally sound until more attention is paid to more of the "lesser" male poets and to all of the women poets of that era.

APPENDIX

Additional Poems Showing Influence from Milton's Shorter Poems

1. Anonymous, "A Maske of the Gentlemen of Graies Inne, and the Inner Temple, by Mr Francis Beaumont," G6–H1v, in *Poems, by Francis Beaumont, gent.* (London, 1653), with influence from and partial imitation of *Comus*.

2. Nahum Tate's "Hor. Ode 5th, lib. 3," which owes something to Milton's version although not form, which is Havens's reason for assigning a poem to influence from the "Fifth Ode" (it is added to the second edition of *Poems Written on Several Occasions, by N. Tate* [London, 1684], 155–56).

3. "The E. of Essex's Ghost. 1687," p. 22, in *A Third Collection of the Newest and Most Ingenious Poems, Satyrs, Songs, &c. against Popery and Tyranny, Relating to the Times. Most of which never before published* (London, 1689), imitation of the beginning and ending of *Comus*.

4. Nahum Tate, *A Pastoral Dialogue. A Poem* (London, 1690), showing influence from *Comus*, passim.

5. William Walsh's three "Pastoral Eclogues: Eclogue I, Daphne; Eclogue II, Galatea; Eclogue III, Damon," 110–13, 113–16, and 117–20, respectively, all with influence from *Lycidas*, in *Letters and Poems, Amorous and Gallant* (London, 1692).

6. Anonymous, "Against Sloth, When the King was at Oxford," with influence from *L'Allegro*, found in Dryden's collection, *Examen Poeticum: Being the Third Part of Miscellany Poems* (London, 1693), 175–77.

7. William Congreve's "The Mourning Muse of Alexis," in *The Mourning Muse of Alexis. A Pastoral. Lamenting the Death of Our Late Gracious Queen Mary of Ever Blessed Memory* (London, 1695), with influence from *Comus* and *Lycidas*.

8. *An Ode, on the Death of Mr. Henry Purcell; Late Servant to His Majesty, and Organist of the Chapel Royal; and of St. Peter's Westminster. The Words by Mr. Dryden, and Sett to Musick by Dr. Blow* (London, 1696), with influence from *Lycidas*.

9. John Pomfret, *The Choice. A Poem. By a Person of Quality* (London, 1700), an imitation of the companion poems, which would be classified as "generally known and of much importance."

10. John Hughes, *The Court of Neptune. A Poem* (London, 1700), with influence on its beginning from the language of *Lycidas* (1).

It should also be mentioned that Thomas Yalden's "A Hymn to the Morning. In Praise of Light. An Ode," pp. 127–31, and "A Hymn to Darkness," pp. 132–37, in *Examen Poeticum*, although owing debts to *Paradise Lost*, exhibit the kind of contrast that the companion poems presented for their audience. Such contrastive poems are also exemplified by William Mason's imitations of *L'Allegro* and *Il Penseroso* respectively, "Il Pacifico" and "Il Bellicoso"; the first is included in George Pearch's version of Dodsley's *Collection of Poems in Two Volumes. By Several Hands* (London, 1768), 1.180–86, and both in his 1775 edition in four volumes. See 1.204–10, for the second, and 211–16, for the first. (Compare Havens, *The Influence of Milton*, 459–60, on Mason.)

Three similarly contrastive hymns in octosyllabic couplets, broken into quatrains, but decidedly not Miltonic in execution, are Thomas Ken's "A Morning Hymn," "An Evening Hymn," and "A Midnight Hymn"; see *Morning Evening Midnight 3 Hymns by Thomas Ken* (New York: P. and K. Oliver, 1937), 13–16, 19–22, 25–28, respectively. They were first published in Ken's *A Manual of Prayers . . . for Winchester College* (London: Printed for Charles Brome, 1697).

"A Maske" is, of course, not by Beaumont; it was reissued in 1653 and 1660 and reprinted in 1711 (and later). "The E. of Essex's Ghost" is printed three more times in 1690, 1697, 1699; it is also called "Lord Lucas's Ghost." It appears in six manuscripts, one having the title "A detestable Libell." It reappears in 1702, and forward. A similar poem, "Rawleigh's Ghost," found in a Bodleian manuscript, also employs the beginning of *Comus*. Tate's poem has an allusion on page 27, and is revised and published in *Poems on Affairs of State* (1707) as "A Poem, Occasion'd by the late Discontents and Disturbances in the State, 1691." Walsh's three "Pastoral Eclogues" were published in the reprint of Dryden's *Fourth Part of Miscellany Poems* (1716), 389–95; and in *The Works of Celebrated Authors, Of Whose Writings There Are But Small Remains* (London, 1750), 2.130–36.

The first reprint of Dryden's *Examen Poeticum* collection was in 1706; "Against Sloth" appears a few more times in the century. Congreve's poem was frequently reprinted in the seventeenth and eighteenth centuries (1709 onward); all Havens notes is: "In his *Mourning Muse of Alexis* (1695, *ib.* 836) there is a reference to '*Comus* Feast' (Good, p. 141)" (16 n. 4). The ode on Purcell reappears in *Orpheus Britannicus. A Collection of All the Choicest Songs for One, Two, and Three Voices, Compos'd by Mr. Henry Purcell* (London, 1698), with further editions in 1706 and 1721, as well as in a manuscript songbook owned by George Forman (in the Folger Shakespeare Library), copied from the first edition. The Pomfret poem had two further editions in 1700, and 1701 saw the first of numerous eighteenth century printings. There is also Benjamin Church's *The Choice: A Poem, After the Manner of Mr. Pomfret* (Boston, 1757), which thus imitates *L'Allegro* to some extent and includes an allusion and comment. Griffin, *Regaining Paradise*, notices the Pomfret poem (dating it 1704) as relating to the Edenic myth of retirement (108). The Hughes poem was reprinted in 1735. Yalden's poems, beginning in 1706, are reprinted frequently in the first half of the eighteenth century.

2 • John Milton, Lucy Hutchinson and the Republican Biblical Epic

David Norbrook

In a recent book, *Writing the English Republic*, I tried to situate Milton in a larger grouping of republican writers who, whatever their limitations and the limitations of their moment, offer a present challenge in an England newly open to political change.[1] On questions of gender, however, the charge that Milton is indeed a monument to dead, patriarchal ideas poses a continuing challenge and difficulty. Joseph Wittreich has addressed that difficulty in a series of studies which have opened up contradictions and resistances in Milton's prose and poetry, and have drawn attention to contemporary women readers who responded admiringly to his writings.[2] The fact remains that many of the leading women poets of the later seventeenth century were strongly royalist in their political views. Germaine Greer has found "a contrast between royalist and republican culture that could be traced from the beginning of the century to the triumph of masculinism in the Whig supremacy," with royalist culture being more sympathetic both to female agency and to female sexuality.[3] Mary Astell's attack on Milton may seem to clinch the argument that republicanism or Whiggery was antagonistic to the most advanced women thinkers of the time.

That assumption, however, has become fixed too easily. It was in an attempt to rethink its empirical base that I was led to explore the writings of Lucy Hutchinson (1620–1681), long known both as a republican and as a woman writer of some distinction, as the author of a celebrated biography of her regicide husband. Further exploration has revealed that Hutchinson was in fact the author of a much wider range of poetry, including an epic poem on the book of Genesis which, though unfinished, reached to about four-fifths the length of *Paradise Lost*. This poem, *Order and Disorder*, was arguably the most ambitious poem composed by an Englishwoman down to that time, and it emerged from the center of the republican ideology which Milton affirmed. To set the two poems against each other is to find a striking convergence in theme and poetic strategy. In some sense, however, *Order and Disorder* may indeed be argued to prove the rule of which it is an exception: it is much less overtly feminist than many contemporary writings by women, and indeed it has been traditionally assumed to be the work of a man, Hutchinson's brother Sir Allen Apsley. The poem in fact belongs to that large class of texts which were published anonymously and were subsequently assumed to be by a male author. The assumption in this particular case, by the strongly Tory Anthony Wood, lacks evidence, and a far stronger combination of factors identifies the author as Apsley's sister, Lucy Hutchinson. Ironically enough, the only critical attention the poem has attracted is from Wittreich himself, in a stimulating survey of Milton's immediate reception.[4] His reading is colored by

Wood's attribution to the conservative Apsley; the reascription offers new evidence for precisely the kind of cooperative though critical dialogue between Milton and his female readers that Wittreich has so imaginatively explored. Rather than opposing an infinitely open Milton to a rigid and closed Hutchinson, I believe that it is more realistic to expect both poets to be at once constrained by and open to their age's questioning of different orthodoxies; there are common elements in both poets, which I shall consider before turning to the undoubted points of difference that Wittreich has noticed.

The first five cantos of *Order and Disorder* narrate the Creation and Fall; the remaining 15 cantos follow the major landmarks in Genesis from Cain and Abel to the story of Jacob, Rachel and Leah, at which point the poem breaks off abruptly in midline. Thus the poem effectively reverses the proportions of *Paradise Lost*, giving the majority of its space to the events that are presented in inset narratives in Milton's last two books. *Order and Disorder*, too, belongs to the genre of biblical or hexameral epic, with a mingling of biblical and classical conventions, though the latter are mainly confined to the occasional extended simile, and the style often moves from high prophetic passion to a plain, meditative note. The subtitle of the printed edition, *Meditations upon the Creation and the Fall; as it is recorded in the beginning of GENESIS*, indicates its discursive character.

Unfortunately, much still remains obscure about the poem. It survives in a version in two scribal hands in a manuscript book that belonged to Anne Wilmot, Countess of Rochester, and which bears the date 1664 — though the date may apply to the table book rather than the poem it contains; another manuscript, now lost, contained an extract which the early eighteenth century compiler believed to have dated from 1664.[5] The first five cantos were printed anonymously as late as 1679, two years before Hutchinson's death. It is unclear how much — if any — had been completed by 1664. The 1679 preface views the poem as a recantation of her "youthful" translation of Lucretius; that translation seems to have been still in progress in the late 1650s. John Shawcross lists the poem in his bibliography as strongly indebted to *Paradise Lost*.[6] There are indeed a number of verbal parallels, with the opening and closing lines of Milton's epic especially prominent in Hutchinson's, as will be further discussed below. Overall, however, we do not find in Hutchinson the kind of close imitation of Miltonic vocabulary that characterize later verse imitators of *Paradise Lost*, and the parallels derive more from independent reworking of Genesis material from a comparable ideological perspective, and with comparable literary models, than from slavish imitation. In principle it is even possible that the influence worked in the other direction. Her friend and patron Arthur Annesley, earl of Anglesey, supported Milton in 1660 when his life was in danger and later helped him with the publication of the *History of Britain*; it was in a similar capacity as a royalist who maintained close links with dissenters that he aided Hutchinson. It is not entirely implausible to imagine Milton's having some passages from *Order and Disorder* read to him, or conversely Hutchinson having early access to a manuscript of *Paradise Lost*. It remains most likely, however, that she began work some time after the first publication of Milton's epic. Andrew Marvell, who contributed a notable commendatory poem to the 1674 edition, had probably used Anglesey's library to work on his *The Rehearsal Transpros'd*, which came to the defense of the Congregationalist divine John Owen about the time Hutchinson would have been translating one of Owen's books. Hutchinson dedicated her translation of Lucretius to Anglesey the following year and would have had access to the same library.[7]

While *Order and Disorder* probably constituted a response to *Paradise Lost*, we should not assume that Milton would have had for Lucy Hutchinson the awesomely canonical status he enjoys today. She is likely to have viewed him with at least mixed feelings, as one who had wavered in the Cromwellian period from devotion to the republican cause, and whose views on divorce and — if she was aware of them — on theology she would have regarded as heretical. Marvell's hints at possible heterodoxy in Milton may conceivably have emboldened Hutchinson to attempt a more strongly Calvinist account of the Fall. If *Order and Disorder* does show the influence of *Paradise Lost*, it is not at a simple verbal level but in deeper forms of ideological affinity.

On many levels, *Order and Disorder* fits the model of republican poetics that I outlined in *Writing the English Republic* (chap. 10). That poetics was consciously and polemically anti-Augustan. Hutchinson intervened directly in such polemic. During the 1650s she composed a line-by-line response to Waller's *Panegyric of My Lord Protector*, the pioneering statement of literary Augustanism.[8] The classic anti-Augustan epic was Lucan's *Pharsalia*. Hutchinson alludes to Lucan in her autobiography and draws heavily on the *History* of Lucan's translator, Thomas May — though censuring him because he gave "more indulgence to the King's guilt than can justly be allow'd."[9] In general, however, she does not follow Milton's Lucanian strategy of evoking Augustan epic machinery in order to discredit it; she is far more concerned than Milton to reject all pagan fictions in the name of biblical truth. The whole episode of the fallen angels' war in heaven is dismissed as "circumstances that we cannot know / Of their rebellion and their overthrow" (4.43–44). Where Milton is ready to evoke the imaginative resonance of pagan myth, if only then to dispel the charm (compare *PL* 1.507–21, 738–47), Hutchinson confines herself to denouncing the "some truths, wrapped up in many lies" of pagan myths (4.48).

Hutchinson's remarkable description of the destruction of Sodom, however, recalls both Lucan and Milton. Milton's allegory of Sin and Death reworked monarchist triumphal imagery and associated death with kingship; Hutchinson works in a distinct but comparable way:

> Divine Vengeance had her troops arrayed
> And ready for quick execution made.
> That day she in a fiery chariot sate
> On whom the armèd elements did wait,
> Each in the head of their own furious bands
> Attending to receive her dire commands.
>
> . . . .
>
> The goddess' scarlet robes in blood were dyed.
> Dreadful portents before her chariot ride:
> Pale Horror, wild Amazement, ghastly Fear,
> Despair and Sorrow her attendants were;
> Her weapons flame, darts, savage teeth, keen swords,
> Whatever plagues heaven, earth, or sea affords.
> Ruin and Desolation followed her.
> Pale Death, like a triumphant conqueror
> With funeral blazes crowned, marched in the rear,
> And fatal shafts did in her quiver bear.
>
> (13.187–92, 201–10)

Hutchinson relishes the irony of using courtly imagery as a metaphor both for pride and for its destruction; as in Milton, the crown becomes an image at once of kingship and of death:

> The stately palaces and temples burned;
> Whatever the flame seized, to flame was turned.
> Each turret had a blazing coronet
> Where fiery floods which fell from heaven met
> The flames that did from burning beams aspire
> And raised their unopposèd triumphs higher;
> Yet were they but like sacrifices crowned:
> Their fatal splendour burned them to the ground.
>
> (13.227–34)

Hutchinson seems to have no direct precedent in deploying the courtly image of the triumphal car in this context, and the closest parallel is with the chariot of the Son in *Paradise Lost*, book 6, lines 750–66, which fuses courtly imagery with Ezekiel's vision of the fiery chariot. In linking Vengeance with the four elements Hutchinson is probably borrowing from

Ezekiel 1:42–48, as Milton did with his "four Cherubic shapes, [with] Four faces each" (*PL* 6.753).

Like Milton, Hutchinson associates extreme artifice with the sterility and tyranny of monarchical rule. Like him, though in different ways, she aims at a poetics which will come closer to the natural — and hence to God's sublime primal act of creation. Interestingly, her most explicit statement of this point comes where she is describing the clouds with their forms that ever change, never resolving themselves into a fixed entity:

> Scorn, princes, your embroidered canopies
> And painted roofs: the poor whom you despise
> With far more ravishing delight are fed
> While various clouds sail o'er the unhousèd head,
> And their heaved eyes with nobler scenes present
> Than your poetic courtiers can invent.

> (2.21–26)

Hutchinson aims at poetic sublimity not through Milton's expansive blank verse but through fluid, open pentameter couplets, the syntax of which is often hard to confine within the boundaries of modern punctuation conventions. Though linking poetic form with political ideology needs care, her onslaught on Waller, a leading pioneer of the smoothing of the closed couplet, does suggest that there was an ideological edge to her resistance.

Hutchinson's poetic universe, however, is a degree less open than Milton's, as emerges from a comparison between the following accounts of the Creation:

> then founded, then conglob'd
> Like things to like, the rest to several place
> Disparted, and between spun out the Air,
> And Earth self-balanc't on her Centre hung.

> (*PL* 7.239–42)

> Now, the great fabric in all parts complete,
> Beauty was called forth to adorn the seat;
> Where Earth, fixed in the centre, was the ground,

A mantle of light air compassed it round;
Then first the watery, then the fiery wall,
And glittering Heaven last involving all.
(Order and Disorder, 2.71–76)

Milton's caesura gives his pentameter line a sense of closure
that is slightly undermined by the active "hung," just as when
he speaks of fixed bodies he will then undercut the claim ("the
fixt Starrs, fixt in thir Orb that flies," 5.176). Here and elsewhere, Hutchinson gives her cosmos greater fixity —"fixed"
is one of her favorite words — with none of Milton's juxtaposition of Ptolemaic and Copernican cosmologies and relish
of unexpected motion. An interesting study could be made
of the two writers' differing uses of the word "fix," though
a postmodern preference for fluidity would be likely to exag-
gerate the differences. Politically radical writers generally
need some point of stability from which they can launch a
critique. Both writers took pride in the firmness of their adherence to basic principles, and there are close affinities between the pride with which Hutchinson records Clarendon's
comment that her husband was "the most unchang'd person
of the party" after the Restoration *(Memoirs,* 256) and Milton's
"I Sing . . . unchang'd" *(PL* 7.24).

Insofar as Hutchinson does have more difficulty with the
unfixed, it is because in *Order and Disorder* she was reacting
sharply against a cosmology more dangerously open than either
of those alternatives. Philip Hardie has suggested that the
Miltonic sublime had a strong Lucretian element, and indeed
that Marvell's poem on *Paradise Lost,* which evoked Lucan,
also evoked Lucretius.[10] Milton had placed Lucretius on his
ideal syllabus in *Of Education,* and his description of Creation
as a formation not ex nihilo but from preexisting matter draws
on the *De rerum natura.* Hutchinson did not share Milton's
heterodoxy over Chaos, and in later life she came to believe
that her translation was a sin that urgently needed expiation
by the composition of her new poem. She turned firmly against
Lucretian cosmology to a traditional Christian one, rejecting

"the foppish casuall dance of attoms" for God's "most gratious, ever active Providence, upholding, ordering and governing the whole Creation."[11]

She reacted so strongly, however, precisely because she had saturated herself in Lucretius more than any contemporary, by composing the first English translation of the entire poem. Her description of heaven "leading back all ages to the womb / Of vast Eternity from whence they come" (1.163–64) recycles her rendering of *De rerum natura*, book 5, line 259, as "Earth for her part made by her fruitfull womb / The generall mother, is the common tomb" (Hutchinson's translation, 5.272–73); Milton renders the same passage as "The Womb of nature and perhaps her Grave," *PL* 2.911). Though Protestants abhorred Lucretius's atheism, they could find in him a certain kindred spirit in the vehemence of his attacks on priestcraft and superstition. He can be viewed in many ways as an anti-Augustan poet, whatever Virgil's complex relationship with his verse.[12] Lucretius opposed political activism, and could thus chime in with the mood of disenfranchised royalists like John Evelyn, who began work on a translation when in exile. However, he had no admiration for the emergence of royalist tendencies in Roman culture and his supporters tended to oppose Caesar. His language resists the courtly polish that was to emerge under imperial patronage. He had a primitivistic side, and Hutchinson's later attacks on courtly luxury sometimes borrow phrases from her Lucretius translation. Again and again she attacks courtly artifice and insists that the good life is one lived in close harmony with the natural world (for example, 2.308–10). *Order and Disorder* pushes such proto-primitivism to a degree unusual in its time in its protests against sports like cock-fighting. As Reid Barbour has pointed out, she would have responded positively to Lucretius's call for a return to first principles, the term by which she translates his *principia rerum*: a return to first principles, a remodeling of society to get back to lost premises, was a central feature of republican vocabulary of the 1650s.[13] Evelyn never published the later books of his translation and his annotations to the manuscript revealed that he had some ideological difficulties with them, finding it necessary to affirm "against our poet, that the first Legislatiue power was not in the people."[14]

Hutchinson continually opposes a divinely created natural order to a social order that has become unbalanced by monarchical artifice. In Milton, I have argued, there is a consistent opposition between the sterile harmony of courtly artifice and the more open, sublime *concordia discors* of divine creation. Hutchinson's title evokes a comparable opposition. It may have been designed to help get the poem past the licenser, for on its publication in 1679 the poem may well have looked on the bookstalls as if it were a promonarchist engagement in the escalating Exclusion Crisis. In fact, the title carried a degree of grim irony, for Hutchinson was one of those who believed that if the Puritan revolution had turned the traditional order upside down, that was because it had previously been the wrong way up. Milton's usurping Satan lacks a sense of the common good and his defense of "Orders and Degrees" (*PL* 5.792) privileges hero worship rather than humility, thus revealing itself as the basis of the postlapsarian princely order; in Hutchinson, too, the quest for a prelapsarian order leads to a mordant critique of established power.

If the natural world still reveals some of that primal order and beauty, after the Fall it has become much harder to sustain the sublime proportion, and it is more common for political and religious orders to subvert it in the name of a narrow tyranny and uniformity. Kings should observe "fair order," but often they "pluck up and destroy / Those plants whose culture should their cares employ" (3.634–38). The rulers

> whom God did institute to curb
> The world's disorders, did the world disturb,
> To murder and to slaughter led whole hosts
> Till searèd conscience made their crimes their boast.
>
> (8.321–24)

Even before the Fall, the divine order was not quite naturally balanced, in the sense that Eden needed human labor to cultivate it — a point on which Hutchinson insists as strongly as Milton:

> Who formed, could have preserved the garden fair
> Without th'employment of man's busy care,
> But that he willed that our delight should be
> The wages of our constant industry.
>
> (3.635–38)

The emphasis on labor extends, in Hutchinson as in Milton, to the heavenly order: using the striking oxymoron "vulgar angels," Hutchinson contrasts the "vain pride" of men with angels' willingness to serve "poor worms" (1.279–82). At the same time, like Milton, Hutchinson insists that the angels' hard work should not make them vain, since they were created "not for need, but for majestic state" (compare *PL* 8.239).

In sharp contrast with such divine and natural order and proportion is the order of the fallen angels:

> An order too there is in their dire state,
> Though they all orders else disturb and hate.
> Ten thousand thousand wicked spirits stand
> Attending their black prince at his command,
> To all imaginable evils pressed
> That may promote their common interest.
> Nor are they linkèd thus by faith and love,
> But hate of God and goodness, which doth move
> The same endeavours and desires in all,
> Lest civil wars should make their empire fall.
>
> (4.85–94)

The republican term "common interest," which Hutchinson also uses in the *Memoirs* (16), here takes on a sharp irony: the interest of the fallen angels — and of the tyrannical civil and religious orders they will sustain on earth — is intrinsically private, self-interested; they manage to suppress the evils of civil war, but at the cost of suppressing all public good. The use of such language in a republican context closely parallels Milton's

> O shame to men! Devil with Devil damn'd
> Firm concord holds, men onely disagree.
>
> . . . .
>
> Yet live in hatred, enmity and strife
> Among themselves, and levy cruel wars.
>
> (2.496–97, 500–501)

Though there is no equivalent in Hutchinson of Milton's Satan, there is a glimpse of his tragic self-division in her portrayal of fallen men like Cain: "If men the reigning power of sin admit, / Hell enters them, and they abide in it" (6.305–6) — lines which of course recall Satan's "Which way I fly is Hell; my self am Hell" (*PL* 4.75).

In the second part of *Order and Disorder*, earthly kingship and priestcraft are traced back to the progeny of Cain, the founders of the "Wordly State," and are contrasted with the elect members of the Gospel Church. As in *Paradise Lost*, monumental architecture is associated with tyranny and idolatry: the elect praise God "in woods and fields," rejecting "stately temples" (15.18–20). This piety is contrasted to the idolatry of those who tie God's boundlessness down to particular places,

> When even Heaven, which doth this globe embrace,
> Cannot hold him who yet fills every place,
> Still present in the earth, the sea, the air,
> Not bounded, nor excluded anywhere.
>
> (15.35–38)

(These lines closely parallel a passage in *Paradise Lost* [11.335–38] which itself echoes Lucan [9.578–80]). After the Flood, the monarchical desire to "fix your own great name" (10.47 — here, as in Milton, fixity in the fallen world is associated with an imperial, monumentalizing impulse — motivates the building of the Tower of Babel. In a move closely parallel to Milton's reappropriation of Virgil's bee imagery in his description of Pandaemonium (*PL* 1.768–75), Hutchinson describes the architecture in ironically Augustan terms; both poets allude to the *Aeneid*, book 1, lines 430–36, but Hutchinson comes close to paraphrasing Virgil:

> So when the bees a colony send out,
> The new swarms soon disperse themselves about
> And several labours busy every one:
> Some search for honey, some expel the drone,
> Some suck the flowers, some carry their loads home,
> Some take what they bring in, some work the comb:
> All various toils with diligence intend,
> Yet in one public work their labours spend.
>
> (10.71–78)

If John Beale objected that Milton's description of Nimrod showed that he "holds to his old Principle,"[15] he would have had no difficulty in deriving a similar conclusion from Hutchinson's comment that "the first mighty monarchs of the earth / From Noah's graceless son derived their birth" (10.19–20).

Against the perverted fixity of civil and ecclesiastical tyrannies, Hutchinson, like Milton, sets the figure of God as heavenly legislator. The parallels between civil and heavenly polities, it must be said, are much less marked in Hutchinson than in Milton because of her reluctance to speculate about the heavenly order: in her poem God remains a remote figure. She thus avoids a problem that concerned Milton, that of negotiating the differences between heavenly and earthly kingship: she applies the word "king" only three times in a long poem to God and Christ, and the form her imaginative iconoclasm takes is of refusing to visualize God in human terms. She does, however, share in the republican vocabulary of "restoration," of breaking down corrupt or tyrannical orders in order to restore a primal freedom. The idea of restoration turned republicans back to narratives of origin, both to Genesis and to Ovid's *Metamorphoses*; in accordance with this pattern, Hutchinson supplemented her Genesis epic by translating the description of the first men in *Metamorphoses*, book 1, lines 89–103.[16] And though she did not share Milton's unorthodox views of Chaos, she similarly linked her own experience in the process of composition with the Spirit's shaping of order from Chaos (1.21–30; *PL* 1.6–10). The language of restoration appears most pointedly in the description of the Flood, where a vivid description of divine destruction gives way to a lyrical moment of renewal and the poet asks: "What will full Restoration be, if this / But the first daybreak of God's favour is?" (8.27–28). We are reminded, however, that such a "restoration" is never more than provisional and can always be destroyed by a lapse into tyranny, in which case "Your new-restorèd glory shall expire" (8.51).

In many central respects, then, *Order and Disorder*, far from representing a conservative reaction against *Paradise Lost*, closely parallels that poem in its literary and ideological projects. In two ways, however, the poem can be seen as significantly more conservative. Both involve Hutchinson's commitment to a less adventurous biblical hermeneutic than Milton or other more radical Puritans. First of all, there can be no doubt of the poem's rigid adherence to orthodox Calvinist theology. To Hutchinson, fidelity to the principles of Parliament's cause involved total fidelity to the high Calvinism of its inception. In the continual spiritual voyaging of the revolutionary period, she did not travel as far or as fast as Milton. She came to reject an exclusive state church but her closest affinity was with John Owen, who retained an attachment to some form of public national church. Though ready to tolerate religious dissent, she shared none of Milton's excitement at the growth of sect and schism, and wrote a treatise to try to dissuade her daughter from joining a sect. And she never wavered in a strong belief in the Trinity and in double predestination. In revising *Order and Disorder* for publication, she greatly enlarged a passage on the Trinity in the opening pages, to leave the reader in no doubt as to where she stood (1.85–122, and textual notes). In the current debates over Milton's authorship of *On Christian Doctrine*, some scholars have argued that there is no evidence for anti-Trinitarianism in *Paradise Lost* as opposed to the treatise. On the evidence of *Order and Disorder*, however, Hutchinson would probably have considered that poem's lack of overt reverence for the Trinity to be in itself suspect, and she may have enlarged the Trinity passage to distinguish her Genesis poem from Milton's. Hutchinson's poem again and again insists that human agents appear as the unconscious players in a divinely plotted drama. Following Calvin, she uses the story of Jacob and Esau to insist on the utter inscrutability of God's judgments, "To make his boundless will and free grace known" (18.78–88). Here she stands in firm opposition to Milton's questioning of Calvinist readings of Jacob and Esau.[17]

Does such theological conservatism necessarily lead to a political conservatism? In the political context of the mid-seventeenth century, just what counts as conservative needs careful definition. Calvinism had appealed to many precisely because it offered a firm point outside the traditions and institutions of the church as a basis for a complete transformation. Though Milton implicitly equated a predestinarian God with a tyrannical king, not all Parliamentarians would have accepted this analogy. In the *Memoirs*, Hutchinson presents John Hutchinson's two spiritual crises, just before the civil war and after the Restoration, as moments simultaneously of increased understanding of Calvinist theology and of heightened dedication to Parliament's cause. Such beliefs had been utterly orthodox among the initial leaders of Parliament's struggle with the king, and had hardly deflected them from political action. Indeed, outside her poetry Hutchinson could be more insistent on specifically political agency than Milton. Her variety of republicanism was in certain senses less radical, but to the same extent it implicitly placed greater faith in the agency of the existing political community. Milton became thoroughly disillusioned with the traditional "ancient constitution" and looked for a radical transformation of political culture. This made him ready to support Cromwell's dissolution of the Long Parliament in 1653 and to consider at least tentative support for the second military dissolution in 1659. (The army might prove to be a providential agent in remodeling the nation from above.) Hutchinson, by contrast, steadily opposed any further military interference with Parliament after Pride's Purge, which her husband had accepted only with great misgivings. Where Milton warmly greeted the recall of the Long Parliament in 1659, at the cost of such inconsistency as to have led scholars who stress his loyalty to Cromwell into some very contorted readings, Hutchinson, while welcoming the demise of the Cromwellian dynasty, records her distaste at the fact that Parliament had returned so much at the behest of the army (*Memoirs*, 214). Though she adopted some of James Harrington's historical analysis in her account of the revolution in the *Memoirs*, she never accepted his proposals for radical constitutional reform, believing that a republic would eventually emerge as a logical extension of the existing parliamentary system. In the *Memoirs* she passes on to her children their father's advice, not that rebellion was to be rejected, but that it should be undertaken only when it was solidly grounded in the political community, rather than being preempted by self-appointed agents of the millennium (269). It was because he was wrongly accused of taking part in a rising he clearly considered premature that he died. His wife reserved some of her harshest criticisms for figures like Cromwell and Lambert who used millennial rhetoric to justify the destruction of civil government. A passage in *Order and Disorder* strikingly presents her consistent hostility to "priestcraft" when it takes on military garb:

For when the priests war's silver trumpets sound,
Cruelty rages without any bound,
And none more ardently pursue those fights
Than impious and dissembling hypocrites,
Ravished with joy to find that fair pretence
A cover for their native violence.

(20.109–14)

These differences of emphasis within the two writers' common republican principles emerge in the poems' different representations of political agency in the fallen world. Both *Paradise Lost* and *Order and Disorder* may seem to fit a traditional paradigm according to which the Puritans turned away from wordly action once the revolution had failed and sought a paradise within. Recent work on Restoration history, however, is revealing more and more how much opposition continued, and thus offers new contexts for the later careers of both writers.[18] The central conception of *Paradise Lost*, in any case, predated the Restoration, while the date of Hutchinson's poem remains too uncertain for firm conclusions about its immediate context. We do know that the huge setback of 1660 did not ultimately quash her belief that "the last gasps of expiring Monarchy" were at hand; the political crisis shortly before her death in 1681 may have confirmed her in that view (*Memoirs*, 41). She never wavered in her belief in an impending millennium which would redeem the prelapsarian order externally as well as internally, and her papers show that she was prepared to justify armed rebellion under certain circumstances.

Neither poem, it is true, celebrates the achievements of the Puritan revolution, and both present secular history as a bleak process in which early simplicity and liberty speedily give way to successive phases of tyranny and idolatry. If anything, Milton's portrait is bleaker, for his condensed narrative in books 11 and 12 leaves little space for positive achievements.

This may, however, reflect not a post-Restoration pessimism about politics but rather the very radicalism of his distaste for existing political institutions, which from the 1640s onwards had made him all the gloomier about the English people's capacity to change them. Hutchinson's poem insists with a Calvinist rigor on universal depravity; but in retailing general corruption she tends to focus on the wealthy and the noble, and there is a certain populist coloring in *Order and Disorder* that is not found so sharply in her other writings. The poem again and again looks forward to an impending millennial destruction of tyranny. It does not, it is true, examine the human agency that would forward the millennium, which is figured by natural forces like the Flood or allegorical figures like Vengeance. This hesitation is compatible with Hutchinson's anxiety about premature millennial activism. At the same time, once we start decoding the allegory of Vengeance, we can see that a space is indeed left for human agency. In the poem, as opposed to her prose writings, Hutchinson does not feel herself constrained to spell out exactly how that agency might function.

In comparing Milton with Hutchinson on their political commentaries, of course, we need to bear in mind the question of censorship. Milton could not be fully outspoken in a poem for the public press, and he encountered difficulties with his passage about the eclipses that perplex monarchs (*PL* 1.594–99). Hutchinson's comparable passage is more militant in its reference to the Dissenting "saints," which makes an identification of Charles II with the "tyrant" (the manuscript, slightly more cautiously, reads "tyrants"):

> Even those stars which threaten misery and woe
> To wicked men, to saints deliverance show:
> For when God cuts the bloody tyrant down,
> He will their lives with peace and blessings crown.
>
> (2.205–8)

The political point is reinforced by marginal glosses that point us to Deborah's and Barak's song of victory over Sisera (Judges

5). The glosses in the 1679 *Order and Disorder* would make a study in themselves; with some ingenuity they invite subversive application, but only in those very well versed in the saints' favorite passages. Hutchinson did not venture into print until 1679, when censorship was about to collapse in the onslaught of the Exclusion Crisis, and even then she printed only the first five cantos, which are relatively muted in their political comments. Nonetheless, there is arguably more seditious matter in this book than in *Paradise Lost*; and the later cantos, with their savage prophecies of impending doom to courts, would have had little prospect of reaching print.

Rather than aligning *Order and Disorder* as clearly conservative and *Paradise Lost* as clearly radical in political terms, then, it is perhaps more fruitful to explore the poems' differing strategies and tactics in a political trajectory where much is shared. A similar approach helps to illuminate both poems' gender politics. Hutchinson's greater concern to avoid her own invention does leave her in several respects closer to the more restrictive aspects of Genesis as interpreted by Saint Paul. "Whether [Adam] begged a mate it is unknown" is her comment on a topic on which Milton expatiated at length (*Order and Disorder*, 3.312; *PL* 8.379–97); "We can but make a wild uncertain guess" (5.262) at the fallen couple's emotions. Insofar as she does depart from Scripture, at one point it is to favor the status of the male: where Genesis, and Milton's Raphael (*PL* 7.519–20), have God "make man in our image . . . and let them rule," implying that the rule applies to man and woman, Hutchinson has

> "Let us," said God, "with sovereign power endued,
> Make man after our own similitude,
> Let him our sacred impressed image bear,
> Ruling o'er all in earth and sea and air."
>
> (3.9–12)

The difference is not huge, for in *Paradise Lost*, the 'them' quickly gives way to the statement that it was Adam who was created "in the Image of God" (7.527), though Milton's more indirect narration leaves some latitude for deciding how far Raphael's voice is authoritative.

Hutchinson and Milton unite in idealizing the companionate marriage, "Though perverse men the ordinance reject, / And, pulling all its sacred ensigns down, / To the white virgin only give the crown" (3.436–68; compare *PL* 4.744–46). Like Milton, Hutchinson makes God test Adam in his desire for a mate: "God could at first have made a human pair, / But that it was his will to let man see / The need and sweetness of society" (3.238–40). Adam's need for an "equal mate" (3.233) stems from his desire for conversation (3.386). While this word may at this point retain some of its Latinate overtones of "sexual intercourse" (as in Hutchinson's "brutish conversation," *Order and Disorder* 3.261), in both poets the word becomes generalized and sublimated (compare *PL* 8.418, *Order and Disorder*, 3.290, 386). If the mate Adam is in fact given appears to have been decreed by God to be less than fully equal, this is as true of *Paradise Lost* as of *Order and Disorder*. On the cosmic level of conversation, Wittreich points out that there is an important difference between Milton's and Hutchinson's understandings of the limits of the cosmic conversation: Hutchinson denies that prelapsarian mankind was "sublime" enough to gain access to "angelic converse" (3.291–93). In the unpublished, postlapsarian parts of the poem, however, she does show the human and divine worlds in constant interaction, and the episode of the divine visitation to Sarah (*Order and Disorder* 12.193–264) closely recalls, and may be patterned on, Raphael's visit to Adam and Eve (*PL* 5.298–505). Hutchinson's cosmos does lack the excitements, and the tensions, of Milton's explicitly more sublime and unbounded cosmos. Nevertheless, it shares Milton's strong emphasis on the importance of mutual conversation in relations between man and woman.

Hutchinson's account of the making of Eve is far less narratologically complex than Milton's; with her normal reluc-

tance to introduce nonscriptural action, she amplifies the
episode instead by allegorization. In doing so, she conspicuously refuses one traditional allegorization for Eve's creation out of Adam's side: that this showed her to be inferior.
Hutchinson's first allegorization, ignoring the question of
hierarchy, focuses on the fact that Adam was asleep, an
emblem of Providence's power to aid us even when we are
unaware (3.457–66). Her second allegorization introduces the
favorite Puritan motif of the Song of Songs as an allegory for
the relations between Christ and the church and blends it with
Adam's relation to Eve. Milton makes polemical use of the
couple's nakedness to defend unfallen sexuality and perhaps
also to evoke a republican delight in stripping away false
customs.[19] Hutchinson deals with the couple's nakedness
rather differently (3.493–502): the allegorical meaning of the
nakedness, as a stripping away of types and shadows in the
face of the truth, comes before we are allowed a brief glimpse
of the couple themselves.

Hutchinson does not offer us an equivalent of Milton's
famous blazon of Adam and Eve together (*PL* 4.288–318);
instead, there is an extensive blazon of Adam and nothing
whatever is said of Eve's appearance other than that she is
beautiful. This could be read as another sign that *Order and
Disorder* is more patriarchal than *Paradise Lost*; once alerted
to the poem's authorship, however, we may expect a more
complex situation. Hutchinson confines physical description
to Adam and emphasizes Eve's spiritual beauty, thus qualifying
the very definite hierarchy of spiritual and physical qualities
established in Milton's blazon with its "Hee for God only,
shee for God in him" (*PL* 4.299). We might almost claim
Hutchinson as anticipating modern feminist critiques of the
objectifying masculine gaze when she cautions us against
forgetting our originary dust "while we gaze upon our own
fair frame" (3.123). In fact, Hutchinson certainly did not reject
the genre of the blazon as such, for she used it extensively to

praise her husband in the "Elegies," but the terms of her praise always ultimately qualified the merit of physical beauty.[20] The praise of Adam becomes a generalized praise of the human body, lacking Milton's clear distinction between masculine and feminine physiques: contrast his description of Adam, whose "fair large Front and Eye sublime declar'd / Absolute rule" (*PL* 4.300–1), with Hutchinson's "The brows Love's bow and Beauty's shadow are" (3.111). If in Milton sublimity is allocated to the male and aesthetic beauty to the female, in Hutchinson Adam's beauty is described in terms that a male poet might well have applied to a woman.

When we come to the narration of the Fall, the differences between Hutchinson and Milton again do not bring out a clear pattern of radicalism and conservatism. The Fall itself is passed over very quickly, with none of Milton's elaborate buildup of suspense. Eve is condemned for "unbelief," "dissatisfaction with her present state" and "fond ambition of a Godlike height" (4.205–8). And yet the main moral drawn by the narrator is a lot more concerned with everyday advice in the fallen world than with a primal female disorder: the concluding advice to the female reader is "Hence learn pernicious counsellors to shun." In introducing the Fall the narrator stresses the present-day analogues for the situation of Eve, in women who expose themselves to "flattering whispers" by shunning the counsel of friends, and who are now more culpable because they should know better (4.171–84). Rather than locating in womankind the heinous primal sin that causes all later evil, this analysis actually excuses Eve on the grounds of "unexperience" — a sentiment which may to some degree be implicit in *Paradise Lost* but which it is hard to imagine coming from Milton's narrator.

Nevertheless, the analysis does reveal Milton and Hutchinson as being at one in having severe reservations about women's capacity for full rationality. The biblical texts in Hutchinson's margin at this point are those she also cites in the preface to *Order and Disorder* where she is recanting her own earlier error in translating Lucretius, and in the treatise she addressed to her daughter to warn her against being seduced by heresies. There can be no doubt that she was sincerely haunted by guilt at her earlier translation; and the lament she gives to Eve after the Fall, lamenting the "spots" of her "sin-defiled self" and blaming herself for her husband's fate, is so close in sentiment to some of her own confessions of error that an early reader of one manuscript believed it to be auto-biographical ("Elegies," IIA; *Order and Disorder*, 4.401–40).

Hutchinson does not offer the complex interplay between Adam and Eve after the Fall which Wittreich has explored so illuminatingly in *Paradise Lost*. As he observes, Hutchinson firmly gives Adam the last word. Yet the effect is not quite as conventional as a bald summary might suggest. The narrator glosses Eve's curse with a long passage that offers a view of woman's role in marriage never found in Milton: there are bitter elements in

> The best condition of the wedded state,
> Giving all wives sense of the curse's weight,
> Which makes them ease and liberty refuse,
> And with strong passion their own shackles choose.
> Now though they easier under wise rule prove,
> And every burden is made light by love,
> Yet golden fetters, soft-lined yokes, still be
> Though gentler curbs, but curbs of liberty,
> As well as the harsh tyrant's iron yoke;
> More sorely galling them whom they provoke
> To loathe their bondage, and despise the rule
> Of an unmanly, fickle, froward fool.
>
> (5.135–46)

The narrator does not question the need for "wise rule," but her opposition of marriage to "liberty" is nonetheless striking. She goes on to say that the desire for children, while often reconciling women to a bad marriage, leads to its own torments.

Adam, it is true, is given a lengthy reply to Eve's complaints in which he calms her with biblical texts. But it is noteworthy that he does not cite any of Paul's censures on women; when he declares that "we shall trample on the serpent's head" (5.574), he is uniting male and female agency, taking up an earlier use of the line (5.252) in the voice of the narrator herself; he proceeds to describe their activity as bringing about a "birth" (580). His reply comes to its climax in saying that she is blaming herself excessively, and extenuating her fall as proceeding not from sin but merely from ignorance, a sentiment which it is hard to imagine coming from Milton's Adam (5.579–84). Adam concludes by reminding her that God "promised thee salvation in thy seed." This speech is followed by a striking narratorial intervention: "Ah! Can I this in Adam's person say, / While fruitless tears melt my poor life away?" (5.599–600). This is the closest the narrator has come to revealing a personal dimension, and in breaking the poem's frame it reminds us that Adam's voice is her own creation. After a further consolatory meditation the first part of the poem concludes:

> Return, return, my soul to thy true rest,
> As young benighted birds unto their nest,
> There hide thyself under the wings of Love
> Till the bright morning all thy clouds remove.
>
> (5.699–702)

The narrator identifies herself, here and elsewhere (compare 8.189–94) with the dove; such passages connect with her opening invocation of the Holy Spirit to lay claim to prophetic authority for her verse. There she had compared poetic to divine creation in language that closely recalled Milton's invocation of an androgynous Spirit (*Order and Disorder*, 1.21–30; *PL* 1.6–26). This passage was immediately succeeded by a declaration of humility that closely borrowed from Adam's final speech to Michael (compare *Order and Disorder*, 1.38–44 and *PL* 12.553–60); Adam's "Beyond which was my folly to aspire" (560) becomes Hutchinson's "Let not my thoughts beyond their bounds aspire" (42). (That the closing lines of *Paradise Lost* were especially important to her is indicated by the close concurrence of the phrases "wandering steps" and "happy seat" [*Order and Disorder*, 14.330–33; *PL* 12.646–69], and the appearance of "natural tears" [*PL* 12.645] in Hutchinson's consolation [5.657].)

From Milton, Hutchinson could derive a combination of prophetic audacity and resigned humility that suited her own artistic and ideological purposes. Her lines avoid any element of the apology for female composition found in so many women's texts of the seventeenth century, including Hutchinson's own. Anonymous publication may have been a way of sidestepping accusations of immodesty, but it was also a way of having her writing treated as a significant intervention in contemporary debates. The preface to *Order and Disorder* is full of penitence at the earlier sin of translating Lucretius, but though the wording suggests that Hutchinson expected at least some readers to be aware of her identity, there is no suggestion that the sin was specifically female. Instead, she situates herself in the long Christian tradition in which poets apologize for earlier, sinful works — a tradition that always had an element of rhetorical convention, and that might be felt to remind readers of how powerful those earlier writings must have been for their ill effects to occasion such penitence. There can be no doubting Hutchinson's sincere belief that women were particularly liable to intellectual error, but she clearly also believed that she had been granted unusual powers that would enable her to exorcise her own error. That she did not do so explicitly on behalf of her own sex means that she certainly does not qualify as an early feminist; but she writes with an assurance that is informed both by her Calvinist sense of election and by a republican sense of independence from received customs and traditions.

In the later, postlapsarian sections of the poem, Hutchinson's representation of female characters becomes much more vivid. For a full consideration of Hutchinson's representations of female agency we should have to take account of her Sarah, Hagar, Rebecca and Rachel, which space does not here allow. It would be interesting to develop the parallels with Milton's early drafts of tragedies, which show that he shared Hutchinson's interest in the problematic, challenging women of Genesis; he considered two different treatments of Sarah.[21] On questions of gender, as in so many other areas, Milton and Hutchinson share a common ideological perspective, though with important differences of emphasis. In both, Puritan republicanism led to a suspicion of some forms of female agency, notably in courtly contexts where private will was the less exposed to the countervailing pressure of public institutions. But both, in different ways, were also informed by the universalizing claims of radical Protestantism and of early modern republicanism, claims which meant that the status of women needed to be reexamined from the beginning rather than being read off from customary paradigms. The fact that Hutchinson expressed so much unease about women's status does indicate the particular strains that were placed on women writers occupying her particular place in the ideological spectrum: committed enough to biblical fundamentalism to be unable to share the feminism either of Margaret Cavendish, with her decidedly heterodox religious skepticism, or of the Quaker women who felt greater freedom in claiming the support of the Spirit over against Scripture. Yet despite her intense self-criticism, she did produce one of the most intellectually ambitious bodies of writing of any seventeenth century woman, and in doing so she was empowered as well as limited by a republican milieu.

Hutchinson comes closest to acknowledging herself as a writer toward the end of the surviving text of the poem, when she is describing Jacob's vision of the ladder:

> the next day brought on his early dawn,
> When with like diligence as dames that feel
> The spur of urging need rise to the wheel,

Rake by the cinders, and rush-candles light,
Calling their drowsy maids up while 'tis night,
Then ply their tasks and labour hard to gain
An honest maintenance for their small train,
The son of Isaac from his hard bed rose,
The stone on which he did that night repose
Erects and consecrates unto the Lord,
And like a pillar sets it to record
The memorable vision.

(19.102–13)

Here there is a striking distance between tenor and vehicle: the young, active male hero and the working women. The hidden figure of the woman writer is what bridges the gap. Women had traditionally been supposed to turn to the spinning wheel instead of the pen. In her Lucretius dedication, Hutchinson had tried to integrate the different spheres of activity by declaring that she had numbered the syllables of her translation by the threads of the canvas she was working on.[22] Jacob is seeking to immortalize his dream with his stone; Hutchinson is doing so in verse. This moment, shortly before the poem breaks off, recalls the final simile of *Paradise Lost*, where the figure of the laborer returning homeward evokes the poet finishing his poem, a simile likewise linking manual with intellectual labor (*PL* 12.628–32). Here, perhaps, the two poets find solidarity. Miltonists will of course recognize another parallel, with the strikingly disjunctive simile where Satan's glimpse of the ladder ascending to heaven recalls Jacob (3.511–15). Hutchinson may not have been an unreserved admirer of Milton, but in this androgynous simile she finds common cause with her fellow visionary poet.

3 • "Pleasure by Description"

Elizabeth Singer Rowe's Enlightened Milton

Sharon Achinstein

Alexander Pope's 1713 recipe for an epic poem advises that for the language, "it will do well to be an Imitator of Milton, for you'll find it easier to imitate him in this than any thing else."[1] As Pope's mockery made clear, even early in Milton's afterlife, his peculiar use of language spawned a generation of bad imitation in the eighteenth century. The Tory Anglican Francis Peck, who dared to write a Miltonic imitation in an encomium to Queen Anne, cataloged in his *New Memoirs of the Life and Poetical Works of Mr. John Milton* some 49 features of the Miltonic style, complete with examples and admiration, especially calling attention to his obscure, Latinate or archaic vocabulary, the excessive use of circumlocutions and syntactic inversions. When R. D. Havens explored the influence of Milton on English poetry in a 1922 study, the

primary elements of his analysis were also diction and versification. Blank verse was an obvious starting point, and yet to
write unrhymed lines was not enough to distinguish an author
as "Miltonic"; what the non-Miltonics missed, according to
Havens, was his prosody: the irregular breaks within the lines,
his diction and vocabulary, a penchant for obscure, Latinate
and obsolete words.[2] The diction peculiar to the poet gloried
in inversions, repetitions and circumlocutions, but came to
be disliked amongst twentieth century critics in the great
"Milton controversy."[3] While recently students of Milton's
Whig or radical legacy have focused on the content of his works
and on Milton's "Visionary poetics," here I shall return to the
question of poetic style, exploring how "style" itself could
contribute to a radical, dissenting literary tradition, suggesting
additional directions for accounting for Miltonic radicalism
in the eighteenth century. The Miltonic "style" bore contradictory political or ideological meanings, serviceable to a
variety of occasions and interests, even as his political identity
remained clearly antimonarchical during this time.

This essay looks at one experience of Milton's stylistic
influence upon one Whig writer, Elizabeth Singer Rowe (1674–
1737), who, writing her Miltonic imitation well before the
Romantic Milton of James Thomson and Joseph Warton, saw
Milton not as the arid exponent of a dead language, but rather
as the poet of nature, sublimely infused with God's inspiration.
Rowe's is among the many now-forgotten names compounded
in John Shawcross's collection of Milton criticism from the
eighteenth century as an imitator of Milton's "style."[4] Elizabeth Singer Rowe disrupts the story told by feminist historians
of political thought of a demonized liberal or republican tradition; her first publication praised the Glorious Revolution,
showering King William in glory in 1691 with her "Upon King
William's Passing the Boyne," which announced her poetic
ambition to sing for the Protestant king. Admirers called her
"Madam Laureate."[5] Ever loyal to that monarch, even when

radical Whigs were abandoning him, Rowe was committed to his internationalist, militant Protestant vision. Her poems sing repeatedly of the liberty of the English people, the self-restraint and valor of their leaders, and praise the violence of military success against Jacobites, the French, and themselves, in a moral and political campaign against the decadence and irreligion of the times. A patriotic poem on the great Whig hero-martyr John Hampden ("his soul with freedom fir'd") remains in manuscript among her works.[6] As if imitating Milton's career, Rowe penned "A Pastoral on the Nativity of our *Saviour*," which contains Miltonic echoes. Of interest here is her "A Description of Hell. In Imitation of Milton," which will be an excellent case through which to investigate what counted as "Miltonic" in the early eighteenth century, as well as to investigate how a woman writer coped with the legacy of that strong forebear. Writing in the Miltonic tradition, Rowe seems not at all interested in the matter of Eve's responsibility for the Fall, as so many women were in ages succeeding Milton; indeed, her interests were moral, social, literary and political. If in *Feminist Milton* Joseph Wittreich has directed our view to Milton's female readers in order to explode the caricature of Milton as the woman writer's Bogey, this essay turns from a feminist Milton to a political Milton in the hands of a feminist. Rowe's feminism is not in a pro-woman reading of Milton; rather, the feminism is Rowe's assertion of her right to write as a woman, to inherit a major writer in her own attempts at epic verse. With Rowe, we see how the Whig Milton could be, in addition to a defender of political liberty, also a religious Dissenter.

Elizabeth Singer was born in Somerset in 1674, the eldest of three daughters of Walter Singer, a nonconformist minister, and his wife Elizabeth Portness. Her father, who had a fair estate in the neighborhood of Frome, had been imprisoned in his early life for nonconformity and he first met his wife when she was visiting prisoners there as an act of charity. Elizabeth was educated religiously, practiced music and drawing, and wrote verse from an early age, including a feminist screed defending her authority as a poet against traditional "polite" women's learning.[7] In 1694 and 1695 she was anonymously published in John Dunton's *Athenian Mercury*, and her *Poems on Several Occasions by Philomela* was brought out, also anonymously, in 1696. Included among her suitors and friends were pious men, the poet Matthew Prior, the nonjuring Bishop Ken, the Dissenter Isaac Watts, and the New England divine, Benjamin Colman. When she married, it was in 1710 to Thomas Rowe, 13 years her junior, son and grandson of ejected Nonconformist ministers. Thomas was a classicist and staunch Whig writer, having translated Plutarch's *Lives* with its biographies of antityrannical heroes. The couple moved to London; her husband died in 1715 and was buried in the great Nonconformist burial ground in London, at Bunhill fields. After her husband's death, Rowe returned to Frome where she had inherited a small property from her father, remaining there for the rest of her life, writing devotional poetry and publishing these and other literary works, while maintaining a close friendship with Frances Thynne, the countess of Hertford, later duchess of Somerset. Rowe died in 1737; her *Miscellaneous Works in Prose and Verse* were published in two volumes in 1739.[8] A devout dissenter, Rowe spent half her yearly income in charity, in support of her Rook Lane Congregational Meeting at Frome, where she spent most of her life and where she was buried next to her father. Rowe's poetry developed from youthful lyric effusions published by John Dunton to the mature writing of a ten-book biblical heroic poem; she was enamored of the Italians, translated bits of Tasso and made adaptations of Ovid, Crashaw, Drayton and a biblical paraphrase of Song of Songs. With her poetic meditations and experiments in narrative fiction, Rowe crossed the genres of poetry and prose. She was well regarded in her own day; in response to her Pindaric ode, the "Athenians" hailed her as William III's laureate; Elizabeth Carter saw her as a spokesperson for all women; the major publisher John Dunton was ever a backer. Her literary ambitions were great, and her ten-book biblical poem *The History of Joseph* (1736) was a publishing success, running to seven editions, including a German translation.[9]

Elizabeth Singer Rowe was an avid reader of Milton. In letters to her friends, in her poetic allusions and in her poetic form, Rowe looked to Milton as a model; he was enough of an everyday companion that she cited him to greet the morning, quoted him while moralizing to her sister-in-law, and noted her eagerness for the arrival of Signor Rolli's Italian translation. In an age where the rhyming couplet reigned supreme, Rowe wrote 42 blank verse poems, her "Soliloquies," and she overtly imitated Milton in her "Description of Hell," first published in 1704.[10] Rowe's very literary identity was founded upon Milton's — her pen name, "Philomela," was chosen after Milton's figure in *Il Penseroso*, and she used it in publications in John Dunton's *Athenian Mercury* in the 1690s as well as in her romantic correspondence with her husband.[11] In a letter, Rowe recollects a young lady who was so absorbed in reading Milton in the park that she did not notice her approaching lover.[12] Rowe was an excellent devotional poet; in stressing her position as a woman writer, and ignoring her political and religious aims, her recent biographers have misunderstood the power of that religiosity to achieve a radical identity.[13] In exploring Rowe as a reader of Milton, I hope to understand how Milton's was not simply an aesthetic style to imitate, but a set of concerns, an orientation toward the natural world and its inhabitants, and a moral perspective on artistic creation.

Milton, Whig and Tory

Milton, to be sure, bore heavy ideological weight in Rowe's time. Tonson's 1688 folio edition gave John Milton to a new period in English history, breathing life into the poet's reputation at a moment when the history of seventeenth

century radical religion and antimonarchical politics could
be braided together for a newly anointed king. The reign of
William III was a boon era for Milton rehabilitation, as the
poet was transformed from republican to Whig and then
became something of a splintered mirror in splintered Whig
polemic, refracting different political and religious partisan
views after the Glorious Revolution. Milton was enough of a
household name in 1692 for the Whig *Athenian Mercury* to
run the question, "Whether Milton and Waller were not the
Best English Poets?"[14] Milton in the 1690s was a changing
identity, caught up in the politics of Williamite propaganda
and policy as a string of Whig publications after 1688 brought
out Milton's works. After the Glorious Revolution, Milton
the republican was transformed into Milton the Whig, as
Nicholas von Maltzahn has shown, and was made to serve in
the Standing Army controversy in later political discussion.[15]

After the accession of Anne, however, with the eclipse of
Whig supremacy and further unrest over the status of Dissenters, it was Milton the poet rather than the politician who
received widespread praise. The Anglican Tory Mary Astell,
stinging the Lockean, and as she saw it, Miltonic, principles
which had inaugurated the reign of William and Mary, quoted
Milton's *Eikonoklastes* in her tracts opposing toleration for
Dissenters. In her support for high church, absolute monarchy, and the conservative politics of Queen Anne, Astell
begrudgingly professed that Milton "was a better Poet than
Divine or Politician."[16] But for his politics, Astell would grant
no such praise; her view was that dissent was a dangerous
cloak for political rebellion, and that claims for sovereignty
based upon natural liberty, such as those of Milton and Locke,
were fraudulent. Her advice to Anne was to roll back the
recently won toleration for Dissenters.

While for political Whigs after 1688, Milton stood against
tyranny and for liberty, literary critics on both sides of the
political fence of the early eighteenth century seemed most

interested in fashioning Milton as a poetic "style," putting him to use in the various culture wars of early English criticism: as a religious poet against atheistic libertine poetry; as a modern against the ancients; and, above all, as standing for a sublimity and expansiveness as against narrow Augustanism. Vaunting the potency of Milton the sublime writer, and praising his religious themes, Whig and Dissenting writers were convinced that Milton was a revolutionary poet — poet of revolutionary poetics, not politics. The Dissenting minister and hymn writer Isaac Watts praised blank verse for its "variety of Cadence, Comma, and Period, which Blank Verse Glories in as its particular Elegance and Ornament" (even as in his own verse Watts often preferred rhyming heroics) in his *Horae Lyricae* of 1706.[17] Watts saw Milton as a strong forebear, one whose muse "Breaks all the Criticks Iron Chains, / And bears to Paradise the raptur'd Mind."[18] Milton, "The noble Hater of degenerate Rhyme / Shook off the Chains, and built his Verse sublime, / A Monument too high for coupled Sounds to climb" (*Horae Lyricae*, 212).

Milton is an inspiring presence for Watts, the Milton who "knows no Rule but native Fire" (*Horae Lyricae*, 213), and who "shall be for ever honour'd as our Deliverer from the Bondage" of rhyme, whose "works contain admirable and unequall'd Instances of bright and beautiful Diction, as well as Majesty and Sereneness of Thought" (ibid., xx). Yet Milton was also a problem for Watts, who complained of the poet's "length of his Periods, and sometimes of his Parenthesis," which "runs me out of Breath: some of his Numbers seem too harsh and uneasy." In addition, Watts abjures Milton's archaisms and roughness: "I could never believe that Roughness and Obscurity added any thing to the true Grandeur of a Poem," he wrote, and in his own poetry refused to "affect Archaisms, Exoticisms, and a quaint Uncouthness of Speech, in order to become perfectly *Miltonian*" (ibid., xx–xxi). Even as Watts praised Milton's revolutionary blank verse he disliked

the jarring roughness of his numbers; and that Rowe and Watts
alike preferred the rhymed couplet shows Milton could bear
an ambivalent poetic legacy.

Milton, Poet of Darkness

Rowe's Milton was recognizable as a style, but hers was a
Milton of extreme states, a poet of darkness and loss, as well
as a moral center in an irreligious age. Rowe's "Description of
Hell" begins with Milton's rhetorical penchant for epanalepsis:

> Deep, to unfathomable spaces deep,
> Descend the dark, detested paths of hell,
> The gulphs of execration and despair,
> Of pain, and rage, and pure unmingled woe;
> The realms of endless death, and seats of night,
> Uninterrupted night, which sees no dawn.
>
> (1–6)

These first six lines strain our sense of the syntax; with
a delayed subject for the verb "descend," Rowe imitates
Milton's inversions of adjectives, verbs and subjects: "deep . . .
descend . . . the paths of hell." It is an ambiguity, and Milton
delighted in ambiguity, as if Rowe might be speaking in the
second person, commanding the paths of hell to descend, deep.
But there is a sense of perversity, too, an inverted invocation
perhaps to begin a poem not asking for inspiration from
above but seeking that from below. Indeed, Rowe inverts
Milton's general architectonic movements from low to high,
making that inversion a theme of her poem, as even in slight
verbal details Rowe negates Milton's negations: her hell is
"uninterrupted night"; Milton's Eden was "uninterrupted joy"
(*PL* 3.68).

Rowe's verse is, however, stiffer than Milton's. As if to
further insist upon her thematic inversions, the next lines in
the poem offer something of a Miltonic exclamation, a private
comment in parentheses, as she hails not "holy light" but

> Prodigious darkness! which receives no light
> But from the sickly blaze of sulph'rous flames,
> That cast a pale and dead reflection round,
> Disclosing all the desolate abyss,
> Dreadful beyond what human thought can form,
> Bounded with circling seas of liquid fire.
>
> (7–12)

This 86-line homage has begun with an extended description, not of the descent of fallen angels, but of the paths of hell leading downwards; absent are any actors in the scene. There are Miltonic echoes, the "desolate abyss" reminds us of *Paradise Lost*, book 4, line 936, but in many ways the poem doesn't read like Milton's. Despite her efforts to imitate his diction, theme and mood, the extended description of hell is a passage of nearly pure description, an enumeration of sights and sounds:

> Aloft the blazing billows curl their heads,
> And form a roar along the direful strand;
> While ruddy cat'racts from on high descend,
> And urge the fiery ocean's stormy rage.
> Impending horrors o'er the region frown,
> And weighty ruin threatens from on high;
> Inevitable snares, and fatal pits,
> And gulphs of deep perdition, wait below;
> Whence issue long, remediless complaints,
> With endless groans, and everlasting yells.
> Legions of ghastly fiends (prodigious sight!)
> Fly all confus'd across the sickly air,
> And roaring horrid, shake the vast extent.
>
> (13–25)

In Rowe's hands, unlike in Milton's, the language draws attention to the objects described, not to the writer doing the describing. Although Rowe delights in her parentheses (two "Prodigious sights!"), and rhetorical parataxes, there are no oxymorons here, no "darkness visibles" or unconsumed burning sulphur. Similes lead to things seen: fire is an ocean, as the passage creates a visual match between ocean and fire, a pyrotechnic hydrographia: the register is somehow made more, not less, vivid by language. For Rowe, Milton offers material to *hear* as well as to *see*: endless groans, everlasting yells, roaring horrid. So in Rowe's image the senses lead us toward understanding the picture more fully. In moving back and forth between the registers of the visual and the aural, Rowe produces an aural correlate for a visual image, not only synesthesia but catachresis. These elements comprise her attempt at a Miltonic sublime.

Even as she, in a Miltonic moment, doubts her ability to represent ("Dreadful beyond what human thought can form"), nonetheless in her sublime poetic attempt Rowe strikingly does not betray any mediating consciousness (human or angelic) to filter the description. Impending horrors may *frown* and weighty ruin *threaten* from on high, but a judging Christian deity and a sentient being to receive that judgment are both absent thus far from the poem, as is the allusion to the story of Satan's sin. With Milton, seeing is always marred by the viewer, and sometimes things can not be seen at all (the best things, sometimes). While in Milton's hell, the landscape is filtered through individual consciousness ("regions of sorrow"), even humanized (satanized?), here the scene is rendered more distant: a work of art, to be sure, as it depicts not a visible region but an imagined one. But that imagined picture is ab-sent characters' perceptions. Verbs indicating personification render the mighty natural forces as actors: the billows roar; the cataracts urge; snares, pits and gulfs wait. The sounds are disembodied and nasty. Rowe's hell fits a scheme of the objective more than it does the psychologized perspective of Milton's poetry.

Rowe's interest in Milton the scene painter was not simply an instance of the eighteenth century's love of the pictorial, as Jean Hagstrum surveyed in *The Sister Arts*, that penchant for perceiving an analogy in the arts of poetry and painting.[19] Rowe herself was an amateur painter, and her friend the

Countess of Hertford was also a lover of pictures and an amateur painter as well. But nature, for Rowe, was no mere painterly challenge: hers was a religious appreciation of the natural world. To her sister-in-law, Mrs. Sarah Rowe, she wrote of her appreciation of the countryside:

> I have been just taking a solitary walk, and entertaining myself with all the innocent pleasures, that verdant shades, painted flowers, fragrant breezes and warbling birds can yield. If I could communicate my pleasure by description, I would call the muses to assist me; but I am afraid 'twould be insipid to you, that are but moderately fond of the country. Yet I am sure you would relish any pleasure that heighten'd your devotion; and what can more effectually raise it, than viewing the beauties of nature? I have been pulling a thousand flowers in pieces, to view their elegance and variety, and have a thousand times with rapture repeated *Milton's* lines
>
> *These are thy glorious works, Parent of good,*
> *Almighty, thine this universal frame,*
> *Thus wond'rous fair; thyself how wond'rous then!*
> *Speak, ye, who best can tell, ye sons of light,*
> *Angels; for ye behold him.—*
>
> They indeed behold the great original; but 'tis not deny'd me to trace his footsteps in the flowery fields, and hear some faint echoes of his voice in the harmony of birds, or meet his gentle whispers in the softness of the evening breezes; yet this only raises my impatience to be admitted to the blissful vision of uncreated beauty.[20]

As Rowe quotes from Adam and Eve's evening prayer (*PL* 5.153–55, 160–161), she turns her country walk into an ode of adoration of God. Indeed, she becomes as Eve, ever associated with flowers. But that relation is a violent one; a scientific admiration that kills the flower even as it studies it. The minute observation of the flower is also a reflection on the handiwork, the artistry of God: also a figure for the poet's own handiwork. What beauty can be observed is a sign of God's care in the world, and her view incites ardent devotion to God's works, even as it dismembers them in observing more closely. For Rowe, the empirical observation, even as it approaches a scientific objectivity, leads to spiritual devotion. In picking apart delicate flowers to view their variety, Rowe is no detached observer, to be sure, but an admirer of a world infused with divinity. Her attentive viewing of the "art" visible in the natural world, reflected in the art of the poet she cites, all serve to honor God and to make room for the artistry of humans.

If the art of "description" is the poetic model here, then the scene is rendered more immediate than it ever could be in Milton. For Milton, to contrast, objective description is not to be found in hell; his hell is conspicuously psychologized and moralized — or rather, demoralized — in its every aspect. Satan is hurled with his horrid crew into a hell designed just for them; the landscaper of hell is not simply physical but psychological as well ("the hell within him"). Milton's portrayal of hell shows a place overpowering the human ability to construe it, but with each physical description, psychological affect and moral judgment are rendered:

> At once as far as angels' kenn he views
> The dismal Situation waste and wild,
> A Dungeon horrible, on all sides round
> As one great Furnace flam'd, yet from those flames
> No light, but rather darkness visible
> Serv'd only to discover sights of woe,
> Regions of sorrow, doleful shades, where peace
> And rest can never dwell, hope never comes
> That comes to all; but torture without end
> Still urges, and a fiery Deluge, fed
> With ever-burning Sulphur unconsum'd:
> Such place Eternal Justice had prepar'd
> For these rebellious, here thir Prison ordain'd
> In utter darkness, and thir portion set
> As far remov'd from God and light of Heav'n
> As from the Center thrice to th' utmost Pole.
> O how unlike the place from whence they fell!
>
> (*PL* 1.59–75).[21]

Satan is undeniably the medium for cognition here, as Milton gives the vision from his perspective of a fallen angel, the tormented viewer whose sights of this geography incite his first lamenting speech, "If thou beest he; but O how fall'n!" (1.84). T. S. Eliot had noted these lines on hell as "difficult to imagine" for its paradoxes: but the passage, as Carey and Fowler note, "is not intended merely as a physical description."[22] The point of Milton's images was not simply to represent objective reality, but, as later critics saw it, to prompt specific affective states: wonder, terror, revulsion. John Dennis, who defended Christian poetry in his *Advancement and Reformation of Poetry* (1701), had praised Milton's "noble Images, which *Milton* has shewn in such wondrous Motion . . . at the same Time that the Eye is ravishingly entertain'd, Admiration is rais'd to a Height, and Reason is supremely satisfied."[23] Condensing anguish, loss, lament and inspiration, Milton presented a geography of darkness that could inspire Satan's renewal of energy and tempt readers to partake in sin. The paradoxes of Satan's sight reflect his inner world bereft of the goodness of order and harmony.

Rowe's landscape of hell is rendered an immediate vision, however, without such theological and ontological paradoxes; strikingly, her scene in this early part of the poem lacks a viewer, either satanic or Miltonic. Without an agent whose emotional compass could chart the place, whose "baleful eyes" (56) might witness a vision of torture or who might receive the moralizing judgment of a victorious deity, Rowe establishes a different poetic affective relation to the reader. Unlike Milton, Rowe not only refuses to supply the references of biblical or classical sources, but also denies her vision any mediation through a personal perspective.[24] Her poetry is, rather, to be a transparent medium of a description, a representation of physical landscape in its sublime objectivity. At its core, this is an aesthetic theory which renders a harmonious relationship between things in the world and things as they are perceived. In Milton's aesthetic vision, to contrast, there is often a mismatch: landscape cannot reveal moral truth, since language itself is a fallen medium; moral truth may be disclosed or mediated only through the fallen language since "shadowy types" are the closest thing to real knowledge. Unlike Rowe's his is always the mediation of a fallen vantage point, a result of an overpowering awareness of human frailty: this is a profound ontological difference. For Rowe's mediating poetry, there is no fallen impediment to true sight: hers is an enlightened confidence in the ability of human powers to conceive and perceive the world around her: a Lockean moral and cognitive universe, not a Miltonic one. This is an enlightened religious outlook, arising from an optimistic base of human capability.

Although she differs in her tools for the construction of a moral vision, hers is like Milton's, an affective poetic nonetheless; she hopes to awaken conceptions, to make an impression upon her readers. Both Rowe and Milton seek to elicit readers' emotional response; however, Rowe solicits her readers not through sympathetic identification with their feelings, but through mastery of objective technique, an emblematic rather than a subjective view. Her physical description represents a scene which should inspire or evoke imaginative sensations: terror, horror, judgment. Rowe reveals a new emphasis in English poetry, as she translates Miltonic subjective states, fallen mediations, into a mode of pure, immediate description. Evoking horror, rue or blame, Rowe chooses a representational mode with a stable point of reference.

Rowe does at last represent hell's inhabitants, but their perspective does not supply the moral vantage point of view:

> Pale, meagre spectres wander all around,
> And pensive shades, and black deformed ghosts.
> With impious fury some aloud blaspheme,
> And wildly staring upwards curse the skies;
> While some, with gloomy terror in their looks,

> Trembling all over, downward cast their eyes,
> And tell, in hollow groans, their deep despair.
>
> (26–32)

Although we do not know which edition of Milton Rowe drew upon for her image, it is striking to compare Rowe's scene painting with the engraving for book 1 found in Tonson's 1688 volume. The pictorial representation of hell, as Roland Mushat Frye has documented, has a long and varied tradition: yet Rowe's hell is quite unlike that of the Western European artistic tradition. Her hellish creatures are, like Milton's, humanized, that is, they are not monsters; nor do they experience torture or physical punishment. Their requital, on the other hand, is mental, their sin signified by verbal, not physical, gestures: blasphemy, impiety, or despair.[25] Both Rowe and Tonson's engravers are interested in chiaroscuro effects; Tonson's illustration for book 1 is lit from below and that glare lights up the demonic faces. Rowe, too, was interested in the "sickly blaze of suph'rous flame." However, the resemblance between her vision and that of the 1688 volume ends there. The 1688 illustration offers nothing of the dimensional perspective we are made to perceive in Rowe's version. Tonson's prospect is horizontal, with a flat plane receding: in the foreground, angels crowd on a burning lake of fire, and further back are other pools of fire. Even further back is a neoclassical structure where a group of figures are clustered around a throne; above a sky threatens. Rowe's perspective, on the other hand, is vertical: she offers "deep . . . deep . . . deep," with gulfs, pits, paths, ruddy cataracts. This is a romantic, mountainous landscape, quite unlike that of Tonson's in which no clear boundaries exist between ground and sky. The greatest difference, however, is the classicism of the 1688 engraving, as Satan and his crew wear Roman armor, and the building in the background is in the neoclassical style (this has been interpreted as a satirical portrait of the dethroned James II).[26] Rowe contains nothing of this Roman fascination, and it is hard to see a particular target of her satire. Her image is much closer to the 1749 illustration of Francis Hayman, rather, where Satan summons his legions, a fully Romanticized version.[27]

For Rowe, Milton was a scene painter of extraordinary power and vividness. Using the new tools of an enlightened religion, Milton, for Rowe as he would be for Thomson, Warton and Wordsworth, has become the great poet of direct, natural description, where nature could become the expression of the divine. This is a very different Milton from that described by Addison who had bested the classics by outclassicizing them. It is also a different Milton from that of Samuel Johnson, who opined that Milton saw nature only through the spectacle of books. In the natural divinity that suffuses Rowe's poetic, Milton's nature could be seen distinctly, just as God could be apprehended in its workings. Her interpretation was not simply the victory of empiricism, natural landscape over politics or psychology; we have come to see that natural description often expresses an ideological point of view. Landscape moralized: this was the central aesthetic plank of country poetry stretching from the seventeenth to the eighteenth century, from Marvell's "Appleton House" and its "naked equal Flat which *Levellers* take pattern at," in a context of civil war conflict, or, under the Hanoverians, an aesthetic correlate to the country Whig faction exemplified by James Thomson's *Seasons*. In the early modern period, descriptions of prospects were often not simply descriptions, but rather embodied political or ideological meanings. *Cooper's Hill*, as James Turner puts it, "presents ideological statements as aesthetic masterpieces."[28] The Augustan Georgic which represented rural life and labor also made statements with social implications, offering idealizations in order to mask or mediate changes in rural economies, land ownership and political power. As contemporary cultural critics have attended to the ways that images of place, and specifically of country life, mediate or mask social relations, they have read landscape and country representations as stories about other significant economic and social relations, for instance, the colonial slave trade, consumerism, urbanism, enclosure and the effects of capitalism upon the rural poor.[29]

For Rowe, landscape is ideological, but in a different way. Hers is not a benevolent landscape, but rather one of grand indifference to those who observe it. Objective scenes could be the background upon which subjects could view themselves truly, immediately, and arrive at an understanding of the harmony of a sensible cosmos.[30] Unlike Milton, Rowe searches for an objective, empirical medium through which the just order of things might become evident, a poetry of description with great emotional impact, one through which objective moral states could be expressed in a realistic, not a morally subjective view. For Milton, the experience of landscape varied according to the viewer, but the eighteenth century critics who admired him were drawn to his mastery of picture painting. As Rowe viewed landscape as separate from consciousness of the viewer, often emptied of people, her primary goal was to evoke emotional states through direct representation of object to viewer. Above all, Milton, for Rowe, is a poet of scene painting, a moral realism with a morally stable point of view.

Milton Moralist

If Rowe learned scene painting from Milton, an appreciation for an immediate poetry of nature, her "Imitation of Hell" does in the end pick up the great theme of *Paradise Lost*, religious morality and social comment. The second half of her "Imitation" poem brings us a Miltonic catalog of devils, echoing Milton's passage that had so charmed eighteenth century critics; Addison praised the "Abundance of Learning in it, and a very agreeable Turn of Poetry." Addison explains that the greatness of the passage "rises in a great measure from its describing the Places where they were worshipped, by those beautiful marks of Rivers so frequent among the Ancient Poets. The Author had doubtless in this place *Homer's* Catalogue of Ships, and *Virgil's* List of Warriors in his view."[31] Rowe's catalog, however, refuses the learned tradition so admired by Addison. For Rowe, the view to the topography of hell does at last yield an engagement with social or political themes, but the vision is objectified and denuded of its classical and biblical pasts.

As Rowe turns to the Miltonic roll of fallen angels, she shifts from her scene painting to present a point of view; indeed, she becomes the satirist against contemporary morality. Rowe's demons are individuated, each given his (and her) own little hell.

> Convinc'd by fatal proofs, the atheist here
> Yields to the sharp tormenting evidence;
> And of an infinite eternal mind,
> At last the challeng'd demonstration meets.
>
> (33–36)

Rowe offers an empirical religion and, with it, an empiricist poetics: the atheist comes to experience the truth of God by specific tormenting proofs. Similarly, the repentant Eve in *Paradise Lost* had come to know by "sad experiment" what she had done (*PL* 10.967); however, Rowe's poem as a whole works at a register of proof that is quite unlike that of Milton, whose aim was to "justify the ways of God," not to prove God exists. Milton's *Paradise Lost* has been called a "poetry of experience," but that experience, as Stanley Fish has explained, is personal: only Satan is the spokesperson of an empirical, self-sufficient, mode of knowledge.[32] For Rowe, however, the empirical is a means of revealing theological truths. Her poem turns into moral satire, that most beloved of Augustan genres, with its familiar character types: the atheist, the libertine, the wanton beauty, the fool and, last of all, the "execrable persecutor" (67).

In line with his effort to make Milton the great British epic poet, Addison called attention to those aspects of *Paradise Lost* that resembled Homer and Virgil, as well as praising the correctness of his allusions to the Bible. Addison, finding that Milton's representation of these deities conformed with authority, proved his point by corroborating the vision with Henry Maundrell's *A Journey from Aleppo to Jerusalem* (1703). John Dennis had also admired the "most delightfull and most admirable Part of the sublimest of all our Poets, is that which relates the Rebellion and Fall of these Evil Angels, and their dismal Condition upon their Fall, and their Consult for the recovery of their native Mansions, and their Original Glory."[33] For Rowe, on the other hand, there was no such interest in classical or biblical allusions, no need to situate the historical geography of *Paradise Lost*'s hell in any specific location, no desire to have Milton compete with the classics for poetic stature, or even to use Milton's example as an opportunity to show off her own classical learning. Instead, her Milton is the inspired poet, authorized by divine (not literary-traditional) authority. Instead of Addison's classicizing, she presents general character types. Although they emerge from her specific moment in history evoking the politics of religion in Rowe's day, where religious persecution of Dissenters at home and of Protestants on the Continent was still a live issue, these figures are nonetheless universalized into types:

> Beyond them all a miserable hell
> The execrable persecutor finds;
> No spirit howls among the shades below
> More damn'd, more fierce, nor more a fiend than he.
> Aloud he heav'n and holiness blasphemes,
> While all his enmity to good appears,
> His enmity to good; once falsly call'd
> Religious warmth, and charitable zeal.
> On high, beyond th'unpassable abyss,
> To aggravate his righteous doom, he views
> The blissful realms, and there the schismatic,

The visionary, the deluded saint,
By him so often hated, wrong'd, and scorn'd,
So often curs'd, and damn'd, and banish'd thence:
He sees him there possest of all that heav'n,
Those glories, those immortal joys, which he,
The orthodox, unerring catholic,
The mighty fav'rite, and elect of God,
With all his mischievous, converting arts,
His killing charity, and burning zeal,
His pompous creeds, and boasted faith, has lost.

(66–86)

This is the end of the poem. With her use of rhetorical suspension ("which he . . . has lost"), Rowe imitates Milton's grammar, yet with a twist: this loser is not to be pitied or offered grace, as were Adam and Eve: instead the "unerring catholic" deserves unremitting punishment. Here Rowe has the persecutor suffer his just punishment, her sketch also evoking the thematic moment of Satan, who gazes longingly upon the good ("Sometimes towards *Eden* which now in his view / Lay pleasant, his griev'd look he fixes sad, / Sometimes towards Heav'n and the full-blazing Sun," *PL* 4.27–29), and also Satan's moral perversion ("Evil be thou my Good," *PL* 4.110). Of all the fallen creatures, the persecutor receives most of Milton's Satan's affect, as his punishment is to look upon those he once persecuted and to view their ultimate victory. Gone are marks of Satan's passions which "betraid him counterfet" (*PL* 4.116–17); Rowe's persecutor suffers for real without eliciting our sympathy. We have, instead, a moral emblem for an irreligious age, done up in Miltonic "style" that is at once aesthetically and politically charged.

Indeed Rowe read the catalog of fallen angels very differently from Addison: she has erased classical and biblical allusion in order to create universal types, fitting for a moral diatribe for her own day, a pronounced defense of religious unorthodoxy. Addison, in contrast, in his praise for the hellish catalog in

Paradise Lost, had highlighted the learned and vivid details which gave life to Milton's powerful character sketches. Moloch's "preferring Annihilation to Shame or Misery, is also highly suitable to his Character . . . becoming the bitterness of this implacable Spirit"; Mammon's "Speech in this Book is every where suitable to so depraved a Character."[34] For Addison, Milton was a great fabricator of interior states of being as well as a judicious scholar, fashioning motives for his devils that seemed plausible and breathing new life into dusty arcana.

For Rowe, Milton was a sublime poet and a moralist ready to issue thundering condemnation, not the sapient classical and biblical scholar who gave new, British life to ancient traditions through vivid portraiture and elevated or unnatural style. Rowe, in refusing the neoclassicism of Milton's epic catalog, rife with its density of reference to learning, chooses a purer, more abstract relation, honed to the minimum of detail. Indeed, in contrast to her first half of the poem, this portion of the poem presents virtually nothing of concrete detail about the physical nature of these fallen creatures; it is simply Milton denuded of his learning, a purged Milton. Instead, Rowe highlights the moral anguish of the damned creatures, intensifying the contrast in perception between unfallen and fallen states by giving their vantage point upward, toward a lost heaven. In a just reversal, these damned inhabitants now look up to the airy realms in which those whom they had cast down are now elevated. With her stylistic repetitions echoing Milton's habits, Rowe hammers home the reversed morality that is the just end: "while all his enmity to good appears, / his enmity to good." Milton, of course, had emphasized the freedom of his angelic creatures, who can "execute thir aerie purposes / And works of love or enmity fulfill" (1.430–31). It is a Miltonic imitation, to be sure, but more in theme than in method.

Participating in a cultural campaign against arid neoclassicism, against the leeching of Milton's religious moralism for his political commitments to liberty, Elizabeth Rowe, as did many Dissenting writers, sought to return poetry to its source in the divine, to reclaim religion in poetry. In an age of Pope, they fought an aesthetic battle that was also allied to a country party, an anticourtly politics, positioning themselves against the urbane, decadent wits; they were to be the defenders of religion, nature, ethics and justice. As Elizabeth Rowe's friend and patron Lady Hertford wrote to Isaac Watts, "I think everybody must wish a muse like Mr. Pope's were more inclined to exert itself on divine and good-natured subjects; but I am afraid satire is his highest talent."[35] Watts wrote that he wished "Would not Mr. Pope, that bright genius and that supreme poet, more happily entertain and improve mankind, could he be persuaded to turn his pen to such sort of lyric odes, than by all his satiric imitations of Horace?"[36] Hertford subscribed to an alternate Miltonic literary tradition, support-ing the publication of the poetry not only of Elizabeth Singer Rowe but of John Hughes, Stephen Duck, James Thomson and Isaac Watts. Rowe's poetic tastes were broad and ecumenical; she found enough in Pope to praise. But for her, Milton was the living poet. Well before the charges of unnatural prosody in the twentieth century Milton controversy, before Eliot's and Leavis's charges of arid pomposity and remoteness of image, Milton was at one time seen as the poet of lively nature, a country writer, a writer at odds with the cold formality of a neoclassical, stylized pastoral. The poetic effect of direct inspiration, Milton's poetry was to some in the eighteenth century the ample author of wild scenes; the Milton of Eden, hell, the unformed world, of primitive nature and of extreme feeling. The Miltonic style was sublime: direct, and a sharp contrast to the urbane, cultivated artifice of wags and wits. Moreover, Milton was simply a defender of political liberty, but a rebuke to irreligion in a libertine age, a moral center in a stable universe.

Rowe returned to the Miltonic scene of hell as she composed her heroic poem *The History of Joseph*, the first eight books of which were published in 1736. There she tells the story of the enslavement and ultimate restoration of a Christ figure. Although in this biblical epic Rowe chooses rhyming couplets, there are many implicit allusions to Milton. In her poem, Rowe also returned to the subject of hell, as Milton did, as the first place of action in the first book:

> In *Hinnon's* vale a fane to *Molock* stood,
> Around it rose a consecrated wood;
> Whose mingled shades, excluded noon-day light,
> And made below uninterrupted night.
> Pale tapers hung around in equal rows,
> The mansion of the sullen king disclose;
> Seven brazen gates its horrid entrance guard;
> Within the cries of infant ghosts were heard:
> On seven high altars rise polluted fires,
> While human victims feed the ruddy spires.
> The place *Gehenna* call'd, resembled well
> The native gloom and dismal vaults of hell.
>
> (66–77)

Hell has become not otherworldly; it is, rather, the local parish church. As Rowe composes her hell in this poem, she evokes a contemporary obsession with the dangers of priestcraft, not simply as anti-Catholicism, but as a Dissenter negating the ceremonialism of the Anglican church, with its royal control and its religious props: candles, altars and the rite of baptisms. Rowe takes the opportunity to attack a superstitious and tyrannical religious regime.

Rowe's poem is also aware of the international setting for confessional disagreement: these are "apostate princes," not simply fallen angels:

> 'Twas night, and goblins in the darkness danc'd,
> The priest in frantick visions lay entranc'd;
> While here conven'd the *Pagan* terrors sate,
> In solemn council, and mature debate.
> T'avert the storm impending o'er their state.
> Th'apostate princes with resentment fir'd,

> Anxious, and bent on black designs, conspir'd
> To find out schemes successful to efface
> Great *Heber's* name, and crush the sacred race.[37]

As Rowe tells the story of the fall, rise and restoration of Joseph, she parallels the history of the biblical people of Israel with the English nation. Milton's poem is clearly a model for her imaginative shaping of biblical material, and of her topical application to contemporary history. In her *Joseph*, "a virgin Muse" sings her "virgin theme" (1:44): daughter of Milton, inheritor of his dissenting vision.

Milton's poetic reputation was secured long before his political and radical religious legacies were accommodated; indeed, the recognition of "the poet" was also an elevation of the question of style to a realm *beyond* political faction and religious sectarianism, and toward national inclusiveness. It had been as a poet with an instantly recognizable style that Milton had found recognition early and swift after his death in 1674. John Dryden had long recognized his stature, but the process of avoiding Milton the defender of king-killing in favor of Milton the great poet was a complex one. His works were revived in both a Whig political agenda as well as in a Tory backlash. He was inspiration both for those advocating a neoclassical aesthetics, as did Joseph Addison, as well as for those claiming a divine poetics, as did John Dennis, Isaac Watts and Elizabeth Singer Rowe. Theorists of the sublime in the early eighteenth century often turned to Milton as an exemplar.[38] Yet the Whig literary tradition could find different varieties of inspiration from Milton; a more careful exploration of Whig poetry, politics and aesthetics could help us disentangle the many ways Milton held significance for his heirs. For Rowe, Milton could serve as both sublimely inspired poet of affective description as well as the stern moralizer, not only a defender of political liberty, but a prophetic voice against religious persecution. As early Milton admirers and detractors knew, "There are many *Miltons* in this one Man."[39]

4 • Inventing Postcolonialism

Edmund Burke's Paradise Lost and Regained

Annabel Patterson

This essay follows the steps of Joseph Wittreich who followed the steps of John Milton into the eighteenth and nineteenth centuries with a creative zest of his own. I offer a Miltonic contribution to what is often called the "Burke problem"; the vexed relation between Edmund Burke's defense of the American Revolution in the mid-1770s and his attack on the French Revolution in the early 1790s. This trajectory from undeniably liberal principles to an eloquent but extreme conservativism has naturally been celebrated by as many or more than have regretted it. It has been "explained" in psychological terms by Isaac Kramnick, as the not-inconsistent behavior of someone who was always "a believer in political and constitutional balance" by David Bromwich, and as the frustrated response of a man whose talents were never rewarded by any significant public office, and whose influence in the House of Commons had waned significantly after the death of his patron Rockingham in 1782 when he was no longer seen as "the mouthpiece, and perhaps also the brain, of one of the wealthiest landowners under the crown."[1] But the overall effect of the "Burke problem," in our own academic culture, has been to privilege the *Reflections on the Revolution in France* as an intellectual event and rhetorical performance, in whose shadow the speech on conciliation of the American colonies, delivered in the House of Commons on March 22, 1775, and extraordinarily celebrated in its own time, has rather languished. The central myth of the *Reflections*, that the French Revolution destroyed beauty, order and custom to no good purpose, has effectively and affectively prevailed over the central myth of *On Conciliation*, which this essay will offer to restore.[2]

Until the later twentieth century, *On Conciliation* must have been one of the best known and best conserved political speeches of all time. Published on May 22 by J. Dodsley, who had five years earlier published five editions of Burke's *Thoughts on the Cause of the Present Discontents*, it went through three English editions in 1775 and was also published in New York by James Rivington in that year. This was no accident. As a member of the Opposition party in the Commons, the Rockingham Whigs as they are usually known, who were always depressingly in the minority, Burke knew in advance that his proposals would be voted down, and that the main purpose of his speech was to consolidate pro-American feeling in England at large (of which there was very little) and to reassure the American leaders that they had articulate support in the mother country. Since then, the speech appeared not only in editions of Burke's collected works, but in many separate editions in both countries, some of these explicitly for use in schools; by 1895 it had evidently become a classic in the United States; by the 1990s it was a forgotten one.[3]

Perhaps this also stemmed from the way *On Conciliation* had been adopted in America. Thomas Jefferson had, of course, purchased the 1776 New York edition and placed it among his huge collection of tracts on Anglo-American relations.[4] But from 1895 onward it was deployed either as a paradigmatic oration for the rhetorical instruction of advanced students or the occasion for inculcating an important block of Anglo-American history. But somehow the two sides of this endeavor, the rhetorical and the historical-contextual, have not enlightened each other. We can see that this speech (even more than the *Thoughts on . . . the Present Discontents*) crystallizes the dilemma of the Rockingham Whigs, who with Burke as their Cicero attempted to define a cause around which they might rally; but the extraordinary *tone* of *On Conciliation* and its underlying myth have almost eluded us.[5] I call that myth, with Burke's authorization, *Paradise Lost*. Much later in his life, Burke would be scathingly associated with Milton's poem, when, after Rockingham's death in 1782, James Sayers published a cartoon showing Burke and Fox as Adam and Eve, excluded from Paradise, over whose locked gate is the sculptured, gloating head of William Petty, earl of Shelburne, to whom George III had offered the ministry. F. P. Lock has suggested in his definitive biography that "*Paradise Lost* more truly expresses Burke's plight in 1784," when the rout of the Fox-North coalition in the election of that year completed the collapse of his political career, but in 1775 Milton's epic did not express his "plight" at all.[6] Rather, it represented his now fully developed philosophy of the Western empire, part tragic, part epic, part utopian foresight.

By 1775 Burke had almost reached the conclusion that the colonies, like Paradise itself, were effectively lost. He was trying to avert an event already predetermined by precedent mismanagement, not to mention greed and stupidity. His argument was that George III and Lord North were attempting to punish heroic entrepreneurialism in the colonies, and to wipe out resistance motivated, according to Burke, by essentially Whig principles; and one of his strategies was to marshal feelings, at the subliminal level, by casting his speech as a complex reworking of Milton's *Paradise Lost*. Far from being merely decorative, his allusions to Milton's poem constitute, as it were, a second-level hermeneutics by which we can understand why he delivered it, and why he delivered it then. The role that the American colonies and the struggle with the mother country played in Burke's own intellectual and imaginative development (later to be replaced by an equally idealistic but less realistic commitment to the Eastern empire) was more profound than we can deduce by merely following his arguments and identifying his positions. But we can get closer to plumbing its psychological and ideological depths if we attend to his invocations of Milton — already established, in Burke's 1757 *Philosophical Enquiry into the Origin of Our Ideas of the Sublime and Beautiful*, as the greatest modern source of the sublime.

Burke had a vast amount of Milton in his library. He had a precious copy of the 1691 edition of Bentley and Tonson's *Paradise Lost*, "adorn'd with Sculptures." He owned two copies of Newton's edition of *Paradise Lost*, the first published in Dublin in 1751 in two volumes, the second published in London in 1754 (erroneously cited as three volumes in the sale catalog of his library). He owned a 1740 edition of Paoli Rolli's two-volume Italian translation, supposedly from "Parigi" (Paris), volume 1 having first been published in "Londra" in 1729 and both volumes in "Londra" in 1735; as well as William Dobson's two-volume Latin-English edition, published in Oxford in 1750 (volume 1) and 1735 (volume 2). More significantly, he evidently recognized, as was rare in the eighteenth century, the whole Milton, the republican and regicide Milton, not just the author of the great poems, for he owned the 1753 edition of the prose works edited by Richard Baron; and, as a more specialized acquisition, the special edition of *Eikonoklastes* produced by Baron in 1756. A still more telling item is John Toland's *Life of Milton* in the 1761 edition sponsored by

Thomas Hollis, who sent Burke this copy in one of his famous red morocco bindings. Hollis at least assumed that Burke was an appropriate recipient of the Milton legacy.[7] As if this were not enough, Burke continued his Milton collection well past the era of *On Conciliation*, indeed, into the era of the *Reflections on the Revolution in France*, for his library contained a 1793 edition of *Paradise Lost*, presumably purchased five years before his death.[8] Even in a collection as deep and as catholic in its tastes as Burke's, which was of course well supplied in the Whig classics of the seventeenth century, this cluster stands out as something special.

In 1775, so did *On Conciliation*. Of course this was not the first time that Burke had delivered a major speech involving British policy toward the colonies. The first occasion was his *Observations on a Late State of the Nation*, Burke's response to William Knox, who had taken it upon himself to defend the policies of the Grenville administration, which had ended in 1765, and to argue that those of Rockingham's administration were plunging the nation into a financial recession. Burke's response, also published by Dodsley, appeared in February 1769, and in its last third mocked Knox's proposals for raising 200,000 pounds a year by some form of taxation of the American colonies.[9] This gave Burke the opportunity to review the history of the notorious Stamp Act, already repealed during Rockingham's brief administration, and to give a clear indication of his pro-American sympathies. The second occasion was Rose Fuller's motion of April 19, 1774, proposing the repeal of the tea duty, a motion supported by both the Chatham and the Rockingham wings of the Opposition, but which would be characteristically defeated by a huge majority, 182 votes for the North administration, as against 49 for the other side.[10] Despite this legislative rout, Burke's speech on American taxation made a lasting impression, primarily by virtue of its brilliant political character sketches of Townsend and Grenville, now dead; of Chatham, Rockingham's rival for leadership of the anti-North parties; of Rockingham himself, who is presented as an ideal figure of rectitude; and, much more briefly, of General Henry Conway.

These sketches evince Burke's extraordinary gift for both personalizing politics and pressing beyond the local contingencies to the broadest formulation of the issues. In the case of Grenville, presented as an honest and hardworking administrator, his failings consisted in too great a belief in the powers of regulation and a certain jealousy of American success in the trade markets (2:432–33). In the case of Townsend, Burke delivered a devastating satire of his personality as the "delight and ornament" of the Commons, a phrase that rapidly acquires a dandyish inflection. Townsend "conformed exactly to the temper of the house; and he seemed to guide, because he was always sure to follow it"; "He every day adapted himself to [its] disposition; and adjusted himself before it, as a looking glass." He so far avoided "the vice which is most disgustful," in politics, that is to say, obstinacy, that he changed his mind and his policies at the drop of a hat. "To please universally was the object of his life; but to tax and to please, no more than to love and be wise, is not given to men" (2:452–55).

In the case of Chatham, who was alive to hear of these criticisms, it was his cynical view of human nature, Burke suggested, that led him to construct an administration designed to substitute for probity and principle a system of checks and balances:

> He made an administration, so checkered and speckled; he put together a piece of joinery, so crossly indented and whimsically dovetailed; a cabinet so variously inlaid; such a piece of diversified Mosaic; such a tesselated pavement without cement; here a bit of black stone; and there a bit of white; patriots and courtiers, kings friends and republicans; whigs and tories; treacherous friends and open enemies: that it was indeed a very curious show; but utterly unsafe to touch, and unsure to stand on. (2:450)

This parody of nonparty government (which was also, probably, a parody of a similar architectural metaphor developed by Milton in *Areopagitica* to argue for the value of diversity of opinions) simply led to chaos: "When his face was hid but for a moment, his whole system was on a wide sea, without chart or compass" (2:451).[11]

One can already see, in this passage usually quoted for its political theory, the Miltonic talent for metaphor, never more obviously metaphorical than when employed in the immediate service of political theory, supposedly a purely rational discourse. In addition, the portrait of Chatham is introduced by way of a quotation from Lucan's *Pharsalia*, a text sharply appropriate to Burke's increasing conviction that the nation was engaging in a civil war with its colonies. In 1766 (though Burke does not give the date) "the state . . . was delivered into the hands of Lord Chatham — a great and celebrated name; a name that keeps the name of this country respectable in every other on the globe. It may truly be called, '*Clarum et venerabile nomen / Gentibus, et multum nostrae quod proderat urbi.*' " How many of Burke's audience or readers recognized this quotation from Lucan's epic, one must wonder, and of the handful that did, how many would have taken the trouble to trace these lines to their source in book 9, lines 202–3, of the *Pharsalia*, where back in Rome Cato employs them in his lament for Pompey the Great, murdered in Egypt on Caesar's instructions? In the Loeb translation, they read: "His name is illustrious and revered among all nations, and did much service to our own State." But, Cato continued, "Sincere belief in Rome's freedom died long ago, when Sulla and Marius were admitted within the walls; but now, when Pompey has been removed from the world, even the sham belief is dead."[12] This was an extraordinary way to honor the twilight glory of the elderly Pitt, who had been out of action through illness for three years, and was now, as it were, to be buried alive in Burke's Roman analogy. This strategy of oblique criticism was enhanced by the hidden biblical quotation from Isaiah 54:8, "In a little wrath I hid my face from thee for a moment," which, when used as above to describe the chaos that broke out when Pitt's high instincts failed and his competence slackened, not only made him an Old Testament deity, but also, on too many occasions, an aloof and prickly one.

This demonstration of Burke's hidden agenda in his quotations should help to make plausible my account of an even more remarkable move, which was seemingly to praise and actually to destroy General Henry Conway, who was seated in the House and to whom Burke pointed on more than one occasion. Conway had been Rockingham's secretary of state during his brief ministry, and had been given the distinction of moving the repeal of the Stamp Act in 1766. Burke recalls that moment as, ostensibly, one of glory:

> I remember, Sir, with a melancholy pleasure, the situation of the Hon. Gentleman who made the motion for the repeal; in that crisis, when the whole trading interest of this empire, crammed into your lobbies, with a trembling and anxious expectation, waited, almost to a winter's return of light, their fate from your resolutions. When, at length, you had determined in their favour, and your doors, thrown open, shewed them the figure of their deliverer in the well-earned triumph of his important victory, from the whole of that grave multitude there arose an involuntary burst of gratitude and transport. They jumped upon him like children on a long absent father. They clung about him as captives about their redeemer. All England, all America joined to his applause. Nor did he seem insensible to the best of all earthly rewards, the love and admiration of his fellow-citizens. *Hope elevated and joy brightened his crest.* (2:443)

Now, while this epic description might seem hyperbolic with respect to the person who, after all, had merely *moved* what turned out to be a highly popular repeal, there is something more than exaggeration in the quotation in the italicized last sentence at which my citation pauses. These words come from Milton's epic, and not, as one might guess, from the description of the Son's return to heaven after his defeat of the fallen angels, but, the very opposite, from the description of Satan in the form of the serpent at the moment of his successful temptation of Eve. We need their fuller context also:

> Hee leading swiftly roll'd
> In tangles, and made intricate seem straight,
> To mischief swift. *Hope elevates, and joy*
> *Bright'ns his Crest*, as when a wand'ring Fire,
>
> . . . .
>
> Hovering and blazing with delusive Light,
> Misleads th'amazed Night-wanderer from his way
> To Bogs and Mires, and oft through Pond or Pool,
> There swallow'd up and lost, from succor far.
>
> (9:631–34, 639–42)

Anyone who knew *Paradise Lost* as well as Burke did must have become an amazed night-wanderer at this moment, wondering where the *ignis fatuus* was leading.

How was this sinister allusion to fit with what immediately follows, a comparison of Conway to Saint Stephen at the moment of his stoning; "his face was as if it had been the face of an angel." But Satan, too, had had the face of an angel for some time after his fall.

One possible reaction to this disturbance in our readerly expectations is to say that it means nothing; that it *could* not mean what it seems to imply; that Burke was merely rolling familiar phrases around on his tongue, not stopping to consider what freight they carried with them. This seems unlikely, however, in that "Crest," though conceivably appropriate to the helmet of an ancient warrior, would surely have reminded Burke that its usage in Milton was part of an ornately visual description of a serpent, elsewhere described as bowing "his turret Crest" before Eve. What makes his allusion more suspicious, however, is the fact that before introducing it Burke *twice* referred to a rumor that Conway, even as he moved the repeal, "had another sett of resolutions in his pocket directly

the reverse of those he moved" (2:441). While ostensibly
mentioning this rumor in order to discredit it, and asserting a
moment later that "far from the duplicity wickedly charged
on him, he acted his part with alacrity and resolution" (2:442),
Burke may in fact, but very indirectly, have been seriously
undermining Conway's integrity. In November 1770, he had
attacked Conway in the House, an event which F. P. Lock reads
as "part of a larger pattern of attacks on Conway, [which]
suggests that their mere political differences, real as those were,
were exacerbated by deep personal resentment."[13] And later,
in November 1776, in a debate in the Commons moved by
Lord John Cavendish and seconded by Burke on the impossible
motion "for the revisal of all the Laws by which the Americans
think themselves aggrieved," he attacked Alexander Wedder-
burn for *his* inconsistency in debate with an unmistakably
Miltonic comparison.

> On that memorable occasion he lay, like Milton's devil,
> prostrate "on the oblivious pool, confounded and astounded,
> though called upon by the whole Satanic host. He lay prostrate,
> dumb-founded, and unable to utter a single syllable, and suffered
> the goads of the two noble lords to prick him till scarcely
> betrayed a single sign of animal or mental sensibility. Why,
> Sir, would he not be silent now."[14]

In what follows, I shall argue that Burke's allusions to *Paradise Lost* in *On Conciliation* were not random memories,
but instead well-considered supports for his emotionally
powerful philosophy of empire. It is worth pointing out that
On Conciliation, like the other speeches published by Dodsley,
is rhetorically polished to a very high sheen, and seems more
fully premeditated than the two previous "American" produc-
tions; that Burke had announced his intention to present a
bill at the opening of the session on November 30, 1774; that
he had tried to introduce it on March 16, 1775, but it was
mysteriously tabled until March 22; and that it was not
published until May 22, so that he had two months to polish

it still further. Unlike the two previous "American" speeches, it contains none of the obsessive concerns with fiscal detail that might have distracted a reader outside the house, nor does it dwell obnoxiously on the inconsistencies of the Townsend and North policies. With one remarkable exception, it does not rely on ad hominem argument, however indirect, nor attribute the coming disaster to individual ministers. It eschews the individual political portraits of *American Taxation*, eulogistic, falsely eulogistic or grandly retributive, and substitutes for them one of the most extraordinary accounts of national character — American national character — that either country had ever read. It was indeed an epic performance; Burke spoke for a full three hours. And the whole is placed within a grand adaptation of Milton's *Paradise Lost*, the premise being that there remains only the faintest chance that the story of England and its Western empire will turn out, instead, to be the story of *Paradise Regained*.

How soon could a very attentive reader have grasped this? Perhaps in Burke's opening moves. For after having explained the "providential favour" that had caused the Lords to return to the Commons "the grand penal Bill, by which we had passed sentence on . . . America," the great luck, as it were, of a second chance, he explains the nature of the challenge: "We are therefore called upon, *as it were by a superior warning voice,* again to attend to America; . . . surely it is an awful subject; or there is none so on this side of the grave."[15] Only an ear tuned to Miltonic echoes, probably, would have caught that first echo, from the opening lines of *Paradise Lost*, book 4:

> Oh for that warning voice, which he who saw
> Th'Apocalypse, heard cry in Heav'n aloud,
>
> . . . .
>
> *Woe to the inhabitants on Earth!* that now,
> While time was, our first Parents had been warn'd.
>
> (1–2, 5–6)

Of what should they have been warned? Of the approach of Satan, winging his way toward the "new created World" intended to replace the space left in creation by the expulsion of the fallen angels. Burke would certainly have been aware that the New World of the American colonies was often described in terms directly or mediately derived from Milton. The threat to be averted is that the New World will also be corrupted.

But anyone who missed this, and most would, would also be given a second chance at right reading when, following directly on Burke's efficient and startling comparison between the volume of English trade to the colonies in 1704 and 1772, he came to the following long (and for purposes of quotation, indivisible) passage:

> Mr. Speaker, I cannot prevail on myself to hurry over this great consideration. It is good for us to be here. We stand where we have an immense view of what is, and what is past. Clouds indeed, and darkness, rest upon the future. Let us however, before we descend from this noble eminence, reflect that this growth of our national prosperity has happened within the short period of the life of man. It has happened within Sixty-eight years. There are those alive whose memory might touch the two extremities. For instance, my Lord Bathurst might remember all the stages of the process. He was in 1704 of an age, at least to be made to comprehend such things. . . . Suppose, Sir, that the angel of this auspicious youth, foreseeing the many virtues, which made him one of the most amiable, as he is one of the most fortunate men of his age, had opened to him in vision, that, when, in the fourth generation, the third Prince of the House of Brunswick had sat Twelve years on the throne of that nation, which (by the happy issue of moderate and healing councils) was to be made Great Britain, he should see his son, Lord Chancellor of England, turn back the current of hereditary dignity to its fountain, and raise him to an higher rank of Peerage, whilst he enriched the family with a new one — If amidst these bright and happy scenes of domestic honour and prosperity, that angel should have drawn up the curtain, and

unfolded the rising glories of his country, and whilst he was gazing with admiration on the then commercial grandeur of England, The Genius should point out to him a little speck, scarce visible in the mass of the national interest, a small seminal principle, rather than a formed body, and should tell him — "Young man, There is America — which at this day serves for little more than to amuse you with stories of savage men, and uncouth manners; yet shall, before you taste of death, shew itself equal to the whole of that commerce which now attracts the envy of the world. Whatever England has been growing to by a progressive increase of improvement, brought in by varieties of people, by succession of civilizing conquest and civilizing settlements in a series of Seventeen Hundred years, you shall see as much added to her by America in the course of a single life!" If this state of his country had been foretold to him, would it not require all the sanguine credulity of youth, and all the fervid glow of enthusiasm, to make him believe it? Fortunate man, he has lived to see it! Fortunate indeed, if he lives to see nothing that shall vary the prospect, and cloud the setting of his day! (3:114–16)

Burke's parliamentary audiences by this time must have learned to beware the approach of his complimentary mode. This piece was designed to set up the Bathursts, father and son, Alan and Henry, as examples of the kinds of men, avid Tories, friends of Lord North, who, in the words of Burke's modern editors, "had done very well by the Brunswick line which of course they were known originally to have opposed" (3:115 n. 4). Of the younger Bathurst, created lord chancellor in 1771 more or less by default, the old *Dictionary of National Biography* reported that "by a universal consensus of opinion . . . Bathurst is pronounced to have been the least efficient lord chancellor of the century." In the same year, and surely not by coincidence, the elder Bathurst received the earldom which in due course (very due, as it turned out) the son would inherit. In fact, the elder Bathurst died in December at the age of 91, probably unaware of the trick that had been played on him.

Burke's primary weapon was irony, some of it merely verbal. The process of getting an earldom into the family is described as "turning back the current of hereditary dignity to its fountain" and "these bright and happy scenes of domestic honour and prosperity." The vision of America he is granted in this imaginary geography lesson, a "small seminal principle" in "the mass of the national interest," is the view of the colonies, Burke suggests, that Tories would naturally hold — a view of the New World as existing entirely for the economic interests of the English. And there are literary allusions, before the vision really opens, that deserve to be more than merely identified. Burke suggests that all the members of the House of Commons have for a moment been granted epistemological eminence. Will they be able to use it well? "It is good for us to be here," cites Saint Mark's account of the transfiguration of Christ on "an high mountain" (9:2–6), a vision which Peter characteristically fails to understand in other than conventional, institutional terms. "Clouds indeed, and darkness, rest upon the future," may be a quotation from the most famous Whig play of the century, Addison's *Cato*, at the point where Cato, having decided that the world belongs to Caesar, prepares for suicide.[16]

But the major allusion — the vision of the future delivered to a young man by an angel — is still more ironic, more literary and more provocative. It derives from the end of *Paradise Lost*, where the archangel Michael reveals to Adam the future history of the world; but it also, inevitably, would remind good readers of Milton of the parallel scene in *Paradise Regained* where Satan carries the young Jesus to the top of a mountain to show him all the empires of the earth in order to tempt him with material dominion. Burke's version is, ethically, a blending of the satanic vision, which the young hero must categorically reject, with the angelic vision, whose message, though depresssing, must be accepted by Adam if he is to live with any integrity in a fallen world. Burke's exhortation, "Let us . . . before we descend from this noble eminence, reflect," recalls how Michael closed down his lecture to Adam, "Let us descend now therefore from this top of Speculation; for the hour precise exacts our parting hence" (12:587–90). But it is the imperialism of Satan's temptation that really fits the context of Burke's adaptation, its focus on material wealth and nationalism conceived as expansionism.

The "purple" aspect of this passage about the angel was drawn to the attention of Samuel Johnson by Hester Thrale, who, as she tells us in her memoirs, was in 1775 "venturing to praise" Burke's speech as a whole and this piece of virtuosity in particular. Johnson's anonymous anti-American pamphlet, *Taxation no Tyranny*, had just appeared.[17] On March 16 Charles Pratt, now Lord Camden (who as chief justice had ordered the release of John Wilkes in 1763 in the case of the *North Briton*) delivered a speech in the Lords against the bill for restraining American trade. In it he mentioned "a pamphlet published a few days ago, called 'Taxation no Tyranny,'" as one of the provocations in the press which required a response.[18] This places Johnson's pamphlet at the end, perhaps, of the first week of March. By the end of the month, Johnson could have read Burke's speech, which (perhaps to Johnson's irritation) makes no mention of his pamphlet, and proceeds to make several of the arguments on which Johnson had poured scorn. Johnson was predictably indignant. Unlike Mrs. Thrale, he was not deceived by Burke's irony, and proceeded to offer his own rebuttal, choosing definitively between angelic and satanic prospects, and turning the trick against the Whigs in an imaginary parliamentary riposte:

> Suppose Mr. Speaker, that to Wharton or Marlborough, or some of the most eminent Whigs in the last Age the Devil had — not with any great Impropriety — consented to appear, he would perhaps in these words have commenced the Conversation.
>
> "You seem my Lord to be concerned at the judicious Apprehension, that while you are sapping the Foundations of Royalty, and Propagating the Doctrines of Resistance here

at home, the distance of America may secure its Inhabitants from your Arts though active; but I will unfold to you the gay Prospects of Futurity: the People now so innocent, so harmless, shall draw their Sword upon their Mother Country and break its Point in the blood of their Benefactors: their people now contented with a little; shall then refuse to spare what they themselves could not miss; and these Men, now so honest and so grateful shall in return for Peace and for Protection *see their vile* Agents in the house of Parliament, there to sow the seeds of Sedition, and propagate Confusion Perplexity and Pain. Be not dispirited then at the Contemplation of their present happy state; I promise you that Anarchy Poverty and Death shall carry even across the spacious Atlantick — and settle even in America the consequence of Whiggism."[19]

Thus Johnson rewrote the Miltonic script once more, unveiling the ironies of Burke's version and reappropriating the Pisgah prospect to demonic use.

I take Johnson's understanding of this famous passage as confirmation that Tory members of the house would not have been deceived, as was a recent commentator, into reading this "tribute" to Bathurst's "heroic gaze" as an appeal to a broad consensus of gentlemanly opinion. Can we really suppose that Burke selected Bathurst *because* "his association with the Tories, rather than Burke's Whig associates, guarantees the comprehensiveness and impartiality of the vision ascribed to him by placing it beyond narrow party interests?"[20] That Pope should have "mythologized" the elder Bathurst in his *Epistle to Burlington* (lines 177–18) in 1731 (de Bruyn's main argument rests on this, though the *Epistle to Bathurst*, which had attacked avarice, would have been more pertinent) would scarcely in itself be a reason for Burke's idealizing him in 1775; and we have already seen, from his attack on Chatham's unstable "Mosaick" constructions, what Burke thought of the merits of supposedly nonparty government.

In his reference to "their vile Agents in the house of Parliament" Johnson may also have included a personal jab at

Burke, whose official, paid position as agent for the New York assembly had begun in 1770. By 1774 it had become something of a political liability to him, casting a shadow over his vaunted independence. In June 1775 Burke wrote to the New York assembly a long letter explaining how the petition they had sent him had been refused acceptance in the Commons but successfully presented in the Lords, due to the good offices of the dukes of Manchester and Richmond, Rockingham, Lord Camden, and the earl of Effingham. It is not without significance that this letter was intercepted and copied by the government.[21]

In any case, once we are aware of the Miltonic perspective, it would seem fair to suggest that other references to Milton in *On Conciliation* would bear rather more weight than the several Shakespearean allusions (though all are from the tragedies) and the several classical quotations (though five references to Juvenal's satires may also subliminally set the tone). Two of the quotations from *Paradise Lost* suggest that the Commons, and England in general, are in danger of assuming the posture of the fallen angels in Milton's hell. Refusing once again to encounter the argument for or against taxation of the colonies from a legal or theoretical position, Burke remarked:

> These are deep questions, where great names militate against each other; where reason is perplexed; and an appeal to authorities only thickens the confusion. For high and reverend authorities lift up their heads on both sides; and there is no sure footing in the middle. The point is the *great Serbonian bog, betwixt Damatia and Mount Casius, old, where armies whole have sunk.* I do not intend to be overwhelmed in that bog, though in such respectable company. (3:135)

Although he had used it years before, in a draft of a response in the *Public Advertiser* (March 1768) to the debates on "Nullum Tempus" (2:86), and there, too, as an analogy to the swamps of public policy, in *On Conciliation* it gathers to it, by way of more extensive quotation, the whole threatening landscape of hell as Milton understands it:

> Beyond this flood a frozen Continent
> Lies dark and wild, beat with perpetual storms
> Of Whirlwind and dire Hail, which on firm land
> Thaws not, but gathers heap, and ruin seems
> Of ancient pile; all else deep snow and ice,
> A gulf profound as that Serbonian Bog
> Betwixt Damatia and Mount Casius old,
> Where Armies whole have sunk.
>
> (2:587–94)

If we know the context, we know that the "such respectable company" eschewed by Burke at this moment are the fallen angels, on a voyage of exploration to see what *their* new world in the underworld can offer.

But Burke also acknowledges that, from another perspective, it is the colonists, the rebels, who occupy the satanic position. Arguing against the latest version of the North plan for taxation, and in favor of returning to the era where the colonies made voluntary contributions, Burke wrote: "whatever is got by acts of absolute power ill obeyed, because odious, or by contracts ill kept, because constrained; will be narrow, feeble, uncertain and precarious. *'Ease would retract vows made in pain, as violent and void'*" (3:163). The speaker here is Satan, at the beginning of book 4 of *Paradise Lost* (which opened with the appeal for "that warning voice" and which contains Satan's soliloquy on the motives for his initial rebellion and its continuance). Here we have a still more subtle test case of how the context of a quotation affects and rounds out the new usage. Satan himself admits that his response should have been one of gratefulness to his sovereign (the frequently reiterated position of those who spoke in Parliament against the colonists as ingrates), but speaks of that gratitude as "a debt immense of endless gratitude, / So burdensome, still paying, still to owe," (4.52–53), a deep psychological truth that can readily be converted into the taxation issue. And the lines about vows made in pain belonged originally in a framework of demonic self-analysis that suggests (once translated into the new context of Burke's speech) that conciliation of the rebels would only lead to new kinds of resistance — precisely the position asserted by those who favored penal laws against the colonists:

> But say I could repent and could obtain
> By Act of Grace my former state; how soon
> Would highth recall high thoughts, how soon unsay
> What feign'd submission swore: *ease would recant*
> Vows made in pain, as violent and void,
> For never can true reconcilement grow
> Where wounds of deadly hate have pierc'd so deep:
> . . . .
> This knows my punisher.
>
> (4.93–99, 103)

Does this mean that Burke, at the deeper level of his myth, was admitting the very arguments against which his speech was marshaled? Or does it mean only that *punishment*, as distinct from true conciliation, would be rebarbative? For any reader of *On Conciliation* who was sufficiently puzzled by Burke's Miltonic quotation to track it to its source, this quandary would be politically and psychologically enlightening.

If the previous two instances have placed the House of Commons (and behind them, all England) in the position of fallen (but possibly redeemable) Adam and the Americans in the position of the fallen angels, we are teetering on the edge of an almost conveniently trite political allegory. There is, however, one further twist to Burke's redeployment of Milton, which unsettles such conventional parallelism. This occurs in the famous central section of the speech where Burke explains why force will not work on the Americans, because of their national character. As a transition to this claim, Burke inserted an epic description of the American fishing industry:

And pray, Sir, what in the world is equal to it? Pass by the other parts, and look at the manner in which the people of New England have of late carried on the Whale Fishery. Whilst we follow them among the tumbling mountains of ice, and behold them penetrating into the deepest frozen recesses of Hudson's Bay, and Davis's Streights, whilst we are looking for them beneath the Arctic circle, we hear that they have pierced into the opposite region of polar cold, that they are at the Antipodes, and engaged under the frozen serpent of the south. . . . Nor is the equinoctial heat more discouraging to them, than the accumulated winter of both the poles. We know that whilst some of them draw the line and strike the harpoon on the coast of Africa, others run the longtitude, and pursue their gigantic game along the coast of Brazil. No sea, but what is vexed by their fisheries. No climate that is not witness to their toils. . . . When I contemplate these things, when I know that the Colonies in general owe little or nothing to any care of ours, and that they are not squeezed into this happy form by the constraints of a watchful and suspicious government, but that through a wise and salutary neglect, a generous nature has been suffered to take her way to perfection: when I reflect upon these effects, when I see how profitable they have been to us, I feel all the pride of power sink, and all presumption in the wisdom of human contrivances melt, and die away within me. My rigour relents. I pardon something to the spirit of Liberty. (3:117–18)

This writing raises the American fishing industry to the level of a sublime victory over nature. The point was acknowledged by Herman Melville in *Moby Dick* (chap. 24, "The Advocate") when his defense of the grandeur of the whaling industry includes the rhetorical question and answer: "And who pronounced our glowing eulogy in Parliament? Who but Edmund Burke!"; a move immediately followed by the claim that the whalers have better than royal blood in their veins, being all descended from Benjamin Franklin's grandmother.[22]

This heroic transition prepares audience and reader for an account of American national character that is itself heroic, and, moreover, heroically Whig. The colonists have been bred in the spirit of liberty, specifically that strain of English liberty that has always defined itself around the question of taxation rather than, as in classical commonwealths, on the "right of election of magistrates; or on the balance among the several orders of the state" (3:120). They are also Protestants, of a particularly oppositional kind. (Burke would deal, rather uncomfortably, with the obvious counterargument — that the Southern colonies had a very different religious constituency — by arguing that as slaveholders the Southerners were as equally committed to their own liberty as their Northern colleagues). But in his zesty account of it, New England Protestantism became a version of Whiggism:

> The Church of England . . . was formed from her cradle under the nursing care of regular government. But the dissenting interests have sprung up in direct opposition to all the ordinary powers of the world; and could justify that opposition only on a strong claim to natural liberty. Their very existence depended on the powerful and unremitted assertion of that claim. All protestantism, even the most cold and passive, is a sort of dissent. But the religion most prevalent in our Northern Colonies is a refinement on the principle of resistance; it is the dissidence of dissent. (3:121–22)

Finally, the importance to the colonists of education, especially their self-education in law, has made them especially well equipped to survive this conflict. "The profession itself is numerous and powerful. . . . The greater number of the Deputies sent to the Congress were Lawyers. But all who read, and most do read, endeavour to obtain some smattering in that science" (3:123). Copies of Blackstone's *Commentaries* are in hot demand. This study makes the Americans *anticipate* problems with their rulers. "They augur misgovernment at a distance; and snuff the approach of tyranny in every tainted breeze" (3:124).

This essay in anthropology, brilliantly overstated, has a single purpose: to persuade the members of the House of

Commons that none of their proposed solutions to the rebellion *except* conciliation can have the slightest effect on the colonists' determination. But there are two other irreversible factors, more basic, more fundamental still than these cultural conditions. Both involve problems of scale. One is the sheer breadth of the Atlantic, which renders government at a distance unwieldy and desperately slow; the other is the colonists' extreme reproductive ability — there are so very many of them. "While we spend our time in deliberating on the mode of governing Two Millions, we shall find we have Millions more to manage" (3:111).

Most of these points, remarkably, had been anticipated and discredited by Johnson's *Taxation No Tyranny* a fortnight or so earlier. Johnson had complained:

> we are then told that the Americans, however wealthy, cannot be taxed; that they are the descendants of men who left all for liberty, and they have constantly preserved the principles and stubbornness of their progenitors; that they are too obstinate for persuasion, and too powerful for constraint; that this will laugh at argument, and defeat violence; that the continent of North America contains three millions, not of men merely, but of Whigs, of Whigs fierce for liberty, and disdainful of dominion; that they multiply with the fecundity of their own rattle-snakes, so that every quarter of a century doubles their numbers. (4)

Did Burke read this pamphlet? If so, he never deigns to address it directly, but rather steers straight ahead down the path that Johnson excoriates. And on the subject of American fertility, he has one last great Miltonic (and biblical) move to make. To counter the argument that, in order to curtail the population growth, the Crown should make no further grants of land in America, Burke declares simply that "the people would occupy without grants":

> If you drive the people from one place, they will carry on their annual Tillage, and remove with their flocks and herds to another. Many of the people in the back settlements are already little attached to particular situations. Already they have topped

the Apalachian mountains. From thence they behold before them an immense plain, one vast, rich, level meadow; a square of five hundred miles. Over this they would wander, without a possibility of restraint; they would change their manners with the habits of their life; would soon forget a government, by which they were disowned; would becomes Hordes of English Tartars; . . . Such would, and in no long time, must be, the effect of attempting to forbid as a crime, and to suppress as an evil, the Command and Blessing of Providence, "Encrease and Multiply." Such would be the happy result of an endeavour to keep as a lair of wild beasts, that earth, which God, by an express Charter, has given to the children of men. (3:128–29)

Thus Burke creates a new and innocent status for the colonists, as a series of Adams and Eves at the beginning of the story, before the Fall has taken place. Burke knows that moment has passed, and that "Tillage" is not only Miltonic but post-lapsarian. Perhaps he glances in his scenario of landlessness at the story of Abraham, the first nomad, who, however, had divine mandate for his behavior:

> I see him, but thou canst not, with what Faith
> He leaves his Gods, his Friends, and native Soil
> Ur of Chaldaea, passing now the Ford
> To Haran, after him a cumbrous Train
> Of Herds and Flocks, and numerous servitude;
> Not wand'ring poor, but trusting all his wealth
> With God, who call'd him, in a land unknown
>
> (12:128–34)

But the conclusion of Burke's advice to Parliament is benign. It echoes the song of the angels that sums up book 7 of *Paradise Lost*, the book of the creation of the world, which ends with God's *other* mandate:

> [God] blessed Mankind, and said
> Be fruitful, multiply, and fill the Earth,
> Subdue it, and throughout Dominion hold
> Over Fish of the Sea, and Fowl of the Air,

And every living thing that moves on the Earth,
Wherever thus created, *for no place*
Is yet distinct by name.

(7.530–36; italics added)

This sense of a world without borders and boundaries is what Burke, with deliberate unrealism, opposes to the complex proposals of the North government with respect to the treatment of individual American states.

But we have now to move on to the winter of 1776, when the Rockingham group decided to secede from parliamentary business in protest against the failure of all their attempts to move toward conciliation with the colonies. Now Burke was debating with himself and his friends in Rockingham's inner circle the effect of the Whig secession (which could itself be interpreted as Achilles sulking in his tent) on the future of the Whig party. On January 6, 1777, Burke wrote to Rockingham a long and very revealing letter expressing both his support of and his doubts about the secession, and urging that the Rockingham group, rather than seceding in misinterpretable silence, should send an address to George III explaining their actions. In this letter Burke mentioned Benjamin Franklin's arrival in Paris, his assumption that Franklin had been sent to negotiate with Lord Stormont, the British ambassador in Paris, and his hope that it was "not wholly impossible that the Whigg party might be made a sort of Mediatours of the Peace." As to the secession,

> after rolling the matter in my head a good deal, and turning it a hundred ways, I confess I still think it the most advisable; notwithstanding the serious Objections which lie against it; and indeed the extreme uncertainty of the Effect of all political Maneuvres; especially at this time. It provides for your honour. I know of nothing else which can do this. It is something; and perhaps all that can be done under our present Circumstances. . . . However such as it is, (and for one I do not think I am inclined to overvalue it) both our Interest and our Duty

make it necessary for us to attend to it very carefully as long as we act a part in publick. The Measure you take for this purpose may produce no *immediate* Effect; but with regard to the *party*, and the *principles*, for whose sake the party exists, all hope of their preservation, or recovery, depends upon your preserving your Reputation. (3:311)

The "Measure" Burke has in mind is sending to the king the address he himself has written; and the latter part of the letter is devoted to imagining the consequences, none of which Burke seemed to have thought would fall directly on himself. He wonders aloud what either the Parliament or the court would do in revenge. "Though they have made some successful Experiments in Juries, they will hardly trust enough to them, to order a prosecution for a supposed Libel." Parliament might attempt an impeachment, as in the case of Henry Sacheverell, or a Bill of Pains and Penalties, as in the case of Francis Atterbury, bishop of Rochester. The court, on the other hand,

> may select three or four of the most distinguished among you for the Victims; and therefore nothing is more remote from the Tendency of the proposed at, than any Idea of retirement or repose. On the contrary, you have all of you, as principals or auxiliaries, a much hotter and more dangerous conflict in all probability to undergo than any you have yet been engaged in. The only question is, whether the risque ought to be run for the chance (and it is no more) of recalling the people of England to their antient principles, and to that personal Interest which formerly they took in all publick affairs? (3:313)

Given this dark prognosis, it is hardly surprising that Rockingham decided against their doing anything of the sort.

Thus began, I suggest, the Burke problem; prevented by his patron and employer from writing the script for a rebellious gesture of epic proportions, Burke began the slide into wounded self-esteem. In 1780 he lost his seat in the House for his Bristol constituency and had to make do with the far less important borough of Malton, which was within Rockingham's gift.

When Rockingham took office in 1782, Burke was not offered the cabinet post he had hoped for. Although technically a member of the Privy Council as paymaster general of the forces, he seldom attended meetings and felt himself excluded from the inner circle. When Rockingham died, the hopes of the Whig party, as Burke had understood it, died with him. This was the moment of the *other* visual allusion to *Paradise Lost* as a paradigm of Burke's career, since it was shortly after Rockingham's death that James Sayers published his cruel cartoon. In July of that year Burke joined Fox, Lord John Cavendish and a few others in an ill-judged resignation from Parliament. In the 1784 elections the party of Fox was decimated — and Burke, who was reelected, became daily more intemperate and more isolated. F. P. Lock, to whose biography this summary of a decline is indebted, happens to have closed the first volume with the following pertinent allusion. "These incidents illustrate one of Burke's more heroic qualities, in the words of Milton's Satan, 'the unconquerable will . . . and courage never to submit or yield.' Still possessed of vast energies of mind and capable of intense application, once recovered from the shock of the 1784 election, he would find new causes to champion" (1:544). One of those new causes was his crusade against Warren Hastings; the other was his crusade against the French Revolution.

But it will be evident by now that I take a somewhat less heroic (or even heroically demonic) view of the later Burke than do his apologists. Of the three explanations for his change of direction mentioned at the outset, the most persuasive seems to be Thomas Copeland's hypothesis that after the series of disappointments and diminishments that preceded and followed Rockingham's death, Burke needed to find a cause that would move him from the impotent left to the respectable center right, a stance that would bring him, in place of the friendship of Charles James Fox, the gratitude of George III. To those who argue (as Burke did) that the principles declared in the *Reflections* were those of the revolution of 1688, I am inclined to reply, as did the *Gazeteer and New Daily Advertiser*, on November 4, 1790,

> in his argument on the *right of choice* in the people, which he refines upon so as totally to extinguish, he establishes a doctrine that would have kept England, and would keep the whole world in a state of villainage. If his principles had had weight on the public mind, at the time of the Reformation, they would have prevented the Reformation. . . . They would equally in 1688, have prevented the glorious Revolution.

5 • Gratitude and *Paradise Lost*

A Neglected Context

Peter E. Medine

That great man *Philo* the Iew, in the booke he hath entitled *Noes plant,* figureth vnto vs a certayne tradition of the Sages of his nation, to wit, that God the creator, after he had framed the world as a Scucheon of his Nobility, a contracted Table of his titles, a mirror of his greatnesse and wisdome, demaunded of the Prophets, or the Angels, assisting his glory, what they thought of this worke; and that one among them, after he had highly commended the architecture of this goodly Vniuerse, sayth freely, that he also therein yet required a Perfection, to fixe a seale vpon so many braue, and rich inuentions. What is it (sayth the eternall Father?) I would desyre a strong voyce, powerfull, harmonious, which borne vpon the winges of the winds and cloudes, vpon the chariot of the ayre, should replenish all the partes of the world, and incessantly *Eccho* forth night, and day in prayses, and thanks-giuing for your incomparable benefits.

— Nicolas Causin, *The Holy Covrt; or, The Christian Institvtion of Men of Qvality*

1

In a recent essay on the place of *Paradise Lost* within the Renaissance exegetical traditions, Joseph Wittreich writes that although "Milton's poems may emerge from sometimes monolithic biblical traditions and enunciate their interpretive commonplaces, they also belong within the orbit of literary hermeneutics and dialogic discourse, thus promoting open rather than closed readings."[1] I examine in this essay the idea of gratitude in *Paradise Lost* and its exploitation by Milton in his interpretation of the biblical materials. Gratitude is a subject that has received virtually no attention from commentators on Milton and comparatively little attention from historians of ideas. I therefore begin by sketching some of the biographical, theological and scriptural contexts. Turning to Milton's thematization of gratitude within the poem, I then discuss the ways in which gratitude and ingratitude inform the characterization of Adam, Eve and Satan, and are fundamental to the depiction of the fallen and unfallen states. Milton's appropriation of gratitude in this case is fairly orthodox and serves both to humanize the characters and lend focus to the poem's theological questions, such as the nature of godhead, theodicy and free will. I turn last to the education of Adam and the expulsion from Eden. I suggest that Milton qualifies Adam's expressions of gratitude in book 12 and intensifies the ambiguities of the expulsion through clashing perspectives on the prospects of achieving the Christian ideal and the paradise within the postlapsarian world. I conclude that in the final analysis rather than advancing a particular reading of the myth of Creation and Fall, Milton's interpretation opens its meanings and renders the conclusion of *Paradise Lost* very much a ground of contention.

2

The epigraph above from Philo of Alexandria summarizes the essential characteristics of gratitude as it was to develop over the next millennium and a half. Gratitude is fundamentally the acknowledgment of God's originary power in creating the universe; in the nature of things, gratitude is literally a universal debt, and the perfection of the universe depends on its expression in hymns of thanks and praise. The passage implies that besides completing God's design, gratitude reflects the universe's divine beauty and finally becomes a dynamic transaction in which God, man and creation are integrated in one magnificent celebration.

Gratitude is not the first virtue we associate with John Milton. Nevertheless he opens *The Second Defense of the English People* (1654) with the assertion that, "In the whole life and estate of man the first duty is to be grateful to God and mindful of his blessings, and to offer particular and solemn thanks without delay when his benefits have exceeded hope and prayer."[2] Milton specifies several benefits he enjoys, including his being born in revolutionary times in England and his recent triumph over a royalist adversary. Milton wrote this in late 1653 or early 1654, a time when events in his personal life might suggest that he had little to be grateful for. By February 1652, he had become completely blind and for his remaining 22 years would struggle with this disability. Milton's wife and one-year-old son John died later in the spring of 1652. These circumstances must have tried Milton's patience and strained his capacity for gratitude, the virtue he calls in the passage quoted from the *Second Defense* man's "first duty" to God. Some critics have seen Milton's personal struggle reflected in his choice of the eight psalms he translated in August 1653, seven of which are laments and petitions for relief and the eighth a Joblike thanksgiving for God's mysterious power.[3]

Trial and strain are recurrent themes in Milton's life and writing. Often the tension derives from Milton's distinct sense of God's gifts and the obligations they carry, and the equally distinct sense of the limitations and deprivations of the human condition. Such limitations can lead to a questioning of the "strictnesse" with which Milton believed God "requires the improvement of these his entrusted gifts," as he puts it in an allusion to the parable of the talents (Matt. 25:14–31) in *The Reason of Church-Government* (YP 1:801). The most famous lyric expression of this tension appears in *Sonnet 19*, the so-called sonnet on his blindness, the conjectured date of which is autumn 1655. The sonnet presents a personal struggle with God. In the first seven and a half lines the speaker inclines toward murmuring against the Almighty for endowing him with gifts and then depriving him of one — that "talent" of seeing — and so undermining his efforts to serve. The subjective utterance gives way to an objective voice in line 8, that of patience, the personification of the capacity to suffer:

> but patience to prevent
> That murmur, soon replies, God doth not need
> Either man's work or his own gifts, who best
> Bear his mild yoak, they serve him best, his State
> Is Kingly. Thousands at his bidding speed
> And post o're Land and Ocean without rest:
> They also serve who only stand and wait.[4]

Patience offers the hard, humbling advice of submitting to God's will. Readers have often read the words of Patience as a resolution of the problem articulated by the speaker of the octave. But increasingly Patience's words have come to sound like a voice that is not necessarily normative and that does not necessarily refute or cancel the troubled questioning of the speaker-poet. Many would feel that the tension remains and perhaps increases with the last line.

However this may be, for the next 20 years or so, Milton stood and waited. Disappointment revisited him regularly. He remarried in 1656, and his second wife died two years later; another child, a daughter, died the same year. The year 1660 must have been especially trying, as the Commonwealth government gave way to the restoration of the monarchy of Charles II, the conviction and execution of whose father Milton had defended. Milton naturally lost his post as Latin secretary. Although he escaped the death penalty under the Act of Oblivion in August, he was imprisoned for a two- or three-month period in the autumn.

Throughout these two decades, Milton also continued to serve. He wrote a dozen treatises on political, theological and historical subjects, and he completed *Paradise Lost* as well as *Samson Agonistes* and *Paradise Regained.* The record is heroic: an aging, frequently ill, blind man, beset with problems of every sort, who continued to endure and to write. What is remarkable is the fascination that gratitude held for Milton in the work that occupied him principally in this conclusive period of his life.

3

Thomas Aquinas provides a comprehensive theological rationale of gratitude. He begins by discussing it within the Aristotelian framework of commutative justice, which deals with contractual relations between parties. Aquinas's premise is that all human indebtedness is to God, who is the source of all good (*primum principium omnium bonorum nostrorum*).[5] He then distinguishes between a legal debt (*debitum legale*) and a debt of gratitude, the preeminent example of which is what humans owe to their Creator. Although legal debt can be discharged exactly with the agreed upon repayment, no one can repay God in this way. The obligation of gratitude originates not in an external contractual arrangement but within the individual: "Sed ad virtutem gratiae sive gratitudinis retributio pertinet quae fit ex solo debito honestatis quam scilicet aliquis sponte facit" [But in the case of the virtue of gratitude, repayment pertains to a debt of honor which obviously one fulfills of his own free will] (*ST* 2a2ae.106, 1). The corollary to this view is that gratitude can never be compelled externally, a point that Aquinas illustrates with a reference to Seneca's *De Beneficiis* (3.7): "Unde et gratitudo est minus grata, si sit coacta" [Whence gratitude is less grateful if it is forced] (*ST* 282ae.106, 1). Gratitude is by nature heartfelt. It is experienced and expressed willingly and freely — a condition that Milton's God regards as essential in book 3, lines 103–11.

Aquinas moves gratitude still further from the quantitative and legalistic framework of commutative justice to the moral realm, where human feelings and actions are dynamic rather than static, and relative rather than absolute (*ST* 2a2ae.106, 3, 5). The benefit or favor — *gratia* is Aquinas's preferred word — depends not simply on the "size of the gift" (*ex quantitate dati*) but on the benefactor. Aquinas illustrates by pointing out that the debt resulting from the forgiveness of sins is comparatively greater than the debt resulting from the gift of innocence, since forgiveness is extended freely (gratis) and to the undeserving: "cum enim esset dignus poena, datur ei gratia" [for although he (the sinner) is worthy of punishment, grace is given to him] (*ST* 2a2ae,106, 2). The value of a gift lies chiefly in the attitude of the benefactor, a claim Aquinas underlines with a pointed sentence from Seneca: "Beneficium non in eo quod fit aut datur consistit, sed in ipso dantis aut facientis animo" [A benefit is not in what is done or given but in the mind of the giver or doer] (*ST* 2a2ae.106, 5). By the same reasoning, the value of gratitude lies chiefly in the disposition of the person responding gratefully: "Sicut enim beneficium magis in affectu consistit quam in effectu, ita etiam recompensatio magis in affectu consistit" [For just as the significance of a benefit lies more in the heart than in the deed, so also repayment lies more in the heart] (*ST* 2a2ae.106, 3).

By locating the source of gratitude within the individual and in his personal responses, Aquinas establishes the morality rather than the legality of gratitude. He also provides the rationale for the essential inwardness of gratitude.

Aquinas suggests the specifically theological dimension of gratitude in a comparison to a law of physics. Claiming that every effect in nature turns back to its cause (*ad suam causam convertitur*), Aquinas cites Dionysius's theological version of the principle: "Deus omnia in se convertit, tanquam omnium causa" [God turns all things back to himself as the cause of all things] (*ST* 2a2ae.106, 3). From this principle it follows that as the benefactor / beneficiary relationship is causal, so the beneficiary must necessarily respond in a way that is appropriate to his relationship to the benefactor. In other words, gratitude is another of the principles — or moral virtues — that tie the universe together, integrating humans among themselves and binding them to God. Milton develops this idea in Raphael's postprandial discussion of the moral cosmos with Adam and Eve in book 5, lines 469–505. From this point of view, gratitude is an *obligation* in the etymological sense: a bond that ties.

Strictly (or legally) speaking, the fulfillment of the obligation of gratitude may be impossible, as in the case of the parent / child or divine / human relationship. One cannot return to his parents exactly what he has received from them — his very life and (presumably) rearing — or any reasonable equivalent. But as we have seen, morally speaking everyone is capable of gratitude. Aquinas's example is conclusive: "Dicendum quod etiam pauper ingratus non est, si faciat quod possit. Sicut enim beneficium magis in affectu consistit quam in effectu, ita etiam recompensatio magis in affectu consistit" [It ought to be said that even a pauper is not ungrateful if he does what he can. For just as the value of a benefit consists more in the feelings of the benefactor than in the thing itself, so also repayment consists more in the feelings of the beneficiary] (*ST* 2a2ae.106,

3). Gratitude is thus an empowering virtue: *si faciat quod possit*, even the pauper *can* — that is, *is able to* — repay the greatest of gifts. Aquinas returns to the example of the indebtedness of child to parent and concludes: "Si autem attendamus ad ipsam voluntatem dantis et retribuentis, sic potest filius aliquid major patri retribuere, ut Seneca dicit. Si tamen non posset, sufficeret gratitudinem recompensandi voluntas" [If, however, we look at it from the point of view of one giving and repaying, a son can thus repay his father even more, as Seneca says. But if that would not be possible, the will to repay would still meet the needs of gratitude] (*ST* 2a2ae.106, 6). Such empowerment increases individual responsibility, for everyone has a will and a heart. The empowerment also provides great potential for the individual, so long as the will is not perverted and the heart not hardened. Theologically speaking, if one recognizes and acknowledges God's benefits, he can — will? — respond with gratitude, that is, respond *gratis*, which is a mirror image of God's actions toward mankind. The response becomes religious in the deepest sense, an exertion of ultimate freedom: it makes one godly — godlike — and reveals the state of grace. In the long soliloquy at the beginning of book 4, lines 32–113, Satan's unwillingness merges with the inability to be grateful and reveals enthrallment and damnation.

4

Aquinas nowhere cites the Book of Psalms in his discussion of gratitude. But the general sense of gratitude as a moral virtue that is inward and subjective runs throughout the psalms, both those that are lamentory and those that are celebratory. The Old Testament does not, however, have any distinctive idea of or particular word for "gratitude" or "thanks" as distinguished from "praise," "glorifying" or "magnifying." Two Hebrew words carry the meanings: the verb *yadah* (to confess,

to acknowledge, to sing) and the derived noun *todhah* (confession, acknowledgment, vow). The fundamental meaning
of the Hebrew root in both words is "confess." They are used
in two basic ways: (1) confessing, acknowledging or declaring
God's attributes and works; and (2) confessing sins. The object
of *yadah* is always Yahweh. In the case of the psalms, the
Authorized Version most often follows the Geneva Bible and
translates *yadah* as "praise" rather than "thank."[6]

The evidence from the Geneva Bible suggests that the
concept of the Hebrew original including both "thank" and
"praise" remains in English, though only one word might be
used. The Geneva translation frequently uses "praise" in the
text of the Psalm while a headnote or side note comments on
the "thanksgiving." The translation of Psalm 9 uses "praise"
for *yadah* in the opening verse, "I wil praise the Lord with my
whole heart."[7] The headnote summarizes the first part of the
psalm as consisting of David's giving "thanks to God for the
sundrie victories that he had sent him against his enemies."
The Geneva translation of Psalm 56:12 is "Thy vowes are vpon
me, O God: I wil rendre praises vnto thee," while the side
note paraphrases: "Hauing receiued that which I required, I
am bounde to paye my vowes of thankesgiuing." The headnote
to Psalm 136 comments that it is "A moste earnest exhortation
to giue thankes vnto God," and the translation of *yadah* in
the original of the first line is "Praise ye the Lord, because he
is good."

Now in discussing the psalms, we may regard "thanks" as
the "state of being grateful," and "praise" as the consequent
expression of that feeling in words, song, and even deeds. So
the combination of the meanings of "thanks" and "praise" in
single Hebrew words that basically mean "acknowledgment"
is of more than lexical interest and extends to both the form
and content of the psalms.

To begin with content. The psalmist naturally adduces
reasons for gratitude. Most basic is the fact of Creation itself,

a fact that most of the celebratory psalms imply and that many acknowledge explicitly, as Psalm 33: "By the word of the Lord were the heavens made; and all the host of them by the breath of his mouth. He gathereth the waters of the sea together as a heap: he layeth up the depth in storehouses" (Ps. 33:6–7).[8] The headnote in the Geneva translation draws a clear connection between the fact of Creation and the universal debt of praise that humans owe, pointing out that the psalmist "exhorteth good men to praise God for that he hathe . . . created all things, and by his prouidence gouerneth the same." The debt of gratitude deepens in view of God's creation of man and gift of the created world. Psalm 8, for example, observes the miracle of God's being mindful of man and the fact that God "made him a little lower than the angels . . . [and] to have dominion over the works of thy hands . . . [and] put all things under his feet" (Ps. 8:5–6). The side note to the Geneva translation comments on the point and focuses on man's unworthiness with the image of dust: "It had bene sufficient for him to haue set forthe his glorie by the heauens, though he had not come so low as to man, which is but dust." Milton uses this image several times in *Paradise Lost* as he elaborates the notion of man's incalculable debt to his maker (see *PL* 4.416, 7.525, 10.743). Throughout the poem, we shall see that Milton uses the fact of Creation and God as the originary force as a matrix within which he presents gratitude and ingratitude.

In adducing reasons for man's debt of gratitude, the psalms often center on the recognition and thence the acknowledgment of God's power and deeds. The Geneva headnote to Psalm 8 explains that the psalmist considers the "excellent liberalitie and fatherlie prouidence of God towards man, whome he made . . . [and the psalmist] doeth . . . giue great thankes." It is an apt comment on the crucial verse, "When I consider thy heavens, the work of thy fingers, the moon and the stars, which thou hast ordained; What is man, that thou art mindful of him?" (Ps. 8:3–4). The point about man's obligation to acknowledge the Creator is made explicit in the Geneva headnote to Psalm 92: "This psalme was made . . . to stirre vp the people to acknowledge God and to praise him in his workes." The opening verses of the psalm announce the theme: "It is a good thing to give thanks unto the Lord, and to sing praises unto thy name, O Most High: To show forth thy loving-kindness in the morning, and thy faithfulness every night" (1–2). Very often, the acknowledgment includes a subjective, emotional response. After rehearsing his deliverance by the Lord, the psalmist says in Psalm 40, "I delight to do thy will, O my God: yea, thy law is within my heart" (8), and similarly in Psalm 138, "I will praise thee with my whole heart" (1). Milton's translation of Psalm 8 makes the perception strongly subjective: "When I behold thy Heav'ns, thy Fingers' art / The moon and Starrs which thou so bright hast set / In the pure firmament, *then saith my heart,* / O what is man that thou remembrest yet, / And think'st upon him?" (9–13; my emphasis).

Frequently the emotional response extends to wonder and admiration, as in Psalm 96, "O sing unto the Lord a new song: sing unto the Lord, all the earth . . . Declare his glory among the heathen, his wonders among all people" (1, 3), and Psalm 98, "O sing unto the Lord a new song: for he hath done marvelous things" (1). Occasionally such statements remark on the mystery of God's powers, as in Psalm 145, "Great is the Lord, and greatly to be praised; and his greatness is unsearchable" (3). In the case of Psalm 40, "Many, O Lord my God, are thy wonderful works which thou hast done, and thy thoughts which are to us-ward: they cannot be reckoned up in order unto thee" (5), the Geneva side note comments on the response of the psalmist: "Dauid goeth from one kinde of Gods fauor to the contemplation of his prouidence ouer all . . . & confesseth that his counsels towards vs are farre aboue our capacities: we can not so much as tel [count] them in ordre." Quite often the responses acknowledging the wonder of God become exultant and expressive of great joy. Even the lamentory Psalm 71 affirms, "My lips shall greatly rejoice when I sing unto thee; and my soul, which thou hast redeemed" (23). The more celebratory psalms often bring out the expressiveness through repetition that survives in translation, as in Psalm 95: "O come, let us sing unto the Lord: let us make a joyful noise to the rock of our salvation. Let us come before his presence with thanksgiving, and make a joyful noise unto him with psalms" (1–2). The headnote to Psalm 92 in the Geneva Bible summarizes many of these aspects of the psalmist's perception of and response to God: "This psalme was made to be sung on the Sabbath, to stirre vp the people to acknowledge God and to praise him in his workes: the Prophet reioyceth therein." In short, acknowledgment, subjectivity and joy all figure prominently in the substance of the psalmist's thanks.

These responses receive appropriate expression in the psalms' lyric form, which is basically an expression of praise. The side note in the Geneva Bible to Psalm 71:23, "My lips shall greatly rejoice when I sing unto thee," explains that "there is no true praising of God, except it come from the heart." The explanation isolates the essence of lyric: A heartfelt expression of an emotional state in the first person. The spontaneity is conventional, and the lyric form reveals a high degree of artifice and self-conscious rhetoric. The notes in the Geneva Bible to Psalm 19, "The heavens declare the glory of God," remark on the specifically rhetorical aim. The side note to the first verse asserts that the psalmist "reprocheth vnto man his ingratitude." The headnote comments that to "the intent he might moue the faithful to a deeper consideration of Gods glorie, he setteth before their eyes the moste exquisite workemanship of the heauens with their proportion, and ornaments." So besides having the aim of "reproaching" and "moving" the audience, the psalm relies on mimesis, representing and celebrating the accomplishments of God in his creation.[9]

The method of such psalms is often highly figurative. For example, in the first six verses of Psalm 19, the heavens "declare" and the firmament "uttereth." The side notes in the Geneva Bible explicate the metaphors with still other figures, noting that the "heauens are a scholemaster" and that they are "as a line of great capital letters." Psalm 148, which also focuses on the fact of Creation as reason for praising God, varies the metaphoric expression: "Praise ye him, sun and moon: praise him, all ye stars of light. Praise him, ye heavens of heavens, and ye waters that be above the heavens. Let them praise the name of the Lord: for he commanded, and they were created" (3–5). The trope of inanimate objects of nature praising God for their creation results in hyperbolic expression and elevates gratitude to a universal law. In the words of the Geneva Bible note to Psalm 19, the metaphorical statement also constitutes a reproach to human ingratitude by "seing the heauens, which are dumme creatures, set forthe Gods glorie." Milton will use not only the substance but also the rhetoric of these psalms in the morning hymn he gives Adam and Eve in book 5, lines 153–208, showing that in their prelapsarian state they are certainly no "dumme creatures."

We may conclude discussion of the psalms by considering the psalmist's treatment of sacrifice, the formal enactment of gratitude. Stemming from prebiblical times, sacrifice is literally a "making sacred," a setting aside of something from the human, secular realm and dedicating it to the Divine. The act is a physical expression of acknowledgment of godhead and accordingly entails praise and thanksgiving. A recurrent critique is that sacrifice had become legalistic and ritualistic, and so the psalmist is concerned to redefine it. In Psalm 69 the psalmist promises to "praise the name of God with a song, and . . . [to] magnify him with thanksgiving. This also shall please the Lord better than an ox or bullock that hath horns and hoofs" (30–31). The side note in the Geneva translation comments that "There is no sacrifice, whiche God more

estemeth, then thankesgiuing for his benefites." The identification of "thankesgiuing" as the supreme form of sacrifice
shifts the sacrificial act from the external to the internal, from
the physical to the spiritual.

Sacrifice so defined bears both on the conception of godhead
and on the responsibilities of the individual as a free agent.
This conception regards God as intrinsically divine. Psalm 50
invokes Yahweh in a voice reminiscent of the Book of Job as
He rejects traditional sacrifices and "burnt offerings" and
asserts: "I will take no bullock out of thy house, nor he goats
out of thy folds: For every beast of the rest is mine, and the
cattle upon a thousand hills. . . . If I were hungry, I would not
tell thee: for the world is mine, and the fulnes therof. Will I
eat the flesh of bulls, or drink the blood of goats?" (9–10, 12–
13). The irony, verging on sarcasm, points to the divinity of
Yahweh for whom a physical sacrifice is meaningless, if not
blasphemous and potentially idolatrous.

In so acknowledging godhead, the psalmist also points to
the responsibilities humans have to act in accord with their
own condition. This begins in self-knowledge and leads to
humility and contrition. In Psalm 51, the psalmist asserts
that the Lord delights "not in burnt offering" and that the
"sacrifices of God are a broken spirit." He concludes that a
"broken and a contrite heart, O God, thou wilt not despise"
(16–17). The verses bring out the intense emotionality and
self-reflexivity of contrition. While inward in this way,
contrition results from a sense of the divine which can be
grasped only through faith. As the side note in the Geneva
Bible glosses the above verses, contrition is a "wounding of
the heart, proceding of faith, which seketh vnto God for
mercie." Faith requires volition; but it also requires God's
prevenient grace. Even though painful, contrition leads to a
reconnection with Yahweh, to restoration of the broken
relationship between man and God — and to a state of mind
and soul that becomes grateful, that is, literally full of grace.

For this reason the psalmist celebrates such sacrifices as most pleasing to God. Milton accordingly casts his expression of Adam and Eve's prayers of contrition in explicitly sacrificial terms (11.14–20). The prayers are mediated by the Son and preliminary to the Father's provision of a future that may lead to a "second Life, / Wak't in the renovation of the just" (64–65). It is a life that Adam and Eve may anticipate with gratitude, though, as we shall see, the poem's larger ironies greatly qualify their anticipation.

The emphasis on song and on inwardness appears in the dispensation of the New Testament. There the concept of gratitude includes very much the salient features we have found in the Old Testament: acknowledgment, praise and thanksgiving to God for benefits received. From this perspective, gratitude is the most fundamental of religious acts. As the author of the epistle to the Hebrews puts it: "Wherefore we receiving a kingdom that cannot be moved, let us have grace, whereby we may serve God acceptably with reverence and godly fear" (12:28).

The primary terms for "thank," "thankful," "thanksgiving" and so forth in the New Testament are ευχαριστεω and its cognate noun ευχαριστια and the adjective ευχαριστος. A related noun χαρις (grace or favor) is also used for "thanks" and "gratitude." The common locution εχω χαριν "have thankfulness," recurs in the synoptics and the epistles. These terms nearly always refer to thanks directed to God rather than to other human beings.

Thanksgiving and gratitude are conspicuous features in the accounts of the institution of the Eucharist: Matthew 26:26–28, Mark 14:22–24, Luke 22:17–20, and 1 Corinthians 11:24–26. Occasionally, earlier redactions use ευλογεω, meaning something like "to pronounce a blessing," but ευχαριστεω prevails. Without digressing into the complexity and obscurity of the accounts of the Last Supper, we can say that it depended on Jewish custom, and Jesus' actions and words of blessing represent his thankfulness for God's deeds of salvation that the new dispensation was introducing. Early on, certainly in the Pauline communities, the Eucharist appears to have become liturgical (1 Cor. 14:16–18, 1 Thess. 5:18), and Paul enjoins the Ephesians to be "speaking to yourselves in psalms and hymns and spiritual songs, singing and making melody in your heart to the Lord; Giving thanks always for all things" (5:19–20).

By far the largest number of references to gratitude in the New Testament occur in the epistles of Paul, the apostle and theologian of thanksgiving. In the introduction to his epistles, he typically expresses thanksgiving to God and relates the thanksgiving to the particular subject. In fact, to give "honor and thanks" to God is the primary way by which we acknowledge God and show devotion, as in the following from Romans 1:20–21: "For the invisible things of him from the creation of the world are clearly seen, being understood by the things that are made, even his eternal power and God-head: so that they are without excuse: Because that, when they knew God, they glorified him not as God, neither were [they] thankful." Paul extends the sheerly meditative and liturgical dimension of gratitude to the realm of the ethical. Just as ευλογεω (praising or blessing) is man's proper response to God's ευλογια (blessing), so he says in 2 Corinthians 4:15 that ευχαριστια (thanksgiving) is his response to the χαρις (grace or gracious gift) of God. Indeed χαρις (in the sense of the grace of vocation to the apostolate) must bear fruit in the ευχαριστια (thanksgiving) of those who have converted. Through gratitude and thanksgiving, activities that are themselves indifferent become consecrated for the most exalted aim of life. Through gratitude things are literally *sacrificed* — that is, made sacred. This applies both to words and deeds, as Paul says in Colossians 3:17, even to eating and drinking. Paul writes to Timothy: "For everything created by God is good, and nothing is to be rejected if it is received with thanksgiving. For then it is consecrated by the word of God and prayer" (1 Tim. 4:4–5). Even prayers of petition must be constantly intermingled with thanksgiving (Phil. 4:6; Col. 4:2). Not surprisingly, Paul expresses gratitude for faith, hope and charity (Rom. 1:8, for faith; Philem. 1:4–6 for faith and love; 1 Thess. 1:3 for works of faith, the self-sacrifice of love, the steadfastness of hope).

At the risk of overly schematizing, let me summarize briefly some of the recurring features of the concept of gratitude or thanksgiving which the preceding survey of Scripture brings out. Fundamentally, gratitude stems from recognition and acknowledgment of godhead. In this respect the concept retains the root senses of the Hebrew *yadah* and *todhah*. Although such acknowledgment obviously entails perception, the process is not exclusively intellectual or ratiocinative; one does not simply reason one's way into a mode of thanksgiving and gratitude. Gratitude is distinctly emotional, stemming from the heart, and brings with it an exultant joyousness. From fairly early Jewish times, the expression of gratitude was liturgical and the special liturgical form was song. Typically these expressions brought out admiration and awe for the ultimately mysterious nature of the benefactor, that is, God.

5

In turning to *Paradise Lost* we see that love, praise and thanksgiving, and joy define the condition of humans in their unfallen state. We see that their opposites — hatred, complaint and ingratitude, and misery — define the fallen condition.

Let us begin with the creation of man in book 7, where Raphael relates his version of the hexameral account:

> There wanted yet the Master work, the end
> Of all yet don; a Creature who not prone
> And Brute as other Creatures, but endu'd
> With Sanctitie of Reason, might erect
> His Stature, and upright with Front serene

> Govern the rest, self-knowing, and from thence
> Magnanimous to correspond with Heav'n,
> But grateful to acknowledge whence his good
> Descends, thither with heart and voice and eyes
> Directed in Devotion, to adore
> And worship God Supream, who made him chief
> Of all his works.
>
> (7.505–16)

The passage continues with Raphael's direct quotation of the Creator:

> Let us make now Man in our image, Man
> In our similitude, and let them rule
> Over the Fish and Fowl of Sea and Air,
> Beast of the Field, and over all the Earth,
> And every creeping thing that creeps the ground.
> This said, he formd thee, *Adam*, thee O Man
> Dust of the ground, and in thy nostrils breath'd
> The breath of Life.
>
> (7.519–26)

The passage conflates and embellishes Genesis, chapters 1 and 2, and Milton underlines the biblical association of Adam and the earth — dust — reproducing the wordplay of the Hebrew of Genesis 2:7, ʿ*adham* (man) and ʿ*adhamah* (earth): "thee O Man" in line 524 and "Dust of the ground" in line 525. By elaborating the grandeur and nobility of God's creation from dust, Milton expands upon the Genesis account, enhancing the image of the miracle and adding the quality of gratitude. Although God makes man "magnanimous to correspond with Heav'n," he makes him "grateful." The syntax and meter align the two qualities and underline their potential opposition — magnanimous "[b]ut" grateful. The characterization of Adam as "magnanimous to correspond with heaven" suggests the loftiness of his moral and intellectual gifts, which enable him to communicate with as well as be appropriate to heaven. The adjective "magnanimous" recalls the heroic virtue described by Spenser as "magnificence" in his letter to Ralegh prefatory to *The Faerie Queene* and stems from Aristotle's μεγαλο-ψυκια.[10] Significantly, Aristotle explains that the magnanimous person abjures receiving benefits from another since he would require gratitude and so relegate him to a position of relative inferiority (4.3.1124b). In characterizing Adam as "magnanimous" but "grateful," Milton suggests an ideal that is broadly comprehensive.

Milton is explicit in this passage about Adam's distinctive quality of gratitude. God creates Adam first of all to acknowledge whence his good originates — which points to the intellectual dimension of gratitude. Adam is also grateful in his loving worship and prayerful hymns, which reflect the subjective, emotional dimension of the virtue expressed in liturgical acts of thanks and praise, as in the morning prayer declaimed by Adam and Eve in book 5. Milton could not be more precise: God creates Adam inherently grateful, and if he had remained so he would not have fallen. We shall not be surprised when we turn back to book 3 and hear God's particular denunciation of the fallen Adam.

Subsequently, in book 8, Adam describes his first response to his creation. It is perfectly grateful and dramatizes much of what we have been tracing of Milton's depiction of Adam's original nature as created in the prelapsarian state. Adam relates how he awoke into existence in a balmy sweat and then:

> Strait toward Heav'n my wond'ring Eyes I turn'd,
> And gaz'd a while the ample Skie, till rais'd
> By quick instinctive motion up I sprung,
> As thitherward endevoring, and upright
> Stood on my feet; about me round I saw
> Hill, Dale, and shadie Woods, and sunnie Plains,
> And liquid Lapse of murmuring Streams; by these,
> Creatures that liv'd, and mov'd, and walk'd, or flew,
> Birds on the branches warbling; all things smil'd,
> With fragrance and with joy my heart oreflow'd.
> My self I then perus'd, and Limb by Limb

> Survey'd, and sometimes went, and sometimes ran
> With supple joints, as lively vigour led.
>
> (8.257–69)

The recollection describes an apprehension of the external, phenomenal world in which Adam's response is appreciative as well as apprehensive. Physicality and naturalness predominate in the depiction of Adam's surveying of his person and actively exerting himself. Above all, Adam's response expresses the joyousness of the perception — "all things smil'd, / With fragrance and with joy my heart oreflow'd."

The primary response — the apprehension of nature and himself — extends to a metaphysical and thence theological inquiry, as Adam inquires into his origins:

> Thou Sun, said I, fair Light,
> And thou enlight'n'd Earth, so fresh and gay,
> Ye Hills and Dales, ye Rivers, Woods, and Plains
> And ye that live and move, fair Creatures, tell,
> Tell, if ye saw, how came I thus, how here?
> Not of my self; by some great Maker then,
> In goodness and in power praeeminent;
> Tell me, how may I know him, how adore,
> From whom I have that thus I move and live,
> And feel that I am happier then I know.
>
> (8.273–82)

The periodic repetitions of the verse move toward a climactic sense of deity. The movement is intellectual and at the same time wholly subjective: deeply felt and deeply joyous. The passage recalls and contrasts with Satan's address to the sun at the beginning of book 4. It also recalls (or anticipates) the psalmic hymn of thanksgiving that Milton gives to Adam and Eve in book 5. Here Adam asks the creatures of nature to "tell" him of his origins, of his creator. In the hymn, Adam and Eve enjoin the creatures of nature to sing their thanks and praise to their creator.

Adam's inherently grateful desire to know the maker is then satisfied when the Divine Presence appears and Adam responds as follows:

> Rejoycing, but with aw,
> In adoration at his feet I fell
> Submiss: he rear'd me, and Whom thou sought'st I am,
> Said mildly, Author of all this thou seest
> Above, or round about thee or beneath.
> This Paradise I give thee, count it thine
> To Till and keep.
>
> $\qquad\qquad\qquad\qquad\qquad$ (8.314–20)

Adam enacts perfectly and naturally prayerful thanksgiving. He knows God aright, and as a result of his submissive prostration God raises him to a new height and vouchsafes him new gifts, the ultimate one being Eve.

Milton provides a more extended image of perfect gratitude in the first presentation of Adam and Eve together in book 4, lines 411–91. Gratitude figures not only in the joyous relationship between the unfallen couple but also in their regard of God. The image emerges from an exchange that approaches lyric expression, a virtual love duet of harmony and mutuality. Adam's address to Eve is both heartfelt and intellectual:

> Sole partner and sole part of all these joyes,
> Dearer thy self then all; needs must the Power
> That made us, and for us this ample World
> Be infinitely good, and of his good
> As liberal and free as infinite,
> That rais'd us from the dust and plac't us here
> In all this happiness, who at his hand
> Have nothing merited, nor can perform
> Aught whereof hee hath need.
>
> $\qquad\qquad\qquad\qquad\qquad$ (4.411–19)

The subjectivity comes from the intimacy of Adam's initial words to Eve, the almost colloquial repetition of "Sole partner and sole part." At the same time, Adam's address entails a strictly intellectual apprehension of God. The phrase "needs must" and the inductive thought process suggest logical inference of the Creator's goodness from the facts of experience:

the ample, beautiful world given them, their creation from mere dust, and their inability to do anything "whereof he [their creator] hath need." The inference leads to a wholly reasoned sense of the miracle of divine beneficence and liberality. The point and the consequent wonder result from the unfathomable gap between the infinite goodness of God and the essentially undeserving nature of humans. As Adam completes his address, he moves through the conclusion of his theological reflections to a deeply subjective assertion:

> But let us ever praise him, and extoll
> His bountie, following our delightful task
> To prune these growing Plants, and tend these Flowrs,
> Which were it toilsom, yet with thee were sweet.
>
> (4.436–39)

Adam concludes that the debt of gratitude to God is ongoing, and echoes the traditional liturgical terms of "thanks" and "praise." He ends on a highly romantic note: that the mere presence of the beloved can transform what is toilsome into something sweet. The wonder and power of his personal love merges with his grateful sense of the miracle of Creation.

Eve's response to Adam is equally grateful and picks up his specific terms of thanks and praise: "O thou for whom / And from whom I was form'd flesh of thy flesh . . . what thou has said is just and right. / For wee to him indeed all praises owe, / And daily thanks" (4.440–45). The register of Eve's response differs, however. She, too, is intensely intimate and subjective. But where Adam tended to be logical and analytical, Eve's response is a highly personal narrative. In the first place it substantiates the gender hierarchy of the early characterization of the couple, "Hee for God only, shee for God in him" (4.299). Eve acknowledges Adam as her source and authority — "my Guide and Head" — even as she confirms his conclusion that it is "just and right" for them to express gratitude to their Creator. Her narration of staring at her reflection in a pool and of God's leading her to Adam suggests a relatively enclosed space, domestic and conjugal, and maintains her primary focus on Adam. The narrative concludes the exchange between Adam and Eve and marks their perfect union, as Eve recalls Adam's romantic plea to her that she is "neerest [his] heart" and "Part of [his] soul" and his "other half."

Perhaps the fullest expression of gratitude in the poem occurs in book 5, lines 137–208, the morning prayer sung by Adam and Eve after he consoles her upon waking from her troubled dream. Like the exchange in book 4, their prayer is lyric, but it is neither responsory nor harmonious but in unison. The narrative voice calls attention to the prayer's musicality and suggests the purity of its lyricism by emphasizing its unmediated and spontaneous nature. Each morning Adam and Eve undertake a prayer

> In various style, for neither various style
> Nor holy rapture wanted they to praise
> Thir Maker, in fit strains pronounc't or sung
> Unmeditated, such prompt eloquence
> Flowd from thir lips, in Prose or numerous Verse,
> More tuneable then needed Lute or Harp
> To add more sweetness.
>
> (5.146–52)

The purity of the lyric utterance reflects the unfallen condition of Adam and Eve and deepens the heartfelt sincerity of the expression of gratitude. Of course the prayer is not actually spontaneous, any more than the prayers by the psalmist are. Opposed to the intimacy and occasional colloquial cadences of the exchange in book 4, Adam and Eve's prayer is self-consciously formal and recalls readings assigned in *The Book of Common Prayer* for morning prayer, that part of the daily office which most occupies itself with thanks and praise.[11]

The prayer's often-commented-on formality is evident in the gross structure. It falls into three distinct parts, which may be described in rhetorical terms: (1) exordium, lines 153–59; (2) narratio, lines 160–204; and (3) peroratio, lines 205–8.

The exordium establishes both the premise of the prayer — that, in the words of Psalm 19, the heavens declare the glory of God — and its rhetorical strategy — that thanks and praise receive expression through an elaborate celebration of the created world.[12] Like all thanksgivings, the prayer is fundamentally an acknowledgment of deity, "Him first, him last, him midst, and without end" (5.165), as creator and sustainer of the universe.

The narratio employs the rhetoric of praise from Psalm 148 and presents the evidence for God's beneficence through a litany of enjoinders to praise.[13] It consists of nine apostrophes in eight sentences in the imperative mood. These urge animate and inanimate creatures alike to raise their voices in praise and range from the morning star (5.166–70) to Adam and Eve themselves (5.202–4). The litany spans the created universe in a catalog that suggests perfect comprehensiveness. The perfection of the statement receives reinforcement from the numerological subtext. There are nine imperative clauses and eight sentences. The numbers eight and nine are traditionally used to suggest the idea of perfection owing to the fact that nine is the number of all the whole integers, and eight the number of natural pitches in the musical scale. The harmony, if not the music of the narratio, also emerges from the repetition in each of the apostrophes of the word "praise," initially as a finite imperative verb and successively as a noun in the objective case.

The peroratio maintains the imperative grammatical mood but modulates the statement from the narratio's rhetoric of musical celebration to direct address:

> Hail universal Lord, be bounteous still
> To give us only good; and if the night
> Have gather'd aught of evil or conceald,
> Disperse it, as now light dispels the dark.

(5.205–8)

The vocative address to the "universal Lord" is personal and direct, and completes the lyric logic of the prayer by acknowledging the Creator of the world celebrated in the narratio. The acknowledgment moves to petition that the speakers be preserved; it is a petition that follows rhetorically and substantively from the recognition of the Creator and their own dependence on him. In this way the prayer concludes with a return to the beginning, "These are thy glorious works, Parent of good" (5.153), and perfects the whole.

The harmony and music that result from the formal structure of the morning prayer are distinctive in their ritualistic, ceremonial qualities, recalling most obviously the service prescribed in *The Prayer-Book*. These qualities are appropriate to the fundamentally religious character of the utterance, which in its expression of gratitude reveals Adam and Eve's sense of deity. As the narrator stresses, there is no service prescribed in Paradise. Adam and Eve pray spontaneously, and the prayer is naturally harmonious and musical. It is natural that they engage in such celebration of the world, in such praise, and in such thanks upon rising every day; they have been created grateful. The prayer is also spontaneous since their perception and experience of the created world is so immediate and complete that it leads them every day to a renewed recognition and acknowledgment of their God. The resulting relationship is one of concord: differences are reconciled in an orderly and indeed beautiful way: man, creation, and God. All is in accord with the divine plan and man's wishes. It is fitting that the prayer receives musical expression.

6

As we have seen, God creates man grateful. So when we watch God foresee the Fall, we hear him denounce man's disobedience as ingratitude. He surveys Satan winging his way toward the new world to see if he can destroy or, as he says,

> By som false guile pervert; and shall pervert;
> For Man will heark'n to his glozing lies,
> And easily transgress the sole Command,
> Sole pledge of his obedience: So will fall
> Hee and his faithless Progenie: whose fault?
> Whose but his own? ingrate, he had of mee
> All he could have; I made him just and right,
> Sufficient to have stood, though free to fall.
>
> (3.92–99)

Nowhere does the imputed irritability of Milton's God resound more clearly than in the fuming repetition of the verb "pervert" and the phrases "sole command," "sole pledge," and the angry exclamation "ingrate," which may be one of the earliest uses of the word as a substantive.[14] Especially notable is the juxtaposition of the exclamation that man is ungrateful with the observation of what man had been given: "he had of mee All he could have." Significantly, God indicates not the world and Paradise but the moral qualities he had endowed humanity with — "I made him just and right" — and the moral strength those qualities provide — "Sufficient to have stood though free to fall." Thus Milton links man's endowment to his supreme challenge, the challenge to be free. It is an endowment that the Father believes man should be grateful for.

Milton then supplies a negative example, one that embodies ingratitude and the concomitant loss of joy and liberty. Right before the poem's first image of Adam and Eve in Paradise, Satan appears in soliloquy at the beginning of book 4, lines 31–113, and reflects candidly on his lot as leader of the rebellion. He admits that God

> deserv'd no such return
> From me, whom he created what I was
> In that bright eminence, and with his good
> Upbraided none; nor was his service hard.
> What could be less then to afford him praise,
> The easiest recompense, and pay him thanks,
> How due! yet all his good prov'd ill in me,

And wrought but malice; lifted up so high
I sdeind subjection, and thought one step higher
Would set me highest, and in a moment quit
The debt immense of endless gratitude,
So burdensome still paying, still to ow;
Forgetful what from him I still receiv'd,
And understood not that a grateful mind
By owing owes not, but still pays, at once
Indebted and discharg'd; what burden then?

(4.42–57)

Satan first observes that his debt to God is absolute: he owes God his existence. The language of gratitude pervades the speech: service (45), praise (46), thanks (47), debt (52), and the word "gratitude" itself (52). Satan's understanding of his debt to God is standard and orthodox. It is a debt that is endless, one that necessitates paying still and owing still; but it is also a debt that by one's very owing of it one discharges it. That is, by *feeling* the debt one repays it. As we have seen in Aquinas's analysis, besides being rational, legal and just, gratitude is emotional and heartfelt. It is a frame of mind in the widest sense. That frame of mind depends on recognition and acknowledgment of the basic reality of God's beneficent creation and the individual's undeserved creation. Satan recognizes and acknowledges this reality, but he cannot accommodate himself to it. He thinks that doing so would entail inferiority. He disdains subjection and inferiority; he aspires to superiority. The result is profoundly ironic: perfect misery and complete loss of freedom, as the conclusion of Satan's soliloquy makes plain:

Me miserable! Which way shall I flie
Infinite wrauth, and infinite despair?
Which way I flie is Hell; myself am Hell;
And in the lowest deep a lower deep
Still threatning to devour me opens wide,
To which the Hell I suffer seems a Heav'n.

(4.73–78)

Satan makes the important point that he is not just fallen; he is continually falling.

If Satan reveals thorough understanding of gratitude in his soliloquy, he reveals thorough hypocrisy in his public debate with Abdiel at the end of book 5, lines 772–907, where he argues for action that is perfectly ungrateful.[15] Satan denies the Father's right to elevate the Son above the heavenly host and to require of them the Son's adoration since they "live by right / His equals, if in power and splendor less, / In freedom equal" (5.795–97). Abdiel contests Satan's argument and summarizes Satan's personal offense and particular ingratitude:

> O argument blasphemous, false and proud!
> Words which no ear ever to hear in Heav'n
> Expected, least of all from thee, ingrate
> In place thyself so high above thy Peers.
>
> (5.809–12)

Like the Father condemning Adam and Eve as ingrates in book 3, Abdiel bases his objection on the gift — in Satan's case his hitherto preeminence — received from the Father. Abdiel continues his analysis of Satan's blasphemous ingratitude by asserting the authority of the Father, which he traces to his originary act. "Shalt thou give Law to God," Abdiel asks, "who made / Thee what thou art, and form'd the Pow'rs of Heav'n / Such as he pleas'd, and circumscrib'd thir being?" (5.822–25). Abdiel repeats the point and invokes the scriptural tradition of the Son as the creative word, by whom "the mighty Father made / All things, ev'n thee, and all the Spirits of Heav'n" (5.836–37). Satan responds sarcastically to Abdiel's assertions of the Father and the Son's authority by flatly denying the angels' status as creatures of God: "That we were formd then saist thou? and the work / Of secondarie hands, by task transferd / From Father to his Son? strange point and new!" (5.853–55). Satan rewrites history and utters the ultimate blasphemy against God the Creator, the doctrine of which he continues to call into question:

> who saw
> When this creation was? rememberst thou
> Thy making, while the Maker gave thee being?
> We know no time when we were not as now;
> Know none before us, self-begot, self-rais'd
> By our own quick'ning power.
>
> (5.856–61)

In denying God's originary act, Satan denies God's authority and so becomes completely ungrateful. He has arrogated to himself God's unique and defining power. Characteristic of the poem's irony, Satan's presumptuous claims and attempts to aggrandize himself make him ever less godly and he continues his fall.

The final instance of Milton's rendition of the fallen state I wish to consider is the postlapsarian Adam in book 10. He is not Satan, but he has fallen and Milton suggests that he is in some ways satanic. Adam is alone in book 10, alienated from God and Eve, and his words recall Satan's soliloquy from the opening of book 4:

> O miserable of happie! is this the end
> Of this new glorious World, and mee so late
> The Glory of that Glory, who now becom
> Accurst of blessed, hide me from the face
> Of God, whom to behold was then my highth
> Of happiness: yet well, if here would end
> The miserie, I deserv'd it, and would bear
> My own deservings.
>
> (10.720–27)

Like Satan, Adam is miserable; and like Satan in his soliloquy, Adam analyzes his own predicament clearly. He admits that he deserves his fate, but the admission does little to relieve the pain he experiences from falling from the state of being "blessed" to the state of being "accurst." He is no longer capable of celebrating (of blessing) creation and his God but only of complaining.

Now he must suffer a fate of being cursed for all time. Indeed, Milton develops Adam's complaint with ironic variations on the curse motif. Adam exclaims:

> All that I eat or drink, or shall beget,
> Is propagated curse. O voice once heard
> Delightfully, *Encrease and multiply*,
> Now death to hear! for what can I encrease
> Or multiplie, but curses on my head?
> Who of all Ages to succeed, but feeling
> The evil on him brought by me, will curse
> My Head, Ill fare our Ancestor impure,
> For this we may thank *Adam*; but his thanks
> Shall be the execration.
>
> (10.728–37)

The gift of life and of generating life, of creating the human race and the future made Adam godly. The gift has now become a curse. For the "gift" of life will be cause not for gratitude but its opposite, as Adam contemplates his children's bitter irony of extending him not thanks but execration. The gift that was a source of joy and hope has now become a source of grief and despair.

As his agony deepens and the complaint intensifies, Adam does not blaspheme or deny God's originary actions as Satan does. But he does call into question the justice of those actions and become decidedly ungrateful:

> Did I request thee, Maker, from my Clay
> To mould me Man, did I sollicite thee
> From darkness to promote me, or here place
> In this delicious Garden? as my Will
> Concurd not to my being, it were but right
> And equal to reduce me to my dust,
> Desirous to resigne, and render back
> All I receav'd, unable to perform
> Thy terms too hard, by which I was to hold
> The good I sought not. To the loss of that,
> Sufficient penaltie, why hast thou added
> The sense of endless woes? inexplicable
> Thy Justice seems.
>
> (10.743–55)

The same biblical imagery that earlier had expressed the miracle of creation from dust figures here in Adam's wish to reject God's gift. The wish amounts to a quarrel with God's ways and recalls Satan's impulse to "give law to God." Adam is rejecting God's plan and in the process rejecting God's love. He has become an ingrate indeed.

The ingratitude extends to God's last, best gift, Eve. Adam's frustration and despair turn to anger and aggression directed toward Eve:

> Out of my sight, thou Serpent, that name best
> Befits thee with him leagu'd, thy self as false
> And hateful; nothing wants, but that thy shape,
> Like his, and colour Serpentine may shew
> Thy inward fraud, to warn all Creatures from thee
> Henceforth; lest that too heav'nly form, pretended
> To hellish falshood, snare them. But for thee
> I had persisted happie.
>
> (10.867–73)

Adam is quite wrong here since, as the narrative makes explicit in book 9, he was "not deceaved, / But fondly overcome with Femal charm." So his words and actions are unjust and patently self-serving. They are also ungrateful. Eve comes to Adam out of love and compassion in an effort to allay his affliction and fierce passion, and he rebukes her cruelly. Adam compounds his ingratitude as he turns his complaint back to God:

> O why did God,
> Creator wise, that peopl'd highest Heav'n
> With Spirits Masculine, create at last
> This noveltie on Earth, this fair defect
> Of Nature, and not fill the World at once
> With Men as Angels without Feminine,
> Or find some other way to generate
> Mankind?
>
> (10.888–95)

In his anger Adam rewrites history. In book 8 he recounts to Raphael that he had asked for Eve. As he puts it to God, "In solitude what happiness, who can enjoy alone?" God complies with his request and provides Adam with his wish, exactly to his heart's desire. Now Adam responds not with gratitude but with cruel hatred toward Eve. He becomes the world's first misogynist. Though Adam may not be irretrievably damned, his ingratitude is complete.

If critics have sometimes found Milton's depiction of Paradise and Adam and Eve in their prelapsarian state unrealistic, they almost always find their depiction in the postlapsarian state compellingly realistic, all too faithful to the fallen human condition. Milton thus presents Paradise and Paradise lost, innocence and experience, joy and sorrow. They are dichotomies he develops through the pervasive juxtaposition of gratitude and ingratitude.

7

The narrative is not finished, however. As we know from book 3, God has provided for a second miracle, one equaling and perhaps surpassing the miracle of Creation: salvation and grace in the miracle of the Incarnation and redemption. This surely is a miracle to elicit joy, praise and gratitude. As Adam receives a vision of the future, of what awaits humanity from the first generation to the Second Coming, he gradually takes heart. The encouragement appears in five passages in book 12 in which Adam breaks in and responds to the second miracle, the miracle of salvific grace. In the fourth of these passages, at the prospect of the Resurrection of the Son, Adam declares:

> O goodness infinite, goodness immense!
> That all this good of evil shall produce,
> And evil turn to good; more wonderful
> Then that which by creation first brought forth
> Light out of darkness! full of doubt I stand,
> Whether I should repent me now of sin
> By mee done and occasiond, or rejoyce

Much more, that much more good thereof shall spring,
To God more glory, more good will to Men
From God, and over wrauth grace shall abound.

(12.469–78)

Adam's reviving spirits and joy, increasing acknowledgment
of God's beneficence, sense of wonder, and expression of
praise — all recall the gratitude that characterizes the response
of Adam and Eve to their creation and life together in the
prelapsarian state. The gratitude here would seem to point to
closure of the narrative in which Adam and Eve leave Paradise
educated and spiritually fortified. This has been the judgment of most critics. Barbara Kiefer Lewalski represents the
consensus when she concludes that Adam has acquired a
"comprehension of spiritual things . . . that is necessary for
eternal salvation and the true happiness of life."[16] History
might suggest that Adam's enthusiasm is naive, and in fact
Adam himself almost immediately expresses misgiving: "But
say . . . what will betide the few / His faithful? . . . will they
not deal / Wors with his followers then with him they dealt"
(12.479–84). "Be sure they will," says Michael, though God's
people will enjoy "from Heav'n . . . a Comforter" (12.479–86).

The poem itself offers further qualification of Adam's
reaction. In the fifth of his responses, Adam foresees the Second
Coming and declares:

Greatly instructed I shall hence depart,
Greatly in peace of thought, and have my fill
Of knowledge, what this Vessel can contain;
Beyond which was my folly to aspire.
Henceforth I learn, that to obey is best,
And love with fear the onely God, to walk
As in his presence, ever to observe
His providence, and on him sole depend.

(12.557–64)

Adam says he has learned his lesson, and the lesson is hearten-
ing. It is suffused with resolution, hope, as well as recognition

and acknowledgment of godhead. The claim is implicitly but
nonetheless eloquently grateful. Michael commends Adam
with the forthright statement, "This having learnt, thou hast
attaind the sum / Of wisdom" (12.575–76). Still there is history,
and history shows that the lesson is hard to put into practice.
Even after commending his attainment of the sum of wisdom,
Michael provides a condition that Adam must do more:

> *onely* add
> Deeds to thy knowledge answerable, add Faith, .
> Add Vertue, Patience, Temperance, add Love,
> By name to come call'd Charitie, the soul
> Of all the rest: then wilt thou not be loath
> To leave this Paradise, but shalt possess
> A Paradise within thee, happier farr.
>
> (12.581–87; my emphasis)

Michael summarizes a comprehensive Christian ideal, uniting
the performance of works with the realization of the Pauline
theological virtues of faith, hope and charity. But the context
of the entire poem qualifies and even subverts the expression
of that ideal as a normative statement. God had made Adam
originally just and right and provided him with instruction.
He was sufficient to have stood but nevertheless fell. Now
Adam faces a far greater challenge: realizing the Christian ideal
in a fallen world. The word "only" in the above passages
deepens the irony: Adam *only* has to realize the complete
Christian ideal, he *only* has to emulate the Messiah. Michael's
conditional endorsement of Adam's acquired wisdom thus
casts Adam's enthusiasm, joy — and certainly his gratitude —
in a highly ironic light.[17]

   The poem seems to ask: Is this situation, this condition of
humanity something to be grateful for? Rather than a definitive
answer, the poem provides images, the most famous of which
bears on the question:

> They looking back, all th'Eastern side beheld
> Of Paradise, so late thir happie seat,

Wav'd over by that flaming Brand, the Gate
With dreadful Faces throng'd and fierie Armes;
Som natural tears they drop'd, but wip'd them soon;
The World was all before them, where to choose
Thir place of rest, and Providence thir guide:
They hand in hand with wandring steps and slow,
Through *Eden* took thir solitarie way.

(12.641–49)

The image distills the ambiguities, ironies and clashing perspectives that pervade Milton's rendition of the biblical narrative. There are apocalyptic suggestions from the "waving Brand," the "dreadful Faces" and the "fierie Armes"; poignant suggestions of nostalgia from the "natural tears"; but also hopeful suggestions from their wiping of the tears and stepping out into the world and history with Providence their guide. Unlike Satan, who is always falling and always choosing to do so, Adam and Eve are fallen but may choose to rise — in gratitude of course.[18] Gratitude may well be the most difficult of the virtues — as Milton would certainly say, *only* add a grateful spirit. The gratitude that was once natural and spontaneous must now be actively willed and for the most part arduously achieved. That certainly is a loss to be regretted, like the loss of innocence. It is also occasion for rejoicing, celebrating and gratitude, that much more good thereof may spring.

6 • Paradise Enclosed and the *Feme Covert*

Lynne A. Greenberg

> We shall see how the stalking pageant goes
> With borrow'd legs, a heavy load to those
> That made and bear him: not, as we once thought,
> The seed of gods, but a weak model wrought
> By greedy men, that seek to enclose the common,
> And within private arms impale free woman.
>
> — Thomas Carew, "A Rapture"

Thomas Carew's "A Rapture" inextricably weds property and women, private ownership and control, suggesting that men who enclosed land necessarily and naturally enclosed women as well. The poem voices a common paradigm of the seventeenth century, as debates about property rights often associated images of dominion and power in the land with dominion and power over women.[1] A range of discourses, poetic, political and religious in nature, envisioned men's relationships with their wives as comparable to men's interests in property. As one proponent of enclosure queried: "Doth not every man covet to have his own alone? Would any man admit of a partaker in his house, his horse, his oxe, or his wife, if he could shun it?"[2] Hotly contested during the period, the enclosure movement pitted local customs, equitable practices and commonly held rights against national rules of law and individual proprietorship. The institution of marriage enclosed women within the common law system of coverture; the ramifications of which parallel that of enclosure, literally and figuratively fixing walls or restrictive boundaries around permissible gender roles and additionally limiting women's ownership of property. Thus, one of the "grounds of contention" of the period included England's actual grounds and the extent of individuals' rights in and to these grounds. The debates over law, land and women would ultimately culminate by the end of the seventeenth century in changes to the division and definition of property and to women's rights in this property. The metaphor of enclosure, thus, framed and mapped paradigm shifts in parallel proprietary systems of unequal and exclusionary power. Milton's *Paradise Lost* in its extended discussions of enclosed spaces and marital relations participates in seventeenth century struggles over both property and gender.

This analysis is indebted to Joseph Wittreich's discussions of the multiple, often conflicting, discourses of gender politics "mapped by" the poem and seeks to respond to his call for a "revaluation of *Paradise Lost* in its historical moment."[3] Historicizing Milton's poem has led to progressively more nuanced readings of the poem's gender politics, as scholars have cautioned that one should consider *Paradise Lost* in relation to early modern, rather than contemporary, interpretations of Genesis and conceptions of marital and gender relations.[4] These historical readings have not focused, however, on the legal constructions underpinning these relations that, arguably, framed societal conceptions. As legal scholars have long argued, law operates as ideology, producing and reproducing dominant social constructs.[5] Its definitions define, perpetuate and enforce a range of social customs, beliefs, moral values and cultural expectations of a given community and period. Generally understood as representing the dominant hegemony, these legal definitions thus operate in themselves as enclosing devices, structuring and delimiting a particular dominant hegemonic construct at the expense of others.[6]

By foregrounding the legal constructions enclosed within *Paradise Lost*, this essay insists that juridical and legal discourse is critical to an understanding of the historical context of the poem, and further, that the poem's confrontation with and depiction of these conflicting legal discourses possibly gesture to a conclusion suggested by Wittreich that "*Paradise Lost*, instead of codifying, conflicts with patriarchy."[7] The poem explores the changing visions of property and married women's rights in a vision of a prelapsarian Eden that embodies seventeenth century legal reforms and, remarkably, anticipates the consequences of this new system. Exploring the legal consequences of Milton's depiction of Paradise and of paradisal marriage ultimately uncovers the poem's embedded critiques of the enclosed fields of England and of the married woman's enclosure by her husband, as both became relegated to private spheres of ownership and control.

1

> But suppose you will say, you . . . become one body, and so do use your Common as an inseparable spouse, to be your helper: why are you then so cuckolded by Foreigners and strangers . . . indeed (while you make it a common prostitute to every lust) how can you help it? . . . were it not better therefore and more secure to take her home to your chamber, and keep her with a guard . . . which you may do by distinguishing each ones part property to himself?
>
> — Adam Moore, *Bread for the Poor*

One of the most important geographical and proprietary changes to the Early Modern English countryside was the enclosure of the wastelands and common fields. Topographically, enclosure transformed the land into a patchwork of geometrically precise plots, clearly separated from each other by hedges and fences. Control of the wastelands was transferred by voluntary agreement in the seventeenth century from villagers, who once held communal rights in the land, to a small percentage of landowners, who were to privately and exclusively own the property. As part of the larger agricultural revolution that took place over several centuries and did not culminate until the nineteenth century, the enclosure movement participated in the rise of a developing market economy that eroded the established moral economy structured around manorial estates intended for production and sustenance.[8] By the end of the seventeenth century, "[i]ndividual property rights based on written title replaced ancient custom. . . . A conception of land as a commodity to be exploited for profit, protected by absolute rights of ownership, had triumphed over an older one under which ancient custom had guaranteed rights of access and use by the community."[9] The bounded fields emblematized the end of feudal notions of land ownership and the beginning of a new era, one in which we still live, that privileges the private rights of individuals over the collective rights of communities.

Upon the execution of King Charles I, parliamentary agrarian reforms and legislation were sweeping and included not only enclosures, but also the drainage of fens, sequestrations, confiscations, compositions, forced sales of estates and fine and tax increases.[10] Political debates raged throughout this period over the propriety of agrarian legislation and who should acquire rights in crown, church, royalists' and common lands subjected to such legislation.

Milton participates only tangentially in these debates, although he clearly supported reforms that protected the private ownership of property.[11] His arguments against tithes, for example, stress the injustice of "seis[ing] out of mens grounds, out of mens houses thir other goods."[12] He also critiqued James Harrington's economic reform, as articulated in *Oceana*, that called for limitations on the value of individual estates. Milton argued that his own plan "requires no perilous, no injurious alteration or circumscription of mens lands and proprieties" (7.445). He shared with proponents of agrarian reform an interest in improving wastelands. In *Of Education*, addressed to his friend Samuel Hartlib, a supporter of enclosure, Milton emphasized that reading the classical authors of agriculture would "be an occasion of inciting and inabling men hereafter to improve the tillage of their Country, to recover the bad Soil, and to remedy the waste that is made of good" (2.389). He rarely suggested specific economic or agricultural improvements in his prose tracts, but in *Proposalls of Certaine Expedients for the Preventing of a Civill War Now Feard, & the Settling of a firme Government*, he specifically advised that should the government provide for "the just division of wast Commons . . . the nation would become much more industrious, rich and populous" (7.338).

Political arguments over agrarian reform commonly resorted to Scripture and "deeply rooted religious rationale[s]" to justify their positions.[13] For example, certain radical sects, such as the Diggers, blamed the Fall for a system of private property ownership and envisioned the earth as a "common Treasury."[14] Thomas Rainsborough, in contrast, assured Henry Ireton during the Putney debates that the Levellers did not seek to destroy the system of private property, as it was firmly rooted in the biblical commandment, "Thou shalt not steal."[15] Royalists and anti-enclosure tracts bewailed the loss of "Eden," as the countryside, parceled out to the few, led to the depopulation of villages, emigration, homelessness, day labor and poverty.[16] Improvers seeking to encourage enclosure (referred to in one such tract as "commonwealths-m[e]n") made the connection between Paradise and England explicit, arguing that: "It was once Adam's happiness . . . to dress the Garden, and . . . it was his great unhappiness to be thrust out into the large field of the World. . . . What's the matter with us in England, that we labor not to remove the curse, and reduce those large briary and thorny Commons . . . if not into a Paradise, yet into pleasant Gardens, goodly fields of Corn, feeding pastures for all sorts of Cattel."[17]

The prevalence of the Genesis story to enclosure debates invites a consideration of whether Milton's *Paradise Lost*, the definitive reading of the Genesis story in the period, participates in these debates, and, if so, how the poem constructs the ideal proprietary order. Strikingly, the topographical descriptions of Paradise bear a marked resemblance to the newly bounded pastures of England. The poem repeatedly stresses the "hallowd limits" and "narrow room" of the garden, "all bound / Of Hill or highest Wall."[18] In three separate instances, the poem specifically refers to Paradise as enclosed.[19] Adam describes the prospect of the garden as: "A woodie Mountain; whose high top was plain, / A Circuit wide, *enclos'd*, with goodliest Trees" (8.303–4). He also depicts the property as comprised of both a cultivated garden, complete with "flowrie Arbors" (4.626), "Planted, with Walks, and Bowers" (8.305), and a "field" (5.292), rather than a waste area of uncertain usages. Satan too refers to the garden as an "enclosure wild" (9.543). The enclosures themselves are legion. Satan

>   to the border comes
> Of *Eden*, where delicious Paradise,
> Now nearer, Crowns with her *enclosure* green,
> As with a rural mound the champain head
> Of a steep wilderness, whose hairie sides
> With thicket overgrown, grottesque and wild,
> Access deni'd; . . .
>
>   . . . .

> Yet higher then [the trees'] tops
> The verdurous wall of Paradise up sprung: . . .
>
> . . . .
>
> And higher then that Wall a circling row
> Of goodliest Trees.
> > (4.131–37, 142–43, 146–47; emphasis added)

The poem then frames Paradise not with a simple divider but with layer upon layer of thicket, hill, wall and tree, all designed to create inaccessible borders.

The poem contrasts Paradise with all that rests beyond its idyllic bounds. Immediately outside Paradise stretches Eden, a "rural seat of various view" (247), comprised of "open field" (245) and "Bowrs" (246), "wood" (538), "Hill and Dale and Plain" (243). Importantly, Eden, unlike Paradise, includes "waste" (538) lands, a subtle example of the poem's implicit favoring of enclosed spaces of certain usage. The most important alternative proprietary order compared to the privately enjoyed and enclosed Paradise is the publicly accessible hell, a landscape described as "waste and wild" (1.60). Satan maintains that all should hold nonexclusive interests in hell: God "gave it me, / Which I as freely give" (4.380–81). Rather than seeking to exclude individuals from hell, Satan seeks to provide common and unlimited rights of access: "Hell shall unfold, / . . . her widest Gates, / . . . there will be room, / Not like these narrow limits, to receive / Your numerous ofspring" (4.381–85). Satan does not confine this vision to hell, as he also seeks to obtain free admittance to the earth, "either with Hell fire / To *waste* his whole Creation, or possess / All as our own" (2.364–66; emphasis added). He reiterates this goal of "Wasting the Earth" (2.502), drawing once again upon an agrarian term in dispute within the period. The poem describes his sins themselves as "transgressions" (4.879), that is, etymologically, the crossing of boundaries, or the failure to remain "bound" (4.897) by the will of God. As God describes, "our adversarie, whom no bounds / Prescrib'd, no barrs of Hell, nor all the chains / Heapt on him there, nor yet the main Abyss/Wide interrupt can hold" (3.81–84).

By juxtaposing satanic boundlessness to divine boundedness, the poem unequivocally privileges the enclosed. Notably, feminist legal scholars have characterized the system of enclosed and privately owned property as "founded primarily on the right to control and exclude; and 'right' itself — the right way of doing things."[20] Raphael's description of God's creation encapsulates both of these uses of the word "right," envisioning the universe as limited spaces of certain ownership and of their intrinsically just nature: "He took the golden Compasses . . . / to circumscribe / This Universe, and all created things: / . . . And [God] said, thus farr extend, thus farr thy bounds, / This be thy just Circumference, O World" (7.225–27, 230–31). The careful attention to demarcating the rightful perimeters of the world has a contemporary analogue in seventeenth century surveying manuals that increasingly stressed the landowners' need to know the proper limits of their property rights.[21] According to Bottomley, "Spatial techniques, new forms of mapping and measurement, are fundamental to the development of modern law, making possible and necessary the rule of law in the construction of ownership."[22] God's "golden Compasses" prefigure those innovative surveyors' tools used in the seventeenth century to measure property systematically and to clarify boundaries. Milton also relied on this figure in *The Reason of Church-Government* to stress the right nature of bounded property: "The state also of the blessed in Paradise, though never so perfect, is not therefore left without discipline, whose golden survaying reed marks out and measures every quarter and circuit of new Jerusalem" (1:752). Interestingly, these passages also echo Sir Edward Coke's often-quoted argument that individual rights and obligations, like property itself, should "be measured by the golden and straight metawand of law, and not the incertain cord of discretion."[23] The new surveyor's measure, more precise at parceling out individual units of property, serves as an apt metaphor, then, for the increasingly systemized common law that stressed private ownership of property.

The poem describes Adam and Eve's bower as the most enclosed of the bounded spaces within Paradise:

> it was a place
> Chos'n by the sovran Planter, when he fram'd
> All things to mans delightful use; the roof
> Of thickest covert was inwoven shade
> Laurel and Mirtle, and what higher grew
>
>   . . . .
>
> Fenc'd up the verdant wall.
>
>   (4.690–94, 697)

Here, the poem subtly alludes to the gendered nature of place, as the term "covert" suggests the system of coverture of which men made "delightful use" in the early modern period (as described more fully in section 3 below). In the physical description of the bower, the reader surveys the walling off of the private from the public sphere at its genetic moment. The historical birth of the separation, or sequestration, of the private from the public sphere has been dated to the early seventeenth century. As former Master of the Rolls Lord Evershed explained: "It was in the year 1604, not far removed from the date that Shakespeare wrote the lines from *The Taming of the Shrew* ["I will be master of what is mine own: / She is my goods, my chattels; she is my house, / My household stuff, my field, my barn, / My horse, my ox, my ass, my any thing"] . . . that, according to [Sir Edward] Coke's report of the judgement in Semayne's Case, it was judicially laid down that the house of everyone is to him as his castle and fortress."[24] As feminist legal theorists have argued, this construction of private space serves not only to wall in its inhabitants, but also to wall off any scrutiny, regulation or legal protection of its inhabitants from the outside world.[25]

Paradise Lost dramatizes this process, as

> other Creature here
> Beast, Bird, Insect, or Worm durst enter none;
> Such was thir awe of Man. In shadier Bower
> More sacred and sequesterd, though but feign'd,
> *Pan* or *Sylvanus* never slept.
>
> (4.703–7)

So, too, the "steep wilderness, whose hairie sides / With thicket overgrown . . . / Access denied" (4.135–36) conceals and sequesters Paradise. By blocking views into the bower and into Paradise itself from the other vantage points of Eden, the "natural" boundaries serve to isolate the inhabitants in a zone not only of protection, but also of nonregulation, save the divine.[26] God's panoptical, all-seeing vantage point situated at the center "in his Meridian Towr" (4.30) permits the only full perspective of Paradise.[27]

Enclosure, as argued previously, is constructed on a notion of exclusion, on the right to control absolutely what resides within its borders and the converse right to "exclude" (4.584) those deemed not to have a right to enter. The poem does not describe these rights as coming naturally. Rather, the "secure" (791) and "inviolable" (843) Paradise requires vigilant defense. Satan attributes his eventual success to the garden's vulnerability — "ill secur'd" (370), because "Ill fenc't for Heav'n to keep out such a foe" (372). The poem emphasizes the militaristic nature of the defense of the garden's boundaries, depicting the angels, at "strictest watch" (783), standing "armd / To thir night watches in warlike Parade" (779–80). When faced with Satan's entry into the garden, the angels use fear (or "awe" [705]), intimidation and "threats" (968) of physical violence to accomplish their charge. Ithuriel first acts violently, "with his Spear / Touch'd lightly" (810–11) Satan, while the "guards" stand close "in squadron joind / Awaiting next command" (862, 863–64). When Gabriel, described by Satan as a "limitarie cherub" (971) speaks, he employs the rhetoric of enclosure, censoring Satan for having "broke the bounds prescrib'd / To thy transgressions" (878–79). The angels further emblematize the workings of enclosure, as they finally "began to hemm him round / With ported Spears" (979–80). This confrontation culminates, as Richard J. DuRocher has noted, in an extended simile comparing the angels' formation to a "field" (980), thereby directly alluding to the processes of enclosure.[28]

The militaristic language used to describe the guarding of Paradise suggests that a discourse of imperialism lies submerged within the politics of this enclosure.[29] As W. J. T. Mitchell has argued in a discussion of the semiotic features of landscape painting, the "Enclosure movement . . . [is] an internal colonization of the home country, its transformation from what Blake called 'a green & pleasant land' into a landscape." To Gillian Rose, landscape constitutes a "visual ideology," encompassing understood hegemonic cultural codes that are themselves embedded in social power structures. The poem describes Paradise as a "Lantskip" twice (4.153, 5.142), thus, arguably, participating with landscape painting, a genre that interestingly emerged in the seventeenth century, in the conveyance and enforcement of colonizing values and power structures.[30] The poem, as this discussion has maintained, depicts as originary, and therefore idyllic, a landscape enclosed within clearly demarcated boundaries. Yet, "[t]he boundary metaphor permits us to indulge in focusing on the experiences we can have in, on, and with our property . . . and ignore the patterns of relationship shaped by the power to exclude," ones that ultimately require "power and domination."[31] Because Milton's poem depicts this bounded, and therefore idyllic, landscape as necessitating dominating and violent tactics to ensure its boundaries, the poem not only incorporates a changed vision of property distribution within its boundaries but also dramatizes the underlying power effects of this vision.

2

Concurrent changes in the legal definition of landed property in the seventeenth century made possible the changing economic division of property ownership, signified by the increasingly enclosed commons. This legal meaning began to construct property as a "public" rather than a "private resource," consistent with the socioeconomic changes from a feudal to a market economy.[32] The 1624 edition of John Rastell's treatise of legal terms, *Les termes de la ley*, first announced a definition of property that comprehended the notion of absolute, not merely possessory, rights in land. Rastell defined property as "the highest right that a man hath or can have to any thing, which in no way dependeth upon another mans courtesie" and divided property rights into three categories — "absolute," "qualified" and "possessory."[33] Nevertheless, this definition remained restricted to rights, that is, uses or interests in and not ownership of land, consistent with the feudal understanding that "none in our kingdom can be said to have in any lands, or tenements, but only the king in the right of his Crowne. Because all the lands through the realme, are in the nature of fee, and doe hould either mediately or immediately of the Crowne."[34] The Long Parliament's 1646 ordinance abolished wardship and other royal feudal tenures, thereby dismantling this restriction on private ownership of property.

Thereafter, legal commentators began to give accounts of the standard incidents, that is, the rights and entitlements, of ownership. They interpreted "the highest right" in property as including the unqualified and exclusive privilege to possess; enjoy; use and derive all income from the property; manage the property, including the power to decide who has license to use the property; and dispose or alienate the property. These commentators also understood such interests as "gained by Industry," rather than simply by feudal privilege.[35] The confirmation of the abolition of wardship and feudal tenures at the Restoration in 1660 further confirmed a vision of property as individually owned and controlled. Interestingly, by the early eighteenth century Lockean political defenses of private property began to appear in legal terminology, concluding that "Every man . . . hath a Property and Right which the Law allows him to defend his Life, Liberty, and Estate; and if it be violated, it gives an Action to redress the Injury, and punish the Wrong-doer."[36] The language of absolute and private property ownership thus constituted a sweeping paradigm shift, both encoding and delimiting a perceptual change in the social customs and values of seventeenth century England.

By interrogating the particular construct of property articulated in *Paradise Lost*, one can glimpse how the poem itself encloses the concurrent paradigm shift within its boundaries. The seventeenth century emerging notion of private property ownership operates as the relevant model for evaluating Adam's relationship to the land. The land until Adam's creation corresponded to pure common ground, as no creature in the community was forbidden to trod there. Upon God's transfer of the land, Adam became its absolute owner. The poem's grant of property rights, it should be emphasized, goes far beyond that of the biblical account that gave man the right to "subdue" and "rule . . . ouer all the earth, and ouer euerie thing that crepeth & moueth on the earth" (Gen. 1.28, 26).[37] In Milton's poem, God grants the property to Adam in language that directly implicates the seventeenth century legal definition of proprietary ownership. As Adam relates, God stated:

> This Paradise I give thee, count it thine
> To Till and keep . . .
>
> · · · · · · · ·
>
> Not onely these fair bounds, but all the Earth
> To thee and to thy Race I give; as Lords
> Possess it, and all things that therein live.
>
> (8.319–20, 338–40)

Likewise, Michael clarifies Adam's proprietary rights after the Fall as:

> All th' Earth he gave thee to possess and rule
> No despicable gift; surmise not then
> His presence to these narrow bounds confin'd
> Of Paradise or *Eden*;
>
> . . . .
>
> God is as here, and will be found alike
> Present, and of his presence many a signe
> Still following thee, still compassing thee round.
>
> (11.339–42, 350–52)[38]

Adam also has "power and rule" (4.429) and "Dominion" (430) over Eden, "Free leave so large to all things" (434). His rights in Paradise are even characterized as "absolute" (301), consistent with the seventeenth century notion of ownership of, rather than merely qualified or possessory rights in, the property.

The land transfer also rests on a reciprocal duty on Adam's part; that is, God gave Adam ownership of Paradise in exchange for Adam's promise to tend it and his ancillary promise not to trespass on that part of the property, the Tree of Knowledge, still retained exclusively by God. Adam obtains exclusive proprietary rights in these previously common grazing lands, then, through voluntary, contractual means, requiring reciprocal duties from both parties consistent with the legal understanding that one should gain ownership of property "by Industry," rather than privilege alone. The contractual nature of this transfer corresponds historically to the voluntary nature of enclosure in the seventeenth century, as only in the eighteenth century did enclosure occur through involuntary acts of Parliament.[39] One can understand Adam's and Eve's exile from the Garden after the Fall, then, not simply as divine punishment but also as God's revocation of the property agreement and confiscation of the property in light of Adam and Eve's failure to keep the terms of their agreement. Thus, upon the Fall, "The Princely Hierarch / In thir bright stand,

there left his Powers to seise / Possession of the Garden"
(11.220–22). Michael's words further support this reading by
advising Adam that, though he has lost his ownership of the
garden, he still retains ownership of the rest of the world
(11.339–42).

Adam also gains those incidental rights in the land consistent with ownership, including control over its use. Adam can
exclude others from the land and restrict others' admittance
to the land. In effect, one can read the separation scene in
book 9 as an extended negotiation for and achievement of a
license, as Adam grants Eve access rights to certain parts of
his territory. She frames her offer to work separately in rhetoric consistent with the legalistic language of a license agreement. She requests to gain admittance to a specific area of the
property for only a limited duration of time, while simultaneously acknowledging that he has fuller access rights to all
of the Garden:

> Let us divide our labours, thou where choice
> Leads thee, or where most needs, whether to wind
> The Woodbine round this Arbour, or direct
> The clasping Ivie where to climb, while I
> In yonder Spring of Roses intermixt
> With Myrtle, find what to redress till Noon.
>
> (9.214–19)

Eve disputes Adam's initial reluctance to grant her such
license in proprietary terms: "If this be our condition, thus to
dwell / In narrow circuit . . . / How are we happie" (322–23,
326). She characterizes Adam's eventual acceptance of this
license as his having granted her "permission" (378), again
relying on the legal language of property licensing.

The poem, in contrast, describes Satan's entry into the Garden as "Unlicenc't" (4.909), likening it to an "assault" (4.190)
by a "Thief" (4.188). So, too, the poem describes Eve's taking
of the fruit from the Tree of Knowledge as a "fatal Trespass"
(9.888), as does Satan (9.693) and God (3.122). These legal

terms — "unlicensed entry" and "trespass" — were intimately tied to changing notions of property ownership in the late seventeenth century. The courts no longer considered the admittance onto common fields as the customary right of a villager, but rather associated it with an illegal intrusion onto private property. By the end of the seventeenth century, causes of actions and prosecutions for trespass, not surprisingly, multiplied at an unprecedented rate, in keeping with the heightened emphasis on private ownership in the period. These prosecutions could also prove "fatal," indeed, as the judicial system deemed trespass a capital punishment. Legal historians have characterized the paradigm shift from a feudal to a market economy as accompanied by a parallel shift in perceptions of the main purpose and goal of criminal law. By the early eighteenth century, the justice system no longer concerned itself primarily with regulating order and preserving religious conformity but became concerned mainly with the defense of property.[40] The Black Act of 1723, which created approximately 250 categories of property-related crimes, represents the apotheosis of this paradigm shift. Milton's poem, in its characterization of Satan's and Eve's crimes, then, anticipates and participates in the shift to a view of government, in John Locke's words, as having "no other end but the preservation of property."[41]

Consistent with nascent agricultural improvement ideas and changing views of husbandry, Adam also has the obligation — the "easie charge" (4.421) and "delightful task" (4.437) — not merely the right, to improve his property. As he directs Eve: "With first approach of light, we must be ris'n, / And at our pleasant labour, to reform / Yon flowrie Arbors" (4.624–26). His discussions with Eve repeatedly center on such reform, enrichment and improvement of the property's natural resources. Anthony Low, in his study of the Georgic influences of the poem, discusses the extent to which the depiction of Adam's improvements and work also corresponds to the period's changing models of agrarian reform and husbandry.[42] The term "husbandry" is an important one in the context of this essay, suggesting once again that men's marital and proprietary relations were somehow comparable. The following discussion will interrogate to what extent *Paradise Lost* concurs with this analogy.

3

A garden inclosed is my sister, my spouse: a spring shut up, a fountaine sealed.

— The Song of Solomon 4:12

Milton's poem juxtaposes the private and exclusive relations between humans to the communal and unbounded relations between animals: "Hail wedded Love, mysterious Law, true sourse / Of human ofspring, sole proprietie / In Paradise of all things common else" (4.750–52). By linking marriage, law and property, the poem encodes a vision of marriage as a legalistic and proprietary relation over which mankind has absolute rights of ownership. This frame, then, invites an analysis of how the laws of marital relations interpolate the laws of property within *Paradise Lost*.

The moment a marriage became legally binding during the early modern period, the woman found herself radically transformed by the common law doctrine known as "coverture," a legal fiction whose source and justification derived in part from the scriptural understanding of a man and wife as *una caro*.[43] As explained by the nineteenth century legal historian W. S. Holdsworth, the married woman's legal position with respect to her husband, "[u]p to comparatively recent times, and especially during the Middle Ages, [was] coloured by the canonist's conception of marriage as a sacrament which makes the husband and wife one flesh, and gives the husband dominion over the wife."[44] While canonists debated the extent of men's domination over women,[45] legal commentators appropriated this "divine" inequality with unqualified ease to set the perimeters of the legal relationship between husbands and wives: "God has divided reasonable creatures into two sexes. . . . The male is superior, the female inferior."[46] Therefore, the wife, "by the Law of GOD and of the Land, is put under the Power of the Husband, and is bound to live in Subjection to him."[47] Thus, particularly Pauline canonical interpretations often justified early modern legal constructions important to women's place in society.

The eighteenth century legal commentator William Blackstone, in his famous explication of coverture, delineated its practical effects as follows: "By marriage, the husband and wife are one person in law: that is, the very being or legal existence of the woman is suspended during the marriage, or at least is incorporated and consolidated into that of the husband: under whose wing, protection and *cover* she performs everything and is therefore called in our law French a feme covert, or under the protection and influence of her husband, her *baron*, or lord."[48] As one legal commentator described the particular power relations underlying the descriptions "baron" and "feme": "A woman as soone as she is married is vailed, as it were, clouded and over-shadowed . . . her new selfe is her superior, her companion, her master."[49]

The consolidation of the woman's legal identity into that of her husband led to her placement in the same legal category under the common law as wards, lunatics, criminals and idiots. Legal historians are in some disagreement as to whether this legal classification and the consequences of coverture technically constructed *femes covert* as chattels, that is, property.[50] One informal customary practice used from the early modern period to the late nineteenth century does indicate that in some circumstances women were treated literally as property. Known as a "wife sale," the husband could formally sell his wife for money through a cattle dealer to another man, publicly ending the first marriage and thereby circumventing the law's refusal to recognize divorce.[51] As described in an eighteenth century legal treatise: "if the man had a mind to authenticate the intended legal separation by making it a matter of public notoriety, thinking with Petruchio, that his wife is his goods and chattels, he puts a halter around her neck, and thereby leads her to the next market place, and there puts her up for auction as though she was a brood-mare or milch-cow." The earliest such "sale" actually took the form of a gift, for no pecuniary reward.[52]

Regardless of whether coverture led to the *feme covert*'s status as a mere chattel, it certainly led to the suspension of legal rights or "civil death" of the woman during her married state.[53] Practically, it led to the automatic relinquishment of nearly all of her private rights. The economic consequences of coverture, in particular, were grave. The *feme covert* could no longer own property in her own name, nor could she accept grants, even from her husband, or legacies. All of her real and personal property became subject to the control of her husband. Her "leasehold property" (land held for a fixed term of years) became the husband's property outright during the marriage, freely disposable by the husband during his lifetime. Any personal property owned by a woman at the time of her marriage also became her husband's property outright, as did any personal property given to a wife after her marriage. Legal commentators justified these property disablements by arguing that "[i]n the contemplation of our law, the wife is scarcely considered to have a separate existence. . . . It is for [this] same reason, namely the unity of the persons of husband and wife, that the property is placed under the controul and management of one of them; and the law has selected the husband as being more worthy of this trust. 'The husband is the head of the wife, and therefore all that she hath belongs to him.' "[54]

Paradise Lost encloses the marital relation within the framework of the unity of person, as Adam recalls having uttered to Eve upon her creation: "And they shall be one flesh, one Heart, one Soul" (8.499).[55] Here, Milton undoubtedly reproduced the language of Genesis ("Therefore shal man . . . cleaue to his wife, and they shalbe one flesh" [Gen. 2:24]); yet, it is the central argument of this essay that one should read the phrase "one flesh" as referring not only to its canonical interpretation, including as James Grantham Turner, among others, has so beautifully articulated, its often contradictory exegesis, but also to its legal interpretation, so critical to the very basis of the relationship between husband and wife from the thirteenth century through the early modern period.[56]

As other critics have analyzed, Adam understands Eve's status in proprietary terms. He describes her as "Heav'ns last best gift" (5.19) and the "fairest this / Of all thy gifts" (8.493–94).[57] This designation conforms to such seventeenth century customary practices as wife sale and, more tellingly, to the strictures of coverture (property cannot own property). The legal framework of coverture itself imbues the poem. First "covertly," in the narrator's description of Eve's "vail" (4.304) of hair "which impli'd / Subjection" (4.307–8), and more forcefully in Eve's description of women's legal status, one that, it should be noted, accurately reflects women's foreclosure from participation in the law during the seventeenth century: "God is thy Law, thou mine" (4.637). Adam's descriptions of their marital relations likewise rely on the discourse of coverture, seeming to replicate the language of legal commentators:

> leave not the faithful side
> That gave thee being, still shades thee and protects.
> The Wife, where danger or dishonour lurks,
> Safest and seemliest by her Husband staies,
> Who guards her.
>
> (9.265–69)

Yet, it is Milton's deviation from coverture's practical effects on married women that illustrates not Milton's patriarchal but rather his more egalitarian vision of gender relations. Milton both records the legal inequities of the system of coverture and a critique of this system.

The poem constructs Eve's equal access to proprietary rights in the land ambiguously. In Adam's rendition of his creation, God's grant of the property occurs prior to Eve's creation. Her absence thereby problematizes whether one can understand her as a party to, or the beneficiary of, this land transfer. Nor does she provide an alternative account of her creation that would mediate the seemingly exclusive and private nature of the grant to Adam. She instead confirms that Adam alone is "all Earths Lord" (9.273). Adam does indicate that Eve shares in the possession of the property: "Two onely, who yet by sov'ran gift possess / This spacious ground" (5.366–67). As legal commentators made clear in the period, however, possessory rights in property did not constitute absolute ownership of the property. Adam also states in a discussion with Eve:

> God hath pronounc't it death to taste that Tree,
> The only sign of our obedience left
> Among so many signes of power and rule
> Conferrd upon us, and Dominion giv'n
> Over all other Creatures that possess
> Earth, Air, and Sea.
>
> (4.427–32)

Yet, here, while emphasizing that he and Eve share in dominion over the animals, he does not directly address the issue of their ownership rights in the property.

Raphael's account of the property transfer from God to Adam does not lead to a more definitive understanding of Eve's participation, either. As Raphael states, God spoke to his son:

> Let us make now Man in our image, Man
> In our similitude, and let them rule
> Over the fish and Fowl of Sea and Air,
> Beast of the field, and over all the Earth,
> And every creeping thing that creeps the ground.
>
> (7.519–23)

This language faithfully recites Genesis (1.260). The term "Man," as critics have emphasized, is used to refer to a plural "them" (7.520) and functions as gender neutral both in this passage and in Genesis, thereby incorporating "woman" within its meaning.[58] Yet rule over the animals of the earth, once again, does not necessarily imply ownership of the property itself. Nevertheless, other passages in the poem also refer to Adam and Eve in the plural as "lords" (8.339), "lords of the world" (1.32) and "lords of all" (4.290, 9.658). This repeated use of the plural is particularly significant, seeming to disagree with Eve's characterization of Adam as "all Earths Lord" (9.273). Ultimately, however, the poem never explicitly states that God has granted Eve ownership rights in the property equal to those of Adam.

Nevertheless, her position does not correspond to that of the *feme covert* or married women in English seventeenth century law, foreclosed by the doctrine of coverture from holding any rights in property at all during her marriage. Indeed, the poem depicts one parcel of the property, the "Nurserie" (8.46) as unequivocally owned exclusively by Eve. She "Rose, and went forth among *her* Fruits and flowrs, / To visit how they prosper'd, bud and bloom, / *Her* Nurserie" (8.44–46; emphasis added). This characterization explicitly characterizes her private and exclusive ownership rights in the property. The poem also depicts Eve as primarily responsible for tending the flowers of Eden. She is variously described as nurturing, pruning, watering, supporting and improving the flowers, providing further indicia of her incidental rights in the property consistent with the seventeenth century definition of legal ownership.[59] The "Nurserie," then, represents a sphere that the poem has carefully carved out as Eve's individual and absolute property.

This instance of the poem's mitigation of the harsh consequences of coverture in fact transcends even the most liberalizing legal development of the late seventeenth century. Enforced only in the equity courts and not recognized by the common law of England, trusts for the sole and separate estate of *femes covert* became a method for women to retain some access to capital in their property that would otherwise, under coverture, have fallen into their husbands' control. Throughout the latter half of the seventeenth century, individuals utilized these increasingly complex agreements to protect the individual property rights of *femes covert* during their marriages. The *femes covert*, as mere beneficiaries of such trusts, however, did not have direct control over or ownership rights in the property, as these rights legally resided with the trustees. Eve, then, has a degree of ownership in property that a seventeenth century *feme covert* would have found unattainable even using the most sophisticated trust arrangements. Milton's poem, by envisioning such female control over property, erodes the restrictive covering of coverture and offers a radically novel vision of property ownership.

Eve also names the flowers: "O flowrs / . . . which I bred up with tender hand / From the first op'ning bud, and gave ye Names" (11.273–77). One can interpret Eve's naming of the flowers, generally used by critics as indicating her innate reason and Milton's elevation of her status, as further evidencing her proprietary rights in the "Nurserie."[60] Parallel to the privilege granted to engrafters to name their hybrids, Eve's ownership of the flowers entitles her to name them. Eve's naming of the flowers also comprises an important concept critical to feminist legal theory. As described by Ann C. Scales, through the process of "Naming," "we discover what we really think and express it, we give words and the world new meaning. . . . For us, 'Naming' is a political term. 'Naming' means rejecting the Adam myth that the world was made for males to discern; it means reclaiming our world and our own experiences."[61] Eve's naming, then, not only constitutes an explication of the vagueness of Genesis but also anticipates a contemporary critique of the originary myth's link to patriarchy. Milton's poem grants Eve proprietary rights that, while not unequivocally equal to those of Adam, were absolute and individual to her. The poem thereby "rejects the Adam myth" as forcefully as it retells the myth, or, alternatively it incorporates an "Eve myth" alongside the "Adam myth."

4

To have been one
Of many ribs
And to be chosen.
To grow into something
Quite different
Knocking finally
As a bone knocks
On the closed gates of the garden —
Which unexpectedly
Open.

Linda Pastan's poem, "Aspects of Eve," beautifully evokes the transgressive power of *Paradise Lost*.[62] Milton's poem depicts the "closed gates" of enclosure and coverture, only to "open" them, by anticipating the effects and future critiques of these parallel systems of proprietary control. The poem records the metaphors, arguments and language of seventeenth century agrarian debates and gender politics, and "grow[s] into something / Quite different" in depicting the consequences of private property ownership and the figure of a married woman property holder, an individual who would not be historically conceived until the Married Women's Property Acts of 1870 and 1882 ended coverture. This essay has approached the issue of Milton's gender construction — not as scholars have traditionally done by examining the extent of Eve's subordination and the poem's articulation of patriarchal attitudes — but through a back gate, so to speak. Eve's actual proprietary rights in the Garden mitigate the language of female inferiority embedded in both the poem and the legal framework of coverture. Milton's poem tests the boundaries of this construct and, ultimately, "unexpectedly," breaks through them to give place and space, even if only covertly, to myths of both Adam and Eve.

7 • Choice and Election in *Samson Agonistes*

Susanne Woods

Joseph Wittreich, in the most comprehensive reading thus far of *Samson Agonistes*'s context and critics, presents us with a fallible and unregenerate Samson who defies efforts to turn him into Samson Triumphantes. In Wittreich's reading, Milton embraces contemporary commentary and "prophesyings" about the Samson legend which emphasize the difficulties and ambiguities of Samson's character.[1] Barbara Lewalski, in her recent critical biography of Milton, respects Wittreich's approach but sees Samson learning from his tragic situation and his encounters in the course of the drama, and understanding, at last, his tragic destiny. In Lewalski's reading, Samson has to learn to get it right, but he does in the end, and in the process "judges" and teaches the Chorus who represents the Hebrew people.[2] Both critics view *Samson* in relation to its publication with *Paradise Regained*, with Lewalski's Samson a public hero in contrast to the private Jesus of the preceding poem and Wittreich's Samson modeling interior struggle in contrast to Jesus' assured vision. For these learned and sophisticated readers, if Samson is a Christian hero he is not simply a regenerate messenger of God but a complex figure whose marriages may have owed as much to human lust as divine direction, and whose brutality and desire for revenge will not fall neatly into orthodox typology. He is a divinely gifted man who is influenced by a fallen nature and has made some terrible choices.

The Wittreich and Lewalski readings, I believe, show that Milton achieved exactly what he wanted: two members of his fittest audience choose their differing, individual readings with full attention to the poem's context. In the course of the dramatic poem, Samson's choices create the very calling for which he is presumed to be born; what he elects affirms his election. Samson, though blind and enslaved, is an example of freedom in a providential world. Similarly, Milton's readers, though limited by the linguistic and cultural contexts they confront, are invited to enact their own freedom in their interpretive choices, to find their own relationships to Milton's liberal God. In this essay I want to explore two related premises: that *Samson* is preeminently about choice, and that Milton invites readers to make choices as part of their own calling to understand and enact God's word.

Milton's preface, "Of that Sort of Dramatic Poem which is Call'd Tragedy," draws attention to his choice of genre even as it modifies generic expectations. The preface suggests that the reader's involvement is central to the purposes of Milton's poem, as he gives primary place to tragedy's ability to raise "pity and fear, or terror, to purge the mind of those and such like passions" (573). Unlike Aristotle, whom he purports to follow, Milton only secondarily centers his tragedy on plot, which he lumps with "style and uniformitie" to offer an example of authorial choice: "Plot, whether intricate or explicit, . . . is nothing indeed but such economy or disposition of the fable as may stand best with verisimilitude and decorum." Here, too, Milton's knowing reader is invited to participate, to decide on that verisimilitude and decorum, as "they only will best judge who are not unacquainted with *Aeschylus, Sophocles,* and *Euripides,* the three Tragic Poets unequall'd yet by any, and the best rule to all who endeavour to write Tragedy" (574).

Samson's entrance begins with choice and chance, which the drama will reveal as the interplay of reason and Providence. As Christopher Hill notes, *Samson's* opening echoes and extends the conclusion of *Paradise Lost,* where the delicate integration of a providential guide and a world all before them where to choose defines the human condition Adam and Eve confront at their exit from Paradise.[3] Samson, pertinent son of those first parents, needs the "guiding hand" to lead him to the bank where he may find "choice of sun or shade" (1, 3). The respite from his prison labor, where even the air is "imprison'd also," brings him "The breath of Heav'n fresh-blowing, pure and sweet," allowing him to "feel amends" though at first he is able to think only of his fall and blindness (8–10).

Samson's first speeches interrogate his choices and his fate: "why . . . what if . . . whom . . . what is?" (30–54). His blindness and imprisonment figure his internal confusion, so that initially he is unable to see beyond his own lack of understanding ("highest dispensation . . . / Happ'ly had ends above my reach to know" [61–62]) and lack of agency ("My self, my Sepulcher, a moving Grave" [102]). Samson is no intellectual; his choices come from his feelings, and they have apparently betrayed him. Yet even in his unpraiseworthy marriage choices, Samson was aware, as he will be again, of recognizing providential direction: "what I motion'd was of God; I knew / From intimate impulse" (222–23).

If the tragedy is about choice, it must begin with Samson's recovering his own sense of agency. This he does when he takes responsibility for what others see as his unhappy fate. When the Chorus presents God's reasons as inscrutable and Manoa presents them as unfair, Samson rejects their conclusions. He assents neither to the Chorus's "Down Reason, then, at least vain reasonings down" (322) nor to Manoa's "Alas methinks whom God hath chosen once / To worthiest deeds . . . / He should not so o'rewhelm" (368–70). In countering his father, Samson is able to declare responsibility for his ills: "Sole Author I, sole cause" (376).

From this point forward, Samson tests and corrects his partial understandings and misunderstandings. Both friends (Chorus, Manoa) and foes (Dalila, Harapha) provide the foils through whom he develops understanding and recovers his moral, as well as his physical, strength. The Danite chorus, Samson's eyes, feed him the outward shape of what approaches him, but miss the point repeatedly in interpreting it. So they describe Dalila's approach effectively (710–31) but misinterpret her new meaning to Samson. His encounter with Dalila re-forms the choices he made in marrying and trusting her, as he rejects her effort to bring him "home" to her spousal care ("It fits not; thou and I long since are twain" [929]), and is emphatic in his distance from her ("At distance I forgive thee, go with that" [954]). The chorus, dwelling on the dangers to which Samson once had fallen prey but that he has now chosen to step beyond, meditates unhelpfully on the power of female beauty and the necessity for male domination (1003–7, 1025–60).

His encounters with Manoa and Dalila lead Samson to recognize and accept his folly and failures. Harapha's cowardly boasting provokes Samson's physical courage and helps him see that his bad choices, his self-accusation, and his misery do not separate him entirely from his God:

> these evils I deserve and more,
> Acknowledge them from God inflicted on me
> Justly, yet despair not of his final pardon
> Whose ear is ever open; and his eye
> Gracious to re-admit the supplicant;
> In confidence whereof I once again
> Defie thee to the trial of mortal fight,
> By combat to decide whose god is God.

(1169–76)

Samson's renewed trust in God and in his God-given physical strength reveal Harapha to be a blustering coward, but Harapha's bluster has enabled Samson to revise his choice, from abject despair to a renewed sense of God's chosen champion.

Increasingly over the course of the poem, though without a clear line of progress, Samson is able to choose what Providence guides, until the choice to go with the Philistine officer to Dagon's feast fulfills, at last, his divine calling. The play begins with Samson's physical blindness as a metaphor for his lost freedom, which he takes initially as absolute powerlessness:

> the vilest here excel me,
> They creep, yet see; I dark in light expos'd
> To daily fraud, contempt, abuse, and wrong,
> Within doors, or without, still as a fool,
> In power of others, never in my own.
>
> (74–78)

It ends with Samson's confidence that "Commands are no constraints. If I obey them, / I do it freely" (1372–73), the position from which the "rouzing motions" invite him, and Samson is able to choose, to go along with the Philistine messenger (1382, 1384).

Whether or not another reader sees the progress of the play in just this way, I think it would be difficult not to see the issue of choice, along with related questions of reason, fate and agency, as recurrent and persistent. The play's concern with choice and with the recognition and exercise of free will is consistent with Milton's own lifelong interest in liberty, and his Protestant reading of the relation between free will and the Fall.[4] This is no news to Miltonists, although we may disagree on details. What remains fascinating and problematic about Samson's developing sense of his own choices, however, is the tentativeness and uncertainty with which it is achieved, the ambiguities that remain unresolved, and the complexities that refuse to simplify themselves into a clear understanding of God's calling or Samson's election as God's hero, however flawed. These complexities and uncertainties encourage readers to make choices that involve us in the process of the play. Milton's drama may be designed for reading rather than performance, but it is nonetheless drama, and his readers comprise an audience whom he seeks to engage actively in the play's evolution.

In *Samson Agonistes* Renaissance humanism and Reformation Protestantism mingle in a discourse as rich and uneasy as an experience of radical times. The drama not only tells a powerful tale, it invites the reader to live within each moment's ambiguities as that tale unfolds.[5] Ultimately, Milton involves the reader directly in Samson's evolving choices, and so invites and empowers the reader's own exercise of choice and of freedom. These techniques, part of what I have called "elective poetics," have a history in the developing self-awareness of the Renaissance humanist meritocracy, and reach their fullest and most explicit statement in Milton's work. They are particularly interesting in *Samson* because, through them, Samson rediscovers his vocation — that moment when election as Samson's choice of action and election as God's choice of Samson at last come together.

Among the literary techniques in *Samson* that tend to invite or provoke the reader to make choices (as well as to observe the process of Samson's choices) are disjunction ("Acknowledged not, or not at all consider'd / Deliverance offerd" [245–46]), interrogation ("Can this be hee, / That Heroic, that Renown'd, / Irresistible *Samson*?" [124–26]), qualification ("a living death, / And buried. . . . / Buried, yet not exempt / By privilege of death and burial / From worst of other evils" [100–1, 103–5]), the conditional ("had I sight, confus'd with shame, / How could I once look up" [196–97]), and litotes. This last, a sometimes self-deprecating understatement that presents a positive by means of a negative, is common in Milton's prose, including the preface to *Samson*, as if the author were backing away from rhetorical directive: "Nor is Nature wanting in her own effects to make good [Aristotle's] assertion"; "The Apostle *Paul* himself thought it not unworthy to insert a verse of *Euripides* into the Text of Holy Scripture" (573); and, with specific though indirect application to the author himself, "Heretofore Men in highest dignity have labour'd not a little to be thought able to compose a Tragedy" (573–74).

These techniques were to a large extent the common currency of the recent tradition Milton inherits, and I have argued elsewhere that they reflect a largely conscious effort to provoke reader choice on the one hand and avoid direct confrontation with entrenched power on the other.[6] Like Spenser's allegorizing in *The Faerie Queene* or Sidney's use of numerous stories to shade themes of love and power in the *Arcadia*, the meritocratic humanist uses devices of ambiguity and dislocation to teach and empower his fit audience though few, while evading the wrath of the unfit though powerful. If *Samson Agonistes* is (among other things) a commentary on the failure of the revolution and if the Philistines are to be associated with the Restoration royalists, for example, then those are inexplicit interpretive choices the reader may or may not choose to make.[7]

The Chorus is prone to disjunctions, often combined with rhetorical questions: "Or do my eyes misrepresent? Can this be hee?" (124). If disjunctive interrogatories such as this are largely for rhetorical emphasis, other uses of disjunction more clearly display the ambiguous confusion of the Chorus in its roles as friend to Samson and slightly misguided Hebrew voice. So, for example, after the encounter between Manoa and Samson, the Chorus leads itself to an essentially classical vision of a God who throws down the hubris of his heroes:

> God of our Fathers, what is man!
> That thou towards him with hand so various,
> Or might I say contrarious,
> Temperst thy providence through his short course,
> Not evenly.

. . . .

Nor do I name of men the common rout.

. . . .

But such as thou has solemnly elected
With gifts and graces eminently adorn'd
To some great work.

. . . .

Yet toward these thus dignifi'd, thou oft
Amidst their height of noon,
Changest thy countenance.

. . . .

Nor only dost degrade them.

. . . .

But throwest them lower then thou didst exalt them high.
(667–71, 674, 678–80, 682–84, 686, 689)

"Various" or "contrarious"? Not only "degrade," but "throwest them lower"? Which is it? Either, both, neither? Here, as elsewhere, the Chorus seems to reflect what has gone before (in this case, Manoa's effort to bring comfort to his son, infused with both Manoa and Samson's efforts to understand the hero's current plight). Yet the Chorus never quite echoes Samson's understanding of the situation, nor is it a reliable authorial commentator. Like Samson, or Job's friends, it keeps trying to get things right only to show not only its own limitations, but the limits on human knowledge and reason. The reader is, of course, free to read the Chorus as a commentary — but of what kind?

The interrogative mode, in which I have just indulged, allows us to try out solutions without committing to any, or establish problems without directing solutions. Like the Chorus and Samson, Manoa uses it both for rhetorical emphasis ("O miserable change! is this the man, / That invincible *Samson?*" [340–41]) and for voicing the confusions and ambiguities on which the play depends:

> Why are his gifts desirable, to tempt
> Our earnest Prayers, then giv'n with solemn hand
> As Graces, draw a Scorpions tail behind?
> For this did the Angel twice descend?
>
> (358–61)

They also allow him to pose his own desire for his son's return as a theological question, and so seek to avoid offending the terrifying God in which Manoa and the Chorus appear to believe:

> Who knows
> But God hath set before us, to return thee
> Home to thy countrey and his sacred house,
> Where thou mayst bring thy off'rings, to avert
> His further ire, with praiers and vows renewed.
>
> (516–20)

Dalila the temptress is Samson's principal foil, allowing him to test the boundaries of his own responsibility and weakness. At the same time, her magnificence and rhetorical skill convey something of what Samson was up against. She knows how to make the argument from weakness and self-effacement, and her speech to Samson begins with an example of litotes:

> With doubtful feet and wavering resolution
> I come, still dreading thy displeasure, *Samson*,
> Which to have merited, without excuse,
> I cannot but acknowledge.
>
> (732–35)

She dwells in ambiguities, including those that reside in disjunctions: "I may, if possible, thy pardon find / The easier towards me, or thy hatred less" (771–72). When Samson rejects her various pleas, she responds with a rhetorical question ("Why do I humble thus myself?" [965]) that leads ultimately to her claim of patriotic pride. She leaves as she began, with litotes, but this time transformed into triumphant enjoyment of her role as a Philistine heroine: "Nor shall I count it hainous to enjoy / The pubic marks of honour and reward / Conferr'd upon me" (991–93).

Dalila presumably reveals her personal duplicity in language such as this, yet her arguments have a human reason and rhetorical force almost as persuasive as the Chorus's rejection of a rational God. Both Philistine and Hebrew live in ambiguous times, and their respective views from positions of power and weakness have their logic. Just as it is too easy to see the Chorus or Manoa as Samson's comforting voices, it is too easy to see Dalila (as the Chorus does) as pure evil. Samson must sort out her treachery and his blame, neither of them simple matters.

Harapha, the bully, is a master of the conditional. His courage depends on what might have been.

> Oh that fortune
> Hath brought me to the field where thou art fam'd
> T'have wrought such wonders with an Asses Jaw;
> I should have forc'd thee soon wish other arms,
>
> . . . .
>
> that honour
> Certain t'have won by mortal duel from thee,
> I lose, prevented by thy eyes put out.
>
> (1092–95, 1101–3)

When Samson challenges him to the test ("Boast not of what thou would'st have done, but do / What then thou would'st" [1104–5]), Harapha resorts to bombastic interrogatives: "Is not thy Nation subject to our Lords?" (1182). How could he fight, he suggests, "With thee a Man condemn'd, a Slave enrol'd, / Due by the Law to capital punishment?" (1224–25). Or again, at Samson's taunting, "can my ears unus'd / Hear these dishonours, and not render death?" (1231–32). No matter what Samson's invitation, however, Harapha chooses to avoid the challenge.

After these several encounters, both the reader and Samson may find the officer sent to take him to Dagon's feast refreshingly direct. Yet this occasion, which at first he rejects, allows Samson to interrogate the moment toward renewed vocational purpose. Samson replies to the officer's order by a series of questions that discover the moral reasons for Samson's refusal:

> *Officer.* Regard thy self, this will offend them highly.
> *Samson.* My self? My conscience and internal peace.
> Can they think me so broken, so debas'd
> With corporal servitude, that my mind ever
> Will condescend to such absurd commands?
>
> (1333–37)

The interrogative mode continues after the officer's first exit, as the Chorus worries for Samson: "who knows how he may report / Thy words by adding fuel to the flame?" But Samson continues to ask questions that soon lead in a surprising direction, from "Shall I abuse this consecrated gift / Of strength" (1354–55) to "But who constrains me to the Temple of *Dagon* . . . / If I obey them, / I do it freely" (1370, 1372–73). The ironic language with which he offers to obey the officer's command shows Samson, at last, in control of his own complex language. Even the Philistine officer, like the Chorus, Manoa and all who would wish Samson well, offers the hope that "By this compliance thou wilt win the Lords / To favor, and perhaps to set thee free" (1411–12). Samson, instead, is moving toward his elected destiny.

Superficial freedom, defined as physical release from slavery and a return home to Manoa, is no match for the freedom of choice that Samson achieves over the course of the play. His internal freedom allows him to respond to a feeling of providential direction, those "rouzing motions in me which dispose / To something extraordinary my thoughts" (1382–83). In the play's most powerful disjunction and dramatic irony, those "rouzing motions" call Samson to a day "remarkable in my life / By some great act, or of my days the last" (1388–89). Here disjunction becomes perfect conjunction, with the great act and the ending of his life the same.

The reader accompanies Samson on his journey from

helplessness, to responsibility, to courage, and finally to renewed agency. Critics will continue to debate how helpless, how responsible, how courageous and, finally, how heroic this Samson is or becomes. Milton's choice of hero and of language invite that debate, invite choices.

This is a sophisticated poet's approach to enacting his own beliefs about human liberty and individual choice, an approach that was not entirely clear to the younger Milton. Samson's final handling of knowledge and election, and Milton's ambiguous terms, are remarkably different from those we find in the Ludlow *Mask*, for example, a work which is also about constraints, choices and freedom. In *Samson*, freedom is an invitation to the reader to make choices. In the *Mask*, freedom is a function of authorial direction and even control.

The *Mask's* Lady may have the freedom of her mind untouched by Comus's magical enchantments (663–64), but she lacks agency. Although Comus is swiftly routed by the arrival of the Lady's brothers, she remains physically bound to his magic chair. Like Spenser's Amoret (*Faerie Queene* 3.12), Milton's Lady is apparently trapped unless her enchanter reverses his magic (814–19); despite the Lady's clear conscience and excellent arguments, she requires intervention in order to be free. Samson, on the contrary, learns over the course of the play that he can act freely, and can make the right choice when the call comes.

There are of course important differences between these two dramatic pieces. One is a celebratory mask with parts for the earl of Bridgewater's three children; the other is a biblical drama with no public performance. One focuses on virginal innocence, the other on flawed experience. Yet the Lady, with her belief in an empowering chastity and the inviolability of conscience, seems a reasonable surrogate voice for the Lady of Christ's, as Samson would be, in some ways, for the blind bard. For whatever reasons, however, whether of genre, occasion, cast or conviction, the author of the Ludlow *Mask* seems unable to invite a solution to the Lady's dilemma; the author must instead impose one.

Specifically and significantly, the Attendant Spirit becomes the mediator of liberty throughout the *Mask*. He brings the brothers to their sister and he invokes the nymph Sabrina to work the counter magic which frees the Lady from her enchantment. At the very end it is again the Attendant Spirit who concludes the *Mask* by directing the audience to "Love virtue, she alone is free," and to affirm that if virtue were to prove weak, "Heav'n itself would stoop to her." Henry Lawes, the *Mask*'s composer, took the role of the Attendant Spirit, suggesting an authorial voice that mediates and directs, delivering the knowledge of freedom ("Love virtue") that will provide providential grace ("Heav'n itself would stoop").

By contrast, through Samson's various encounters and his providential "rousings," he is invited toward his vocation, and the reader is invited, rather than directed, to develop opinions on everything from Samson's freedom to his moral position. It remains possible to be skeptical of Manoa's conclusion that "*Samson* hath quit himself / Like *Samson*" (1709–10), or to understand differently from Manoa or the Chorus what that might mean. From the evidence of the drama itself, a reader may or may not believe that Samson has achieved "Calm of mind, all passion spent" (1758). Milton offers no Attendant Spirit, but only questions and ambiguities.

Wittreich argues that the Romantics were able to see this complexity and "disclose meanings that previous generations resisted, even shielded" (384). I would add that Milton's interrogatives, disjunctive language, litotes and elusive moral stance do anticipate and appeal to the active imagination that the Romantics set at the center of both poetic creation and interpretation. Yet I would put God in the picture more than Witterich does. If, as Milton proposes in *Of Education*, our engagement with learning is meant to repair the ruins of our first parents, teaching us to know God aright, then the complexity and ambiguity of *Samson* are not visionary poetics in a vacuum. Samson's "impotence of mind in body strong" (52) proceeds, through an interaction of choice and call, to strength of mind and his ability to follow the "rouzing motions" that fulfill his divine vocation. As Samson is led to his ultimate choice not because of the Danites and the messenger but through them, so Milton's rhetoric invites us to exercise an individual conscience, led by grace, through the means of the poem.

Samson Agonistes remains an intensely personal experience between the reader and the text, and is arguably Milton's most indeterminate work.[8] I think Milton meant it to be. From at least the time of his own fall into matrimony, Milton was convinced that "God delights not to make a drudge of virtue, whose actions must all be elective and unconstrain'd." Apparently he meant it to be true for the fit reader, as well as for the author called by God to prophesy to a reluctant people.

8 • Milton's Circumcision

John Rogers

1

Even Milton's most forgiving critics have been obliged to agree that the early ode *Upon the Circumcision* is less than entirely satisfying. The justification for this assessment has traditionally been aesthetic. Milton copies for the only time in his career a complex repeated Italian stanza, the specific model being Petrarch's canzone to the Virgin.[1] And he imitates, for the last time in his career, the densely conceited metaphysical style of a Donne or a Cowley.[2] But the long-acknowledged awkwardness of this poem's experiments in form and style surely pales in comparison to the awkward confusion of its theological impulses. *Upon the Circumcision*, written sometime between 1629 and 1633, is by all accounts the poet's first attempt to articulate a theory of the Atonement, the mechanism by which God is reconciled to fallen man, who, mired in original sin, was hitherto deserving only of the punishment of death.[3] Man is justified in God's sight and redeemed, for most Christian theologians, by means of Christ's Crucifixion, an action which is usually seen to satisfy God's demand for justice. Milton famously failed to treat this central event of Christian history in the poem devoted to that subject, *The Passion*, unable, it would seem, to write any more than the eight stanzas of the proem, and none of the actual hymn that would have described the event or its importance. Milton would, for the rest of his life, remain unable to conclude *The Passion: Paradise Lost* would mention the Crucifixion only briefly, and *Paradise Regained* would be able to narrate a Christian redemption, figured as a regaining of Paradise, that overlooked the Crucifixion altogether.

In light of what would become Milton's lifelong poetic neglect of the Crucifixion and its theological implications, it is all the more significant that Milton manages in the poem on Christ's circumcision to touch, however gingerly, on the topic of the Passion, and to speculate on the relation that that event bears to the atonement of man and God after the Fall. So it is with regard to the uniqueness of this accomplishment for the young Milton that I forward an argument here for the pivotal role of this minor lyric in the theological development of the Miltonic canon. I hope, further, to make a case for this poem's unwitting exposure of the troubled origins of the liberal theologies of early modern England.

Twentieth century Milton criticism, riven by competing claims for Milton's orthodoxy or heterodoxy, has predictably bequeathed us two quite disparate views on the matter of Milton's relation to the theology of atonement. The safest of those assessments, one for which Milton's writing can certainly be made to yield evidence, was forwarded by C. A. Patrides, who declared that "there are few opinions that Milton held more sincerely or more consistently than his view of the Atonement."[4] Patrides was opposing in that statement the earlier, more daring, opinion of E. M. W. Tillyard, who gave this explanation, in 1930, of what seemed to him to be Milton's distaste for the subject of the Crucifixion: "Milton would like to believe that Man . . . has it in him to work out unaided his own salvation. But such a belief was so utterly incompatible with Christianity that it was out of the question for Milton to admit it — even to himself."[5] Patrides was right to insist on a strong, generally orthodox energy behind Milton's insistent return, throughout his career, to the general question of divine satisfaction. And Tillyard was right to see in the more specific matter of Milton's neglect of the Crucifixion a provisional faith in man's ability to effect his own salvation, without the help of a sacrificial redeemer; and right to recognize in Milton's provisional belief in self-redemption a theological assumption that had no place in the mainstream religious culture with which critics such as Patrides would wish to identify him. Although it will become clear over the course of this essay that my general sympathies lie with the critical tradition that followed Tillyard in his appreciation of Miltonic heterodoxy, it should also be clear that both Tillyard and Patrides were responding to identifiable strands of Milton's tense and idiosyncratic engagement with Christianity's greatest theological questions. This critical conflict valuably opens our view onto the larger cultural problems Milton struggles to address in his religious verse. Milton's extravagant avoidance of the subject of Crucifixion, that satisfaction of divine justice which was for nearly all Christian faiths the pivotal moment of Christian history, was also a problem that originated in the politically inflected sphere of seventeenth century theological speculation. Not simply a failing of great personal significance, Milton's inability to write about the Passion would come to be, I believe, an ideologically overdetermined response to one of Reformation Europe's most conceptually daring and politically perilous religious movements: Antitrinitarianism.

Early modern Antitrinitarianism arrived at a theory of the rights of the individual by means of a new theology of the Son of God and a consequent denial of an atonement occasioned by his Crucifixion.[6] Theologians throughout early modern Europe struggled with the disjunction between contemporary standards of justice and the seemingly unjust, primitive logic of scapegoating at the heart of the mainstream Protestant justification of the Crucifixion. Behind the Reformation understanding of the Atonement was an increasingly questionable juridical theory of substitutive punishment, by which an innocent party could be legally punished for the criminal's deed (in the case of the Atonement, Jesus was punished for the sins of Adam and his offspring). But this dissociation of corporal punishment from the criminal's own body was, as Debora Kuller Shuger has recently demonstrated, repellent to most of the modern European theories of criminal justice.[7] For many progressive Antitrinitarians, it seemed unfair that anyone but Adam be punished for Adam's sin (the doctrine of original sin was rejected), and if Jesus of Nazareth was crucified, it was at the behest of his Roman or Jewish enemies, and not at the will of a heavenly Father who would demand a revenge sacrifice, a substitutive punishment or any such unethical form of satisfaction.

Interest in Antitrinitarian theologies welled up throughout late sixteenth and seventeenth century Europe, despite the fact that its principal texts, by the sixteenth century heretics Michael Servetus and Faustus Socinus, were everywhere subject to bannings and burnings, its proponents, as in England, subject to execution. The Long Parliament of 1648 passed the Ordinance for the Suppression of Heresies and Blasphemies, which named the denial of the Trinity as a capital offense. In 1652, John Milton was himself to be investigated and summarily dismissed from his government post as state licensor for permitting the publication of the Latin version of the Antitrinitarian *Racovian Catechism*. It was the serious governmental flap that ensued Milton's show of tolerance for the Antitrinitarian catechism which provided the occasion for his sonnets to Cromwell and Henry Vane; and, according to the exhaustive account of the event by David Masson, it was this crisis in 1652 that triggered Milton's alienation from the

Cromwellian government.[8] It is widely agreed that Milton would go on to write his own Antitrinitarian theological treatise, *De doctrina Christiana,* but it was one he was prudent enough not to publish in his lifetime. The most widely read and most controversial of the seventeenth century Antitrinitarian theologies would be that written by the father of modern liberalism, John Locke, whose *Reasonableness of Christianity,* written near the end of his career in 1695, was without question the Lockean text that roused the strongest reaction in the author's lifetime.[9] Grounding his liberal theory of rights in a rewriting of Christian theology, Locke simply wrote the Crucifixion out of the story of redemption and insisted that eternal life was, at least theoretically, a state to which the virtuous individual could claim a *right* on the basis of virtuous behavior. For Locke, the virtuous individual, whose natural right to eternal life was contingent only on his obedience to divine law, need not be dependent on anyone — even a Son of God sacrificed by the Heavenly Father — for his redemption and salvation.

The fact that Milton left unfinished the poem on the Crucifixion at age 21 is one of our first indications that he would precede Locke in entertaining some of the most outrageous and forward-looking principles of Antitrinitarian rationalism. Milton's failure to complete this poem reveals a passion for a topic whose personal, theological and ideological implications were so overwhelming that its complete and coherent exposition would always elude him. But a partial, if incoherent, articulation of the Passion, and its accompanying Atonement, would find expression in the second stanza of the poem *Upon the Circumcision,* written most probably within a few years of the unfinished Passion ode:

> For we by rightfull doom remediles
> Were lost in death till he that dwelt above
> High-thron'd in secret bliss, for us frail dust
> Emptied his glory, ev'n to nakednes;

And that great Cov'nant which we still transgress
Intirely satisfi'd,
And the full wrath beside
Of vengefull Justice bore for our excess,
And seals obedience first with wound smart
This day.

(17–26)[10]

Here in this later lyric Milton fleshes out a theory — actually theories — of atonement throughout the second stanza, but with special care in that stanza's central lines: "And that great Cov'nant which we still transgress / [The infant Jesus] Intirely satisfi'd, / And the full wrath beside / Of vengeful justice bore for our excess" (21–24). In the first two of these lines, Milton forwards the ancient "recapitulation" theory of atonement.[11] In light of this most affable of redemption accounts (it is this liberal theory of atonement on which Milton would rely in *Paradise Regained*), Milton suggests in lines 21–22 that we as fallen creatures continue to transgress the Great Covenant, Abraham's promise of obedience to God's will, a promise sealed by Abraham's circumcision; but someone appears who has never and will never transgress the covenant with God, thereby satisfying entirely the promise made by Abraham when the contract was signed at the Hebrew tradition's first circumcision. The atonement in this narrative is achieved by a recapitulation, with a different outcome, of Adam's test of obedience. In obeying the Jewish law of circumcision and submitting himself to the rabbi's knife, Christ "seals obedience . . . with wounding smart" (25), redeeming mankind by a work of exemplary, Abrahamic obedience that seems simply to overwhelm the disobedience of Adam and his children.

But, as in all of the religious poems Milton composed, at least before *Paradise Regained*, the lyric on the circumcision must learn that the penal system demands not simple restitution but actual retribution. As a consequence of his inability to rest content with an Abrahamic atonement, one almost entirely ethical in its operation, Milton supplements his reference to a liberal theory of a superior obedience with a harsher doctrine, the theory, elaborated so exhaustively by the Reformers, of penal substitution: "And the full wrath beside / Of vengeful Justice bore for our excess" (23–24). Our transgressions, our "excess," must be punished. And since we are clearly not fit to bear the full wrath of vengeful justice ourselves, we must depend on a perfect substitute, in this case Christ, to bear that justice for us. Recapitulation through exemplary obedience, or retribution through penal substitution: these are the central theories of atonement offered in this poem, though they are by no means the only ones. Milton forwards in fact a few others — not all of them compatible — in this lyric of only 28 lines, in the hope perhaps that a scattershot dispersal of multiple atonement accounts would satisfy forever his obligation to this unfriendly topic.

But, of course, all of Milton's hyperattentiveness to the problem of atonement compels us to wonder why these lines are not *Upon the Crucifixion*, but upon the circumcision. Why is it the context of what would have been for Milton, as for any seventeenth century Christian, the grimly exotic practice of circumcision, that enables him to break his youthful silence on the central problems of atonement and redemption? Except for the handful of English Jews, and the occasional sect of Judaizing Protestants, circumcision was never practiced in early modern England.[12] But there were nonetheless great flurries of imaginative investment in the idea of circumcision. In the liturgical calendar, the Feast of the Circumcision is January 1; and for many seventeenth century Englishmen with literary aspirations no New Year's celebration appears to have been complete without some poetic meditation on the removal of Christ's foreskin.[13] Herrick, Quarles and Crashaw are the most prolific circumcision poets, and, like Milton, they seemed to have followed the poet George Wither in exploring the figural alliance between the knife with which the rabbi excised the infant Christ's prepuce and the spear with which the soldier at the Crucifixion gouged Christ's side (John 19:34).

It appears to be Wither's nonce-typological alignment of the little wound of circumcision and the mortal wound of Crucifixion that Milton evokes at the end of his own contribution to the period's growing literature of circumcision. "But O," the speaker concludes, catching himself after musing for so long on the potentially redemptive work of circumcision itself, "ere long, / Huge pangs and strong / Will pierce more near his heart" (26–28). Here, at the end of the poem, Milton abruptly shifts the Atonement narrative he has been charting into the present tense, making clear not merely that the infant Jesus is sealing obedience with his circumcision, but that he "seals obedience *first* with wounding smart / This day" (25–26); a final, more definitive sealing of obedience, we are now led to assume, will not occur until the Crucifixion. As in the other two lyrics written for specific religious holidays — *On the Morning of Christ's Nativity* and *The Passion* — Milton self-consciously, perhaps even stagily, recoils from the full formulation of an atonement achieved without the mortal cost of Christ's Crucifixion, that position identified by Tillyard as Milton's heterodox theological desire for a salvation unaided by Christ's substitutive sacrifice.

The Father in book 3 of *Paradise Lost* will reluctantly remind himself of the Crucifixion with his "But yet all is not done" (3.204), just as the speaker of the Nativity ode would concede that "wisest fate says no"; a full redemptive glory "must not yet be so" (150), until justice is satisfied by Christ's execution.[14] The few scholars who have discussed *Upon the Circumcision* have all accepted the speaker's hurried, tentative forecast of the greater sacrifice of the Crucifixion as the ultimate theological referent of the poem.[15] But if this poem has a serious claim to our admiration, surely it is because it is so capable of leaving the impression, throughout its first 24 lines, that it is the circumcision and not the Crucifixion that satisfies God's demand for justice. It is the circumcision, that painful focus on Christ's "nakednes," that presents itself as the culmination of the sacrificial incarnation of the preexistent

Christ, that *kenosis*, or emptying out, which was itself for some of the Eastern church fathers a sufficient satisfaction of the "rightfull doom" imposed on man by divine justice:

> For we by rightfull doom remediles
> Were lost in death till he that dwelt above
> High-thron'd in secret bliss, for us frail dust
> Emptied his glory, ev'n to nakednes.

(17–20)

The poem proceeds in its elaboration of this action's redemption of us from our rightful doom, suggesting the completeness of the satisfaction of justice achieved at the circumcision. The infant Jesus *"intirely* satisfi'd" "that great Cov'nant" as he acted in accordance with the Abrahamic contract that instituted the practice of circumcision. It was the painful removal of his prepuce, the poem goes yet further to hint in a bold appropriation of the Reformation doctrine of God's retributive and substitutive justice, by which Christ bore "the full wrath . . . Of vengefull Justice." Refusing any syntactical subordination of some forms of atonement to others, Milton employs throughout these lines a disarming parataxis to identify all the major forms of justification and atonement with the circumcision on the first New Year's day: "we by rightful doom . . . were lost in death, till he . . . for us . . . emptied his glory . . . *and* that . . . covenant . . . satisfied . . . *and* the full wrath beside . . . bore for our excess . . . *and* seals obedience . . . this day." With that turn to the present tense, "seals," Milton may be seen, subtly, to be sure, to retreat from the presentation of the circumcision as a final act of atonement: the circumcision might seem here to emerge, belatedly, as merely a part of an ongoing process. But whether a definitive event or the initiation of a gradual process, the justification and atonement central to Christian theology are tied throughout most of this stanza's lines to the work of circumcision: far from the mortal sacrifice on the cross, Christ atoned for our excess sin by a simple excision of his excess skin.

2

Milton's *Upon the Circumcision* derives its energy, as well as its confusion, from the swirl of mutually incompatible meanings that the Western tradition had assigned to that ritual practice. Circumcision had established itself for Christians, as James Shapiro has argued, as a theological and ideological flashpoint. Its role in prefiguring the greater sacrifice of Crucifixion was in fact, it is worth noting, one of its least significant functions in the early modern period. The other of its figural alliances invoked in this poem is the role it is assigned in the Pauline epistles as a symbol for what became in the Reformation the most controversial of all theological categories. Circumcision was the preeminent symbol for the doctrine of the justification by works, works being those obedient, virtuous actions an individual performs in accordance with Mosaic law.[16] Paul, whose epistles are the source for nearly all of Christianity's anxious musings on circumcision, typically dismisses the value of that practice, as well as the general doctrine of the justification by works. The Christian is to be justified not by works of law, by acts such as circumcision, but by faith in the redemptive value of Christ's Crucifixion. The Epistle to the Galatians makes formal and systematic the opposition of circumcision and crucifixion: "For neither they themselves who are circumcised keep the law; but desire to have you circumcised, that they may glory in your flesh. But God forbid that I should glory, save in the cross of our Lord Jesus Christ, by whom the world is crucified unto me, and I unto the world" (Gal. 6:13–14). The seemingly dutiful Jewish circumcisers are wrong, for Paul, to privilege the redemptive power of their obedient works over a faith in Christ's Crucifixion.

Despite Paul's desire to drain circumcision — or any of those actions known as works — of any redemptive efficacy, there is an elusive moment in the Epistle to the Romans that seems at least to suggest that the individual given entirely to virtuous works — entirely to the exemplary behavior embodied in circumcision — earns his own salvation. In a discussion of circumcision, Paul explains the reward to which the patriarch Abraham was entitled by virtue of his works: "Now to him that worketh is the reward not reckoned of grace, but of debt" (Rom. 4:4). The man that worketh, or performs good works, gets his reward not as a favor, as a gratuitous instance of divine mercy, or grace: the man that worketh receives his reward as a debt, as something he is owed, as a benefit that he is entitled to demand as his due. Elsewhere in the epistles, Paul continues the economic metaphor: "circumcision verily is profitable, if thou do the law." But if you place too much faith in circumcision, he would insist in Galatians, "Christ shall profit you nothing" (Gal. 5:2). The reward or profit accrued by the works associated with circumcision is strictly self-generated; it is not conferred on one by Christ. (Paul issued such statements of the profitability of circumcision as admonitions, assuming, I suppose, that his readers would rather be rewarded with grace than paid for their work; but the seventeenth century liberal tradition could read such admonitions as celebrations of independent achievement.)

The antiliberal Calvinist theologians, from the Elizabethan William Perkins to Milton's contemporary, John Owen, devoted considerable energy to their readings of the Pauline treatment of circumcision, forcing all of Paul's statements to speak to the general inadequacy of all human agency. Relying most heavily on the Paul of Galatians, they cited circumcision as the premier emblem of a type of human action intended perhaps to save, but which will always be futile in this world tied to the Almighty's predestinating will. Circumcision began in fact to operate as the code word for the dangerous belief that virtuous human action alone might be sufficient for salvation. This dangerous belief was associated primarily with Catholics, and to a lesser extent Jews, but the faith in "circumcision" and all it entails could also be ascribed to some of

England's most radical non-Calvinist Puritans.[17] England's foremost Judaizing Puritan, John Traske, actually began in the 1620s to circumcise the male infants of his followers, convinced that just such works of virtuous obedience would be pleasing in the sight of God, and therefore redemptive.[18] But other radicals, too, less literal-minded than Traske, would embark on forms of religious and political activism they would figuratively align with the virtue of the Jewish practice of circumcision, but which roused the wrath of conservative Calvinists. In the years of the English revolution, almost any form of radical political intervention was open to denunciation as an act of "circumcision" by pious detractors. There was good reason for the conservative Calvinist clergy to warn their flocks of the dangers of presumptive, "circumcising" action: it was those few moments in the New Testament epistles in which circumcision seemed to be praised that were relied on increasingly for a scriptural justification of independent action, an action whose benefits were earned without the assistance or consent of a higher power. By the end of the century, Locke would turn to the Pauline meditation on circumcision — in Romans 4:4 — to supply the theological grounding of one aspect of the liberal conception of a right: "for righteousness, or an exact obedience to the law, seems, by the Scripture, to have a claim of right to eternal life, Rom. 4:4, 'To him that worketh' (i.e., does the works of the law) 'is the reward not reckoned of grace, but of debt.'"[19]

Few of England's radical protestants would embrace the Hebraic faith in virtuous works with the zeal and the commitment of John Milton, whose polemical defense of divorce in the early 1640s would require him to champion a continued observance of the Mosaic law despite its seeming abrogation at the hands of Jesus. As we might expect, Milton singles out the practice of circumcision in the divorce pamphlets for special praise. In the *Doctrine and Discipline of Divorce* (1643), he admires the Jew for taking such pains to demonstrate his obedience to the law: "That severe and rigorous knife not sparing the tender fore-skin of any male infant, to carve upon his flesh the mark of that strict and pure covnant wherinto he enter'd" (YP 2:302). But Milton, at his most radical in the divorce tracts, would go even further in his praise for the performance of obedient works. Neglecting any mention of the role of Christ in the Atonement, Milton, as Jason Rosenblatt has convincingly shown, insists that sin can be eradicated by works, by the virtuous individual's obedience to the law.[20]

Confronting directly the Pauline disparagement of the law, Milton argues in *Tetrachordon* that "it is an absurdity to say that law can measure sin, or moderate sin; sin is not a predicament to be measur'd and modify'd, but is alwaies an excesse" (YP 2:657).[21] Sin is not an intractable, inevitable feature of fallen life that we can only hope to diminish or temper by an appeal to the law of God. As nothing more than a phenomenon that exceeds the law of God, sin can be eradicated in the believer by a straightforward submission to the law: "If once it square to the measure of Law, it ceases to be an excesse, and consequently ceases to be a sinne" (YP 2:657). Revisiting the peculiar word for sin he had employed so strikingly in *Upon the Circumcision*, Milton systematically proceeds to undo any concession to the retributive theory of penal substitution he had made in the religious lyric of the previous decade. Human "excess," Milton argues, in shocking contradiction to nearly every conceivable stripe of Christian belief, does not require for its elimination any sacrifice by an external redeemer. Refusing here to submit to Protestantism's Pauline derogation of the law, Milton privileges the self-sufficiency of the obedient Christian over the atoning measures of God's supervening grace. Our excess does not, in *Tetrachordon*, require a redeemer to bear the full wrath of vengeful justice; like the superfluous foreskin removed in circumcision, our sinful excess needs simply to be trimmed, made to "square to the measure of Law," for that covenant to be entirely satisfied, for the atonement of God and fallen man.[22]

The Milton of the circumcision ode is not the political and ecclesiastical radical he will become in the 1640s. But something of the divorce pamphlet's faith in the redemptive potential of obedient works, that category of human action best embodied by circumcision, is surely audible in the youthful poem, which devotes the majority of its lines to a lowering of the standard of atonement from Crucifixion to circumcision. Implicit in this descent from the Crucifixion to the more mundane, nonmortal wound of circumcision is an even more daring conclusion: it is not simply Christ's virtuous action, but anybody's virtuous action that could supply the atonement necessary for personal redemption and salvation. To tie the redemption to Christ's circumcision, rather than his Crucifixion, argues naturally against the uniqueness of Christ's atonement. Anyone, or at least any male, can effect an atonement by means of that obedient work.

Milton, in maintaining for so much of *Upon the Circumcision* an implicit argument for the redemptive potential of circumcision itself, takes up the cause of a Judaizing Puritan like the Englishman John Traske, and of the early Jewish Christians, who maintained, despite the fulminations of Paul, their faith in the value of works, their faith in the redemptive potential of human action. According to this serious radicalization of the impact of circumcision, and the impact of works in general, the vicarious atonement of Christ's Passion lies in excess of the simple human virtue that should itself be sufficient to redeem. The extravagance of a sacrificial crucifixion — and its attendant theory of retributive penal substitution — exceeds the work necessary for atonement.

We still have not fully considered why it is the specific act of circumcision that presses itself on Milton as the laudable emblem of virtuous human agency. Certainly the covenant God made with Abraham is striking for the part of the body selected for excision. And it will naturally come as no surprise that theologians had always toyed with the idea that the removal of the prepuce possessed an efficacy beyond its value as an arbitrary sign of a covenant. Moses Maimonides had argued that circumcision was designed as a means of sexual purification, since it seemed to weaken the sexual organ and thereby diminish illicit sexual desire.[23] The Flemish philosopher van Helmont, whose scientific writings Milton would come to admire, would elaborate this thesis, explaining that the removal of the foreskin enabled the good Jew to be made "a Partaker of the less Pleasure . . . [and] Tickling," appropriate for one who "should desire to be registred among the Catalogue of the beloved People of God."[24] The desensitizing work of circumcision acquired its figurative meaning as well, as circumcision could come to signify, as it did for Thomas Browne, a literary process of excision. In a dedicatory poem Browne asks the late John Donne, after Donne's religious poems are printed alongside his earlier erotic verse, "How will [thy readers], with sharper eyes, / The Fore-skinne of thy phansie circumcise?" (5–6).[25] By many accounts the young Milton was committed, throughout a significant portion of the 1630s, to a self-imposed celibacy. And a practice such as circumcision, a ritual of obedience that may well please God by mortifying carnal lust, one additionally associated with a literary process of pious de-eroticization, would inevitably hold a special interest for a poet courting literary greatness by means of the work — both personal and literary — of sexual abstinence.

   To place Milton's interest in circumcision in the context of seventeenth century theological speculation, we would have to say that the atoning work of circumcision for which Milton argues is implicitly founded on the circumcision of the 99-year-old Abraham, whom God had instructed, "And ye shall circumcise the flesh of your foreskin" (Gen. 17:11). (Competing theologies of circumcision were founded on competing scriptural accounts of circumcision.) Milton would actually explain in *De doctrina Christiana* that even for the Hebrews, the practice of circumcision, instituted on the unquestionably mature Abraham, was only effective as a seal of righteousness for adults being circumcised, or more accurately, for adults circumcising themselves; involuntary infant circumcisions were never meaningful to God (YP 6:548–49). Because for Milton circumcision was meaningful only for those who, like Abraham, "believed before circumcision" (YP 6:549), it could provide a satisfactory model of atonement only insofar as it was allied with the willing self-purification and self-redemption associated with the virtuous works of rational adults. It had to be distanced as far as possible from the involuntary filial sacrifice many orthodox Calvinists were so happy to locate in the Crucifixion.

But however far Milton pushes his idealization of the Abrahamic practice of rational adult circumcision, he knows perfectly well that circumcision was rarely performed on adults. As a pediatric procedure it therefore acquired another cluster of associations, one to which Milton in this lyric is painfully alive. The circumcision at stake in this poem is obviously that of the eight-day-old infant Jesus. The vulnerability of the infant circumcisee played a crucial role in the protestant understanding of this ancient Jewish custom, which struck many Anabaptists and Antitrinitarians in particular as cruel and even torturous: the irrational cruelty of infant circumcision seemed to parallel the irrational cruelty of Jesus' adult Crucifixion. Many early modern ethnographers concurred with the rational theologians, and the ethnographer John Bulwer took a special delight, in his 1654 *Anthropometamorphosis*, in characterizing what he considered the savage act of circumcision as one of the most repugnant of all the mutilation practices ever conceived by man's torturous imagination. Not content with his detailed and wrenching accounts of ritual circumcision in the savage lands of Guinea and Patagonia, he went out of his way to distance this act of mutilation as far as possible from the Judeo-Christian tradition. Citing Philo Judaeus, Bulwer notes that "The Egyptians . . . were the first that circumcised their virilities," and he hints that the Hebrews may actually have adopted this practice not on the example of Abraham, but in a weak-minded imitation of their Egyptian masters.[26]

The circumcision ode may, as critics have assumed, comprise the first of Milton's attempts to articulate the atoning work of Christ's sacrifice on the cross; but it functions even more powerfully to rationalize that atonement, to figure an atonement that is something other than the brutal image of the Father's sacrifice of the Son. Milton the pious theologian cannot afford to practice Bulwer's outrageous style of critical historical ethnography. But it is possible nonetheless to see Milton, in *Upon the Circumcision*, struggling to join the rationalizing spirit of a Bulwer as he tries to dissociate the cruelty and torture typically associated with infant circumcision from his theology of atonement. Milton is probably most successful in dissociating the circumcision from the orthodox image of the wrathful father's punishment of his son in what has always been celebrated as the poem's finest passage, the chiastic couplet that begins the second stanza: "O more exceeding love or law more just? / Just law indeed, but more exceeding love!" To suggest that this sacrifice is made in accordance with a just law is already to deny the cruelty of an angry God who requires appeasement. In being circumcised or crucified, Christ is merely subjecting himself to an unavoidable, remediless principle of divine justice.

But this antimetabole takes us even further into a justification of the ways of God. Milton's couplet suggests that it is not simply a just law that necessitates the atoning circumcision, but God's love. In appealing to the power of love as the motive for the circumcision, Milton, in fact, finds himself producing an argument strangely close to that of the Anglican Thomas Fuller, who would in 1653 come to defend paedobaptism by defending the Jewish practice of infant circumcision: "Call not Circumcision Cruelty, but what indeed it was, Mercy, Pity, and Compassion; that such who by nature were *children of wrath*, and deserved damnation, had by Gods mercy, their sufferings commuted into the short pain of *Circumcision.*"[27] Like Fuller, Milton attempts to divert our attention from the seeming cruelty of this action by reminding us how fortunate we are that the damnation we deserve has been, in a merciful show of God's love, "commuted into the short pain of Circumcision." Milton's poem works hard to empty the atonement of its foundation in a logic of blood sacrifice and penal substitution. And the formula he arrives at here, the interaction of law and love with a greater stress on love, is one he will cling to for some time to come; he revisits it 30 years later, when in *Paradise Lost* he is next obliged, in verse, to articulate Atonement: "The law of God exact he shall fulfil / Both by obedience and by love though love / Alone shall fulfil the law" (12.402–4).

It is in light of the attempts throughout this poem to soften, or circumvent, the sacrificial component of Christian atonement theory, that we can best understand the curiously extravagant reference to the Crucifixion that marks the poem's end: "but O ere long / huge pangs and strong / Will pierce more near his heart." Scholars have not been wrong to identify in these lines an image of the spear wound in the side that Christ suffers in the account of the Crucifixion offered in the gospel of John (19:34). Milton's poem concludes with a poetically innovative, if theologically predictable, suggestion that the Judaic circumcision of the foreskin undergone by Jesus will find its ultimate significance in a corresponding, necessarily superior typological fulfillment. But the Crucifixion is only one of the superior actions suggested in these extraordinary concluding lines. If Milton is looking ahead to an action more redemptive than the circumcision, he may have bypassed that Passion altogether. The redemptive act nearer his heart that serves as the typological fulfillment of Christ's preputial circumcision, in other words, might just as easily be the "circumcision of the heart," that inward process of purification, first named in Deuteronomy 30:6, which establishes itself as a trope of inward authority in the New Testament (Rom. 2:28–29). For Hugo Grotius, whose *De veritate religionis Christianae* of 1627 offered a liberal voice of opposition against Calvinist orthodoxy, the figure of a coronary circumcision presented itself as a figure of the virtuous obedience to the law that seemed almost capable of rivaling Crucifixion as a means of justifying fallen man in the eyes of God: preputial circumcision, he writes, "is now nothing worth, but it is the inward *Circumcision* of the heart, the keeping of *Gods Commandments*, the *new* creature, *faith* that is perfected in love, which make Men known to be *true Israelites and mystical Jews*, that is, praisers of *God*, and *commendable* in his sight."[28] If in Milton's poem it makes any sense at all to speak of a "pang" that pierces the heart, that pang can only be said to pierce the heart from within: all of the uses of "pang" charted in the *OED* describe sharp spasms of pain felt from the inside. The huge pangs and strong that will be the ultimate marker of the Christian dispensation are not, in this reading, the piercing pains of nail and spear, but the pangs of conscience, the purified inner space which alone can supply the means by which virtue itself is rewarded with salvation, by which virtue itself entitles one to salvation. The deliberate obliqueness of Milton's "huge pangs and strong," much like the carefully calibrated approximation of closure implied by the awkward comparative "more near," enables this poem to maintain the tension of its theological ambivalence to the very end. While the flexible dialectical figure of circumcision certainly allows Milton, in the orthodox vein affirmed by Patrides, to tie the redemption to the vicarious atonement achieved by Christ's Crucifixion on the cross, it also permits him to express the secret wish, identified by Tillyard, that the individual Christian, heart-circumcised into a state of self-disciplined purity, might actually be capable of redeeming himself.

Only now, having explored Milton's use of circumcision as a conflicted figure for the redemptive potential of unaided human action, can we understand the poem's first stanza, the extravagance of whose opening conceit has proven an embarrassment even for this poem's most stalwart apologists. The most characteristic feature of all of Milton's religious lyrics — with the notable exception of this poem and the unfinished Passion ode — is the speaker's desire that his poem be elevated to the status of divine song, a song sometimes figured as the music of the spheres. This gesture toward transcendence, according to James Holly Hanford, was nothing other than the young Milton's "native theme."[29] The Miltonic speaker typically arrives at this fantasy of joining his voice to the angelic choir by submitting himself to the literary ministrations of a superior, divine power. We are reminded of Milton's beloved topos in the circumcision poem's opening lines:

> Ye flaming Powers, and winged Warriours bright
> That erst with musick, and triumphant song
> First heard by happy watchfull Shepherds ear,
> So sweetly sung your joy the clouds along
> Through the soft silence of the list'ning night,
> Now mourn.
>
> (1–6)

Milton takes care to remind his reader of the earlier Nativity ode, in which the music and triumphant song of the winged angelic warriors are first heard not only by the shepherds at Christ's Nativity, but by the happy, watchful 21-year-old shepherd John Milton. Crucially, though, the similarity of this poem to the earlier, stronger lyrics ends at line 6, as Milton refuses to ask those flaming powers for help in writing the poem, as he refuses any gesture toward joining his voice with theirs. (Milton will, in fact, never permit his poetic persona to sacrifice his poetic autonomy in any poem that directly treats the Passion.)[30] He begins the circumcision ode not by asking the angels for help, but by chiding them for their inability — as angels — to weep at the thought of this painful procedure. If the angels have any intention of mourning properly the sad occasion of the circumcision, then Milton lets them know that they will have to borrow tears wept by the human poet: burning in their fiery essences, they can at the very least count on the process of evaporation to help them assume some of the fleshly signs of mourning that the poet, and only the poet, is capable of producing.

Milton actually offers to *lend* something to the inadequately mournful angels, permitting them graciously to "borrow / Seas wept from our great sorrow." These divine creatures will be indebted to *him*, an inversion of the typical redemption economy (and of the traditional economy of poetic inspiration), an inversion that entitles Milton to the right to claim the profit of this action as his own. Paul had conceded to the Galatians that "circumcision [and the works for which circumcision stands] can be profitable, if thou do the law." Ready to reap what profit, or "excess," he can from his independent poetic effort, Milton is willing to forgo the presumably greater glory Paul had associated with the faith in the vicarious atonement of the Crucifixion.[31] If the conceit of the angelic borrowing of evaporated tears strikes us (as surely it must) as forced, or even desperate, the extent of its hubris speaks to the intensity with which Milton resists the decidedly passive agency that orthodoxy requires the Christian to bring to his redemption. It speaks to the intensity with which Milton has begun his struggle to transform Calvin's Trinitarian theology of supervening grace and human helplessness into the more liberal Arminian, and ultimately Antitrinitarian, theology of free will and rational self-sufficiency. Milton's emergence in the following decade as a political philosopher would be inextricably tied to his emergence as an Antitrinitarian. Even in the mature works of political philosophy, Milton would never fully disentangle his political sense of the individual's right to act from his theological sense of the individual's agency in his own salvation.

3

"But O!" As Milton was forced to back away at the end of the circumcision ode from his liberal nonsacrificial theory of atonement, so I must note here that I, too, am unfinished, having made perhaps in the preceding pages too zealous a case for an ethically conscientious, proto-Unitarian, liberal reading of Milton's early poem. Milton's *Upon the Circumcision*, I have argued, devotes a great deal of energy (and sacrifices a great deal of coherence) for the sake of wrenching from mainstream Protestant theology a meaningfully ethical interpretation of the Christian redemption. And as I have noted, nowhere does Milton appear more successful in this effort than in the lines so frequently cited as the finest in the poem: "O more exceeding love or law more just? / Just law indeed, but more exceeding love!" But the formulaic privileging of "love," which will be repeated so effortlessly in Milton's epic, made a hard-won appearance in the youthful lyric. It is not easy, I submit, to justify the bloody sacrifice of vicarious atonement in an appeal to divine love. A calibration of the stress fractures caused by such an attempt can be made, I propose, by an inspection of the probable literary inspiration for Milton's famous chiastic couplet. Most editors, since the Richardsons in the eighteenth century, have noted the parallel between Milton's couplet and a passage in Virgil's eighth eclogue. But embarrassed no doubt by the implications of the connection, critics have steered clear of commenting on the significance of the tie. Virgil's speaker, Damon, sings of the savage love — "saevus Amor," that savage or cruel little boy Cupid — who led Medea to punish her husband by murdering her two sons:

saevus Amor docuit natorum sanguine matrem
commaculare manus; crudelis tu quoque, mater:
crudelis mater magis, an puer improbus ille?
improbus ille puer; crudelis tu quoque mater.

(*Eclogue* 8, 47–50)

[Savage love taught a mother to stain her hands with the blood
of her own offpsring. Cruel yourself, o mother. More cruel the
mother, or that relentless boy? Relentless that boy: cruel you
yourself, o mother.]

At the very moment that Milton arrives at the formulation
for the Atonement with which he will be satisfied for the rest
of his life, he places it in the formal frame of the clever
antimetabole from Virgil. When placed alongside the Virgilian
original, the divine love that agrees to redeem man's guilt
by an unprecedented sacrifice empties itself of its glorious
generosity and mercy. The more exceeding love that Milton
exclaims begins instead, in the context of the lines from Virgil,
to reflect, rather than correct, the sinful "excess" that is the
state of human depravity; God's more exceeding love comes
eerily to resemble the savage and excessive love that drives
an irrational parent to punish the sinning party by means of a
cruel sacrifice of an innocent bystander. In the Medea story,
Jason may have committed the crime, abandoning his wife,
but it is Medea's two sons who must bear the full wrath of her
vengeful justice. In the story of the revenge sacrifice that lies
behind the poetic scheme that Milton copies for the most
forceful and elegant lines of his poem, we have laid bare before
us the savage logic of revenge and the plight of human helplessness at the emotional core of the Christian Crucifixion.

If Milton can be said to hide the terrible image of a child
sacrifice at the center of *Upon the Circumcision*, he can also
be said to have some practice with this strangely open gesture
of suppression. The young Milton has already struggled, in
his *Ode on the Morning of Christ's Nativity*, to stamp out the
most unethical of the Crucifixion's associations. The speaker

of that poem, as noted earlier, is brought back to his senses
after narrating a view of Christian history that conveniently
omits any mention of the Passion:

> But wisest fate says no,
> This must not yet be so,
> The babe lies yet in smiling infancy,
> That on the bitter cross
> Must redeem our loss.

But the Nativity ode could incorporate this perfunctory mention of the Passion only after it had silenced any of that event's
associations with child sacrifice.

This silencing, I believe, occurs throughout the poem, but
with particular force in Milton's catalog of the pagan gods who
flee their oracles at the birth of the Christian Messiah. We are
told, for example, of Moloch, the brutal God who abandons
his temple, and of his priests, who are left to dance and ring
their ritual cymbals in vain:

> And sullen Moloch, fled,
> Hath left in shadows dread
> His burning idol all of blackest hue;
> In vain with cymbals' ring
> They call the grisly king,
> In dismal dance about the furnace blue.

(205–10)

It has been known at least since the early eighteenth century
that Milton had taken his image of the rites of Moloch from
one of the favorite books of his youth, George Sandys's *Relation of a Journey* (1615), in which the author's descriptions of
his travels through the Holy Land are interspersed with narratives of the practices of the ancient Hebrews. Moloch, Milton
learned from Sandys, was the terrible god whom the most
backsliding of the Hebrews continued to worship, and to whom
they would sacrifice their children by placing them in the arms
of a fiery brass idol. In his account of the ritual sacrifices to

Moloch, Sandys explains, the priests of Moloch, "lest their lamentable shrieks should sad the hearts of their parents, the priests of Molech did deafe their ears with the continuall clangs of trumpets and timbrels."[32] The ringing of cymbals about the burning idol of Moloch was no simple part of a pagan religious ritual. The priests of Moloch clanged continually on their instruments for the sole purpose of deafening the ears of the parents, who would no doubt be overwhelmed with grief to hear the terrible pleas of their tormented children.

Milton, of course, dutifully pictures the priests clanging their cymbals, but, as his eighteenth century annotator Thomas Warton noted, he fails to mention the original function of the cymbals, noting simply that they are being used by the priests, at this hour of desperation, to call back the frightened god.[33] The poet deafens our ears to the facts of child sacrifice for the same reason that he devotes the 27 stanzas of the ode to an outrageous attribution of strength and heroism to this *Christus victor* in swaddling bands: the redemption for which this Christ will be ultimately responsible must be cleansed of all its taint of helpless, unwilling sacrifice. In the brutality of the story of Moloch and the burning children, as in the savagery of the story of Medea's murder of her sons — in all the narratives of sacrifice that Milton evokes only to avert — we gain a glimpse into the initial reasons for which Milton avoided with such passion the poetry of vicarious atonement.

We are in a position now to understand why it was the enormously overdetermined figure of circumcision that not only compelled, but also enabled, Milton to broach the topic of Atonement. As a painful procedure to be performed on eight-day-old infant boys, it presented itself as an image for that aspect of Christian theology that Milton found most repellent, the cruelty of the parental sacrifice of an implicitly unwilling and vulnerable child. The pathetic helplessness of the child circumcisee seemed, too, to figure with distressing clarity the essential passivity that Calvin had asked the individual to bring to the matter of his salvation. But in its role as a sign of virtuous human action, and especially of the actions taken to secure the obedient and chaste submission to the law, circumcision could also present itself as a rational correction to the act of substitutive sacrifice which lay at the heart of Christianity. It is surely this latter, rational set of associations that Milton is struggling to invoke in this earliest bout with the ethical shortcomings of Christianity. But, as the embedded story of Medea should suggest, the cruel power of the wrathful God of the Puritans is never for Milton entirely suppressed, or suppressible. A residue of God's anger and revenge always remains in excess of the ethical strictures to which Milton would like to constrain him. (A Calvinist residue would similarly mar the logic and coherence of Milton's more or less Arminian theological treatise.) Below the surface of one of Milton's earliest expressions of a liberal, enlightened rational theology, we see the troubled encounter with a tyrannical God, and a disquieting identification with that God's dependent, circumscribed creatures.

9 • The Provenance of *De doctrina Christiana*

A View of the Present State of the Controversy

John P. Rumrich

Milton has borrowed more than any other writer; yet he is perfectly distinct from every other writer. — William Hazlitt, *The Round Table*, 1884

The initial challenge to John Milton's authorship of *De doctrina Christiana* was advanced at an International Milton Symposium (Vancouver, 1991) by William Hunter. His challenge was at once probed by a skeptical John T. Shawcross and confidently dismissed by Barbara Lewalski. After these papers were published, Christopher Hill and Maurice Kelley forcefully disputed Hunter's claims.[1] Despite these apparently decisive replies, politic Milton scholars, when citing *De doctrina Christiana*, now include heavily annotated disclaimers. The continuing hesitation owes not so much to Hunter's persistence, however, as it does to the efforts of a self-appointed committee of experts, mostly British, led by Thomas Corns and Gordon Campbell. Six years after Hunter's original challenge, this committee produced a report that brought quantitative analysis to bear on the question of provenance and concluded by denying the reliability of *De doctrina Christiana* as a guide to Milton's beliefs and recommending skepticism as to the authorship of the treatise.

Three of the report's eight conclusions are crucial to the case against using the treatise to elucidate Milton's other works:

(iv) The manuscript [of *De doctrina Christiana*] has two principal strata, an ur-text and a transformation of that text effected by a process of revision which primarily consisted of the accretion of material by Milton.

(v) Some parts of the manuscript show more evidence of Miltonic composition than others; some parts may be wholly of Miltonic origin; others show stylometric characteristics unlike Milton's; much of the manuscript probably constitutes a Miltonic appropriation and transformation that finds precedent in Milton's practice in the production of the *Artis Logicae*.

. . . .

(vii) The relationship of *De doctrina Christiana* to the Milton oeuvre must remain uncertain, since in the case of a work or revision that has halted before completion we cannot know what other changes, especially what deletions of doctrines to which he did not subscribe, Milton would have made in completing his task.[2]

The committee concludes that an "ur-text" underlies *De doctrina Christiana*. The precedent cited is that of *Artis Logicae*, in which Milton indisputably reworks previously published writings on logic and takes authorial credit for the result. Conclusion (vii) reasons that, since we cannot know exactly how far along this process of revision was when Milton stopped work on the "ur-text," we cannot know how accurately the version we possess conveys his own beliefs. This objection to the pertinence of the treatise may be dismissed summarily. As Hunter acknowledges, the manuscript we possess is "essentially finished except perhaps in its discussion of marriage"; "only Gordon Campell has argued its incompletion" (*SEL* 32:130). Campbell is, however, a member of the committee of experts, and specifically responsible for historical sections of the report. This coincidence presumably accounts for the committee's taking a position that no scholar but Campbell has found tenable since Maurice Kelley, more than a decade ago, refuted it.[3]

This essay will address two main topics related to the two other conclusions quoted above. First, it will sketch the reception history of *De doctrina Christiana* and the committee's rationale for resorting to a statistical analysis of the treatise. Then, it will address the adequacy of the stylometric methodology deployed.[4]

Reception History

The committee's most portentous conclusions depend on the results of a complex stylometric analysis, purportedly undertaken to ensure that the report's analysis and conclusions would be unbiased. In a separately published report detailing its methodology and findings, the subcommittee of stylometric investigators explains that it departed from ordinary philological methods and took to counting words "to shift the ground away from intuition and passionately held conviction toward aspects which are more tractable to objective investigation."[5] Difficult as it is to decipher, this statement conveys well enough the stylometricians' intention to bring a quasi-scientific objectivity to their conclusions, as opposed to conclusions that owe in part to "intuition" or "passionately held conviction." The stylometric analysts sought definite, measurable evidence, drawn from the treatise itself, rather than resort to such subjective impressions as, for example, Lewalski's intuitive recognition of Milton's voice: "as I encounter this persona, with or without name and initials and date attached, I can only call him — John Milton" (SEL 32:153). Lewalski relies on decades of study of Milton's writings in forming her intuitive judgment. By contrast, the stylometricians' understanding of Milton, indeed, their ability to comprehend the written word, formed no part of the computational effort.

The intuition of scholars like Hill, Kelley and Lewalski rests on an impressive, and among living Milton scholars very likely unsurpassed, foundation of historical knowledge and literary acumen. Even so, those familiar with the long history of debates around Milton's theology will sympathize with the committee's search for an objective basis for its conclusions. Riddled with heresy, *De doctrina Christiana* has since its discovery given Milton scholars fits, especially those who would like to see Milton as a relatively orthodox Christian who wrote poetry that confirms traditional doctrine. If *De doctrina Christiana* is no longer taken as Milton's work, it becomes possible to construe him as, in Hunter's words, "closer to the great traditions of Christianity, no longer associated with a merely eccentric fringe" (*SEL* 32:166). On the other hand, if Milton is indeed the author of the variously heretical treatise, then his distance from those "great traditions" and affiliation with more than one "eccentric fringe" is evidently far greater than many Milton scholars have been willing to admit. The committee resorted to stylometric methodology as a way to guarantee a disinterested account of the treatise's provenance. The stylometric investigators thus answered Hunter's call for "a definitive stylistic analysis of the Latin prose of the *Christian Doctrine* put beside the Latin prose of the canonical works to see whether under such analysis they are similar or different" (*SEL* 32:166).

The committee recognizes that the treatise "through the 1990s has been the site of fierce controversy"; as a work of systematic theology, it affords relatively plain access to the religious tenets of its author, tenets whose radical political ramifications have become increasingly evident:

> [*De doctrina Christiana*] seemingly extends the possibilities of determining more certainly the details of Milton's theology — and particularly his Christology — than is possible from his major poems or his English prose. Such issues have assumed new vigor as connections have been asserted between religious heterodoxy and political radicalism, and as Milton's revolutionary status and credentials have come under scrutiny. Hence the urgent importance of the provenance of the Latin tract. (*Computing*, 86)

This account of the historical and critical stakes riding on the provenance controversy is undeniable. If the treatise affords an accurate view of Milton's theology, "and particularly his Christology," then Milton scholars will find it exceedingly difficult to deny that he was gravely heretical — and heretical in ways that tend to confirm our growing understanding of his political radicalism. The committee's explanation of the provenance controversy is misleading only in limiting to the 1990s the time frame of the "fierce controversy."

Arguments for and against Milton's authorship of the treatise may be plausibly considered the culmination of a long-standing division in Milton scholarship, one that assumed something like its current shape more than a half century ago, when Maurice Kelley published *This Great Argument: A Study of Milton's "De doctrina Christiana" as a Gloss upon "Paradise Lost."*[6] True, Bishop Thomas Burgess in 1826 disputed Milton's authorship of the treatise, and did so for reasons that anticipated Hunter's, but, as Hunter acknowledges, "[Burgess's] views had been dismissed by everyone concerned with the authenticity of the ascription to Milton" (*SEL* 33:191). As a sturdy proponent of the orthodox doctrine of the Trinity, and as an anti-Catholic who deemed the treatise insufficiently critical of the church of Rome, Burgess was reluctant to accept Milton's authorship and prosecuted his highly tenuous case repeatedly. His persistent challenge was consigned to oblivion because, as Christopher Hill reports, quoting the *Dictionary of National Biography*, Burgess, when he "had some cherished principle or opinion to defend . . . threw away discretion and impartiality" (*SEL* 34:165–66). Burgess's bias was evident to his contemporaries, who dismissed his claims in favor of strong evidence to the contrary. Hunter, however, attributes the quick dismissal of Burgess's opinion to the opposition and intimidation of the Crown, and to a subsequent conspiracy of silence, for which, Hunter suggests, the absence of any trace is evidence. Also, Burgess's publications on Milton cannot be located in any British library, a bibliographical lacuna that similarly arouses Hunter's suspicions (*SEL* 34:202). Whether squelched by a royal conspiracy or merely rejected as inane and so forgotten, Burgess's objection went unseconded until Hunter's revival of it. Milton scholars have instead, until the 1990s, accepted the provenance worked out in compelling historical and documentary detail by David Masson, James Holly Hanford, William Riley Parker and Maurice Kelley. The historical portion of the committee's general report confirms and even adds to the evidence: "the history of the manuscript does not prove Milton's authorship, but it does track the manuscript . . . ultimately, to Milton's desk" (*MQ* 89).

In light of the accumulated historical, bibliographical and philological evidence, no modern scholar before Hunter had disputed the provenance of the treatise. The preliminary skirmishes fought over *De doctrina Christiana* instead concerned the nature of its pertinence to Milton's other writings, especially his poetry. C. S. Lewis dismissed Milton's heretical opinions as "private theological whimsies" that he "laid aside" in composing epic testimony to Christianity's "great central tradition." C. A. Patrides followed Lewis's lead, claiming that Milton was an inept theologian and wisely left *De doctrina Christiana* unfinished.[7] Various others have joined with Patrides in attacking Kelley's initial description of the theological treatise as a "gloss" on his epic poetry — because such a description ignores the integrity of distinct kinds of discourse and turns a deaf ear to the mysteries of poetic expression. Regina Schwartz, for example, though she acknowledges the logic of the treatise's arguments on behalf of the goodness of the first matter, rejects their relevance to the symbolic representation of chaos in *Paradise Lost*, a rejection recently seconded by John Rogers and John Leonard.[8] In their view, chaos is, at the symbolic level, hostile and adverse to life, not "good, and contain[ing] the seeds of all subsequent good," per the explication of matter found in *De doctrina Christiana*.[9] Many other scholars, however — Barbara Lewalski, Dennis Danielson, William Kerrigan, Michael Bauman, Stephen Fallon and Joseph Wittreich notable among them — have refined and fortified Kelley's blunt claim for the correspondence of Milton's theology and poetry. They have done so through credible interpretation of Milton's poetry that depends partly, often crucially, on reference to *De doctrina*. Indeed, it is on the topic of Milton's vitalist materialism that interpretation of *Paradise Lost* informed by the theological treatise has been most fruitful, notably in the work of Kerrigan and Fallon.[10]

Scholars' efforts to avert their eyes from Milton's embrace of the first matter hardly compare with their struggles to dissociate the treatise's Christology from the epic's depiction of the Son. As the authors of the stylometric analysis aver, Milton's Christology has been perhaps the single most prejudicial topic in the long debate over the pertinence of the theological treatise to Milton's epic. The treatise is unmistakably Arian; the epic less overtly so, or even, some have maintained, orthodox. Over the last half century William Hunter, along with C. A. Patrides and a few others, has been especially vigorous in presenting Milton as an orthodox Trinitarian, and, more recently, Gordon Campbell — one of the committee of experts — has repeated and elaborated various of Patrides's arguments.[11] I have claimed elsewhere that this particular critical history, though largely unacknowledged in the committee's report, influences it profoundly.[12] On the other hand, the decision to resort to stylometric analysis was, as we have already seen, intended to neutralize the prejudicial effect of these longstanding debates by affording the committee's conclusions an objective basis. Hence it is to the stylometric analysis of the treatise — the most recent, unprecedented and unexamined contribution to the debate over Milton's theology — that I now turn.

A Discourse on Method

"The Provenance of *De doctrina Christiana*," by Fiona Tweedie, David Holmes and Thomas Corns, offers a specialized and detailed explanation of the methodology behind the stylometric section of the larger committee's general report. It reveals that the investigators applied to a mid-seventeenth century, neo-Latin theological treatise the same stylometric method (the "Burrows technique") previously used for identifying the respective contributions of the multiple authors of the *Federalist Papers*, a late eighteenth century collection of American political essays written in English (*Computing*, 78).

Obviously, the *Federalist Papers* and *De doctrina Christiana* differ significantly, not least in the established state of knowledge concerning them prior to stylometric analysis. Investigators already knew who the authors of the *Federalist Papers* were, for example, and had other examples of Alexander Hamilton's, James Madison's and John Jay's political writings. They aimed only to match specific essays to the known authors on the basis of style. The investigators studying *De doctrina Christiana*, by contrast, did not enjoy prior knowledge of multiplicity in the treatise's authorship, nor did they possess other samples of Milton's style as an exegetical theologian writing in Latin. The quite distinct task the analysts of *De doctrina Christiana* set for the stylometric method was to discover which parts of the theological treatise lie closest to and farthest from Milton's neo-Latin stylistic practice in the polemical Defenses of the early 1650s. A dutiful employee of Cromwell's government, Milton wrote his Defenses very quickly in reply to Continental attacks on the English regicides. The Defenses, furthermore, are often closely modeled on Cicero's attacks on Catiline and Antony and so hardly qualify as examples of Milton's individually distinct style.[13] One might even claim that they represent yet another Miltonic "appropriation and transformation" of an ur-text. As the translator of the *Defensio* for the *Complete Prose Works* stresses, "no one style, in fact, can handle the variety of styles in Milton's Latin" (YP 4:296). As compared to the Defenses, the theological treatise took shape over many years and was continually revised. In short, despite circumstantial and generic differences between the composition of the Defenses and of the treatise, the investigators nevertheless hoped by comparing their styles to determine (1) if Milton was indeed the author of part or all of the treatise and (2) if some unidentified person wrote part or all of the treatise.

Contextual uncertainties necessarily render stylometric investigation of the treatise less conclusive than in the case of the relatively well-defined investigation of the *Federalist Papers*, and the investigators ought to have recognized as much. Although they made allowances for the shift in genre between polemical propaganda and exegetical theology, they did not and perhaps could not fully compensate for the circumstantial singularity of the problem they had set for the stylometric method. It bears repeating: the multiple authors of the *Federalist Papers* were already known; in the case of the *De doctrina Christiana*, by contrast, the investigators were attempting to determine on stylistic grounds whether, or to what extent, Milton was the author. Yet the report of the stylometric investigators acknowledges neither the crucial difference in the state of established knowledge under which the respective investigations were performed, nor the difference in the respective goals set for the same statistical method. Perhaps most crucially, it does not appreciate the vulnerability of the anachronistic premise on which the effectiveness of the methodology depends: that quirks of style make a useful criterion of authorship for a seventeenth century Latin treatise of exegetical theology.

De doctrina Christiana comes late in a centuries-old tradition of systematic Christian theology. The essays comprised by the *Federalist Papers*, by contrast, were written to explain and advocate a freshly invented document of republican governance. They do not address an ancient collection of sacred texts already the subject of massive volumes of commentary, nor were these late eighteenth century political essays composed within an extant tradition of writings justifying freshly invented constitutions of democratic governance. If its prefatory epistle is credible, *De doctrina Christiana* comes self-consciously in a long line of precedent doctrinal systems and offers not a justification of a document of political governance but a sect of one's minutely revised and adjusted statement of faith.

As opposed to the *Federalist Papers*, the theological treatise, according to its epistolary preface, developed from a theological commonplace book such as the one that Milton's contemporaries recall him compiling.[14] Authorship within a commonplace tradition implies readily observable stylistic consequences. The point is straightforward enough. Where *De doctrina Christiana* does *not* disagree with the exegetical tradition, as embodied in the works of Ames or Wollebius, for example, it simply restates it, though — and the import of this authorial contribution should not be underestimated — it often supplements the tradition with additional scriptural citations and fresh or altered arguments. As readers of Maurice Kelley's edition of the treatise can testify, its full and frequent annotation regularly quotes treatises to which *De doctrina Christiana* is indebted, sometimes revealing word for word repetition, and at other times significant departures. This laborious, historically informed, distinctively philological method for assessing an author's indebtedness to his precursors seems more useful than a quantitative measure of the text's deviance from normative Miltonic practice in, for example, the number of times it uses "et" or "in."

For all its heretical tenets, *De doctrina Christiana* is recognizably and categorically an early modern Protestant theological treatise. It is often quite orthodox, and many of its deviations from orthodoxy also depend on precedents within the tradition. Let us assume for the moment that Milton was its author. In that case, the committee's stylometric analysis would indicate only that where a conforming Milton was content simply to repeat some element of the commonplace tradition, the style of the treatise deviates from his own original Latin compositions. The treatise's discussion of the proper interpretation of Scripture, for example, includes the following observation:

> *sensus cuiusque scripturae unicus est; in veteri tamen testamento saepe est compositus ex historia et typo: exempli gratia in his Hoseae verbis, cap xi. 1. cum Matt. ii 15.*

On the same subject, Wollebius had previously written the following:

> *sensus cujusque Scripturae non nisi unicus est: in Veteris tamen Testamenti Vaticiniis saepe est compositus ex historia & typo. Exempli gratia, Hoseae xi. 1.*

One need not be a reader of Latin to see that Milton repeats Wollebius, mostly word for word. Yet, as Kelley observes after quoting these passages in his footnotes, "though Milton has lifted his paragraph from Wollebius, his is the common Protestant position of his age" (YP 6:581). Kelley's note then proceeds to cite other, similarly worded instances of this common Protestant opinion.

If one were to subject the above passage from *De doctrina Christiana* to stylometric analysis and compare the results to an identical analysis of Wollebius's theological treatise and of Milton's Latin defenses, one might suppose that Wollebius, not Milton, wrote the treatise. Analyzing yet another isolated passage according to the same procedure, one might well conclude that Ames or Beza or Bucer, not Milton, was the author. Such a variable, heterogeneous, stylistic profile is a function of authorship within a commonplace tradition, especially one as repetitive and as structurally isomorphic as Protestant systematic theology, or, to cite another generic example, Ramist logic. In making his contributions to these fields, Milton's authorial labor was largely that of a compiler and editor, rather than that of a stylist. The stylometric method deployed so usefully for the *Federalist Papers* can therefore tell us very little regarding the provenance of the treatise. It is rather like attempting to remove a nail with a wrench. Methodologically, statistical analysis of the treatise's style falls far short of providing the illuminating and usefully detailed contextual analysis that Kelley in his deeply informed edition offers.

The stylometric analysts neglect the obvious explanation for the heterogeneity of the treatise's style — Milton's reliance on the commonplace tradition — and assume instead that Milton was redacting some other author's original composition. The authors of the statistical analysis repeatedly appeal to Milton's deeply derivative *Artis Logicae* as an analogue (*Computing*, 78). In some ways the comparison is just. In its circumstantial origins and rhetorical occasion, the book on logic is considerably closer to the theological treatise than the polemical defenses are. The preface to *Artis Logicae* — itself heavily indebted to Downame's *Prolegomena* — acknowledges that the body of the text will consist of Ramus's already extant logical system, edited and interwoven with explanatory commentaries: "I have come to the conclusion that material from Ramus's own *Lectures on Dialectic* and from the commentaries by others necessary for the fuller understanding of the precepts of the art must be transferred to the body of the art proper and woven in there, except where I disagree with what these commentaries say" (YP 8:209–10). As Walter Ong observes in his introduction, "Downame weaves Ramus's text into his own commentary in snippets, sometimes slightly reworded to fit his own constructions, and Milton weaves Downame's text and often Ramus's text into his, sometimes taking Ramus's text in adjusted form from Downame, sometimes from Ramus's own" (YP 8:189). Ong does not hesitate to call the result Milton's "composition" as he traces how Milton, before he published it under his name, revised and adjusted previous Ramist texts to conform to his own, distinctive views about logic (YP 8:197). Hence, the text Milton produced clearly reflects, for example, his "deep-seated, if largely inarticulate, reserve about Ramist logic as it touched, or professed to touch, the persuasive and fictive uses of language" (YP 8:204). Scholars confidently consult *Artis Logicae* for an understanding of Milton's views on logic and cite it to illuminate relevant passages in his other writings.

Disregarding Ong's consistent recognition of Milton's authorship of *Artis Logicae*, as well as the plentiful evidence of its instructive pertinence to Milton's other writings, the stylometric analysts instead draw the following comparative conclusion:

> In the case of the *Artis Logicae*, we are fortunate to have the text on which Milton's work was based, and it is possible to track his emendations. Without access to the underlying text of *De doctrina Christiana*, there is no way of ascertaining which words are those of Milton and which are those of the original author. We have, though, in the *Artis Logicae*, a similar case to that which we have been revealing in this paper, namely a text by another author which Milton was revising, which could well account for the heterogeneity found by stylometric techniques. (*Computing*, 86)

The question-begging assumption is that the systematic theology of an "original author," whose treatise "Milton was revising," lies behind *De doctrina Christiana*. Even in the case of *Artis Logicae* it would be reductive and inaccurate to name Downame as the "original author" per the stylometricians' usage. Downame himself incorporates Ramus's text as well as the work of other commentators, and Ong characterizes Milton's obligations as far more multiple than the stylometricians acknowledge:

> [*Artis Logicae*] consists of the text of the *Dialectic* or *Logic* by the French philosopher and educational reformer . . . Petrus Ramus (1515–72), taken from Ramus's final revision of 1572, virtually intact, amalgamated into a longer explanation of the same material worked up by Milton from George Downame (or Downhame) and other commentators on Ramus and from some ideas of his own, the whole supplemented with an exercise in logical analysis adapted from Downame and an abridgment of the *Petri Rami vita* by Johann Thomas Freige (Freigius). The logic text proper is presented so that the work of Ramus, Milton, Downame, and the other commentators form one continuous text. (YP 8:144)

The situation with regard to *De doctrina Christiana* is even more complicated and multiple, defying complete description, just as the history of protestant systematic theology and scriptural interpretation is of far greater complexity, length and breadth than the history of Ramist logic. The name of the "original author" of *De doctrina Christiana*, I would submit, is legion, and philological scholars like Ong and Kelley have long referred to him under the rubric of the commonplace tradition.

Like the one preceding *Artis Logicae*, the prefatory epistle to *De doctrina Christiana* is forthcoming about the genesis of the work it introduces. Unlike the preface to the book on logic, however, the preface to the theological treatise seems to be indisputably Milton's own composition. With the possible exception of Hunter, everyone agrees on the authorship of the prefatory epistle. The general report of the committee investigating the provenance of *De doctrina Christiana* "most certainly concurs" with Barbara Lewalski's identification of Milton as its persona; its style, the report acknowledges, citing the statistical analysis, lies "close to the core of Miltonic practice" (*Computing*, 84). The same acknowledgment appears in the report devoted to the statistical investigation, which adds the following flat admission: "that Milton should have been wholly responsible for the Epistle to a book of much more complex authorial genesis is a hypothesis consistent with this analysis" (*Computing*, 84). Having quantified the epistle's distinctively Miltonic style, however, the investigators, as they do with the preface to the book on logic, ignore its content, which, as with the preface to *Artis Logicae*, has much to say about just that genesis:

> I made up my mind to puzzle out a religious creed for myself by my own exertions, and to acquaint myself with it thoroughly. . . . I began by devoting myself when I was a boy to an earnest study of the Old and New Testaments in their original languages, and then proceeded to go carefully through some of the shorter systems of theologians. I also started, following the example of these writers, to list under general headings all passages from the scriptures which suggested themselves for quotation, so that I might have them ready at hand when necessary. At length, gaining confidence, I transferred my attention to more diffuse volumes of divinity, and to the conflicting arguments in controversies over certain heads of faith. (YP 6:118–19)

Milton here claims, characteristically, that he began preparing to become the author of this treatise when still a boy, and what he says of his training matches what we already know about his education. If the treatise that follows this epistle is based on the work of someone besides Milton, it seems reasonable to ask why he does not say so — as the epistle to *Artis Logicae* forthrightly does. No precedent in Milton's personal or authorial history justifies the implication of such massive and intricately detailed dishonesty, especially concerning a text evidently so dear to him — his "dearest and best possession" (YP 6:121).

Statistical identification of the epistle's Miltonic style is useful and pertinent, obviously, but stylometric analysis nonetheless remains a limited and anachronistic tool for identifying the authorial distinctiveness of *De doctrina Christiana*. The underlying problem is one of definition, for the committee of investigators never indicates what it means by the term "author." In the epistle of the treatise, as we have seen, Milton admits that he assimilated antecedent systems of theology to establish general headings for his biblical research and to organize evidence on theologically controversial topics. In registering the presence of other writers' styles in the treatise, statistical analysis puts a number on what the epistle already acknowledges and what Maurice Kelley's discriminating philology had previously detailed — that Milton did not choose or on the local level order many of the words that constitute what Milton nevertheless considered his work. Selection and ordering of the words in a text are not useful or pertinent qualifications for authorship of a seventeenth century Latin treatise in exegetical theology. Nor should the measurement of style in any way affect our judgment of whether it can be legitimately considered indicative of its author's opinions.

To hold any of Milton's works to an authorial standard of original diction and phrasing is to misunderstand seventeenth century practices of authorship in general and Milton's method of writing in particular. Many memorable passages in Milton's prose — and poetry — are of questionable origin, things formerly attempted in prose or rhyme.[15] In the case of *Paradise Lost*, the provenance of divine oratory or of angels' hymns is primarily scriptural, though Homer has his moments in God's self-representation. Yet in recognizing Milton's use of his models, we do not ask that students doubt his authorship of the epic or presume that an ur-text lies behind his revision.[16] Renaissance authors' customary method of deploying commonplaces has been historically situated by Walter Ong in his edition of *Artis Logicae*: "no one hesitated to use lines of thought or even quite specific wordings from another person without crediting the other person, for these were all taken to be, and most often were, part of the common tradition" (YP 8:187). Seventeenth century authorship is not a function of diction and syntax.

Stylometric analysis cannot register — is a method oblivious to — the contextual import of the words it counts or the intention of the author who chose to incorporate them. Most critically in the case of Milton's theology, it is a method incapable of assessing the author's use and compilation of evidence. The report of the statistical investigation, like the report of the larger committee that it supports, seems unaware of this limitation. In preparing a sample for analysis, the stylometricians blithely eliminated the strongest evidence of Milton's authorial labor. The general committee's report, confirmed by the stylometric investigators' account, describes the preparation of the sample in two noteworthy sentences: "Minimal pre-processing was carried out: ampersands were converted to 'et,' hyphenations were reformatted and quotations were removed. The last procedure changed the electronic version of *De Doctrina* considerably as the resulting 60,000 words of text were derived from almost 90,000 words of original text" (*MQ* 106). Deletion of one third of the sample, the scriptural quotations, is noted in the same breath as the conversion of ampersands.

To appreciate the methodological blindness of the "minimal pre-processing," mark how the epistle to the treatise, which, it is worth repeating, everyone agrees Milton wrote, distinguishes his treatise from those by other authors:

> Most authors who have dealt with this subject at the greatest length in the past have been in the habit of filling their pages

almost entirely with expositions of their own ideas. . . . I, on the other hand, have striven to cram my pages even to overflowing with quotations drawn from all parts of the Bible and to leave as little space as possible for my own words, even when they arise from the putting together of actual scriptural texts. (YP 6:122)

In *A Scripture Index to John Milton's "De doctrina christiana,"* Michael Bauman, a doctor of theology with expertise in Protestant religious systematics, testifies to the accuracy of Milton's account: "After nearly twenty years of studying Christian doctrine, I have discovered no systematic theology, Protestant or other, that is even remotely as biblically grounded as Milton's. For page after page, the range and number of his biblical references easily outstrip those of every other comparable text." According to Bauman, Milton cites Scripture 9,346 times in his treatise; Calvin, by comparison, offers only 5,574 biblical references in the lengthier *Institutes*.[17]

In contrast to Bauman's relatively modest but shrewdly applied arithmetic, the committee's method precludes notice of Milton's most distinctive authorial practice — his extraordinary dependence on and synthesis of Scripture. William B. Hunter has recently dismissed this objection to the stylometric investigation by noting that inasmuch as Milton is certainly not the author of Scripture, its presence in the treatise is irrelevant to the stylometric investigation.[18] Milton, admittedly, did not compose the various versions of Scripture that appear in *De doctrina Christiana*. But I would argue that we should reverse the conclusion Hunter draws. To the degree that stylometry cannot measure Milton's use of Scripture, the stylometric method, not Scripture, becomes irrelevant to the question of authorship of the treatise. Why should Milton scholars turn for answers to a method that cannot assess such basic evidence of authorial labor? Few writers are more adept or distinctive than Milton in using Scripture. In his theological treatise, Milton may well exceed — as indeed in his prefatory epistle he suggests he will — every other systematic Christian theology in his reliance on Scripture. He crams his pages with biblical verses, leaving as little space as possible for his own words. A method that cannot appreciate this distinctive characteristic of *De doctrina Christiana*, nor account for the influence of the commonplace tradition, must be deemed a severely limited tool for the investigation of its provenance.

Conclusion

The question of authorship remains among the most vexed theoretical issues in literary studies. But if we apply ordinary standards of attribution for seventeenth century texts, Milton may be confidently identified as the author of *De doctrina Christiana*. Ironically, the evidence detailed in the report of the self-constituted general committee, as well as the evidence provided in the special report of the stylometric investigators, confirms this attribution. But the conclusions of the general committee and of the stylometric subcommittee do not take their own evidence into account. The documentary evidence reviewed and usefully augmented by the historical arm of the committee places the manuscript in Milton's possession during the 1650s. The stylometric investigators confirm Barbara Lewalski's intuition when they with mathematical if not Gorgonian rigor identify the chooser of words in the treatise's prefatory epistle as Milton. The statistically certified author of the prefatory epistle — Milton — describes the treatise as his own, and neither the historical nor the statistical side of the committee offers evidence or hypothetical motivation for Milton's deceiving his readers on this score.

It seems that the two sides of the committee investigating the provenance of Milton's theological treatise would have profited from communicating better with each other. The historical side accepts that the author of the prefatory epistle tells the truth when he calls the treatise his own. Hence, the historical portion of the general report asks why the true author would let Milton retain it: "but if it were not Milton's, why, given how important it seems to have been to its author, did Milton retain it?" (*MQ* 97). The only evidence we possess that the treatise was important to its author lies in the prefatory epistle. The report thus tacitly accepts that the author of the prefatory Epistle is as he claims the author of the treatise. The stylometric investigators in turn identify the author of the epistle as Milton, effectively reducing the historical portion's conditional "if it were not Milton's" to a hypothetical condition demonstrably contrary to fact. This curious incongruity between the historical and stylometric portions of the general report was even more pronounced when the report was published electronically in draft form. In this draft report, section 4 of the historical portion, quoting from the prefatory Epistle, asks why the manuscript of the treatise (SP 9/61) would have been entrusted to the untrustworthy Daniel Skinner: "the author of SP 9/61 calls [it] 'my best and richest possession' ('*quibus melius et pretiosus nihil habeo*')."[19] The version of section 4 included in the printed version of the report, however, omits this citation of the epistle and ends abruptly. One wonders why the historical portion of the committee chose to delete the draft's quotation of the prefatory epistle. We may never receive an adequate answer concerning authorial revision of a document of such complex authorial genesis, one that is moreover so internally inconsistent as to be self-contradictory. We are, however, certainly justified in concluding that such a document can hardly be deemed a reliable guide to the provenance of Milton's *De doctrina Christiana*.

10 • Milton and the Socinian Heresy

Michael Lieb

In what appears to be an ongoing tendency in modern criticism, scholars are ever more inclined to align Milton with the various heresies that emerged with renewed vigor during the revolutionary decades of the seventeenth century. Most recently, the fine essays that constitute Stephen B. Dobranski and John Rumrich's collection *Milton and Heresy* suggest the extent to which the "orthodox Milton" has increasingly given way to the "heretical Milton." In the volume's introduction, appropriately subtitled "Heretical Milton," Dobranski and Rumrich distinguish between two constructions of Milton that have arisen throughout the centuries, one orthodox (grounded in the time-honored traditions of Christian humanism), the other heterodox (grounded in the radical crosscurrents of Milton's own age). "It seems absurd," they contend, that Milton "could be heard as a voice of orthodoxy. Yet twentieth century scholars have often understated, explained away, or otherwise soft-pedaled his heretical beliefs."[1] Conceived in this manner,

Milton is one whose works become the repository of either overt or covert heretical views that, sufficiently understood, invite a reassessment of his radical habits of mind. To be sure, such a conception is hardly new. As Christopher Hill's pioneering study *Milton and the English Revolution* made clear more than two decades ago, the conception of a heretical Milton is part of a continuing process of resituating him in the context of the heterodox and often conflicting crosscurrents and movements that distinguish his own radical milieu, one in which Milton himself was a major player.[2] I view the tendency to venture the notion of a heretical Milton not with alarm but with excitement at the potential disclosures that such an approach might yield. At the same time, I am deeply aware that one must resist the temptation simply to "label" Milton as this kind of heretic or that kind of heretic.

Hill himself purports to be sensitive to the dangers of labeling: a great fuss, he avers, is sometimes made concerning the precise heresy with which to label Milton. "Was he," Hill asks rhetorically, "an Arian? A Nestorian? A Monarchian? A Sabellian? A subordinationist? Or was he a Socinian?" As Hill well knows, it is axiomatic that labels of any sort are dangerous. He accordingly maintains that Milton was "an eclectic, the disciple of no individual thinker," or heresy, for that matter.[3] As Janel Mueller reminds us, "heresy," as a "keyword" with its root in *hairesis*, carries the meaning of "seizing" or "taking hold," which then implies "choice" in the sense of an "inclination." At its root, it is neutral in its implications.[4] This is an etymology of which Milton was certainly aware and did not hesitate to articulate in his works.[5] Thus, in his *Treatise of Civil Power*, he maintains that heresy "is no word of evil note; meaning the choice or following of any opinion good or bad in religion or any other learning" (YP 7:247). As Milton argues in *Areopagitica*, right choice involves the exercise of reason informed by a full awareness of the distinction between "good or bad." One way or the other, this choice must be made, not because we follow the dictates of others but because we attend to the dictates of our own judgment. "A man may be a heretick in the truth; and if he beleeve things only because his Pastor sayes so, or the Assembly so determins, without knowing their reason, though his belief be true, yet the very truth he holds, becomes his heresie" (YP 2:543). As much as Milton sought to distinguish between one form of heresy or another, he became painfully aware of the extent to which he himself had to suffer the indignity of being cast as heretical by his enemies. Thus branded heretic for his views on divorce, he portrays himself as one among others "nam'd and printed Hereticks" ("On the Forcers of Conscience," 638) in the "gangraenas" and "heresiographies" of his day.[6] In these vehicles of slander, labels of one sort or another abounded during Milton's own lifetime. As David Masson observes, one always ran the risk of being decried as an "Atheist," a "Mortalist," a "Materialist," an "Anti-Sabbatarian," an "Anti-Scripturalist," an "Anti-Trinitarian" or a "Socinian" or "Arian." Equally appalling, one might (in the same vein) also be branded a "Divorcer" or "Miltonist."[7] Some will no doubt derive a certain satisfaction in realizing that (in Milton's time, at least) to claim oneself a "Miltonist" was tantamount to claiming oneself a heretic. Modern Miltonists (at least, those who view Milton in heretical terms, as opposed to those who view him in orthodox terms) might well consider the label a cause of celebration rather than an occasion of dismay. Instead of writing gangraenas and heresiographies, Miltonists of the heretical bent are producing smart books (like *Milton and Heresy*) that provide a balanced and illuminating assessment of where the heretical Milton stands and why.

In keeping with these studies, as well as with Milton's view of heresy as the product of one's ability to choose wisely through the exercise of reason and informed judgment, I shall focus on one heresy in particular, that of Socinianism (later to be known as Unitarianism), a movement of immense importance to Milton's milieu.[8] As Christopher Hill observes, "there are general histories of Unitarianism and of Socinianism in which Milton's name occurs, but no study [of Milton] in light of this tradition." This is not to say that scholars have been remiss in attending to the Socinian elements in Milton's thought. More than three decades before Hill's own book on Milton and the revolution, H. John McLachlan, the great scholar of Socinianism, produced a study of the religious opinions of Milton, Locke and Newton. Perhaps because of McLachlan's predilections, the "opinions" in question are seen as decidedly "Unitarian," but, despite his inclination to overstate his case at times, McLachlan's work is important in its determination to approach Milton from a decidedly radical perspective.[9] As we shall see, moreover, the notion of pairing Milton's religious views with those of such figures as Locke and Newton is hardly unique to the Unitarian outlook embraced by McLachlan. More recently, Hugh MacCallum has advanced an argument about the Socinian (as well as other radical) elements in Milton's thought that is as illuminating as it is judicious. It lays the groundwork superbly for its own conclusion that Milton's theology "was shaped to a significant extent" by its response to Socinianism.[10]

In keeping with Hill's call for a study of Milton in light of the Socinian tradition and responsive to the important work of scholars such as McLachlan and MacCallum, I shall examine two issues of major import. The first concerns the emergence of Socinianism as a movement and the relationship between that movement and Milton's own doctrinal outlook. The second concerns the afterlife of the movement and the manner in which critics of Milton in the two centuries following upon his death saw fit to interpret his theological views in Socinian terms. What I present here, then, is a contextualizing of Milton and his works in light of the growth of Socinianism, as well as a survey of some significant moments in the critical history of reading Milton as a writer of the "Socinian persuasion." I undertake this essay not with the idea of demonstrating that Milton overtly subscribed to the beliefs that constitute

Socinianism (he most decidedly did not) but to suggest that Hill's astute estimate of Milton as "an eclectic, the disciple of no individual thinker" is as true of his ties to the Socinians as it is of his ties to any one of the sectarian movements that distinguish his radical milieu.

1

The Socinian movement has a long and complex doctrinal history, which can only be summarized briefly here. Especially in the case of Socinianism, a summary of this sort is difficult because so much of what is known about the movement must be derived from its critics and opponents. Like the early Christian heresies (one thinks of Arianism, for example), Socinianism "often suffered from being known largely at second hand." In some respects, Socinianism might be said to have existed as a construction in the works of its enemies. According to McLachlan, "Socinian" was invoked as a general term to encompass different kinds of heterodoxies. Thus, "in an age when nice discrimination between heresies could hardly be expected, 'Socinians' were all who departed radically from the orthodox Christian scheme of redemption or found difficulty with the metaphysical notions enshrined in Catholic doctrinal formulae."[11] The name "Socinus" is derived from the Sienese family known as Sozzini or Sozini. Those opposed to the Socinians invoked the name as a term of opprobrium no doubt with the idea that "Sozzini" as a word has affinities with Italian terms that denote such meanings as "filthy," "nasty," "foul," "obscene" and "polluted."[12] According to Paul M. Zall, detractors spoke of the Socinians with the awareness that "Sozzini" as a term might well imply "filthy little people."[13] Being branded a "Socinian" was accordingly much more demeaning than being branded a "Miltonist."

The history of Socinianism goes back to Lelio Sozzini (1525–1562) and his nephew Fausto Sozzini (1539–1604), who were at the forefront of the Antitrinitarian movement that left its mark on the emergence of religious radicalism in the Reformation. Having established close contacts with Melanchthon, Calvin and Bullinger, Lelio Sozzini was suspected of heresy and obliged to prepare a Confession of Faith, one of the few surviving documents from his hand. At his death in Zurich, he left his library and papers to his nephew Fausto. A student of logic and law, Fausto Sozzini, in turn, produced several important works on biblical hermeneutics, Christology and soteriology. In 1579, he took up residence in Poland, where he became a prominent figure in the Polish congregation (Minor Reformed Church) at Rakow, northeast of Krakow. There, his own theology was later fused with that of the Polish Brethren, who had already devised a Latin *Catechesis* (1574) to express their own Antitrinitarian beliefs. A year after Sozzini's death, a revised *Catechesis* (1605), the work of four ministers who were close disciples of Fausto, was published in Polish, followed by German (1608) and Latin (1609) editions.[14] The 1605 *Catechesis* appeared under the editorship of Peter Statorius Stoinski, assisted by Fausto, as far as his time and strength would permit. It is assumed that Fausto's own *Christianae Religionis brevissimo Institutio* (unfinished before his death) was possibly the first draft of the revised *Catechesis*, but, if so, the draft was entirely recast. Although representing Fausto's views, the 1605 *Catechesis* was both in arrangement and expression the product of others.[15] During the seventeenth century, the work was issued in some 15 editions and translated into several languages (including Latin, Dutch and English) as it made its way throughout Europe.[16] Although customarily ascribed to Fausto Sozzini, the *Catechesis* or *The Racovian Catechism*, then, is a composite (and, to some extent, evolving) work that encompasses a broad range of ideas, not all of them necessarily in accord with Fausto's own views.[17]

Departing from the customary lines and conventional categories of the Protestant confession (such as the Augsburg and the Helvetic confessions), *The Racovian Catechism* bases its doctrines not on earlier systems of divinity or prevailing creeds but on direct recourse to Scripture.[18] As the ultimate source of all belief, Scripture assumes the form of a *corpus juris* through which a mind trained in the legal methods of reasoning is able to explore its teachings inductively, methodically and, above all, rationally. As a result of those explorations, one is able to construct a system of theology entirely consistent with the teachings of Scripture. Those teachings may contain things above reason but not in any sense contrary to reason. Through the exercise of reason in the discovery of the teachings of Scripture, one is able to attain eternal life.[19] The text of Scripture is entirely accessible as a means of arriving at a knowledge of God. The knowledge of God and his will as manifested in Christ provides the way to salvation. What results is very much a text-centered and reason-centered theology. The knowledge of God, in turn, involves the knowledge of both his nature and his will. God in his nature is one and only one, not three.[20] God's nature, moreover, is perfectly just, wise and powerful.[21] There is room in the Racovian system for neither the orthodox concept of the Trinity nor for an inscrutable God whose ways run counter to our understanding. The preincarnate Son does not exist as a person or entity in the godhead, nor, for that matter, does the Holy Spirit, which is understood as the virtue and power of God.[22] Jesus Christ, in turn, is in his nature a real man, not the product of a mysterious union of divine and human.[23] Thus, *The Racovian Catechism* challenges not only the orthodox idea of the Trinity but the notion of the hypostatical union.[24]

If Christ's innate deity is denied, God does bestow upon him an adoptive deity, but only as the result of his successfully and gloriously fulfilling his role as suffering servant in this life. That reward is bestowed after Christ's Resurrection and Ascension. Then, Christ assumes his proper place at the right hand of God, where he shares in God's power over the government of the world.[25] Although Christ possesses a fully human nature in this life, he is nonetheless not an ordinary man. His ability to fulfill God's call in living a life of such sanctity is proof of his holiness. As a sign of his holiness, he is given the power to work miracles. In its soteriology, the *Catechism* as a Socinian document emphasizes, then, not the Crucifixion of Christ as the work of salvation but the Resurrection and Ascension of Christ as a sign of the eventual salvation of his brethren in the fullness of time. The work of salvation, however, is not in any way tied to the doctrine of penal satisfaction. Christ does not die in order to atone for our sins, nor is his willingness to undergo the Crucifixion a sign of that atonement.[26] The purpose of Christ's sufferings is to demonstrate how we might best bear our own sins and work out our salvation through Christ's holy example.[27] The *Catechism*, then, dismisses the traditional, orthodox formulations of Christ's role as savior, a role that presupposes in God the need to maintain justice with the concomitant willingness to accept the death of his innocent Son as a substitute for the punishment of the wicked. There is in Socinian theology no sense of the traditional debate between love and wrath in the godhead as a process culminating in the ultimate expression of grace. Such an idea runs entirely counter to the Socinian view of a mild, reasonable and temperate God.

In the expression of his will, God bestows upon Christ the offices of prophet, king and priest, a traditional paradigm. But not so traditional is the implementation of that paradigm. As prophet, Christ performs his role of teaching his followers the ways of God, but in the capacity of prophet, Christ does not extend his vocation in this life beyond his knowledge as one who is fully human. Christ performs his priestly role not so much as a sacrifice but as an intercessor in heaven after his Resurrection and Ascension have been realized. In his kingly office, he exercises the supreme power bestowed upon him, once again, after he rises from the dead and is seated at God's right hand. In matters of worship, the *Catechism* recognizes only one sacrament, that of the Lord's Supper, which is viewed as an event commemorating the death of Christ. As an outward act through which Christian converts openly acknowledge Christ as their master, baptism is neither appropriate to infants nor possessed of any regenerative value. Other doctrines voiced in the *Catechism* include a belief in the freedom of the will, as opposed to predestination. Nor is there in Socinian thought an acceptance of the doctrine of original sin that infects all mankind as a result of Adam's fall. In the process, Socinus calls into question the notion of a prelapsarian Adam endowed with peculiar gifts bestowed upon him at birth and lost in the Fall.[28] These, in brief, are some of the major doctrinal beliefs articulated in *The Racovian Catechism* and in Socinian thought in general.

As the most authoritative statement of what came to be known as the theology of Socinianism, *The Racovian Catechism* (1605), in its various translations, found its way into Germany, Holland, England and France. In England, it made its first appearance in the Latin edition of 1609. With no doubt the hope of gaining royal sanction, those responsible for the Latin edition published the work with a dedication to James I, who subsequently responded by having it consigned to the fires as a pernicious and heretical document. Its initial presence in England, then, was hardly auspicious. Considering the spirit of intolerance toward any ideas deemed heretical during this period, one need hardly be surprised at the reception that *The Racovian Catechism* was accorded. Intolerance was the order of the day. It was not just works deemed heretical that faced immolation: the very bodies of heretics were in danger of enduring the same fate. Between 1548 and 1612 at least 18 persons were burned at the stake for their heretical (particularly Antitrinitarian) views.[29] The author (or authors) of *The Racovian Catechism* would most certainly have qualified in 1609. About a decade after its first appearance in 1609, *The Racovian*

Catechism was reissued in one or two surreptitious editions, but with little effect. "In all England," Zall comments, "there seems not to have been a Socinian congregation — at least one meeting openly — before 1652/53 when John Biddle ('the father of English Unitarianism') is supposed to have preached to a like-minded group in London."[30]

Shortly after midcentury, however, Socinianism and its doctrines gained greater currency, principally because of the impact of the movement in Holland, where more than 60 Socinian books had been published, either as reprints of Polish originals or in Dutch and English translations. No doubt many of these books found their way to English soil. In fact, even before midcentury, harsh precautionary measures were adopted, in part, to stem the tide of Socinianism, which was well known to be gaining ground. In 1640 a convocation of leading ministers in Parliament sitting as a synod framed a new body of constitutions and canons for establishing true religion. The fourth canon was directed against "the damnable and cursed heresy of Socinianism." Forbidden was the importation, printing and dispersion of Socinian books, as well as the preaching of Socinian doctrines. Books that smacked of Socinianism were ordered destroyed. Although the canons were never enforced, they provide clear evidence that Socinianism was on the rise.[31] Ever vigilant to stem the rising tide of heresy, Parliament passed the so-called Blasphemy Act of 1648.[32] A glance at the act leaves little room to doubt that Socinianism is among the heresies that the act sought to interdict. Those who subscribed to this heresy were to face the possibility of imprisonment or death.[33] In its indictment of Antitrinitarianism (as that which asserts "the Father is not God, the Son is not God, or that the Holy Ghost is not God, or that they three are not one Eternal God"), the act then interdicts any assertion that "Christ is not God equal with the Father." At the same time, the act labels anathema any "that shall deny his [Christ's] death is meritorious in the behalf of Believers; or that shall maintain and publish as aforesaid, That Jesus Christ is not the Son of God." The act also holds as erroneous any assertion "that man is bound to believe no more than by his reason he can comprehend." These blasphemies and others (all of which smack of Socinianism) are branded anathema by the Blasphemy Act.[34]

To counter the spread of Socinianism, writers such as Francis Cheynell, Ephraim Pagitt, Thomas Edwards, John Owen, Bernard Skelton, Francis Fullwood, Edward Stillingfleet and John Tillotson rallied to the cause of orthodoxy in their respective works.[35] Reviewing their works reveals the extent to which Socinianism progressively becomes a label for "heresy" in general, a heresy of danger both to the individual and to the state. Thus, in his tract *The Rise, Growth, and Danger of Socinianism* (1643), Francis Cheynell argues passionately against all the corruptions that the heresy of Socinus represents. These corruptions are reflected in the very subtitle of Cheynell's tract: Socinianism, the subtitle declares, is *"not the pure Protestant religion, but an hotchpotch of Arminianisme, Socinianisme and popery."* According to Cheynell, "the *Socinian* Errour is *Fundamentall.*" Those guilty of it "deny Christs satisfaction and so overthrow the foundation of our faith, the foundation of our Justification." Moreover, "they deny the Holy Trinity, and so take away the very object of our Faith; they deny the Resurrection of these [sic] Bodies, and so take away the foundation of our hope." Still further, "they deny originall sinne, and so take away the ground of our Humiliation; and indeed the necessity of regeneration." Finally, "they advance the power of Nature, and destroy the efficacy of Grace." Socinianism, for Cheynell, is an *"Antichristian* errour, because it takes away the very Essence and Person of *Iesus Christ."* This is the damnable heresy that has infected all of England.[36] Such sentiments are reflected in the writings of other anti-Socinians as well. In sympathy with the kinds of allegations leveled in Cheynell's tract, both Ephraim Pagitt and Thomas Edwards include the Socinians in their respective heresiographies. For

Pagitt and Edwards, Socinianism is to be paired with Arianism, both of which are dreaded forms of Antitrinitarianism, a "gangrenous" heresy sweeping the nation in the 1640s.[37]

The anti-Socinian rhetoric that characterizes the 1640s continued throughout the century. The "hammer of the Socinians," John Owen, is a prime example of one in whom that rhetoric flourished anew. Commissioned by the Council of State, Owen produced his *Vindiciae evangelicae* (1655), in which he pounded not only John Biddle and *The Racovian Catechism* but Hugo Grotius, whom Owen considered something of a Socinian in his views.[38] Among the issues with which the critics of Socinianism were intolerant is what they argued was the fallacious Socinian overdependence on the supreme efficacy of human reason to determine doctrinal matters. In *A Brief Declaration and Vindication of the Doctrine of the Trinity* (1676), Owen asks rhetorically:

> *What Reason* do they [the Socinians] intend? If Reason absolutely, the Reason of things; we grant that nothing *contrary* unto it, is to be admitted. But Reason as it is in this or that Man, particularly in themselves, we know to be weak, maimed, and imperfect; and that they are, and all other Men, extreamly remote from a just and full comprehension of the whole Reason of things.[39]

For Owen and a host of other writers during this period, Socinianism becomes not just a danger but *the* archetypal heresy, one that embodies all other heresies, ancient and modern. In keeping with this view, Bernard Skelton thus maintains in *Christus Deus* (1692) that Socinus, like "that grand Impostor *Mahomet*," was not so much a "*Heretick*" as (what is even worse) "the founder of a new Religion," one that is a "composition of the errors of *Arius, Photinus*, and *Pelagius*," among many other heresies that might be mixed in this anti-Christian brew.[40] Worst of all, however, God in Socinian doctrine is transformed from a Christian to a Judaic deity. The Socinian God, Skelton avers, is indeed "purely *Judaical*," a view (for

Skelton) tantamount to the very *"renunciation of the Christian Religion."*[41]

To be sure, the God of the Socinians is *one God*, an outlook in keeping with their "unitarian" theology. More than that, he is in effect a "person." So John Biddle argues in *The Apostolical and True Opinion concerning the Holy Trinity* (1653): "To talk of God taken impersonally, is ridiculous, not only because there is no Example thereof in Scripture, but because God is the Name of a Person, and signifieth him that hath sublime Dominion or Power; and when it is put for the most High God, it denoteth him who with Soveraign and Absolute Authority ruleth over all."[42] Biddle's God, one might suggest, is very much influenced by the delineation of deity in Hebrew Scripture. If not "purely *Judaical*," the conception is certainly indebted to that rendering. It is a rendering upon which the Socinians would look most sympathetically.[43] The anti-Socinians, on the other hand, viewed this, as well as other Socinian doctrines, with suspicion, if not scorn. At the root of this sentiment was a fundamental concern with the Socinian method of interpreting Scripture as a source of doctrinal belief. If one were confident that all doctrine is entirely accessible through the practical application of the principles of logic to the sacred text free of recourse to faith in higher mystery, there is no telling what absurdities might result.

Centered in the rhetoric of anti-Socinianism, this concern was so widespread throughout the century that it even found its way into the "poetical" mainstream. Thus in his *Religio Laici* (1682), John Dryden asks, "Are there not many points, some needful sure / To saving faith, that scripture leaves obscure? / . . . We hold, and say we prove from scripture plain, that Christ is God"; on the other hand, "the bold Socinian / From the same scripture urges he's but man" (307–15). Conflating Arianism and Socinianism in *The Hind and the Panther* (1687), Dryden follows this assault on Socinian methodology by focusing on the central issue of the Son's divinity. Arius and Socinus, Dryden laments, "disavowed" the Son's "eternal god-head" and "condemned" true doctrine through the blatant misreading of "Gospel Texts." Like all such "hereticks," the Arians and Socinians have used the "same pretence" of piety to "plead the scriptures in their own defence" (150–55).[44] The point is that the controversy over Socinian and anti-Socinian (and, with it, Arian and anti-Arian) modes of thought became a staple of the intellectual life of seventeenth century England and beyond. For those determined to root out Socinian thinking, no one was above reproach. This is true even if one protested his innocence in the face of the charge of allegiance (of whatever sort) to the doctrines associated with Socinianism. In response to the question "Are you now, or have you ever been?," one might exclaim "No!" but be judged guilty nonetheless.

John Locke (1632–1704) represents a major instance of this dilemma. Although he disavowed the Socinian label in public, he has been viewed as a Socinian both by friend and enemy alike. Those sympathetic to the Socinian cause have, in fact, deemed Locke (not without justification) "the Socinus of his age."[45] In accord with the Socinian writings, Locke's works are said to reveal "the same lay disengagement from scholasticism, the same purpose of toleration tempered by prudence, the same interest in the minimising of essentials, and the same recurrence to Scripture, interpreted (that is to say, rationalised) by common sense rather than by profound exegesis."[46] The one work that has elicited this claim is Locke's *The Reasonableness of Christianity, as Delivered in the Scriptures* (1695) a tract that seeks to demonstrate that all that is needful for saving faith is already present in New Testament teachings (as opposed, implicitly, to the extratestamental teachings of the church). Those determined to enlist Locke to their cause have observed that the very title of the work is consistent with the Socinian emphasis upon Christianity as a religion essentially grounded on the rational precepts of Scripture.[47] In keeping with this thrust is a distinction between what might be called "Scriptural Christianity and the Christianity of the Schools." In the work itself, it is significant that "the word *Trinity* is not so much as mentioned," nor is there "the slightest intimation" that the Trinity is to be regarded "as a fundamental doctrine of the Gospel."[48] Along with the erasure of the Trinity is an emphasis upon the Sonship as a result not of the Incarnation but of the Resurrection, by which means, Locke avers, we may find evidence that Jesus became the "Son of God" (7:108). It is this sort of evidence, we are told, that leads the careful reader to the realization that Locke supports the Socinian cause. The extent to which Locke was or was not a "Socinian" is not at issue. What *is* at issue is the way in which those who support the Socinian cause are determined to "read" him as a Socinian.

During Locke's own time, this kind of reading was the distinguishing characteristic of the anti-Socinians. Although Locke mentions nothing of Socinus or Socinianism in *The Reasonableness of Christianity*, such an omission in no way dissuaded the heresy police (ever attentive to the possibility of heterodoxy) from picking up on what they considered a distinctly Socinian frame of mind. Notable in this regard is John Edwards, the stalwart son of Thomas Edwards of *Gangraena* fame. Responding to Locke's *Reasonableness*, John Edwards produced *Socinianism Unmask'd* (1696), through which he takes Locke to task for exhibiting Socinian tendencies. In his tirade, Edwards goes so far as to transform "Socinianism" into a verb: "Socinianize." Even though one does not claim himself a "Socinian," he may be termed such if he (wittingly or unwittingly) "Socinianizes." (One must be careful not to get caught "Socinianizing" in public.) As much as one attempts to hide his Socinianizing tendencies, the truth will out. "The plain truth," the ever-vigilant Edwards exclaims, is that Locke "*Socinianizes*" throughout his work. He does so not directly but obliquely, through a kind of conspiracy of silence. By not mentioning the doctrine of the Trinity, for example, Locke implicitly accepts the Socinian view that such a phenomenon does not really exist. By not mentioning the true doctrine of satisfaction, Locke once again accepts the Socinian view that satisfaction is finally not efficacious. What Edwards lights upon is Locke's "utter silence" concerning sacred matters that are a mainstay of orthodox belief.[49] In short, Edwards reads Locke's silences as evidence of subversive thought; and in the interstices of Locke's exegesis, Edwards sees heresy. It is this criticism by absence that renders Edwards so interesting, for one does not need to be a professed "heretic" before one is in danger of encountering charges of heresy in one's thought and writings.

Locke responded to these charges in two works: *A Vindication of the Reasonableness of Christianity* (1696), followed by *A Second Vindication of the Reasonableness of Christianity* (1697). In both treatises, Locke disavows any ties to Socinianism, its beliefs and its doctrines. Rather, he charges Edwards with trying to frighten people from reading his books by invoking that dreaded bugbear "Socinianism, Socinianism!" Responding to this bugbear, Locke challenges Edwards to "show one word of Socinianism" in his writings.[50] The point, of course, is that the absence of overt statement does not mean that the heresy is not present. Perhaps Edwards is right, after all: Locke Socinianizes in the most subtle of ways, that is, through a subtext of silence. At least, this is how he has been interpreted by those determined to find in his works elements of Socinian belief. Whether or not those elements are present in Locke's writings, his own outlook embraces a latitudinarianism that infuses all his writings but especially his three Letters on Toleration. In the first of these, he declares that, although he has "doubts about the faith of the Socinians," among other forms of heterodoxy, "it is not the diversity of opinions" but "the refusal of toleration to diverse opinions" that has brought about "most of the disputes and wars that have arisen in the Christian world on account of religion."[51] Socinian or not, Locke is a tolerationist who eschews labels. At the same time, his writings are sufficiently complex to suggest (even in their silences) the possibility of "alien" modes of thought.

Locke is not alone in his embrace of doctrines that might well prompt both his friends and his enemies to read Socinianism in his writings. Of a similar frame of mind is Locke's intimate friend Sir Isaac Newton (1642–1727), one who has likewise been thought to subscribe (albeit surreptitiously) to a theology at odds with accepted orthodoxy. Unlike the works that Locke produced on matters of religion, Newton's writings on Christology and soteriology were never made public during his lifetime, perhaps because of fears of reprisal. Accordingly, there was no opportunity for the likes of John Edwards to issue a *Socinianism Unmask'd* in response to Newton's speculations. Although Newton never openly departed from the teachings of the Church of England, his posthumous works and his unpublished papers appear to tell a different story. After Newton's death, his friend John Craig, prebendary of Salisbury, maintained that Newton "was much more solicitous in his inquirys into Religion than into Natural Philosophy," because his thoughts on matters of religion were at times "different from those which are commonly received."[52]

During his lifetime, Newton vacillated about whether to publish any of his theological writings, a notable instance of which is a work in the form of letters exposing as false the customary Trinitarian proof texts of 1 Timothy 3:16 and 2 John 5:7.[53] In 1690, Newton considered the possibility of publishing these letters anonymously in Holland but then presumably withdrew them "in panic" because of his fears of possible repercussions. Although Newton in old age "committed numerous documents to the flames," he nonetheless "spared these letters and scores of other theological manuscripts," among them, "A Short Scheme of True Religion," detailed commentaries on Daniel and Revelation, and an attack on Athanasius entitled "Paradoxical Questions Concerning the Morals and Actions of Athanasius and His Followers." Newton's manuscripts reveal God as one whose servants live "ever under the Taskmaster's eye." For Newton, God becomes a *"dominus deus, pantokrator, Imperator universalis."* Although Christ is present, his role is distinctly "recessive." In his account of the God of Newton's manuscripts, Frank E. Manuel ventures a psychological analysis of such an outlook by suggesting that Newton, as a child born after his father's death, engaged in a search for "the Father" throughout his life. "Overwhelmed by his preoccupation with origins," Newton revealed an "anguished desire" to recover his "lost parent." Questions of theology for Newton were "invested with personal feelings that had their roots in the earlier experiences of childhood." Aware of his special bond to God, Newton looked upon himself as one destined to reveal "the ultimate truth about God's creation." In the words of Alexander Pope, *"God* said: let Newton be! And all was light." Significantly, the phrase *Jeova sanctus unus* became for Newton an anagram for "Isaacus Neuutonus."[54]

However one might respond to such an analysis of Newton's psychological motivations, it is clear that his view of God as Father and Lord is consistent not just with his unpublished writings but with views that he expressed in his published works as well. Of seminal importance is the major theological pronouncement that Newton as an old man publicly issued in the second edition of his *Principia* (1713).[55] Responding to the criticisms of the first edition of the *Principia* (1687) by George Berkeley and Gottfried Wilhelm von Leibniz, Newton articulated his conception of God in the form of a General Scholium to proposition 42 in book 3 ("System of the World") of the *Principia.*[56] In the General Scholium, Newton celebrates "the beautiful system of the sun, planets, and comets," in short, the universe at large, as the creation of the "dominion of One." As we have seen, it is this sense of dominion or lord-ship, with its implications of power and authority, that is crucial to the Newtonian view of God as a being who is the most supreme *"pantokrator"* or *"Universal Ruler."* In his "being-ness," his "livingness," his "oneness," he has a presence and a life over that which he has created. Although God is a being "eternal, infinite, absolutely perfect," we do not, however, substitute his attributes for his "beingness." "We say, my God, your God, the God of *Israel*, the God of Gods, and Lord of Lords," Newton observes; but we do not say, "my Eternal, your Eternal, the Eternal of *Israel*, the Eternal of Gods; we do not say, my Infinite, or my Perfect." To do so would be to call into question our full awareness of God as *Lord*. "It is," Newton declares, "the dominion of a spiritual being which constitutes a God."[57] One might suggest a concurrence here between Newton's view of God and the view expressed by John Biddle, who likewise emphasizes the significance of "dominion" as a primary function of God's "beingness." Like Biddle's "Judaical" God of Hebrew Scripture, Newton's "God of *Israel*" draws upon conceptions that are decidedly Hebraic in outlook.

In the depiction of God that one discovers in the *Principia*, there is no mention of the Son and certainly no sense of the Christological implications of the Son as redeemer. Although it might well be argued that there is no occasion for such consideration within the context of the issues that Newton addresses in his account of the "System of the World," the absence of any allusion to this dimension is not without significance. It might be argued that one must essentially resort to the unpublished material for a sense of Newton's Christology. But even here, one is at a loss. "There are many theological questions on which Newton never settled into a fixed position. Did Christ exist before all worlds and did He create this one at God's command? Was Christ a higher or a lower being than the angels?" Questions of this sort are summarized, but definitive conclusions are not drawn. It is clear that for

Newton Christ was not simply a "mere man": "he was the Son of God, not just a human soul who was sent into the world." There is, to be sure, a distinctly Antitrinitarian bias in Newton's unpublished writings. On the other hand, it would be a mistake to invoke Newton's "Antitrinitarianism" in order to "pigeonhole him in one of the recognized categories of heresy," whether Arian, Socinian or Unitarian. To be sure, Newton's "chief villain" in the early church is Athanasius, rather than Arius. But Newton castigated both for "having introduced metaphysical subtleties into their disputes and corrupted the plain language of Scripture." What is most pronounced in Newton is "a perceptible movement away from the Christological centre of religion." Although Christ himself remains crucial to an understanding of God's providential design, metaphysical distinctions about the nature of the godhead, the hypostatical union, and issues of that sort are relegated to a renewed emphasis upon the "omniscience and omnipotence of God."[58]

However one might be inclined to understand Locke and Newton in the context of the traditions of heterodoxy that flourished throughout early modern England and beyond, it is clear that both reveal an inclination to question the orthodox assumptions upon which the church grounded itself as the century drew to a close. No doubt reflecting his own biases, McLachlan holds that both Locke and Newton "reveal a spirit and temper that closely link them with seventeenth-century Socinianism."[59] As much as this statement is open to question, it does provide a framework through which to examine Milton's own works as the product of a thinker responsive to the heterodox crosscurrents of his time.

2

What is true of Locke and Newton is no less true of Milton: within the interstices of his work, within his silences, one may discover patterns of behavior, attitudes and gestures that on occasion recall aspects of Socinianism. Milton was perhaps one who was "silent yet spake." Are we to interpret from such "utterances" that he might have been "a silent" member of a "small, unorganized," yet "vigorous" movement (interpreted loosely as "Arian" or "Socinian") "that manifested itself openly in the second half of the 1640's and ultimately developed into English Unitarianism"?[60] Our response to this question must be one of extreme caution, for there are equally strong countertrends in Milton's writings that indicate just how removed he was from embracing an outlook that might be labeled "Socinian." Hill is right: Milton was indeed "an eclectic, the disciple of no individual thinker," or heresy. Nonetheless, his writings do at times invite interpretations consistent with certain aspects of a Socinian point of view.

As indicated, I propose to address these aspects not through a detailed examination of specific Miltonic texts. Rather, I shall touch upon both Milton's well-established encounter with Socinianism and his references (both direct and implied) to the movement. I shall explore the history of "Socinianizing" Milton by those determined to enlist him in their cause. At the very least, I hope to demonstrate how misguided is Paul M. Zall's observation that "the connection between Socinianism and Milton" is little more than "a matter of intellectual curiosity."[61]

As is well known, Milton's most immediate contact with Socinianism arose as a result of the publication and licensing of the Latin version of *The Racovian Catechism; or, Catechesis Ecclesiarum quae in Regno Poloniae, et magno ducatu Lithuaniae*, in March 1651.[62] The book was registered on November 13, 1651, to William Dugard, the printer to the Council of State and Milton's friend and publisher.[63] As John T. Shawcross, among others, makes clear, the heretical nature of the work occasioned the arrest of Dugard by the council on January 27, 1652; and two days later Dugard had the registry canceled.

The work was considered sufficiently subversive that on February 4, the council saw fit to appoint a committee to examine Dugard, who, in turn, implicated John Milton as the licenser. According to Shawcross, Gilbert Millington, the chairman of the committee, also reported the existence of a note in Milton's hand licensing the book on August 10, 1650; the note itself, however, has not been located. In a report of his embassy to England, the statesman Lieuwe van Aitzema noted on March 5, 1652, the *Catechesis* and Milton's licensing of it. Aitzema maintains that in his examination by the committee of the council, Milton admitted licensing the book in keeping with the spirit expressed in *Areopagitica*.[64]

The extent of Milton's precise involvement in the licensing of the work and the repercussions of that involvement continue to elicit discussion and debate. Stephen B. Dobranski cautions us to be wary of drawing hasty conclusions concerning the relationship between Milton's own views and his role in the licensing of the *Catechesis*.[65] We would do well in taking to heart Dobranski's cautionary admonitions.Whether Milton's licensing of the *Catechesis* is a reflection of deeply held views concerning the Socinian heresy or simply the product of the circumstances in which Milton as licenser found himself at the time remains to be seen. Dobranski observes that Milton himself "seems to have suffered no consequences for his involvement in the matter"; and, although Dugard was found guilty of publishing "this blasphemous and scandalous Book," Milton continued in his capacity as secretary for foreign tongues. Nor, Dobranski suggests, are we automatically to conclude that the council relieved Milton of his duties as licenser because of the *Catechesis*. That his name does not thereafter appear in this capacity may be the result of his blindness or because he was preoccupied with composing his defense tracts.[66] If the circumstances under which Milton licensed the *Catechesis* and the repercussions that ensued remain uncertain, nonetheless, it is clear that the publication of the *Catechesis* in 1651 is important as a sign not only of the renewed ferment that Socinianism was creating in England at the time but of the bearing that the movement might well have had on Milton's own thought and behavior.[67]

To gauge the precise nature of that bearing on Milton's thought is difficult in the extreme. Milton's own statements about the Socinians are few. In *Tetrachordon*, he refers to the Socinians disparagingly as part of his discussion of Genesis 2:24 ("*Therefore shall a man leav his father and his mother, and shall cleav unto his wife; and they shall be one flesh*"). Responding to those who argue that this verse demonstrates the inseparability of man and woman in all marriages (whether good or bad), Milton credits Adam with the ability to speak metaphorically, that is, with the power to transcend "corporall meaning" in his discourse. To think otherwise, Milton maintains, is to suggest that "*Adams* insight concerning wedlock reacht no furder" than the literal sense of things. To insist that Adam be limited to the literal meaning of his words is, Milton says, to "make him as very an idiot as the Socinians make him; which would not be reverently don of us" (YP 4:604). The Socinians, of course, maintain no such thing about Adam and his limitations, and they certainly don't conceive him as an "idiot." At most, they question the traditional notion of an Adam endowed with special gifts as a result of his so-called unfallen state. Perhaps the idea of an intellectually obtuse Adam might be attributed to the adversaries of the Socinians.[68] If so, Milton's reference to the Socinians' view of Adam as an "idiot" is about as unflattering an allusion to the body of ideas and beliefs of a particular sect within Protestantism as one can imagine. Whether or not Milton drew upon the rhetoric of the enemies of the Socinians, it is clear that in the mid-1640s, at least, he did not hesitate to use Socinus and his followers in a most undiplomatic way.

By the time Milton published *Of True Religion, Haeresie, Schism, Toleration* in 1673, the year before his death, his views had apparently undergone a transformation, at least as far as radical movements such as Socinianism are concerned.[69] It is in *Of True Religion* that we find Milton's most open and direct statements about Socinianism (which Milton, in keeping with the major trends in seventeenth century thought, couples with Arianism). Emerging from a 13-year silence in the publication of tracts on matters of religion and affairs of state, Milton produced a work that, according to an unknown admirer writing some two years later, says more on toleration "in two elegant sheets of true religion, heresy, and schism than all the prelates can refute in seven years."[70] The precise occasion of the tract and the circumstances that provoked it have been treated eloquently by David Masson, William Riley Parker, Keith Stavely and Nathaniel Henry, among others.[71] The milieu through which *Of True Religion* was produced is one of declarations and counterdeclarations on the part of king and parliament to determine the limits of religious toleration throughout the Commonwealth. In 1672, Charles II issued a Declaration of Indulgence that suspended all penal laws in ecclesiastical matters and allowed Protestant Nonconformists to apply for licenses that permitted public worship. On the surface, the act appeared to be a magnanimous gesture indeed. The problem is that the declaration also implicitly extended its "indulgence" to Roman Catholics. (At least, the declaration did not exclude them.) The response to the possibility of Catholicism's regaining power was swift. Immediately upon publication of the declaration, the cry of "no Popery" could be heard in pulpit and pamphlet. Parliament responded by having the declaration canceled and, in its place, passing the Test Act, which (Draconian-like) required all civil and military personnel to take the Oaths of Allegiance and Supremacy, to receive the sacraments according to the rites subscribed by the Church of England, and to renounce the doctrine of transubstantiation. That took care of Catholicism, but it also threatened to compromise the "tender consciences" of the

Protestant Nonconformists.To help mitigate the harshness of the Test Act, the Commons advanced a bill for the "Ease of Protestant Dissenters," which became a subject of ongoing debate in Parliament. This is the environment in which Milton produced *Of True Religion*, a tract that is clearly tolerationist in its support both of Protestantism in general (as we might expect) and of Nonconformists in particular. In keeping with the spirit of the Test Act, however, the tract is entirely opposed to popery. The concluding words of the full title of Milton's tract make this opposition clear: *And what best means may be us'd against the growth of POPERY.* (The typography of the title page is such that the word "popery" is particulary pronounced.)

In his uncompromising hatred of popery, Milton makes it clear in the tract that "Popery is the only or the greatest Heresie: and he who is so forward to brand all others for Hereticks, the obstinate Papist, the only Heretick" (YP 8:421). Such an outlook is consistent with his views of Catholicism throughout his career, including his earlier great tolerationist statement *Areopagitica*. Any attempt to assess the true nature of Milton's attitude toward Socinianism (or any other radical "sect," for that matter) in *Of True Religion* must constantly keep in mind his view of popery. All other sects and schisms that have arisen within Protestantism as the truly "catholic," that is, universal faith, are to be not only tolerated but encouraged as the product of a healthy and energetic church, one in which members seek not to destroy faith but to bolster it. This latitudinarian outlook prevails, as Milton considers Lutherans, Calvinists, Anabaptists, Arminians, Arians and indeed Socinians. Milton's view of them is consistent: "all these may have some errors but are not Hereticks" in the sense of knowingly, voluntarily and maliciously adopting notions that seek to subvert the clear teachings of Scripture. To be sure, there may be elements of error in each of the doctrines advanced by Lutherans, Calvinists and the like, "but so long as all these profess to set the Word of God only before them as the Rule of faith and obedience, and use all diligence and sincerity of heart, by reading, by learning, by study, by prayer for Illumination of the holy Spirit, to understand the Rule and obey it, they have done what man can do." Even if they are "much mistaken" in "some Points of Doctrine," Milton declares, God "will assuredly pardon them" (YP 8:423–24). Such a statement is a sign not that Milton embraces the precise teachings of the movements he mentions (although he might adopt aspects of them) but that he is willing to view them (as he had in *Areopagitica*) as the embodiment of the efforts of those busy in framing the "spirituall architecture" of the "Temple of the Lord" (YP 2:555). Even in the uncertain period of post-Restoration England, the old, long-silent reformer is determined yet once more to break the silence and have his say.

Having expressed this latitudinarian perspective, Milton then provides an account of the contested beliefs of the movements he has named. He does so not to castigate these movements but rather to highlight particular doctrines that, although perhaps open to question, nonetheless do not compromise the movements as a whole and thereby render their members undeserving of salvation. Indeed, if one "calmly and charitably" inquires into "the hottest disputes among Protestants," Milton observes, one will see that those who engage in such disputes have yet "done what man can do" to justify themselves before God, even when certain of their beliefs may be considered erroneous. He then proceeds to catalog such beliefs and those who hold them. Although the Lutheran subscribes to the doctrine of consubstantiation, for example, this is "an error indeed," Milton observes, "but not mortal." If the Calvinist is "taxt" with a belief in the doctrine of predestination that in effect makes God "the Author of sin," this error is committed "not with any dishonourable thought of God, but it may be over zealously asserting his absolute power." Accused of denying infants "their right to Baptism,"

the Anabaptist counters that he "denies nothing but what the
Scripture denies them." The Arminian, in turn, is condemned
for "setting up free will against free grace." But he "disclaims"
that "Imputation" by maintaining that he "grounds himself
largely upon Scripture only." Milton declares that all these
sectarians (including their followers) are not only learned,
worthy, virtuous and zealous men but "perfect and powerful
in the Scriptures." Far from deserting these reformers, God
would both pardon their errors and accept their "pious
endeavours." Following God's example, we too should not
persecute them but, as fellow Protestants, "charitably tolerate"
them, even if we differ with them on certain matters of doctrine (YP 8:424–26).

It is within this latitudinarian context that Milton proceeds
to address Arianism and Socinianism. Once again, Milton's
purpose is neither to blame nor to praise the specific doctrines
these movements profess but to argue on behalf of the idea
that those who subscribe to such doctrines (however erroneous
we might feel them to be) are sincere in their attempts to
ground them in their own reading of Scripture. In his list of
movements, Milton places the Arian and the Socinian in the
penultimate position between Anabaptist and Arminian.
Although the terms of Milton's argument about the various
movements within Protestantism are entirely clear, his statement about the Arian and Socinian movements in particular
has proven extremely difficult to interpret. For this reason, I
quote the pertinent parts of the statement in full:

> The Arians and Socinians are charg'd to dispute against the
> Trinity; they affirm to believe the Father, Son, and Holy Ghost,
> according to Scripture, and the Apostolic Creed; as for terms of
> Trinity, Triniunity, Coessentiality, Tripersonality, and the like,
> they reject them as Scholastic Notions, not to be found in
> Scripture, which by a general Protestant Maxim is plain and
> perspicuous abundantly to explain its own meaning in the
> properest words, belonging to so high a Matter and so necessary
> to be known; a mystery indeed in their Sophistic Subtilties,

but in Scripture, a plain Doctrin. Their other Opinions are of less Moment. They dispute the satisfaction of Christ, or rather the word *Satisfaction*, as not Scriptural; but they acknowledge him both God and their Saviour. (YP 8:424–25)

This is a complex (if not a convoluted) passage indeed. The passage starts out clearly enough: "The Arians and Socinians," which Milton groups together, "are charg'd to dispute against the Trinity." In grouping the two movements, Milton does not aim to raise complex doctrinal distinctions between the Arianism and Socinianism concerning the nature of the Son's preincarnate begetting (for the Arians) and the disbelief in any sort of pre-incarnate Sonship (for the Socinians), among other issues. Rather, Milton states what (he implies) can be agreed upon by all upstanding Protestants: through recourse to the biblical text (and confirmed by apostolic belief)[72] as the one true source of interpretation, both Arians and Socinians believe in the existence and primacy of the Father, Son and Holy Ghost. As for vexed terms of theology such as "Trinity, Triniunity, Coessentiality, Tripersonality," both Arians and Socinians reject them as "Scholastic Notions," a phrase that for Milton, as well as for his contemporaries, certainly smacked of popery.[73] The point is that the enemy here (as throughout Milton's tract) is popery. The pulpit and pamphlet cry of "no Popery" is lurking within the interstices of the passage.

At issue for Milton is the Protestant emphasis upon the primacy of Scripture in contrast to the "corrupt traditions" that arise out of popery. Whereas the former (Protestant belief) is grounded in the idea of Scripture as "plain and perspicuous abundantly to explain its own meaning," the latter (popish belief) is wedded to "Scholastic Notions, not to be found in Scripture." Reflecting the vain attempt to "mystify" the nature of godhead, these "Scholastic Notions" are propounded by the papists as an expression of their "Sophistical Subtilties." Such terms as trinity, triniunity, coessentiality and tripersonality thus assume the aura of a "mystery" in what Milton earlier in

Of True Religion calls "the traditions of men and additions to the word of God" as the defining force of popery (YP 8:421). As opposed to this fabricated mystery (spuriously generated by the papists), the idea of Father, Son and Spirit, then, is revealed as "a plain Doctrin" in Scripture. Accordingly, when Milton refers to "a mystery indeed in *their* Sophistic Sub-tilties" (my emphasis), the antecedent of "their" is that old sophistic-scholastic bugaboo, the Catholic Church (*not*, as some have suggested, the Arians and Socinians themselves).[74] Almost as an afterthought, Milton then addresses another crucial belief, this one associated with Socinianism: "Their other Opinions are of less Moment. They dispute the satisfaction of Christ, or rather the word *Satisfaction*, as not Scriptural; but they acknowledge him both God and their Saviour." In this case, the antecedent of "their" is obviously not the papists but the Socinians. How is one to interpret the afterthought? Is this belief (like those cited earlier) open to question? I see no reason why not, but this is not the point.

The point once again is that all the beliefs of all the movements Milton cites are such that they do not compromise the essential efficacy of the movements themselves. It would be a mistake, moreover, to invoke the foregoing passage as a basis for claiming that Milton was a Socinian, an Arian, or anything else that constitutes his catalog. To endorse the Arian and Socinian interpretative practice (one that grounds itself in the scriptural text) is not necessarily to endorse the beliefs that emerge from this practice. It is simply to say that this is a practice that all good Protestants (no matter what their stripe) adopt to implement their respective hermeneutics. As such, the passage confirms Milton's allegiance to a particular mode of interpretation (the Protestant mode) as the one true foundation upon which to ground belief. Milton's purpose, then, is *interpretive*, not *doctrinal*. He refuses to declare his own doctrinal allegiance beyond maintaining that we should be as accepting of the manifold movements that constitute Protestantism as we are of any group (*except* the papists) who strive to know God aright. It is ironic, he observes, that "we suffer the Idolatrous books of Papists" to be "sold & read as common as our own. Why not much rather of Anabaptists, Arians, Arminians, & Socinians?" (YP 8:437). Again, the question is not a doctrinal one: it is an interpretive one. In interpretation the exegete opens himself to an entire range of ideas with which he may or may not agree. He tolerates these ideas, not because he agrees with them, but because he is open to them. He may embrace certain aspects of them and dismiss others. But they all have something to offer, whether or not we are persuaded by them. "There is no Learned man but will confess he hath much profited by reading Controversies, his Senses awakt, his Judgement sharpn'd, and the truth which he holds more firmly establish't." As the result of allowing controversies to flourish, we shall create an environment in which "falsehood will appear more false, and truth the more true." An attitude of this sort will result not only in the realization of truth but in the confounding of falsehood, which is to say, popery (YP 8:437). This in brief represents Milton's own Declaration of Indulgence, one that suggests both the virtues and the limits of Miltonic toleration.

Although we cannot depend upon *Of True Religion* to provide detailed insight into the complex particulars of Milton's doctrinal beliefs, either pro-Socinian or anti-Socinian, his tract is instructive in suggesting the extent to which such movements as Socinianism were of uppermost concern to Milton later in his career. His willingness to invoke Socinianism in the context of his belief in the direct and unbiased encounter with the biblical text is likewise instructive not only in illuminating the nature of his hermeneutics but in revealing his allegiance to those who adopt a corresponding approach to the discovery of doctrinal truth.

3

It has always been assumed that the best way of gaining insight into Milton's own view of how doctrinal truth is to be delineated in systematic form is to examine his so-called *De doctrina Christiana*, a work about which much has been written and upon which there is hardly universal agreement. Ever since William B. Hunter reopened the whole issue of the Miltonic authorship of this theological tract, moreover, any attempt to confront the question of what positions Milton held regarding precise matters of doctrine have been rendered questionable at best.[75] As much as one might wish to dismiss Hunter's findings with remarkably little fuss, he keeps coming back to haunt the world of Milton scholarship like the little man who wasn't there. Even if Milton may be said to have "authored" *De doctrina Christiana* in whole or in part, the uncertainties surrounding the manuscript (its provenance, its date of composition, its mode of production, its transmission) render the attempt to arrive at definitive conclusions about matters of authorship and text devilishly elusive, if not finally impossible.[76] I take my cue here from what the author of the treatise observes about the difficulties that beset the text of Scripture, especially the New Testament. This document has come down to us "through a variety of hands, some more corrupt than others." We possess, moreover, "no autograph copy [autographum]" and no "*exemplar*" that "we can rely upon as more trustworthy than the others" (YP 6:589; CM 16:276–77). With this caveat in mind, I shall glance at *De doctrina Christiana*, but not to argue that the theology advanced there is definitively Miltonic and therefore an unimpeachable source of investigation into his own theological views. (I no longer think this kind of investigation possible.) Rather, I shall explore how the work might prove instructive in suggesting how the author (perhaps "Milton" in some form) subscribed to views either consistent with or at odds with the kinds of thought that have come to be associated with Socinianism. There is yet another, perhaps more compelling, reason to consider *De doctrina Christiana*. As I shall discuss later in this essay, the remarkable discovery of this work almost a century and a half after Milton's death provided the occasion for renewed interest in the issue of his doctrinal affiliations and the relation of those affiliations to the Socinian or Unitarian outlook.

From the perspective of Milton's emphasis upon Scripture as the sole authority in addressing matters of religious doctrine, it is of more than passing interest that in the prefatory epistle to *De doctrina Christiana* the author claims that he will "adhere to the Holy Scripture alone [libris tantummode sacris adhaeresco]." Referring to his treatise as his "dearest and best possession," he implies that his adherence to Scripture will be his guiding principle. Whether or not such an adherence gives rise to what others deem "heretical" as a result of their "conventional beliefs," he declares that he subscribes to "no other heresy or sect [haeresin aliam, sectam aliam sequor nullam]." In fact, he maintains that he "had not even studied any of the so-called heretical writers" when the mistakes of the "orthodox" theologians prompted him to side with their "heretical" opponents in their judicious (if heterodox) reading of the biblical text. If this be heresy, he, like Saint Paul before him (Acts 24:14), willingly accepts that designation as a sign of the true worship of God grounded in the unswerving belief in Scripture (YP 6:121, 123; CM 14:14, 15).

Evident throughout the treatise, that attitude is delineated in detail in the chapter on the Holy Scripture (1.30). There, the author emphasizes the outlook reflected in *Of True Religion* and other works by Milton that, if studied diligently and carefully, Scripture is entirely "perspicuous [perspicuae]" in everything relating to "salvation" [salutem]. Accordingly, "the rule and canon of faith" is "scripture alone [Regula itaque fidei et canon, scriptura sola est]" (YP 6:574–85; CM 16:249–67).[77] If this sentiment recalls Milton's own statement that

Scripture, by "a general Protestant Maxim," is sufficiently "plain and perspicuous" to "explain its own meaning in the properest words, belonging to so high a Matter and so necessary to be known," it also moves us toward the mainstay of Socinian belief in the absolute sufficiency of Scripture as the exclusive source of all doctrine.[78] On the other hand, the author of *De doctrina Christiana* is, as indicated, aware of the uncertainties associated with the transmission of the text of Scripture (particularly the New Testament), an awareness that leads him to conclude that in matters of belief "the Spirit which is given to us is a more certain guide than scripture, and that we ought to follow it [certiorem nobis propositum ducem spiritum quam scripturam, quem sequi debeamus]." This remarkable turn from text to Spirit is reinforced, moreover, by a recognition of what the author calls a "fallacious" propensity in human reason ("humanas rationes plerumque fallaces") at times to misconstrue the truths of "divine doctrine" [divina doctrina] present in the text (YP 6:583, 589; CM 16:264–65, 278–79).[79] As much as the author of *De doctrina Christiana* emphasizes the ability of reason to arrive at an understanding of the text of Scripture, he likewise reveals an even greater faith in the power of the Spirit to guide us in matters that appear to transcend the ability of reason to comprehend things beyond its sphere. One might say that the author reflects the Socinian propensity to value reason as the means to derive divine doctrine from Scripture but at the same time reflects a profound awareness of the limits of reason in the face of inscrutable circumstances with which the text of Scripture on occasion confronts the reader at least partially as the result of the problems associated with its transmission from the earliest times.

It is particularly in the context of the conception of godhead delineated in *De doctrina Christiana* that both affinities with and departures from Socinianism come into play. Among the attributes of God that the author of *De doctrina Christiana* lists is that of "oneness," the most important aspect of godhead and the one in which all the others culminate. A mainstay of Socinian thought, this uncompromising emphasis upon "oneness" underscores what eventuates as the theology of Unitarianism. To be sure, the assertion of a monotheistic deity is hardly a characteristic that distinguishes the Socinian point of view from mainstream belief, but it is the methodology through which such an outlook is implemented that so compellingly recalls the kind of logic-based methodology characteristic of Socinianism.[80] Citing a multitude of biblical proof texts to support this all-important emphasis upon monotheism, the author of *De doctrina Christiana* poses the rhetorical question: "What could be more plain and straightforward? What could be better adapted to the average intelligence, what more in keeping with everyday speech, so that God's people should understand that there is numerically one God and one spirit [unum numero Deum, unum spiritum], just as they understand that there is numerically one [numerando unum] of anything else." This is a "unitarian" pronouncement that grounds its suppositions in the plain and logical assessment of number available to all. It is not metaphysics: it is just plain sense. This is a sense of godhead "fitting" and "thoroughly in accordance with reason [aequum . . . et rationi summe consentaneum]" (YP 6:146–47; CM 14:50–51). Maurice Kelley is correct is his notation that the conception here is essentially rational and "mathematical" (YP 6:146 n. 51).

The pattern is all-pervasive in the view of godhead endorsed by the treatise. Later in the treatise, the author reasserts his credo concerning the "one true and independent supreme God" that will permit no compromise in this mathematics of oneness, and in the process, the author "personalizes" deity by extolling the "Jews," from whom the concept of "one God" is derived: "God's people, the Jews," he says, "have always interpreted the term 'only one person' [unam duntaxat personam] to mean one in number" (YP 6:213; CM, 6:196–97).[81] Coupled with the emphasis upon "oneness" is a kind of "creatureliness" that finds its ultimate source in what the author of *De doctrina Christiana* associates with the Jews, that is, God's chosen, whose most ancient conception of deity is portrayed in Hebrew Scripture. As we have seen, the move toward the Judaic (or Hebraic) outlook is one customarily looked upon as a signature of the Socinian sensibility.

As much as *De doctrina Christiana* reveals at times characteristics commonly associated with Socinianism as a movement, important aspects of the treatise do suggest a decidedly anti-Socinian point of view. For example, *De doctrina Christiana* makes clear in its discussion of Christ as redeemer (1.14) that although the pre-incarnate Son of God was not "supreme" ("etsi non summus"), he was nonetheless "the firstborn of all creation [omnis tamen rei creatae primogenetus]." It follows, then, "that he must have existed before his incarnation [ante assumptam carnem extiterit necesse est], whatever subtleties may have been invented to provide an escape from this conclusion [ad haec evadenda subtilius excogitarunt], by those who argue that Christ was a mere man [quicquid illi qui Christum merum hominem esse disputant]" (YP 6:419; CM 15:262–63). The not-so-veiled reference, of course, is to the Socinians, with whom the author of *De doctrina Christiana* strongly disagrees at this crucial juncture.[82] Such a disagreement strikes at the heart of Socinian theology, which, in its conception of the *one God*, categorically disallows the existence of the preincarnate Son. Arguing in behalf of the concept of a pre-incarnate Son, the author of *De doctrina Christiana* makes clear that the Son occupies a decidedly subordinated stature in relation to the Father (1.5).

The differences between the theology of the Socinians and of *De doctrina Christiana* extend to the view of the Incarnation as well. Whereas the Socinians view the "historical Jesus" as an individual whose nature is entirely human (although of a remarkable nature indeed), the author of *De doctrina Christiana* views Christ's nature as the product of a hypostatical union, that is, divine and human. "Christ, then, although he was God [Deus cum esset], put on human nature and was made flesh [humanam naturam assumpsit]," yet he "did not cease to be numerically one Christ" (YP 6:418, 420; CM 15:262–63). In his embrace of this concept, the author of *De doctrina Christiana*, in effect, declares his departure from any who would maintain the full humanity of Christ. On the contrary, the incarnate Christ is to be conceived as *theanthropos* in the hypostatic union of divine and human. This view of the incarnate Christ is one that celebrates the *mystery* of the event. In fact, it is an outlook that sides with those who look upon the Incarnation as "by far the greatest mystery of our religion [mysterium religionis nostrae longe maximum esse]." We are obliged to "let such mysteries alone and not tamper with them." Because God has not revealed to us how such a mystery comes about, "it is much better for us to hold our tongues and be wisely ignorant [sapienter potius nescire]" (YP 6:424; CM 15:272–73). This rather Cusanus-like view of the *mysterium* that underlies religious phenomena (in this case, the Incarnation) is one entirely opposed to the Socinian idea of extolling reason at all costs.

By embracing mystery in his treatment of the Incarnation, the author of *De doctrina Christiana* would dispel all notions that might otherwise promote heresy. So the author exclaims: "How many opportunities for heresy we shall remove! How much of the raw material of heresy we shall cut away! How many huge volumes" we shall "fling out of God's temple as filth and rubbish [inquinamenta ac rudera]!" This "cleansing" includes even those who are teachers in the Reformed Church (YP 6:421; CM 15:264–65). For the author of *De doctrina Christiana*, these teachers, one suspects, may well be of the Socinian persuasion. If such is the case, then the act of cutting and cleansing in which the author of *De doctrina Christiana* engages is one that challenges the latitudinarian outlook reflected in *Of True Religion*. The author of the theological treatise is apparently in no mood (at least at this juncture) to "indulge" the errors even of the reformers of his own stripe. Much mistaken in points of doctrine with which the author of the treatise does not agree, these are heretics whom God will assuredly not pardon. Whatever the extent of Milton's own participation in the production of the theological treatise, then, this is a work that further confirms both the embrace and at times the categorical rejection of positions associated with the Socinian point of view.[83]

From the perspective of Milton's overt statements in *Tetrachordon* and *Of True Religion*, as well as of the oblique references in *De doctrina Christiana*, we are given insight not only into his awareness of Socinianism but of his response to it as a movement. This insight is further heightened by Milton's involvement in the licensing of *The Racovian Catechism*, often conceived as the foundational statement of the Socinian doctrinal system. Whatever we might think of Milton's allegiance or nonallegiance to Socinianism, it is clear that, had the likes of John Edwards attacked Milton the way Edwards was to attack Locke, Milton might well have suffered a fate similar to that of the author of *The Reasonableness of Christianity*. John Edwards would surely have "unmask'd" Milton's "Socinianism" by reading both the overt statements and the silences of his works. Doing so, John Edwards would have been eager to follow in the footsteps of his father, Thomas, by rooting out the gangrenous corruptions that plagued the "body" of Milton's heretical works. Fortunately, Milton escaped all such attempts to cleanse the world of any putatively Socinian leanings. Had *De doctrina Christiana* been published in Milton's lifetime, God knows what the repercussions might have been, especially with the issue of authorship not in doubt. This is surely one of the most tantalizing possibilities that offer themselves to those who consider *De doctrina Christiana* as a Miltonic text. For this reason, the afterlife not only of the theological tract but of Milton's works in general represents a fascinating means of understanding both the nature of his writings and of the reception of his theological ideas in the centuries that followed upon his death. Such an understanding is germane to an appreciation of how Milton's poetry (especially *Paradise Lost*) was interpreted both before and after the advent of *De doctrina Christiana*.

4

From the perspective of Socinianism (coupled with that of Arianism), Milton's reputation between the time of his death in 1674 and the publication of *De doctrina Christiana* in 1825 was generally free of the charge of Antitrinitarian heterodoxy. As John T. Shawcross observes, "many people in England seem to have learned their Bible with *Paradise Lost* at hand, for it was considered an exposition of the orthodox creed. This was true for most people during the century." Shawcross makes clear, however, that despite the association of Milton with orthodoxy, charges of Antitrinitarianism were not entirely absent.[84] The foundations of such charges lay in part with the imposing figure of John Toland, controversialist, pamphleteer and Milton biographer. In his "Life of Milton" (1698), first published in a collected edition of Milton's prose, Toland makes no direct reference to the possibility of Socinian leanings, but he does not hesitate to single out, as well as to quote in full, the specific passages from *Of True Religion* on Arianism and Socinianism that we have addressed above. Responding to these passages, Toland endorses Milton's argument that, as Toland says, "no true *Protestant* can persecute any persons for speculative Points of Conscience, much less not tolerat his fellow *Protestant*, tho in som things dissenting from his own Judgment." What Toland is particularly taken with in his reading of the passages he cites from *Of True Religion* is that "nothing can be imagin'd more reasonable, honest, or pious" than the tolerationist sensibility they reflect. The spirit that infuses the argument *Of True Religion* as a whole reminds Toland of the tolerationist position adopted by Locke. Citing works such as Locke's letters on toleration, as well as his *Essay Concerning Human Understanding*, Toland views Milton in the context of a Lockean tradition of latitudinarianism that, according to Toland, all reformers should emulate.

If one takes into account theological issues, it would have been interesting indeed to know what Toland might have thought of *De doctrina Christiana*, had it been available to him. Following hard upon his discussion of Milton's tolerationist point of view in the context of Locke's endorsement of toleration, Toland mentions the existence of Milton's so-called "System of Divinity," the location of which is uncertain and the purpose of which ("whether intended for public view, or collected merely for his [Milton's] own use") Toland is unable to determine.[85] As Shawcross observes, Toland's "Life of Milton" provoked controversy in large part because of the heterodox beliefs (among them, Socinianism) that Toland himself was thought to have held.[86] Judging by such works as Toland's *Christianity Not Mysterious* (1696), one can understand the rationale underlying the questioning of his religious views by those who subscribed to an unwavering orthodoxy.[87]

Following upon Toland, the charge of heterodoxy in Milton appeared thereafter in venues such as John Dennis's "The Grounds of Criticism in Poetry" (1704), Jonathan Richardson's *Explanatory Notes and Remarks on Milton's "Paradise Lost"* (1734), and various items in the *Gentleman's Magazine* and the *Daily Gazetteer* (1738–1739). The tone adopted by those commenting upon Milton's poetry (specifically, *Paradise Lost*) in such venues is either tentative or dismissive, because they are largely founded upon the subtle nuances that arise from the language of the verse, rather than from the systematic process of argumentation that might otherwise distinguish a theological tract. It is interesting, in fact, to see how the critics respond to nuances they discover in the verse, absent the supposedly corroborating evidence that a "System of Divinity" would afford. Citing the angelic hymn to God and the Son in the third book (lines 384–96) of *Paradise Lost*, John Dennis, for example, observes: "I have the rather mention'd these Verses, to show that *Milton* was a little tainted with Socinianism, for by the first Verse 'tis evident, that he look'd upon the Son of God as a created Being."[88]

The verse to which Dennis refers is "Thee next they sang, of all Creation first, / Begotten Son, Divine Similitude" (3.384–85). Although Dennis does not elaborate precisely why this verse leads him to see in Milton the "taint" of Socinianism, one may assume that the emphasis the verse places upon a "created" being in the form of the Son (as "Begotten") suggests to Dennis the presence of Socinian inclinations on Milton's part. Dennis, of course, fails to take account of the fact that in the Socinian doctrinal system, the notion of a preincarnate deity known as the Son does not even exist. But that does not matter, for, as far as Dennis is concerned, the Son is already the incarnate Messiah, even before he becomes the historical Jesus. That the Son is "created" or "begotten" at all is sufficient to convince Dennis of what might be called the creatureliness of the Son as begotten being. Fine theological distinctions simply do not obtain. Nor is there a system of divinity to confirm, clarify or (ironically) further unsettle Dennis's conclusions regarding Milton's unfortunate state of being "tainted."

Perhaps it is the various uncertainties surrounding the matter of Milton's alleged Socinianism or Arianism that led Jonathan Richardson some 30 years later to allude to the contentious environment that prevailed during his own time. In his *Explanatory Notes*, Richardson observes that it is just this environment that "will not permit [him] to Pass over in Silence" the conjecture "that *Milton* was an *Arian*." This conjecture, he observes, "is built on Certain Passages in *Par.*

Lost." Once again failing the presence of an actual system of divinity to which one can resort, charges of heterodoxy must ground themselves in passages from the poetic document. "Some of those [passages]" or perhaps even "all of them for Ought I know," Richardson maintains, "are very Capable of an Orthodox Construction." In other words, these passages can be read either way, as is so often the distinguishing mark of a poetic text. The honesty and forthrightness that such an assertion reflects are refreshing in suggesting Richardson's determination not to accede to readings he considers doctrinaire. In a gesture reminiscent of the admonition to be "wisely ignorant" in *De doctrina Christiana*, Richardson refuses to "Meddle" in a "Dispute" that does not appear to be able to produce indisputable results and that is based solely on "Conjecture" ("Over-rul'd by So many Pious and Learned Divines").[89] Richardson will take the high road and refrain from insisting on heterodoxy in his reading of poetic statement that is open to an entire range of interpretation. No doubt implicit in Richardson's reluctance to proclaim Milton's heterodoxy is precisely the kind of view that arose shortly afterward in the letter of one "Theophilus" in the *Gentleman's Magazine* (1738): Milton "has certainly adopted the *Arian* Principle into his *Paradise Lost.*" I wish we all had the luxury of being so certain about the doctrinal foundation of Milton's poetry. But Theophilus is convinced that in his heterodox views Milton "as little believed the Religion of his Country as *Homer* or *Virgil* did that of theirs." These charges were in turn subjected to countercharges by the likes of "Philo-Spec." and others in succeeding issues of the *Gentleman's Magazine.*[90] Clearly, in the exchange of charge and countercharge, one might be prompted to observe that "Hills amid the Air encounterd Hills" but with little fear that all "Had gon to wrack, with ruin overspred."

Although the whole debate appears to have become quiescent for the remainder of the century, it did not die out completely. In fact, with the growth of Unitarianism, the desire to enlist Milton in the cause flourished with renewed vigor. Theophilus Lindsey represents a notable instance of this renewal. A fellow of St. John's College, Cambridge, Lindsey took Holy Orders after the award of his bachelor of arts in 1747. Having received various ecclesiastical appointments, he adopted latitudiniarian views that prompted him to reassess his position as a cleric. His own allegiance had become decidedly Unitarian, a transition that caused him in 1774 to sever ties with the Church of England. Defending his decision to resign his vicarage, he issued an *Apology* (1774), in which he sought not only to justify his behavior but, in the process, to offer a history of the doctrine of the Trinity and Unitarianism.[91] As one might expect, the treatise elicited both hostile and supportive criticism. To this criticism, Lindsey responded with *A Sequel to the Apology* (1776), a work considered "the most elaborate, and in many respects the most valuable, of his contributions to dogmatic theology."[92]

What is fascinating about these writings is the extent to which Lindsey draws upon Milton to bolster an essentially heterodox Christology, one in keeping with a Unitarian outlook grounded in Socinian principles. *A Sequel to the Apology* is apposite in this regard. In the *Sequel*, Lindsey defends the notion of an essentially *human* Jesus whose youth is distinguished by a remarkable growth in self-awareness and a distinct precociousness. Citing Origen and Grotius as figures whose childhood achievements are deemed remarkable, Lindsey observes that "these and similar instances discover what great things the human mind is capable of, by a careful cultivation, and the divine blessing." But even such exemplary individuals as Origen and Grotius pale beside the young Jesus, whose childhood gives every evidence of "the maturity of wisdom and goodness to which the holy Jesus had arrived in very early youth." At issue is the sense that like Origen and Grotius, Jesus was essentially a man (albeit, an extraordinary man), one whose formative years give every evidence of maturation to a higher plane. His "moral improvements, however gradual and impressive," Lindsey states, "always far surpassed those of any others of mankind." It is this very growth of self-awareness, coupled with the idea of maturation, that leads Lindsey to argue that the Jesus of Scripture was (for all his qualities) a human being, not, at that point at least, the Son of God incarnate.

The foremost poetic exponent of this reading of Scripture, according to Lindsey, is John Milton, whose *Paradise Regained* provides the most profound evidence of a distinctly human Jesus whose early youth is distinguished by a pronounced recognition of his human condition. In keeping with that view, Lindsey offers Jesus' soliloquy having to do with his childhood experiences. Then, "no childish play" was "pleasing" to Jesus. As one "above [his] years," he not only read and delighted in "the law of God" but grew in his knowledge "to such perfection" that, at the ripe age of 12, he was able to propose to the "teachers of our law" in the temple "What might improve [his] knowledge, or their own" (1.201–13). Clearly, this for Lindsey is one of many examples that the Jesus of *Paradise Regained* is essentially human, for "our Lord's condition in this world is constantly represented [in Milton, as in Scripture] like that of other men." It is for this reason that Lindsey takes to task other critics of Milton (such as Thomas Newton) who are "strenuous advocate[s] for the *godhead* of Christ." Jesus must be human in this life, Lindsey argues, for "the *Deity* can never be changed or transformed." Indeed, it is axiomatic that *"God can never become a child, or a youth."* In recognizing this fact in his poems, Milton reveals insight into the true nature of Jesus. "I know scarce any more perfect disciple of *Jesus* than *Milton*," Lindsey declares. In fact, the poet's own life "from the prime of early youth to old age" is consistent with both the maturation and the nobility of Jesus as a man who grows and matures in knowledge and experience. Lindsey even goes so far as to make a distinction between the god-head of *Paradise Lost* as essentially Arian and the Christology of *Paradise Regained* as essentially Socinian. For Lindsey, Milton is respectively of the Arian and Socinian parties in his great epics.[93]

It should be noted, however, that Lindsey subsequently had a change of heart in his reading of Milton. In *An Historical View of the State of the Unitarian Doctrine and Worship from the Reformation to our Own Times* (London, 1783), Lindsey retracted the views about Milton's Jesus that he had expressed in his earlier *Sequel*. Referring to his earlier discussion, he avers that he will now "take the liberty to correct a former inadvertence of [his] own," that is, his all-too-easy "Socinianizing" of the Jesus of *Paradise Regained*. Of the soliloquy from Milton's brief epic that he had cited in the *Sequel*, Lindsey confesses that this passage "too easily persuaded [him], that Milton was at that time come off his former orthodox sentiments, and was become a believer of the proper humanity of Christ."[94] What prompted Lindsey to retract his former interpretation is not immediately apparent. At the very least, Lindsey's change of heart suggests the extent to which the act of reading heterodoxy into texts that yield an entire constellation of interpretations can be (in fact, *is*) a tricky affair. Lindsey was forthright enough to acknowledge that difficulty and did not hesitate to record his altered views as the occasion demanded. However Lindsey's readings are to be judged, he was a critic who struggled with the complex theological nuances of the Miltonic text without whatever "benefit" *De doctrina Christiana* might have afforded.

With Robert Lemon's eventful discovery of *De doctrina Christiana* in the Middle Treasury Gallery, Whitehall, in 1823, and the subsequent publication of the Latin text, along with Charles R. Sumner's English translation in 1825, the issue of Milton's so-called heterodoxies reappeared with renewed vigor. Unlike the pre-1825 critics obliged to labor without recourse to any Miltonic system of divinity, critics now had at their disposal a theological tract, both in the Latin and in an English translation, to squabble over the beliefs that Milton was thought to have held, if not throughout his entire career, then during a good portion of it. It would be an understatement to suggest that the issue of Milton's alleged Antitrinitarianism (whether in its Arian form, its Socinian form, or something of an amalgamation of both forms) loomed large in the discourse of the day. The issue is already present in Sumner's "Preliminary Observations" to his translation of *De doctrina Christiana*. "Doubts have always been entertained as to the real sentiments of Milton respecting the second person of the Trinity," Sumner observes. Now, he says, our suspicions that the Arian and Socinian leanings are discernible in the poetry have been confirmed by the systematic discussions in the theological tract, which establishes without question "the opinions of Milton were in reality nearly Arian" and possibly Socinian as well. As one who subscribes to the orthodoxy of his own clerical calling, Sumner regrets that the great poet exhibits such heterodox views.[95]

As Francis E. Mineka observes, responses (supportive and critical) concerning such matters represent a distinguishing feature of the various periodical reviews that greeted the publication of *De doctrina Christiana*. The treatise at once "shocked the orthodox" and "delighted the unorthodox."[96] Accordingly, one reviewer laments in the *Evangelical Magazine* (1825) that "it is, indeed, harrowing to the feelings to learn, from Milton's own showing, that he believed the Son of God to be nothing more than an exalted creature." To confute Milton's heresies, the *Evangelical Magazine* published a series of articles in 1826 by one "J. P. S." (John Pye Smith) on the subject. It is clear, according to the confuter, that Milton's "generous sympathy with the oppressed would dispose him to the most favourable feelings for the Socinians of Poland."[97] The reviewer for the *Congregational Magazine* (1825) mounted a scathing attack on both the style and the theology of *De doctrina Christiana*. It "cannot be read; and, if it could, would do nobody any good." More than that, it is dangerous, for it contains heresy enough "to delight all the Socinians, Arians, and other triflers with sacred Scriptures, in both hemispheres."[98] In the same vein, the reviewer for the venerable high church and Tory *Gentleman's Magazine* (1825) shudders that in its delineation of God, *De doctrina Christiana* relegates Christianity to Judaism.[99] (This is a criticism that was lodged against the Antitrinitarians from the onset of Arianism in the fourth century through the advent of Socinianism in the early modern period and beyond.)

What was disturbing to the orthodox proved a welcome sign to the dissenters.[100] For the Unitarians, the discovery and publication of *De doctrina Christiana* proved a godsend. Although the Unitarians were uncomfortable with certain aspects of the theology delineated in the treatise, the attack upon the orthodox view of the Trinity prompted them to regard Milton as a valuable ally.[101] Accordingly, the *Monthly Repository* (1825), founded in 1806 to give voice to the Unitarian viewpoint, devoted three issues to provide an extended account of *De doctrina Christiana* as a text that prompted one to align Milton with the mighty names of John Locke and Sir Isaac Newton as foremost Unitarians.[102]

What is true of the English culural climate is no less true of the American, especially on the Unitarian front. William Ellery Channing is a case in point. Deemed "the single most important figure in the history of American Unitarianism," Channing found himself at the very center of the burgeoning Unitarian movement that flourished in New England.[103] Doing battle in his writings against the prevailing theological views and ecclesiastical policies of his Calvinist contemporaries, Channing produced such writings as the pamphlet *Unitarian Christianity* (1819), a latitudinarian document that has since become "the virtual manifesto of the liberal movement in theology, now explicitly Unitarian." A Christian humanist in his own right, he fostered an atmosphere receptive to "the creation of an authentic American literature that would celebrate the dignity and self-awareness of humanity."[104] It is little wonder, then, that Channing's response to the publication of *De doctrina Christiana* would be of more than passing interest. Entitled *Remarks on the Character and Writings of John Milton; Occasioned by the Publication of His Lately Discovered Treatise "Of Christian Doctrine"* (1826), Channing's detailed appraisal is important both in its own right and for what it says about the theological implications of the Unitarian outlook at that time.[105]

Channing's response to the treatise as a whole is muted. Although Channing is not particularly enthusiastic about the work as the product of the great poet and reformer, he nonetheless acknowledges that it must be accorded careful attention as a reflection of the mind and sensibility of the author. These aspects especially interest Channing, who delights in those "passages in which Milton's mind is laid open to us" in a manner that obliges the author to defend the radical nature of his positions (66–68). These include the act of "render[ing] the Supreme Being more interesting by giving him human shape." Although Channing objects to the idea of embodying God in this manner, he is astute in his responsiveness to the materialism that underlies the theology of the treatise (70–71). What most excites Channing is the treatment of the Son of God and the Holy Spirit. We are all aware, Channing observes, that in his delineation of the godhead Milton has "declared himself an Anti-trinitarian, and strenuously asserted the strict and proper unity of God." For Milton, the Son of God is "a distinct being from God, and inferior to him, that he existed before the world was made, that he is the first of the creation of God, and that afterwards all other things were made by him, as the instrument or minister of his Father." The Holy Spirit, in turn, "is a person, and intelligent agent, but created and inferior to God" (75–79). It is this emphasis upon *person,* this *personhood,* in the thought of the author of *De doctrina Christiana* that Channing finds so remarkable. Whether in the form of God, the form of the Son, or the form of the Holy Spirit, the quality of creatureliness is an aspect to which Channing as a Unitarian responds so powerfully. Such creatureliness is for Channing a fundamental aspect of the mind and sensibility of Milton. Even at the risk of imposing an overdetermined reading on the theological tract, Channing is willing to draw conclusions concerning it that reveal as much about his own mind and sensibility as they do about Milton. Thus, Channing brings to the fore elements of the theology that he himself embraces when he remarks that "we are unable within our limits to give a sketch of Milton's strong reasoning against the supreme divinity of Jesus Christ." Although one might have wished Channing to develop this reading in more detail, it little matters, for, as far as Channing is concerned, Milton has sufficiently proven himself the great spokesman of Unitarianism.

This is a triumph that prompts Channing to wax lyrical in his praise. "We must thank God," Channing declares, "that he has raised up this illustrious advocate of the long obscured doctrine of the Divine Unity." In opposition to the "Trinitarian adversaries [who] are perpetually ringing in our ears the names of Fathers and Reformers" to bolster their cause, Channing invokes his own trinity, "the three greatest and noblest minds of modern times," as "witnesses to that Great Truth, of which, in an humbler and narrower sphere, we desire to be the defenders." The minds to which Channing alludes as witnesses to the Great Truth are Milton, Locke and Newton. For Channing, this is the new trinity indeed. "Before these intellectual suns the stars of self-named Orthodoxy 'hide their diminished heads.' To these eminent men God communicated such unusual measures of light and mental energy, that their names spring up spontaneously, when we think or would speak of

the greatness of our nature." "Shackled by no party connex-
ions" and "warped by no clerical ambition," they approached
the subject of the godhead "in the fulness of their strength,
with free minds open to truth, and with unstained purity of
life." Breaking free of the trammels of their own time and
unbowed by the threat of penal law, they refused to discover
in the Scripture a "triple divinity." Rather, they extolled "the
One Infinite Father" and "ascrib[ed] to Him alone supreme
self-existent divinity" and "proper Unity" (75–79).[106] One might
suggest that Channing represents the culmination of the desire
to enlist Milton in the Unitarian cause, a movement that traces
its roots to a time well before the discovery of *De doctrina
Christiana* but is certainly given even greater impetus as the
result of the accessibility of this highly contested work.[107] What
is especially interesting is the inclination to pair Milton with
Locke and Newton, the luminaries of the age of the "new
philosophy" and the "new science." The Unitarian inclination
to situate Milton in this manner suggests once again the extent
to which the traditions that find their ultimate source in the
figure of Faustus Socinus re-emerged in the later periods with
renewed vigor and intensity.

If this essay has attempted to clarify the relationship between Milton and the Socinian heresy both during his own
time and in the later periods, it has also sought to provide
a sense of how the intersection between a writer and his
audience can illuminate our own understanding of what
transpires in his works. It little matters whether we can prove
that Milton accepted "this aspect," as opposed to "that aspect,"
of Socinianism. What does matter is that the Socinian heresy
was a crucial movement in his own time and that he responded
to it at various points in his career. What also matters is
that those who did express their allegiance to the movement
were inclined to draw upon certain elements in Milton's work
to proclaim him as one of their own. They must have seen
something in his delineation of doctrinal matters (either

implicit in the poetry or explicit in the prose) to justify their readings. That *something* became for them even more pronounced after the discovery and publication of the theological tract that the heterodox are determined to claim as *his* and that the orthodox are determined to claim as the work of someone else. The debate over the authorship of *De doctrina Christiana* is deeply implicated in the theological views that Milton's own readers hold. As much as some readers might desire, the debate over the authorship of the tract will not go away; nor will the debate over the heterodox Milton, as opposed to the orthodox Milton. The two debates are inextricably interlinked. I trust that the foregoing exploration provides a means of undertaking future investigations into Milton as a writer whose views gave rise to an entire constellation of interpretive possibilities. At the same time, I trust that we shall have gained a greater sense of Milton's place in the development and afterlife of a movement of the first import to the history of religious thought.

Notes

Notes to Introduction

1. "'He Ever Was a Dissenter': Milton's Transgressive Maneuvers in *Paradise Lost*," in *Arenas of Conflict: Milton and the Unfettered Mind*, ed. Kristin Pruitt McColgan and Charles W. Durham (Selinsgrove, Pa.: Susquehanna University Press, 1997), 21.

2. Joseph Wittreich, *The Romantics on Milton: Formal Essays and Critical Asides* (Cleveland: Press of Case Western Reserve University, 1971), ix.

Notes to Chapter 1/Shawcross

1. Of course, Johnson was not the only important critic to allow political attitudes to color his appraisal. For instance, toward the end of the century even Thomas Warton, in his 1785 edition of the shorter poems, was taken to task for his hostility toward Milton's political position; see *Gentleman's Magazine* 55 (1785): 591.

2. Samuel Johnson, "The Life of Milton," in *The Lives of the English Poets; and a Criticism of Their Works* (Dublin, 1779), 137–230, first separate edition from *The Works of the English Poets*.

3. H. White, letter to *Gentleman's Magazine* 56 (1786): 1109–10.

4. See Steele's *Poetical Miscellanies, Consisting of Original Poems and Translations. By the Best Hands* (London, 1714), 116–19; Thomas Birch, ed., *Complete Collection of the Historical, Political, and Miscellaneous Works of John Milton* (London, 1738), 1: xxxviii; British Library MS Additional 32567 and MSS of the Duke of Portland, reported in His Majesty's Commission on MSS, Fifteenth Report, Appendix, part 4,

vol. 6 [1901], 66; and Samuel Johnson, *The Works of the English Poets* (Göttingen, 1784), 1:259.

5. See *London Magazine* 7 (1738): 356. Raymond Dexter Havens, *The Influence of Milton on English Poetry* (Cambridge: Harvard University Press, 1922; New York: Russell & Russell, 1961), 478–548, discusses the sonnet; he does not cite Pope's hoax, perhaps because it is in ten lines. For discussion of the latter poem, see Dustin Griffin, *Regaining Paradise: Milton and the Eighteenth Century* (Cambridge: Cambridge University Press, 1986), 160.

6. George Friedrich Händel's musical adaptation, with words revised by Charles Jennens, was written between January 19 and February 4, 1740, and published in quarto by Jacob and Richard Tonson, grandnephews of Milton's earlier publisher. It is titled *L'Allegro, Il Penseroso, ed Il Moderato*; the third part does not employ Milton's words. See the holograph manuscript in the British Library, Music Library, MS R.M.20.d 5.

7. For Hoadly, see MS Eb 1737H in the de Beer Collection, University of Otago, and MS 9M73/G906 in the Malmesbury Collection, Hampshire County Record Office. For Yorke, see *The Life and Correspondence of Philip Yorke Earl of Hardwicke Lord High Chancellor of Great Britain. By Philip C. Yorke* (Cambridge: University Press, 1913), 2:147 (first line: "Philip, well versed in the wily Maze"), and 1:292–93 — first line: "Captain, (eftsoons a Colonel I ween)." The March 4 sonnet is in a manuscript at Wimpole. British Library MS Additional 35385, f. 13, transcribes the May 25 sonnet and includes it in a letter from P. Charles Yorke to his brother Sir Joseph Yorke, dated June 19, 1743, with discussion of Milton's Italianate minor poems (the sonnets in particular) and with reference to *Sonnet 8* and the trisyllabification of "Colonel." For "Hope," see *London Magazine* 16 (1747): 382. It is, however, only two quatrains. For Edwards, see Robert Dodsley, ed., *A Collection of Poems in Three Volumes. By Several Hands* (London, 1748), and *The Canons of Criticism, and Glossary; The Trial of the Letter Ψ and Y, and Sonnets* (London, 1758).

8. Havens, Griffin, and Joseph Wittreich have recorded a great number of formerly obscure authors and works, of course; their researches have been notably productive. See Wittreich's *Feminist Milton* (Ithaca, N.Y.: Cornell University Press, 1987), and his "'Under the Seal of Silence': Repressions, Receptions, and the Politics of *Paradise Lost*," in *Soundings of Things Done: Essays in Early Modern Literature in Honor of S. K. Heninger Jr.*, ed. Peter E. Medine and Joseph Wittreich (Newark: University of Delaware Press, 1997), 293–323.

9. Sherburn, "The Early Popularity of Milton's Minor Poems," *Modern Philology* 17 (1919–20): 259–79, 515–40.

10. See 140, but in note 1, he says, "I can find evidence for only nine printings of the complete minor poems before 1740." There were at least

11: 1695, 1705, 1707, 1713, 1720, 1721, 1725, 1730, 1731, 1738, 1739.

11. I gather from his appendices that he refers to 5 from the seventeenth century and 37 from the eighteenth (up to 1742). Of these 42, 32 (3 and 29) are influenced by the companion poems; 2 by *Comus* (one each century), 2 by the Nativity ode (one each century), 3 by the *Fifth Ode*, 2 by *Lycidas*, and one sonnet (all eighteenth century). The sonnet is by Philip Yorke, Lord Hardwicke, and is influenced verbally by Milton's *Sonnet 21*; it is dated June 8, 1741, and was printed in Thomas Park's enlargement of Horace Walpole's *Catalogue of Royal and Noble Authors* (London, 1806), 4:339.

12. See *Miscellany of Poems. Viz. Mully of Mountown. By Dr. King. Phoenix Park. By Mr. Ward. Orpheus and Euridice* (Dublin, 1718), 27–34; Matthew Concannen, *Miscellaneous Poems, Original and Translated, By Several Hands* (London, 1724), 379–91; and George Sherburn's edition of *The Correspondence of Alexander Pope* (Oxford: Clarendon Press, 1956), 1:18. Havens's misreading is curious even if he did not know that Walsh read Pope's own *Pastorals*. Early holograph versions of all four pastorals, dated 1704–1706(?), exist. See Maynard Mack, ed., *The Last and Greatest Art: Some Unpublished Poetical Manuscripts of Alexander Pope* (Newark: University of Delaware Press, 1984); they were first published in 1709 in "Dryden's Miscellany": *Poetical Miscellanies: The Sixth Part*, 721–51. They employ various adaptations from *Paradise Regain'd, Paradise Lost, Sonnet 1, Arcades*, the "Vacation Exercise," *Il Penseroso* and *Comus*. Of course there were also Ambrose Philips's non-Miltonic "Pastorals," first appearing in Elijah Fenton's edition of *Oxford and Cambridge Miscellany Poems* (London, n.d.), variously dated 1706, 1708, 1709, as well as in *Poetical Miscellanies: The Sixth Part* (1709). The first separate edition appeared in (1710), printed by Henry Hills.

13. In *The Fifth Part of Miscellany Poems*, 328–31. The eclogues are reprinted in *The Works of William Walsh, Esq.* (London, 1736), 61–63, 64–67, 67–70 and 81–86.

14. See *Theophilia, or Loves Sacrifice. A Divine Poem. Written by E. B. Esq; Several Parts thereof set to fit airs by Mr. J. Jenkins* (London, 1652); *The First Anniversary of the Government Under His Highness the Lord Protector* (London, 1655); and *Miscellaneous Poems* (London, 1681). Compare what seems to me a strange comment by Havens: "the few borrowings from these early pieces that Grosart points out in his notes to the poems of Andrew Marvell . . . prove nothing, since they are rather less than might be expected from a man who was Milton's friend and assistant. Two are dubious . . . but one . . . is striking" (those for "Upon Appleton House," "Fleckno" and "First Anniversary," respectively), 424 n. 2.

15. Thomas Rymer, *The Tragedies of the Last Age Consider'd and Examin'd* (London, 1678), 143; Havens, chapter 2, "Blank Verse and Rime," 44–53, for a discussion of opposing positions on the question; he

does not, however, mention Rymer; Thomas Shipman, *Henry the Third of France, Stabb'd by a Fryer* (London, 1678), A4v–*1.

16. *A Collection of Poems: viz. The Temple of Death* [etc.] *With Several Original Poems, Never Before Printed* (London, 1701), 393–400, and *A New Miscellany of Original Poems, on Several Occasions* (London, 1701), 212–21.

17. Addison, "Milton's Stile Imitated, in a Translation of a Story out of the Third Aeneid," first published in an augmented edition of John Dryden's *Poetical Miscellanies: The Fifth Part* (1704), 109–17; Anonymous, *The Mohocks: A Poem, in Miltonic Verse: Address'd to the Spectator* (London, 1712) and Anonymous, *On the Death of Mr. Edmund Smith, Late Student of Christ-Church, Oxon. A Poem, in Miltonic Verse* (London, 1712); Anonymous, "On Albanio's Marrying the Incomparable Monissa. By a Youth of Nineteen Years of Age. In Miltonian Verse," *New Miscellaneous Poems* [etc.]. *The Fourth Edition, According to the Original Copy, with Additions* (London, 1716), 40–48.

18. *The Plain Dealer*, no. 46 (August 28, 1724). See also the poem "in Miltonick numbers, on the Wonders of Omnipotence" in *The Plain Dealer: Being Select Essays on Several Curious Subjects* (1730).

19. Anonymous, *Lucifer's Defeat; or, the Mantle Chimney. A Miltonic* (London, 1729); Anonymous, "A Miltonick on Life, Death, Judgment, Heaven, and Hell," *The British Magazine* 4 (1749): 346–48; Samuel Wesley Jr., *Poems on Several Occasions* (London, 1736), 148–50, 151–56, 156.

20. A commonplace of early criticism was that the poem, and Milton as poet, lay long obscure until Lord Somers's edition; that is, Lord Somers as the highest ranking subscriber to the edition kept being accredited with bringing the 1688 edition forth from the publishers Richard Bentley and Jacon Tonson. The assemblage of the edition, however, was primarily the work of Henry Aldrich and Francis Atterbury, centered in Christ Church College, Oxford. Griffin, *Regaining Paradise*, 248–49 n. 8, discusses the matter.

21. Apparently published in Cambridge, Massachusetts, in 1687. A copy of the poem, on one sheet, is owned by Harvard University Library.

22. My translation is as follows:

O Muse who willingly drags along with a limping step
and is pleased with a halting gait like Vulcan's,
and who perceives that in its fitting place it is no less gratifying
than when the flaxen-haired Deiope with well-formed calves
dances before the golden couch of Juno, come hither.

The verses are labeled "Scazontes," which are iambs with a reversed final foot (a trochee or spondee), producing a "limping" effect.

23. Although not published until 1701 (thus 14 years' difference), Philips's poem was written by 1696, when Katherine Butler added a commonplace book of poetic transcriptions, including "In imitation of

Milton" (1–6), to Knightley Chetwoode's transcriptions of John Donne's sermons (St. Paul's Cathedral Library, MS 52.D.14).

24. I use a copy of *The Altar of Love* (1727) in the Henry E. Huntington Library; the edition of 1731 (also in the Huntington) drops the Philips imitation. However, there was a totally different edition of *The Altar of Love* also published in 1727 (copy in the William Andrews Clark Library). Both 1727 volumes were printed for H. Curll.

25. Jonathan Swift, *A Letter of Advice to a Young Poet: Together with a Proposal for the enccouragement of Poetry in This Kingdom* (London, 1721).

26. Joseph Spence, *Essay on Pope's Odyssey: In Which Some Particular Beauties and Blemishes of that Work are Considered. Part II* (London, 1727); see 13–15 on "Miltonick Writers."

27. The remark appears in *Gazette littéraire de l'Europe*, no. 8 (May 2, 1764), and in a letter to Horace Walpole, dated July 15, 1768; see *The Correspondence of Horace Walpole*, vol. 41, ed. W. S. Lewis (New Haven: Yale University Press, 1980), 152–56. Rather similarly, a commentator in *The Dublin Magazine* 2 (July 1762): 399–402, in a piece entitled "An Essay on the Advantages of Rhyme in Modern Narrative Poetry," says that Milton was not "incapable" of rhyme, but was not "formed to it in his youth, and consequently could not command it when he wanted it; or perhaps from laziness, or pride, in considering it as beneath him, and a sort of mechanical servility, he could not prevail with himself to acquire" (400).

28. See William Coward, *Licentia Poetica Discuss'd: Or the True Test of Poetry* (London, 1709), 65–67.

29. "Account of the Progress of Song-Writing in This Country, from the Reign of Queen Elizabeth to the present Time," reprinted in *The New Annual Register, or General Repository of History, Politics, and Literature. For the Year 1784* (London, 1785), 117; see *A Select Collection of English Songs. In Three Volumes*, ed. Joseph Ritson (London, 1783), 1:lx–lxvii. The "songs," however, are from John Dalton's *Comus*.

30. *Correspondence of Horace Walpole*, 31:219–20.

31. *Spectator*, paper no. 297 (February 9, 1712). As Addison goes on to say, it is this which "gave Occasion to Mr. *Dryden*'s Reflection, that the Devil was in reality *Milton*'s Hero." Needless to say, I find Dryden's (and, yes, Blake's) reading not perspicacious; see chapter 4, "The Hero," in my *With Mortal Voice: The Creation of "Paradise Lost"* (Lexington: University Press of Kentucky, 1982). In any case, Addison apparently believed that Milton never intended a hero because Adam (or Adam and Eve) does not emerge as hero under classical rules of literary production; he suggests, if one must have a hero, the Messiah.

32. William Richardson, *Essays on Shakespeare's Dramatic Characters of Richard the Third, King Lear, and Timon of Athens* (London, 1784), 134–35.

33. "Blemishes in the *Paradise Lost*," *The Adventurer*, no. 101 (October 23, 1753).

34. *The Poetical Works of Janet Little, The Scotch Milkmaid* (Air: Printed by John & Peter Wilson, 1792), 113–16. Little reflects Milton in "To Hope" (27–31) (*L'Allegro*); "On Happiness" (32–36) (blank verse); "On the Spring" (72–74) (*Sonnet 1* and perhaps *Paradise Lost* in her "they hand in hand" image); and "An Elegy on the Death of Mrs. ———, Personating Her Husband" (85) (*PL* 3.47–49). There is an allusion in "An Acrostic Upon a Young Woman, Written by Her Lover" (158); the name is Hannah Ivison. Of course, the poem cited here is in octosyllabic couplets.

35. The "Scale" appeared in *The Literary and Antigallican Magazine* (a unique title for this issue of *The Literary Magazine: or Universal Review*) 3 (January 1758): 6–8; in *Edinburgh Magazine* 2 (1758): 26–28; and in *The Scots Magazine* 20 (1758): 72–74. A correspondent to the *Edinburgh Magazine* disputed the positioning and comparisons (106–8).

36. Anthony Ashley Cooper, *Soliloquy; or, Advice to an Author* (London, 1710), 64, 118, 190, and reprinted in *Characteristicks of Men, Manners, Opinions, Time* (n.p., 1711); John Dennis, *Proposals for Printing by Subscription, In Two Volumes in Octavo, the Following Miscellaneous Tracts, Written by Mr. John Dennis* (London, 1721), and *Original Letters, Familiar, Moral and Critical* (London, 1721); Francis Hutcheson, *An Inquiry into the Original of Our Ideas of Beauty and Virtue* (London, 1725), 152 n., 133 n.

37. Leonard Welsted, *The Works of Dionysius Longinus, On the Sublime; or, A Treatise Concerning the Sovereign Perfection of Writing* (London, 1712), 145–59, 171, 175–78, 186; the translation reappeared in 1724. William Smith, *Dionysius Longinus On the Sublime: Translated from the Greek, With Notes and Observations, and Some Account of the Life, Writings and Character of the Author* (London, 1739); it was republished in 1740, 1742, 1743 and 1756. Edmund Burke, *A Philosophical Enquiry into the Origin of Our Ideas of the Sublime and Beautiful* (London, 1757).

38. On Milton as "sublimest Son of the Muses," see J. T., "To Dryden and to 'the sublimest Son of the Muses, *John Milton*'" in *A Letter of Compliment to the Ingenious Author of a Treatise on the Passions, So Far as They Regard the Stage* (London, 1747). The reference is to Dryden's epigram; the author also cites "the *Devil* in the Shape of a Toad at *Eve's* Ear" (13), and *Paradise Lost*, book 1, line 84: "If thou beest he; but O how fall'n! how chang'd" (33). For Milton as the "British Homer," see, for one example, *An Epistle to the Right Honourable the Earl of Orrery, Occasion'd by Reading His Lordship's Translation of Pliny's Epistles. By Henry Jones* (London, 1751), 10, and with reference to Milton's blindness. On Milton as "Prince of our English Poets," see *Universal Magazine of Knowledge and Pleasure* 29 (1761): 13–18.

39. Robert Potter, *An Inquiry into Some Passages in Dr. Johnson's Lives of the Poets: Particularly His Observations on Lyric Poetry, and the Odes of Gray* (London, 1783); "On the Sublime," *The Grub-street Journal*, no. 292 (July 31, 1735), reprinted in *Gentleman's Magazine* 5 (1735): 461.

40. Hugh Blair, *Lectures on Rhetoric and Belles Lettres* (London, 1783). See Lecture 3, on *PL* 2.263–67 (p. 49); Lecture 4, *PL* 1.589–600, 6.643–46 (pp. 69–73); Lecture 13, *PL* 2.879–82, 7.205–07 (p. 267); Lecture 17, various (pp. 348–49), among other places.

41. For Stack's talk see *The Transactions of the Royal Irish Academy. M.DCC.LXXXVII* (Dublin: Printed by George Burham, for the Academy), 12–13, 21. Related to these encomia of Milton's sublimity was a very popular stage show that added representations from the poem. In 1781 Philippe Jacques De Loutherberg created a kind of panoramic moving peep show with various pictures and pyrotechnics, which he called "The Eidophusikon" ("natural shape"). In 1786 he added "The Grand Scene from Milton" and "Satan, Burning Lake, Pandemonium," painted by Edward F. Burney, with Pandaemonium in the background. It was often and continuingly performed; in June 1793 alone, *The Gazetteer, or New Daily Advertiser* carried 12 advertisements for it (nos. 20121 through 20129, June 7 through June 27).

For the most part, remarks on and examples of sublimity in *Paradise Lost* usually reflect human attraction to what is evil and very little interest in what is good. The "exalted" seems not to be enough.

42. Mary Wollstonecraft, *Thoughts on the Education of Daughters: With Reflections on Female Conduct, in the More Important Duties of Life* (London, 1787), 52–53. Wittreich quotes from Moira Ferguson's edition of Wollstonecraft's *The Female Reader* (1789; reprint, Scholars' Facsimiles and Reprints, 1980). The 1787 quotation is reprinted in the 1789 volume (8).

43. Charlotte McCarthy, *The Fair Moralist; or, Love and Virtue. By a Gentlewoman . . . To which is Added, Several Occasional Poems, by the same* (London, 1745).

44. George Colman and Bonnell Thornton, compilers, *Poems By Eminent Ladies*, 2 vols. (London, 1755), 261.

45. *Memoirs of Mrs. Lætitia Pilkington, Wife to the Rev. Mr. Matthew Pilkington. Written by Herself*, 2 vols. (Dublin, 1748–1749); *The Third and Last Volume of the Memoirs of Mrs. Lætitia Pilkington, Written by Herself* (London, 1754).

46. The title in the 1701 edition is *The Ladies Defence; or, The Bride-Woman's Counsellor Answer'd: A Poem. In a dialogue between Sir John Bute, Sir William Loveall, Melissa, and a Parson. Written by a Lady.*

47. Other poems by Anne Finch have been cited, but one should also see "The Musselman's Dream" and "Adam Pos'd" in her 1713 collection

of *Miscellany Poems, on Several Occasions. Written by a Lady,* to which should be added "An Invocation to Sleep" and "To the Honorable the Lady Worsley at Longleat," published by Myra Reynolds in *The Poems of Anne Countess of Winchelsea* (Chicago: University of Chicago Press, 1903). Havens notes *Sick-bed Soliloquy to an Empty Purse* (1735) in connection with Philips but he hadn't seen it (317 n.). I have not found it either and do not know whether the anonymous "Soliloquy on an Empty Purse," printed in the third edition of *Poems by Eminent Ladies* (ca. 1780), is the same. Havens also cites "The Copper Farthing" from *The Poetical Calendar. Containing a Collection of Scarce and Valuable Pieces of Poetry,* ed. Francis Fawkes and William Woty (London, 1763), vol. 10 for October, 48–53.

Havens notes echoes of *Paradise Lost* in Whateley from a review in *Monthly Review* 30 (1764): 449, of *Original Poems on Several Occasions* (1764), where it appears on pp. 72–77. But one should also remark Darwell's "The Power of Destiny" (13–16), "Elegy on a Much Lamented Friend, Who Died in Autumn, 1759" (23–25), "Ode" (72–77), all with allusions in the poems; "To the Rev. Mr. Welchman at Tanworth" (90–94) in blank verse with influence from and allusion to *Paradise Lost*; and "To my Garden" (98–99), in octosyllabics.

48. Elizabeth Griffith, *Essays, Addressed to Young Married Women* (London, 1782), 15.

49. Laetitia Hawkins, *Letters on the Female Mind, Its Powers and Pursuits,* 2 vols. (London, 1793).

50. Their poem is found in Bodleian Library, MS English Poetical d. 47, ff. 84–86.

51. See *The Poetical Works of Anna Seward,* ed. Sir Walter Scott, 3 vols. (Edinburgh, 1810).

52. See pp. 130–38 of chapter 8 of my "Milton in Italy in the Eighteenth Century," *John Milton and Influence* (Pittsburgh: Duquesne University Press, 1991).

53. Poems cited echo and reflect *Comus, Epitaph on the Marchioness of Winchester, Il Penseroso, Paradise Lost, L'Allegro* and *Lycidas.*

54. *Letters from the Mountains; Being the Real Correspondence of a Lady Between the Years 1773 and 1797. The Third Edition* (London, 1807), Letter 51, dated January 2, 1794, 2:267–77.

55. James Burnet, Lord Monbaddo, *Of the Origin and Progress of Language* (Edinburgh: 1789), 5:265–67.

56. See Boerhaden, *Gentleman's Magazine* 49 (1779): 492–93, and James Thomson Callender, *The Deformities of Dr. Samuel Johnson. Selected from His Works* (Edinburgh, 1782), 19, 58n. Milton is also discussed on pages 3, 16, 39, 43–44, 49–50, 53.

57. See *The Poetical Works of Anna Seward; With Extracts from her Literary Correspondence,* ed. Sir Walter Scott (Edinburgh, 1810). Seward

knew Johnson, and James Boswell consulted her in his writing of the biography.

58. See *Gentleman's Magazine* 30 (1760): 611–12 (Supplement).

Notes to Chapter 2/Norbrook

1. David Norbrook, *Writing the English Republic: Poetry, Rhetoric and Politics, 1627–1660* (Cambridge: Cambridge University Press, 1999).

2. Joseph Wittreich, *Feminist Milton* (Ithaca, N.Y.: Cornell University Press, 1987); "'He Ever Was a Dissenter': Milton's Transgressive Maneuvers in *Paradise Lost,*" in *Arenas of Conflict: Milton and the Unfettered Mind,* ed. Kristin Pruitt McColgan and Charles W. Durham (Cranbury, N.J.: Susquehanna University Press, 1997), 21–40; "Receptions (Then and Now) and the Sexual Politics of *Paradise Lost,*" in *Milton and Heresy,* ed. Stephen B. Dobranski and John P. Rumrich (Cambridge: Cambridge University Press, 1998), 244–66.

3. Germaine Greer, *Slip-Shod Sibyls: Recognition, Rejection and the Woman Poet* (London: Viking, 1995), 447.

4. Wittreich, "Milton's Transgressive Maneuvers," 250–52.

5. All quotations from *Order and Disorder* come from my modernized text (Oxford: Blackwell Publishers, 2001); an old spelling edition is in progress. Hutchinson, "Elegies," iiA, in David Norbrook, "Lucy Hutchinson's 'Elegies' and the Situation of the Republican Woman Writer," *English Literary Renaissance* 27 (1997): 468–521.

6. John T. Shawcross, *Milton: A Bibliography for the Years 1624–1700* (Binghamton, N.Y.: Medieval and Renaissance Texts and Studies, 1984). Citations from *Paradise Lost* are from *John Milton: Complete Poems and Major Prose,* ed. Merritt Y. Hughes (New York: Odyssey Press, 1957). For fuller accounts of the manuscript and dating of *Order and Disorder,* see David Norbrook, "'A devine Originall': Lucy Hutchinson and the 'woman's version,'" *Times Literary Supplement,* 19 March 1999, 13–15, and "Lucy Hutchinson and *Order and Disorder*: The Manuscript Evidence," *English Manuscript Studies 1100–1700* 9 (2000): 257–91.

7. Annabel Patterson and Martin Dzelzainis, "Marvell and the Earl of Anglesey: A Chapter in the History of Reading," *Historical Journal* 44 (2001): 703–26. Henry Mortlock, who published *Order and Disorder,* had been involved in the publication of one of the 1668 issues of *Paradise Lost.*

8. David Norbrook, "Lucy Hutchinson versus Edmund Waller," *The Seventeenth Century* 11 (1996): 61–86.

9. *Memoirs of the Life of Colonel Hutchinson,* ed. James Sutherland (Oxford, 1973), 279, 53; future references will be to this edition.

10. Philip Hardie, "The Presence of Lucretius in *Paradise Lost,*" *Milton Quarterly* 19 (1995): 13–24.

11. *Lucy Hutchinson's Translation of Lucretius: "De rerum natura,"* ed. Hugh de Quehen (London: Duckworth, 1996), 24–25.

12. J. D. Minyard, *Lucretius and the Late Republic: An Essay in Roman Intellectual History* (Leiden: E. J. Brill, 1985), passim.

13. Reid Barbour, "Between Atoms and the Spirit: Lucy Hutchinson's Translation of Lucretius," in *Renaissance Papers 1994,* ed. Barbara J. Baines and George Walton Williams (Raleigh: Southeastern Renaissance Conference, 1995), 1–16, and "Lucy Hutchinson, Atomism, and the Atheist Dog," in *Women, Science and Medicine 1500–1700,* ed. Lynette Hunter and Sarah Hutton (Stroud: Sutton Publishing, 1998), 122–37; quote on 130.

14. Commentary on his translation of Lucretius, British Library Evelyn MS 34, fol. 106r.

15. Norbrook, *Writing the English Republic,* 467.

16. Nottinghamshire Archives, DD/HU3, 277.

17. *On Christian Doctrine,* in *The Complete Prose Works of John Milton,* ed. Don M. Wolfe et al., 8 vols. in 10 (New Haven: Yale University Press, 1953–82), 6:168–202.

18. See, for example, Gary S. De Krey, "Rethinking the Restoration: Dissenting Cases for Conscience, 1667–1672," *Historical Journal* 38 (1995): 53–83; De Krey discusses Owen at some length.

19. Norbrook, *Writing the English Republic,* 481.

20. "Elegies," 8.25–36; 9.21–40.

21. See Mary Ann Radzinowicz, "Milton and the Tragic Women of Genesis," in *Of Poetry and Politics: New Essays on Milton and His World,* ed. P. G. Stanwood (Binghamton: Medieval and Renaissance Texts and Studies, 1995), 131–51. For fuller discussion of Hutchinson's women, see Norbrook, *Order and Disorder,* xliii–lii.

22. *Lucy Hutchinson's Translation of Lucretius: "De rerum natura,"* 23–24.

Notes to Chapter 3/Achinstein

1. Alexander Pope, "A Receit to make an Epick Poem," in *The Prose Works of Alexander Pope,* 2 vols., ed. Norman Ault (1936; reprint, Oxford: Basil Blackwell, 1968), 1:120.

2. R. D. Havens, *The Influence of Milton on English Poetry* (Cambridge: Harvard University Press, 1922). The Anglican clergyman, Francis Peck, in *New Memoirs of the Life and Poetical Works of John Milton* (1740), 106–32, catalogs with examples the peculiarly "Miltonic" characteristics of his verse, defining his style by vocabulary, grammar, metaphors and frequent rhetorical tropes, admiring Milton's "mixtures of opposite passions" (129), and finding his imitations of Scriptures "charming" (131). Peck also defended the lack of rhyme in his *Sighs*

Upon the never enough lamented Death of Queen Anne. In Imitation of Milton (London, 1719), xii–xv. See also Havens, *Influence*, 80–85.

3. The instances of "Miltonic" in the Oxford English Dictionary particularly focus on Milton's *diction*; see F. R. Leavis, *Revaluation: Tradition and Development in English Poetry* (London: Chatto and Windus, 1949): "A common, limply pompous Miltonicism" (46). As to his prosody, Leavis accused Milton of an "inescapable monotony of the ritual"; his writing possessed "a certain sensuous poverty," "unexhilarating" (58). As Leavis saw it, "the Grand Style barred Milton from essential expressive resources of English that he had once commanded" (44, 47, 51). Owen Barfield, *Poetic Diction: A Study in Meaning* (London: Faber & Gwyer, 1928), 177, is also cited in the OED: "stale Miltonics, which lay at the bottom of so much eighteenth-century poetic diction." And compare T. S. Eliot, "Milton" (1947), in James Thorpe, ed., *Milton Criticism: Selections from Four Centuries* (London: Routledge and Kegan Paul, 1956), 310–32: "in Milton there is always the maximal, never the minimal, alteration of ordinary language" (320), which is one of the "marks of his greatness" (321).

4. John T. Shawcross, ed., *Milton, 1732–1801: The Critical Heritage* (London: Routledge and Kegan Paul, 1972), 18.

5. Anonymous, *The Athenian Spy* (London, 1704), A2v, 1, 7, and passim, a wonderful lampoon of Singer's assertions of platonic love.

6. British Library Additional Manuscripts. 29,300 ff. 112a–113a.

7. Elizabeth Singer Rowe, "To A Friend who Persuades me to leave the Muses," *Poems on Several Occasions by Philomela* (London, 1696), 6–9.

8. Dictionary of National Biography; Rowe's biography is outlined in Henry F. Stecher, *Elizabeth Singer Rowe, the Poetess of Frome: A Study in Eighteenth Century English Pietism* (Bern: Herbert Lang, 1973), and in the introduction to Elizabeth Rowe, *Miscellaneous Works in Prose and Verse*, 2 vols. (London, 1739), 1:i–xcvii. See also Marjorie Reeves, "Literary Women in Eighteenth-Century Nonconformist Circles," in *Culture and the Nonconformist Tradition*, ed. Jane Shaw and Alan Kreider (Cardiff: University of Wales Press, 1999), 7–25.

9. Earl Wasserman analyses her adaptation of Drayton, *Elizabethan Poetry in the Eighteenth Century* (Urbana-Champaign: University of Illinois Press, 1947), 74–75: "What Mrs. Rowe succeeded in doing was to reduce both colorful extremes to a uniform level of elegant simplicity" (75). Rowe's influence on eighteenth century women writers is discusssed in Stuart Curran, "Romantic Women Poets: Inscribing the Self," in *Women's Poetry of the Enlightenment: The Making of a Canon, 1730–1820*, ed. Isobel Armstrong and Virginia Blain (London: Macmillan, 1999), 161–63.

10. There are no dates for most of her printed letters. Elizabeth Rowe,

The Miscellaneous Works in Prose and Verse, 2 vols., ed. Mr. Theophilus Rowe (London, 1739), 2:97, 58, 82, 111, 198. Rolli's translation appeared in 1729.

11. Rowe, *Works,* 1:xvi: citing Milton's *Il Penseroso* (62), "most musical, most melancholy." R. D. Havens classes Rowe's poetry as "non-Miltonic blank verse," in his appendix B to *Influence,* 626.

12. Cited in Havens, *Influence,* 23 n. 6; Rowe, *Works,* 1:115.

13. The claim of Madeline Forell Marshall, *The Poetry of Elizabeth Singer Rowe, 1674–1737* (Lewiston, Maine: Edwin Mellen Press, 1989), that Rowe chose such topics because "religious writing provided a legitimate way out of the bind of limited female education and consequent literary disqualification" (77), needs correction. I disagree with Stecher, *Rowe,* who sees religion as a kind of safety valve for otherwise unacceptable expressions, and who claims that she wrote "to counteract her unruly imagination, she attempted to concentrate her attention on pious and moral concerns, and to channel the ardency of her feelings into devotional writing" (194). Both of these admirable critics voice the prejudices of a modern, secular society in which religion and the irrationalities expressed by such a writer as Rowe need to be explained as something else. Milton scholars have known for a long time that religious writing was a means of expressing political and personal identities.

14. *The Athenian Mercury* 5, no. 14 (January 16, 1692), n.p.

15. Nicholas von Maltzahn, "The Whig Milton, 1667–1700," in *Milton and Republicanism,* ed. David Armitage, Armand Himy and Quentin Skinner (Cambridge: Cambridge University Press, 1995), 229–53. On the changing meaning of the civil war and regicide in post–1688 England, see R. C. Richardson, *The Debate on the English Revolution* (London: Methuen, 1977), 35–40. On tensions among Whigs and discussions of Commonwealth principles under William, see Henry Horwitz, *Parliament, Policy and Politics in the Reign of William III* (Manchester: Manchester University Press, 1977), 277, 283.

16. Mary Astell, *Moderation Truly Stated* (London, 1704), 80. This emerged in the context of a poetical pamphlet war including William Shippen, *Moderation Display'd: A Poem* (London, 1704), a satirical mock-Miltonic epic against toleration. On religious dissent after the Glorious Revolution, see Michael R. Watts, *The Dissenters: From the Reformation to the French Revolution* (1978; reprint, Oxford: Clarendon Press, 1999), 263–97; B. R. White, "The Twilight of Puritanism in the Years Before and After 1688," in *From Persecution to Toleration: The Glorious Revolution and Religion in England,* ed. Ole Peter Grell, Jonathan I. Israel, and Nicholas Tyacke (Oxford: Clarendon, 1991), 307–30.

17. Isaac Watts, *Horae Lyricae* (London, 1706), preface, n.p.

18. Isaac Watts, "The Adventurous Muse," in *Horae Lyricae* (London,

1709), 212. This second edition is the first that prints Watts's poem on Milton. A discussion of Milton is absent in Watts's 1706 edition. This 1709 edition is hereafter cited in the text.

19. Jean Hagstrum, *The Sister Arts: The Tradition of Literary Pictorialism from Dryden to Gray* (Chicago: University of Chicago Press, 1958), 134.

20. Rowe, *Works*, 2:198 (n.d.).

21. F. R. Leavis, *Revaluation*, castigated this aspect of Milton. In discussing his description of Eden, Leavis remarks, "as the laboured, pedantic artifice of the diction suggests, Milton seems here to be focussing rather upon words than upon perceptions, sensations or things . . . the medium calls pervasively for a kind of attention, compels an attitude towards itself, that is incompatible with sharp, concrete realization" (49–50).

22. John Carey and Alastair Fowler, eds., *The Poems of John Milton* (London: Longmans, 1968), 465 n. See John B. Broadbent, "Milton's Hell," *English Literary History* 21, no. 3 (1954): 161–92.

23. John Dennis, *The Advancement and Reformation of Modern Poetry* (1701), in *The Critical Works of John Dennis*, ed. Edward Niles Hooker (Baltimore: Johns Hopkins University Press, 1939), 1:277. And a little further on, "energetick Image" (277). In *The Grounds of Criticism in Poetry* (1704), in the same volume, 342–56 passim, Dennis takes Milton as his chief case study, defending enthusiasm in his campaign to reform poetry.

24. Indeed, she seems to bypass the long visual tradition of hell representations in Western art explored by Roland Mushat Frye, *Milton's Imagery and the Visual Arts* (Princeton: Princeton University Press, 1978), 125–45. Exploring Milton's absorption with the new science in his depiction of the natural world is Karen L. Edwards, *Milton and the Natural World: Science and Poetry in "Paradise Lost"* (Cambridge: Cambridge University Press, 1999).

25. Milton's hell, too, is absent of physical torture, as Broadbent argued in "Milton's Hell." Frye, *Milton's Imagery*, 71–81, discusses how Milton humanized the devils, in opposition to a "monstrous" tradition.

26. Estella Schoenberg, "The Face of Satan, 1688," in *Ringing the Bell Backward: Proceedings of the First International Milton Symposium*, ed. Ronald G. Shafer (Indiana, Pa.: Indiana University of Pennsylvania Press, 1982), 47–60.

27. John T. Shawcross, "The First Illustrators of *Paradise Lost*," *Milton Quarterly* 9 (1975): 43–46, confirms that the illustrator for the book 1 engraving is Dr. Henry Aldrich. Helen Gardner, "Milton's First Illustrator," *A Reading of "Paradise Lost"* (Oxford: Clarendon, 1965), 121–31; Ernest W. Sullivan II, "Illustration as Interpretation: *Paradise Lost* from 1688 to 1807," in *Milton's Legacy in the Arts*, ed. Albert C. Labriola and Edward Sichi Jr. (University Park: Pennsylvania State

University Press, 1988), 59–92, which covers other elements than those Rowe highlights.

28. James Turner, *Politics of Landscape: Rural Scenery and Society in English Poetry, 1630–1660* (Oxford: Basil Blackwell, 1979), 188; see also Andrew McRae, *God Speed the Plough: The Representation of Agrarian England, 1500–1660* (Cambridge: Cambridge University Press, 1996). For a detailed analysis of the politics of landscape within Whig politics, see Christine Gerrard, *The Patriot Opposition to Walpole: Politics, Poetry and National Myth, 1725–1742* (Oxford: Clarendon, 1994); and Tim Fulford, *Landscape, Liberty and Authority: Poetry, Criticism and Politics from Thomson to Wordsworth* (Cambridge: Cambridge University Press, 1996).

29. See introduction to Gerald Maclean, Donna Landry and Joseph P. Ward, eds., *The Country and the City Revisited: England and the Politics of Culture, 1550–1850* (Cambridge: Cambridge University Press, 1999).

30. Basil Willey, *The Eighteenth-Century Background* (Harmondsworth: Penguin, 1967), discusses this theme in literature in eighteenth century poetics.

31. Joseph Addison, *Spectator,* no. 303 (February 16, 1712) on *Paradise Lost,* in Donald F. Bond, ed., *The Spectator* (Oxford: Clarendon Press, 1965), 3:87; also cited in John T. Shawcross, *Milton: The Critical Heritage* (London: Routledge and Kegan Paul, 1970), 171.

32. Stanley Fish, *Surprised by Sin: The Reader in "Paradise Lost"* (Berkeley and Los Angeles: University of California Press, 1967), 250.

33. John Dennis, *Remarks on Prince Arthur,* in *Works,* ed. Hooker, 1:106. Dennis continues, "Milton, to introduce his Devils with success, saw that it was necessary to give them something that was allied to Goodness. Upon which he very dextrously feign'd, that the Change which was caus'd by their Fall, was not wrought in them all at once" (108).

34. Shawcross, *Critical Heritage,* 174–75.

35. Lady Hertford to Watts, August 8, 1735, Alnwick MS. no. 110, fols. 165–66, cited in Helen Sard Hughes, *The Gentle Hertford: Her Life and Letters* (New York: Macmillan, 1940), 460 n. 13.

36. Dr. Watts to Lady Hertford, June 15, 1738, cited in ibid., 363.

37. Elizabeth Singer Rowe, *The History of Joseph. A Poem* (London, 1737), 1:4–5.

38. See Samuel H. Monk, *The Sublime: A Study of Critical Theories in Eighteenth-Century England* (Ann Arbor: University of Michigan Press, 1960). John Dennis did more than any critic to reconcile Christianity to poetry, ever citing Milton as his best example in *The Advancement and Reformation of Modern Poetry* (1701), in *Works,* ed. Hooker, 1:219. In preferring modern poets to the ancients, Dennis cites the striking image of Satan and the eclipse (*PL* 1.589–601) and defends Milton's vehemence and terror, what he praises as "enthusiasm," in an aesthetic program to couple Christian religion, poetry and reason. Milton,

thus, "excels Virgil" (271), by his "advantage" of Religion; Dennis repeatedly praises Milton's "images" (273, 275, 276).

39. [Richard Leigh, attr.], *The Transproser Rehears'd* (London, 1673), 147. The authorship of this tract is in dispute. In *The Life of John Milton* (London: Macmillan, 1880), 6:704, David Masson ascribes it to Samuel Parker; Nicholas von Maltzahn attributes it to Samuel Butler in "Samuel Butler's Milton," *Studies in Philology* 92 (1995): 482–95.

Notes to Chapter 4/Patterson

1. Thomas W. Copeland, *Our Eminent Friend Edmund Burke* (New Haven: Yale University Press 1949), 73–76. Isaac Kramnick, *The Rage of Edmund Burke: Portrait of an Ambivalent Conservative* (New York: Basic Books, 1977). David Bromwich, ed., *On Empire, Liberty and Reform: Speeches and Letters: Edmund Burke* (New Haven: Yale University Press, 2000), 10. Bromwich also suggests, however, that Burke had been horribly alarmed by the Gordon Riots in London in 1780. A loftier statement of this position is by J. G. A. Pocock, "Burke and the Ancient Constitution: A Problem in the History of Ideas," in *Politics, Language and Time* (New York: 1973), 202–3.

2. The full title is *The Speech of Edmund Burke, Esq., on Moving His Resolutions for Conciliation with the Colonies, March 22, 1775.*

3. One valuable exception is the reprinting of the speech in Bromwich, *On Empire*, 66–134.

4. *Catalogue of the Library of Thomas Jefferson*, 5 vols., ed. E. M. Sowerby (Charlottesville: University Press of Virginia, 1983), 3:259, no. 3097.

5. The exception is a brief discussion in Frans de Bruyn, *The Literary Genres of Edmund Burke: The Political Uses of Literary Form* (Oxford: Clarendon 1996), 138–42. While de Bruyn notes one of the central allusions to Milton in *On Conciliation*, his account of its function virtually upends what Burke, as I shall show, intended.

6. F. P. Lock, *Edmund Burke*, 2 vols. (Oxford: Clarendon 1998), 1:539.

7. For the significance of both Thomas Hollis and Richard Baron in the Whig publishing program, see my *Early Modern Liberalism* (Cambridge: Cambridge University Press 1997). For further discussion of Milton's influence in the founding of America, see the essays in *Milton and the Imperial Vision*, ed. Balachandra Rajan and Elizabeth Sauer (Pittsburgh: Duquesne University Press, 1999).

8. See the catalog of his 1833 library sale in *Sale Catalogues of Libraries of Eminent Persons*, vol. 8, ed. Seamus Deane (London: Mansell 1973), 14, 16, 18, 21.

9. Knox's proposal included a similar one to raise 100,000 pounds a

year by taxing Ireland, a notion which may have first attracted Burke's attention, leading to his interest in the American issue.

10. For these figures, the context of the speech and the speech itself, see *The Writings and Speeches of Edmund Burke*, vol. 2, ed. Paul Langford (Oxford: Clarendon, 1981), 406–63. See especially Langford's remark that "considering that Rockingham had taken particular pains to rally the forces of his party for that day, this represented a crushing defeat for the opposition" (463).

11. The construction metaphor had a long history, originating in the account of the building of Solomon's temple, where he had the stones cut to size before being brought to the construction site so that the quiet of the holy place would not be disturbed. During the English revolution, this was interpreted by Thomas Hill, a conservative divine, to mean "that no noise of contentions and schismes . . . might be heard, . . . and that in his house wee might all thinke and speake the same thing"; see Hill's *The Good Old Way, Gods Way* (London, 1644), 39. In *Areopagitica* Milton reversed this interpretation:

> as if, while the Temple of the Lord was building, some cutting, some squaring the marble, others hewing the cedars, there should be a sort of irrationall men who could not consider there must be many schisms and many dissections made in the quarry . . . ere the house of God can be built. And when every stone is laid artfully together, it cannot be united into a continuity, it can but be contiguous in this world; neither can every peece of the building be of one form; nay rather the perfection consists in this, that out of many moderat varieties and brotherly dissimilitudes that are not vastly disproportionall arises the goodly and the gracefull symmetry that commends the whole pile and structure.

See *Complete Prose Works*, 8 vols., ed. Don M. Wolfe et al. (New Haven: Yale University Press 1953–82), 2:555.

12. Lucan, *The Civil War*, trans. J. D. Duff (Cambridge, Mass.: Harvard University Press 1977), 518–19.

13. Lock, *Edmund Burke*, 300; Lock later noted Burke's peculiar analogy between Conway and Satan as serpent, but without making the connection between it and this constant animosity. Hence his interpretive wavering: "In *Paradise Lost*, however, the crest that is elevated and brightened is Satan's. . . . Had the phrase become entirely detached from its context, or did E. B. mean his hearers to think of Conway as a fallen angel?" (355 n. 12).

14. *The Parliamentary History of England, from the Earliest Period . . .*, 36 vols. (London: Hansard, 1806, 1820), 18:1441.

15. *The Writings and Speeches of Edmund Burke*, vol. 3, ed. W. M. Elofson with John Woods (Oxford: Clarendon 1996), 105; italics added.

16. Addison's *Cato* was staged in 1713. Though mostly written a

decade earlier, it was immediately read as a political allegory by the Whigs, who chose to see Marlborough as Cato. The Tories responded by seeing Marlborough as Caesar. The lines Burke remembered are from act 5, scene 1, lines 13–14: "The wide, th'unbounded prospect, lyes before me; / But shadows, clouds, and darkness, rest upon it."

17. *Thraliana*, 2 vols., ed. K. C. Balderson (Oxford: Clarendon 1942), 1:194. [Samuel Johnson], *Taxation No Tyranny: An Answer to the Resolutions and Address of the American Congress* (London, 1775).

18. *Parliamentary History*, 440–41.

19. *Thraliana*, 194.

20. Frans De Bruyn, *Literary Genres*, 138–39.

21. See *Correspondence of Edmund Burke*, 10 vols., ed. Alfred Cobban and Robert Smith (Cambridge: Cambridge University Press), 6:164–67.

22. There may be little Miltonic echoes in the whaling eulogy which pull the whalers back to the world of the fallen angels; when Sin and Death create the bridge between earth and hell in book 10 of Milton's epic, they do so "as when two Polar Winds blowing adverse / Upon the Cronian Sea, together drive / Mountains of Ice" (290–92). And when they actually create the horrific weather which is the consequence of the Fall, they let loose the winds:

> Now from the North
> Of Norumbega, and the Samoed shore
> Bursting their brazen Dungeon, arm'd with ice
> And snow and hail and stormy gust and flaw,
> Boreas and Caecias and Argestes loud.
>
> (10:695–99)

"Norumbega" was the term, in Milton's culture, for all of northern New England; and this very same catalog of northern winds would later be conjured up (and inaccurately remembered) by Burke in an attack on decayed English courts and palaces that no longer deserve to be maintained. See his speech on economic reform, delivered February 11, 1780, and published by Dodsley, *Writings and Speeches*: "Our palaces are vast inhospitable halls. There are bleak winds, there, 'Boreas, and Eurus, and Caurus, and Argestes loud,' howling through the vacant lobbies, appal the imagination, and conjure up the grim spectres of departed tyrants" (3:510).

Notes to Chapter 5/Medine

1. Joseph Wittreich, *Arenas of Conflict: Milton and the Unfettered Mind* (Selinsgrove, Pa.: Susquehanna University Press, 1997), 22. Epigraph trans. T. H. (Paris: St. Omer, 1626), 84–85; see *Philonis Alexandrini Opera Qva Svpersvnt*, 8 vols., ed. Leopold Cohn (Berlin: Georg Reimer, 1962), 2:158–59.

2. *Complete Prose Works of John Milton*, 8 vols., ed. Don M. Wolfe et al. (New Haven: Yale University Press, 1953–82), 4:548. All quotations of Milton's prose come from this edition.

3. Marian H. Studley, "Milton and His Paraphrases of the Psalms," *Philological Quarterly* 4 (1925): 371, and William R. Parker, "The Date of *Samson Agonistes*," *Philological Quarterly* 28 (1949): 161.

4. *The Complete Poetry of John Milton*, ed. John T. Shawcross (New York: Doubleday, 1971), 242–43, lines 8–14. All quotations of Milton's poetry come from this edition.

5. *Summa Theologiae. Latin Text and English Translation*, 59 vols. (London: Blackfriars, 1972), 23:84 (282ae.106, 1). All quotations of the *Summa Theologiae* come from this edition.

6. The Revised Standard Version very often translates *yadah* as "thank." The Vulgate used the verb *confitebor* almost uniformly, which aptly expresses the concepts of "acknowledge" together with "thank" and "praise."

7. *The Geneva Bible: A Facsimile of the 1560 edition*, ed. Lloyd E. Berry (Madison: University of Wisconsin Press, 1969), 236v. All quotations of the Geneva Bible come from this edition.

8. Unless otherwise noted, all quotations of the Bible come from the Authorized Version.

9. The headnote to Psalm 68 comments similarly that the psalmist "setteth forthe as in a glasse the wonderful mercies of God."

10. *Aristotelis Ethica Nicomachea*, 4.3 (Leipzig: Teubner, 1912), 4.7.4.1124b. All quotations of the *Ethics* come from this edition.

11. Besides Psalms 19 and 148, the prayer imitates the so-called "Song of the Three Children" used as the canticle *Benedicite, omnia opera* in morning prayer. See *The Book of Common Prayer: 1559*, ed. John E. Booty (Charlottesville: University Press of Virginia, 1976), 49–60.

12. These are thy glorious works, Parent of good,
    Almightie, thine this universal Frame,
    Thus wondrous fair; thy self how wondrous then!
    Unspeakable, who sitst above these Heav'ns
    To us invisible or dimly seen
    In these thy lowest works, yet these declare
    Thy goodness beyond thought, and Power Divine.

                                        (5.153–59)

13. Speak yee who best can tell, ye Sons of light,
    Angels, for yee behold him, and with songs
    And choral symphonies, Day without Night,
    Circle his Throne rejoycing, yee in Heav'n,
    On Earth joyn all ye Creatures to extoll
    Him first, him last, him midst, and without end.
    Fairest of Starrs, last in the train of Night,
    If better thou belong not to the dawn,

Sure pledge of day, that crownst the smiling Morn
With thy bright Circlet, praise him in thy Sphear
While day arises, the sweet hour of Prime.
Thou Sun, of this great World both Eye and Soul,
Acknowledge him thy Greater, sound his praise
In thy eternal course, both when thou climb'st,
And when high Noon hast gaind, and when thou fallst.
Moon, that now meetst the orient Sun, now fli'st
With the fixt Starrs, fixt in thir Orb that flies,
And yee five other wandring Fires that move
In mystic Dance not without Song, resound
His praise, who out of Darkness call'd up Light.
Air, and ye Elements the eldest birth
Of Natures Womb, that in quaternion run
Perpetual Circle, multiform; and mix
And nourish all things, let your ceasless change
Varie to our great Maker still new praise.
Ye Mists and Exhalations that now rise
From Hill or steaming Lake, duskie or grey,
Till the sun paint your fleecie skirts with God,
In honour to the Worlds great Author rise,
Whether to deck with Clouds th' uncolourd skie,
Or wet the thirstie Earth with falling showers,
Rising or falling still advance his praise.
His praise ye Winds, that from four Quarters blow,
Breath soft or loud; and wave your tops, ye Pines,
With every Plant, in sign of Worship wave.
Fountains and yee, that warble, as ye flow,
Melodious murmurs, warbling tune his praise.
Joyn voices all ye living Souls, ye Birds,
That singing up to Heaven Gate ascend,
Bear on your wings and in your notes his praise;
Yee that in Waters glide, and yee that walk
The Earth, and stately tread, or lowly creep;
Witness if I be silent, Morn or Eev'n,
To Hill, or Valley, Fountain, or fresh shade
Made vocal by my Song, and taught his praise.

(5.160–204)

14. It antedates by five years the earliest recorded appearance of "ingrate" as a substantive; see *OED* s.v. "ingrate."

15. Since the exchange between Satan and Abdiel in book 5 occurs chronologically before Satan's opening soliloquy in book 4, it might be thought that Satan's later opinions were not held earlier and so the charge of hypocrisy is unfair. On the other hand, Milton does not seem concerned to present a psychological or intellectual development in his narrative.

16. Barbara Kiefer Lewalski, "Structure and the Symbolism of Vision in Michael's Prophecy, *Paradise Lost* Books XI–XII," *Philological Quarterly* 42 (1963): 32; see also Stanley Fish, *Surprised by Sin: The Reader in "Paradise Lost"* (1967; reprint, Cambridge, Mass.: Harvard University Press, 1997), 323; and Georgia Christopher, *Milton and the Science of the Saints* (Princeton: Princeton University Press, 1982), 180. A signal exception to the traditional view of Adam and Eve's education is the study by Regina Schwartz, "From Shadowy Types to Shadowy Types: The Unendings of *Paradise Lost*," *Milton Studies*, vol. 25, ed. James D. Simmonds (Pittsburgh: University of Pittsburgh Press, 1989), 123–39.

17. I elaborate this point in a discussion of Adam's education in the course of books 11 and 12 in "Adam's 'Sum of Wisdom': *Paradise Lost* 12.553–587," in *Reassembling Truth: Twenty-First Century Milton*, ed. Charles W. Durham and Kristin A. Pruitt McColgan (Selinsgrove, Pa.: Susquehanna University Press, 2003), 95–114.

18. I am indebted to my colleague John C. Ulreich Jr. for this suggestion.

Notes to Chapter 6/Greenberg

1. For a wonderful article exploring this link in Cavalier poems and the writings of the Levellers and Diggers, see Christina Malcolmson, "The Garden Enclosed / The Woman Enclosed," *Enclosure Acts: Sexuality, Property and Culture in Early Modern England*, ed. Richard Burt and John Michael Archer (Ithaca, N.Y.: Cornell University Press, 1994), 251–69. Particularly relevant to my discussion are her arguments that the Cavalier poems "used enclosure as a metaphor for marriage" (as in the Carew poem from which she, too, quotes) and that the "bodies of women become analogous to and emblematic of the property whose ownership and government were in dispute in England during this period" (252). My discussion expands this metaphoric link to encompass seventeenth century enclosure tracts and *Paradise Lost*. Contextualizing Milton's poem within the legal discourse of the period reveals that the link served as more than merely a metaphor, but also accurately described the law's parallel treatment of property ownership and marital relations. Epigraph from Thomas Carew, "A Rapture," in *Minor Poets of the Seventeenth Century*, ed. R. G. Howarth (London: Everyman's Library, 1969), 103, lines 15–20.

2. Adam Moore, *Bread for the Poor. And Advancement of the English Nation Promised By Enclosure of the Wastes and Common Grounds of England* (London, 1653), A2.

3. Joseph Wittreich, "'Inspir'd with Contradiction': Mapping Gender Discourses in *Paradise Lost*," in *Literary Milton: Text, Pretext, Context*, ed. Diana Treviño Benet and Michael Lieb (Pittsburgh: Duquesne University Press, 1994), 136; and Wittreich, "'John, John, I blush for thee!':

Mapping Gender Discourses in *Paradise Lost,"* in *Out of Bounds: Male Writers and Gender(ed) Criticism,* ed. Laura Claridge and Elizabeth Langland (Amherst: University of Massachusetts Press, 1990), 47. See also Wittreich, "'He Ever Was A Dissenter': Milton's Transgressive Maneuvers in *Paradise Lost,"* in *Arenas of Conflict: Milton and the Unfettered Mind,* ed. Kristin A. Pruitt and Charles W. Durham (Selinsgrove, Pa.: Susquehanna University Press, 1997), 21–40.

4. See, for example, Wittreich, "'Inspir'd with Contradiction'"; Diane McColley, *Milton's Eve* (Urbana: University of Illinois Press, 1983), 22–62; Philip J. Gallagher, *Milton, the Bible, and Misogyny,* ed. Eugene R. Cunnar and Gail L. Mortimer (Columbia: University of Missouri Press, 1990); Joan Malory Webber, "The Politics of Poetry: Feminism and *Paradise Lost,"* in *Milton Studies,* vol. 14, ed. James D. Simmonds (1980), 3–24; Barbara Lewalski, "Milton on Women — Yet Once More," *Milton Studies,* vol. 6, ed. James D. Simmonds (1974), 3–20; and Susanne Woods, "How Free Are Milton's Women?," in *Milton and the Idea of Woman,* ed. Julia M. Walker (Urbana: University of Illinois Press, 1988), 15–31. For readings of *Paradise Lost* that also situate the poem historically but lead to radically different readings, see Janet E. Halley, "Female Autonomy in Milton's Sexual Poetics," in Walker, ed., *Milton and the Idea of Woman,* 230–53, and Mary Nyquist, "The Genesis of Gendered Subjectivity in the Divorce Tracts and *Paradise Lost,"* in *Critical Essays on John Milton,* ed. Christopher Kendrick (New York: G. K. Hall, 1995), 165–93.

5. See Janet Rifkin, "Toward a Theory of Law and Patriarchy," *Harvard Women's Law Journal* 3 (spring 1980): 83–95. See also Karl E. Klare, "Law-Making as Praxis," *Telos* 40 (1979): 128 (law should be understood as praxis — that is, a form of "practice" through which the social order is defined).

6. See Anne Bottomley, "Figures in a Landscape: Feminist Perspectives on Law, Land and Landscape," in *Feminist Perspectives on the Foundational Subjects of Law,* ed. Anne Bottomley (London: Cavendish, 1996),109–24; and Garrett A. Sullivan Jr., introduction to *The Drama of Landscape: Land, Property and Social Relations on the Early Modern Stage* (Stanford: Stanford University Press,1998), 12–15.

7. Wittreich, "'John, John, I blush for thee!,'" 24.

8. For background on England's change from a moral economy to an "economy of sales and exchanges," see Joyce Oldham Appleby, *Economic Thought and Ideology in Seventeenth Century England* (Princeton: Princeton University Press, 1978), 52–72.

9. David Underdown, *Rebel, Riot and Rebellion: Popular Politics and Culture, 1603–1660* (Oxford: Oxford University Press, 1987), 284. For background on the enclosure movement, see Mark Overton, *Agricultural Revolution in England: The Transformation of the Agrarian Economy, 1500–1850* (Cambridge: Cambridge University Press, 1996); J. A. Yelling, *Common Field and Enclosure in England, 1450–1850*

(Hamden, Conn.: Archon Books, 1977); Robert C. Allen, *Enclosure and the Yeoman* (Oxford: Clarendon, 1992); and Joan Thirsk, ed., *The Agrarian History of England and Wales, 1640–1750*, vol. 5.2 (Cambridge: Cambridge University Press, 1985).

10. For background on the agrarian legislation of the civil war, see Christopher Hill, *Puritanism and Revolution: Studies in Interpretation of the English Revolution of the Seventeenth Century* (New York, Schocken Books, 1964), 153–96.

11. I am grateful to Mary Fenton for allowing me to read her "Hope, Land Ownership, and Milton's 'Paradise Within,'" *SEL* 43 (2003): 151–80. She, too, explores the ways in which *Paradise Lost* encodes the developing discourse of private property rights. However, she and I come to opposing positions, as she situates Satan's understanding of land rights and his critique of God in the developing notion of private property. I, on the other hand, argue here that this discourse also infuses Milton's depiction of prelapsarian rights in Eden.

12. John Milton, *Considerations Touching the Likeliest Means to Remove Hirelings out of the Church*, in *Complete Prose Works of John Milton*, 8 vols., ed. Don M. Wolfe et al. (New Haven: Yale University Press, 1953–82), 7.296. All references to Milton's prose are to this edition and are cited parenthetically in the text.

13. Appleby, *Economic Thought*, 63.

14. Gerrard Winstanley, *A Watch-Word to the City of London and the Armie, The Works of Gerrard Winstanley with an Appendix of Documents Relating to the Digger Movement*, ed. George H. Sabine (New York: Russell & Russell, 1965), 315.

15. A. S. P. Woodhouse, ed., *Puritanism and Liberty: Being the Army Debates (1647–49) from the Clarke Manuscripts with Supplementary Materials* (London: J. M. Dent, 1938), 59.

16. See Anthony Low, "Agricultural Reform and the Love Poems of Thomas Carew: With an Instance from Lovelace," in *Culture and Cultivation in Early Modern England: Writing and the Land*, ed. Michael Leslie and Timothy Raylor (Leicester: Leicester University Press, 1992), 65; and Appleby, *Economic Thought*, 52–72.

17. S. T., *Common-Good; or, The Improvement of Commons, Forrests, and Chases, by Inclosure* (London, 1652), 6. For other references to Paradise and to divine calls to enclose property, see Moore, *Bread for the Poor*, 2; Joseph Lee, *The Inclosure of Catthorp; or, A Vindication of a Regulated Inclosure* (London, 1656), 28; and W. A. Blith, *The English Improver Improved: Or, The Survey of Husbandry Surveyed* (London, 1652), 3. For a brief discussion that ties the rhetoric of agricultural reform and rural labor to envisioning a new "Eden rais'd in the wast Wilderness," see Low, "Agricultural Reform," 67. For "commonwealths-m[e]n," see Arthur Standish, *The Commons Complaint*, 3d ed. (London, 1611), sig. A4b.

18. I am grateful to Jackie DiSalvo's observation that *Paradise Lost* operates as "the great enclosure tract of the seventeenth century," a suggestion that my discussion develops and supports. Quotes from John Milton, *Paradise Lost*, in *The Complete Poetry of John Milton*, rev. ed., ed. John T. Shawcross (Garden City, N.Y.: Doubleday, 1971), 4.964, 207, 181–82. All references to Milton's poetry are to this edition and are cited parenthetically in the text.

19. For the definitive analysis of the scriptural tradition of the garden enclosed, or *hortus conclusus*, see Stanley Stewart, *The Enclosed Garden: The Tradition and the Image in Seventeenth Century Poetry* (Madison: University of Wisconsin Press, 1966), 31–59. As Stewart has emphasized, this trope informs seventeenth century poetic descriptions of gardens. Nevertheless, this trope arguably represents only a partial understanding of the historical nuances of the topography of *Paradise Lost*.

20. Margaret Davies, "Feminist Appropriations: 'Law, Property and Personality,'" *Social and Legal Studies: An International Journal* 3 (1994): 376.

21. Andrew McCrae, "Husbandry Manuals and the Language of Agrarian Improvement," in Leslie and Raylor, *Culture and Cultivation*, 49.

22. Bottomley, "Figures in a Landscape," 119.

23. Sir Edward Coke, quoted in Nicholas K. Blomley, *Law, Space and the Geographies of Power* (New York: Guilford Press, 1994), 93. For further discussion of this quotation, see Bottomley, "Figures in a Landscape," 120.

24. Lord Evershed, foreword to R. H. Graveson and F. R. Crame, *A Century of Family Law* (London: Sweet and Maxwell, 1957), xv. For a discussion of this quotation, see Katherine O'Donovan, "The Male Appendage — Legal Definitions of Women," in *Fit Work for Women*, ed. Sandra Burman (London: Croom Helm for Oxford University Women's Studies Committee, 1979), 141.

25. See Nadine Taub and Elizabeth M. Schneider, "Women's Subordination and the Rule of Law," in *The Politics of Law: A Progressive Critique*, ed. David Kairys (New York: Pantheon Books, 1990), 151–57; and Katherine O'Donovan, *Sexual Divisions in Law* (London: Weidenfeld and Nicolson, 1985), 10–20. For an early example of the law's refusal to invade the private sphere and, more insidiously, its ruling that the private sphere's governance is ultimately determined by the husband alone, see the case of *Manby v. Scott* (1663) reproduced in *A Treatise of Feme Coverts; or, The Lady's Law* (London, 1732), 193, 195: "What a Judicature is set up here, to decide the private Difference between Husband and Wife? . . . the Law makes no Person Judge thereof, but the Husband himself; and in these Cases, no Man is to put his Hand between the Bone and the Flesh."

26. I use the word "natural" here to gesture to arguments used in the early modern period to justify women's relegation to the private sphere

as the "natural" consequence of women's inferiority and their consequent need for protection.

27. The stress on God's panoptical vision derives from Michel Foucault's discussion of the panopticon. See his *Discipline and Punish: The Birth of the Prison* (New York: Vintage Books, 1979), 195–228.

28. Richard J. DuRocher, "Careful Plowing: Culture and Agriculture in *Paradise Lost*," in *Milton Studies*, vol. 31, ed. Albert C. Labriola (Pittsburgh: University of Pittsburgh Press, 1994), 103–4.

29. For a parallel discussion of the defensive strategies of Paradise and Milton's belief in the "division of space via property rights," see Bruce McLeod, "The 'Lordly Eye': Milton and the Strategic Geography of Empire," in *Milton and the Imperial Vision*, ed. Balachandra Rajan and Elizabeth Sauer (Pittsburgh: Duquesne University Press, 1999), 63. McLeod, however, characterizes Milton's conception of space and Paradise as "'evok[ing] not enclosure but panorama'" (64; quoting Chris Fitter, *Poetry, Space, Landscape: Towards A New Theory* [Cambridge: Cambridge University Press, 1995], 301). See also J. Martin Evans, *Milton's Imperial Epic: Paradise Lost and the Discourse of Colonialism* (Ithaca, N.Y.: Cornell University Press, 1996). Evans, however, reads the occupants of the Garden as governed by natural law and, therefore, the "concept of private property is as alien to them as it was believed to be to the native Americans" (96).

30. W. J. T. Mitchell, "Imperial Landscape," in *Landscape and Power*, ed. W. J. T. Mitchell (Chicago: The University of Chicago Press, 1994), 17. See also Ann Bermingham's essay in that volume, "System, Order, and Abstraction: The Politics of English Landscape Painting Around 1795," 77–101. Gillian Rose, *Feminism and Geography: The Limits of Geographical Knowledge* (Minneapolis: University of Minnesota Press, 1993), 90–99.

31. Jennifer Nedelsky, "Law, Boundaries and the Bounded Self," *Representations* 30 (spring 1990): 177, 180.

32. See Appleby, *Economic Thought*, 101; McCrae, "Husbandry Manuals," 56; and Low, "Agrarian Reform," 65.

33. [John Rastell], *Les termes de la ley; or, Certaine Difficult and Obscure Words and Termes of the Common Laws of this Realme Newly Printed* (London, 1624), fol. 261r–v. For helpful background on the changing definition of property in the period, see G. E. Aylmer, "The Meaning and Definition of 'Property' in Seventeenth Century England," *Past and Present* 86 (1980): 87–97, and Andrew Reeve, "Debate: The Meaning and Definition of 'Property' in Seventeenth Century England," *Past and Present* 89 (1983): 139–42. For the classic delineation of what rights, entitlements and duties attend private property ownership, see A. M. Honore, "Ownership," in *Oxford Essays in Jurisprudence*, ed. A. G. Guest (Oxford: Oxford University Press, 1961), 107–47. For background on the concurrent political thought concerning property rights, see Thomas

Allen Horne, *Property Rights and Poverty: Political Argument in Britain, 1605–1834* (Chapel Hill: University of North Carolina Press, 1990).

34. Rastell, *Les termes de la ley*, fol. 261. For a discussion of this definition, see Aylmer, "Meaning and Definition," 90–91.

35. See Honore, "Ownership," 92. Richard Zouche, *Cases and Questions Resolved in the Civil-Law* (Oxford, 1652). For a discussion of this definition, see Aylmer, "Meaning and Definition," 92.

36. John Lilly, *The Practical Register; or, A General Abridgment of the Law* (London, 1719), 2.399–402. For a discussion of this definition, see Aylmer, "Meaning and Definition," 95.

37. *The Geneva Bible, a Facsimile of the 1560 Edition* (Madison: University of Wisconsin Press, 1969). All references to the Bible are to this edition and are cited parenthetically in the text.

38. It is worth noting that the notion of God "compassing thee round" implicates the discourse of enclosure, providing another example of the centrality of this metaphor to an interpretation of the poem.

39. See Michael Edward Turner, *English Parliamentary Enclosure: Its Historical Geography and Economic History* (Dawson, Conn.: Archon Books, 1980).

40. See J. A. Sharpe, *Crime in Early Modern England, 1550–1750* (London: Longman, 1984), 149–50.

41. John Locke, *Two Treatises of Government*, ed. Peter Laslett (Cambridge: Cambridge University Press, 1963), 347. For the definitive study of the Black Act, see E. P. Thompson, *Whigs and Hunters: The Origin of the Black Act* (New York: Pantheon Books, 1975).

42. Anthony Low, *The Georgic Revolution* (Princeton: Princeton University Press, 1985).

43. Legal historians have also offered various practical, technical, economic, sociological and historical explanations for the married woman's position at common law, while generally agreeing that the ideological and canonical interpretations of *una caro* played a significant role in the development of the doctrine of coverture. For brief overviews of these alternative explanations, see O'Donovan, *Sexual Divisions in Law*, 30–35, and Leo Kanowitz, *Women and the Law: The Unfinished Revolution* (Albuquerque: University of New Mexico Press, 1969), 35–38.

44. W. S. Holdsworth, *A History of English Law*, vol. 3 (Boston: Little Brown, 1923), 521.

45. For a helpful distillation of the exegesis of *una caro*, see James Grantham Turner, *One Flesh: Paradisal Marriage and Sexual Relations in the Age of Milton* (Oxford: Clarendon, 1987). While providing a thorough account of the history of sexual relations and the canonical debates embedded within the meaning of this phrase, he does not touch on its legal meaning.

46. Eileen Spring, "The Heiress-at-Law: English Real Property Law from a New Point of View," *Law and History Review* 8 (fall 1990): 282.

See also Mary Jane Mossman, "Feminism and Legal Method," in *Feminist Legal Theory: Foundations*, ed. D. Kelly Weisberg (Philadelphia: Temple University Press, 1993), who explains that legal opinions reflect prevailing cultural and religious views; thus, "even when women and men were regarded as equal in the eyes of God (in the ideas of reformers such as Calvin, for example), women were still treated as subordinate to men" (541). Such inferiority some justices understood as being a consequence of the Fall. As Justice Hyde explained in *Manby v. Scott*: "Presently after the Fall, the Judgment of GOD upon Woman was, *Thy Desire shall be to thy Husband, for thy Will shall be subject to thy Husband, and he shall Rule over Thee. 3 Gen. 16.* Hereupon . . . she is disabled to make any Grant, Contract or Bargain, without the Allowance or Consent of her Husband." See *A Treatise of Feme Coverts*, 179.

47. *A Treatise of Feme Coverts*, 180.

48. William Blackstone, *Commentaries on the Laws of England*, vol. 1 (Oxford: Clarendon Press, 1765), 430.

49. *The Lawes Resolutions of Womens Rights* (London, 1632), 124–25.

50. For a helpful summary of this debate, see Janelle Greenberg, "The Legal Status of the English Woman in Early Eighteenth Century Common Law and Equity." *Studies in Eighteenth Century Culture* 4 (1975): 172 and nn. 1, 2. See also Donna Dickenson, *Property, Women and Politics* (New Brunswick, N. J.: Rutgers University Press, 1997), 2–3.

51. Samuel Pyeatt Menefee, *Wives for Sale: An Ethnographic Study of British Popular Divorce* (Oxford: Blackwell, 1981).

52. *The Laws Respecting Women* (London, 1777), quoted in O'Donovan, *Sexual Divisions in Law*, 51. See 50–52 for information on the first such sale.

53. O'Donovan, *Sexual Divisions in Law*, 31.

54. James Clancy, *A Treatise of the Rights, Duties, and Liabilities of Husband and Wife. At Law and in Equity*, 3d ed. (New York: Treadway & Bogert, 1828), 1–2. For an American judge's embrace of the separate sphere ideology, see *Bradwell v. the State*, 83 U.S. 130, 142 (U.S. Supreme Court, 1872): "The constitution of the family organization, which is founded in the divine ordinance, as well as in the nature of things, indicates the domestic sphere as that which properly belongs to the domain and functions of womanhood. . . . The paramount destiny and mission of woman are to fulfill the noble and benign offices of wife and mother. This is the law of the Creator. And the rules of civil society must be adapted to the general constitution of things."

55. For Milton's explication of "And they shall bee one flesh," see *Tetrachordon*, 2.605–14.

56. See James Grantham Turner, *One Flesh*.

57. See, for example, Nyquist, "The Genesis of Gendered Subjectivity," 172, 180.

58. See, for example, Turner, *One Flesh*, 13, 217; and Wittreich,

"'Inspir'd with Contradiction,'" 137–41. However, some feminist scholars have contested this interpretation. See, for example, Leslie Bender, "A Lawyer's Primer on Feminist Theory and Tort," in Weisberg, ed., *Feminist Legal Theory: Foundations:* "The claim that the masculine terms 'he' and 'man' are generic becomes suspect when we realize that our language does not provide generic feminine terms as well" (61).

59. See Diane Kelsey McColley, *A Gust for Paradise: Milton's Eden and the Visual Arts* (Urbana: University of Illinois Press, 1993), 127–28, and McColley, *Milton's Eve* (Urbana: University of Illinois Press, 1983), 110–39.

60. See, for example, McColley, *Milton's Eve*, 113; and Lewalski, "Milton on Women," 8.

61. Ann C. Scales, "The Emergence of Feminist Jurisprudence: An Essay," in *Feminist Legal Theory*, 55 n. 17. See also Bender, "A Lawyer's Primer": "Men have had the power of naming our world, and giving our words meaning. Naming controls how we group things together, which parts of things are noted and which are ignored, and the perspective from which we understand them. . . . Our language is a male language that reinforces male perspectives, interests, and hierarchies of values" (61).

62. Linda Pastan, "Aspects of Eve," in *Aspects of Eve* (New York: Liveright, 1970), 37, lines 1–10.

Notes to Chapter 7/Woods

1. Joseph A. Wittreich, *Interpreting "Samson Agonistes"* (Princeton: Princeton University Press, 1986).

2. Barbara K. Lewalski, *The Life of John Milton* (Oxford: Blackwell, 2000), 523–36.

3. Christopher Hill, *Milton and the English Revolution* (New York: Penguin, 1979), 431–32. *Samson Agonistes*, in *John Milton: Complete Poems and Major Prose*, ed. Merritt Y. Hughes (New York: Odyssey, 1957), hereafter cited by line number in the text. All poems cited are from this text.

4. For example, from *Areopagitica:* "When God gave [man] reason, he gave him freedom to choose, for reason is but choosing." All prose citations are from *Complete Prose Works of John Milton*, gen. ed. Don M. Wolfe et al. (New Haven: Yale University Press, 1953–82; 1959), 2:527; hereafter cited as YP). Milton admired William Perkins, a Jacobean convert from Catholicism, who often wrote on the topic of free will; typical is this passage from *A Treatise of God's Free Grace and Mans Free-will* (Ffff6v–Iiii6r), (Gggg3v):

> Will, is a power of willing, nilling, choosing, refusing, suspending, which depends on reason. By *power* I meane an abilitie or created facultie: and it is so properly in men and in angells: but in God

only by analogy or proportion. Because his will is his essence or godhead indeed. . . . And in every act of wil, there are two things, *Reason* to guide, and *Election* to assent, or dissent. Will hath his propertie, and that is *Liberty of the will*, which is a freedom from compulsion or constraint, but not from all necessitie. . . . The necessitie of not sinning, is the glory and ornament of will, for he that doth good so, as he cannot sinne, is more at liberty in doing good, than he that can doe either good or evill. When the creature is in that estate, that it willingly serves God, and cannot but serve God, then is our perfect libertie.

5. Compare also Lewalski, *Life*, 523: "Milton . . . emphasizes the ambiguous signs and events of the Samson story. . . . Such ambiguous signs, along with such prominent stylistic features as antithesis and either / or constructions, force readers to weigh and choose, but Milton's literary strategies provide some guide among the interpretive possibilities." I argue that the guide itself remains ambiguous, and that the ultimate effect of Milton's literary strategies is to ask the reader to recognize that vocation occurs only through individual choice. The reader's salvation is not Samson's, but his or her own.

6. Susanne Woods, "The Rhetoric of Freedom in Sidney's *Arcadia*," *Sidney Newsletter* (1987) 8:3–11; "Freedom and Tyranny in Sidney's *Arcadia*," in *Sir Philip Sidney: Quadricentennial Essays*, ed. Michael J. A. B. Allen et al. (New York: AMS Press, 1990) 165–75; "Making Free with Poetry: Spenser and the Rhetoric of Choice," *Spenser Studies* 16, ed. Anne Lake Prescott et al. (New York: AMS Press, 2000), 1–16.

7. See, for example, Jackie DiSalvo, "'The Lord's Battels': *Samson Agonistes* and the Puritan Revolution," *Milton Studies*, vol. 4, ed. James D. Simmonds (Pittsburgh: University of Pittsburgh Press, 1972), 39–62; Lewalski, *Life*, 525–26.

8. And therefore amenable to some critical approaches that not even Milton's Romantic appreciators could have imagined. See, for example, Mary Nyquist, "Textual Over-lapping and Dalilah's Harlot-Lap," in *Literary Theory / Renaissance Texts*, ed. Patricia Parker and David Quint (Baltimore: The Johns Hopkins University Press, 1986), 341–72; and John Guillory, "Dalila's House," in *Rewriting the Renaissance: The Discourses of Sexual Difference in Early Modern Europe*, ed. Margaret Ferguson, Maureen Quilligan and Nancy Vickers (Chicago: University of Chicago Press, 1986), 106–22.

9. *Doctrine and Discipline of Divorce*, YP 2:342.

Notes to Chapter 8/Rogers

1. F. T. Prince, *The Italian Element in Milton's Verse* (Oxford: Clarendon, 1954), 61.

2. J. B. Leishman, *Milton's Minor Poems* (London: Hutchinson, 1969), calls the Donnean conceit in the poem's first stanza "the last and latest thing of its kind in Milton's poetry" (116).

3. C. A. Patrides discusses this lyric in his overview of Milton's atonement theories in *Milton and the Christian Tradition* (Oxford: Clarendon, 1966), 121–52.

4. Ibid., 141.

5. Tillyard, *Milton*, rev. ed. (New York: Collier Books, 1966), 238.

6. The best studies of early modern Antitrinitarianism, and especially of Socinian Antitrinitarianism, are still Earl Morse Wilbur, *A History of Unitarianism: Socinianism and Its Antecedents* (Cambridge, Mass.: Harvard University Press, 1947); and John H. McLachlan, *Socinianism in Seventeenth Century England* (Oxford: Oxford University Press, 1951). In *Catholics, Anglicans and Puritans: Seventeenth Century Essays* (Chicago: The University of Chicago Press, 1987), 186–99, Hugh Trevor-Roper describes the profound dissemination of Socinian ideas and texts throughout the Great Tew circle in the 1620s and 1630s.

7. I am indebted here to Shuger's insightful treatment of the interrelation of judicial and theological theories of punishment in her *Renaissance Bible: Scholarship, Sacrifice and Subjectivity* (Berkeley and Los Angeles: University of California Press, 1994), 89–127.

8. David Masson, *The Life of John Milton, and the History of His Time* (London: Macmillan, 1877), 4:423–53.

9. Dewey D. Wallace Jr., "Socinianism, Justification by Faith and the Sources of John Locke's *The Reasonableness of Christianity*," *Journal of the History of Ideas* 45 (1984): 49–66.

10. All line references to Milton's poetry are to *The Complete Poetry of John Milton*, ed. John T. Shawcross (Garden City, N.Y.: Doubleday, 1971).

11. Patrides offers a useful summary of the recapitulation theory in *Milton and the Christian Tradition*, 132–33.

12. James Shapiro has collected a useful assortment of early modern English references to circumcision in his *Shakespeare and the Jews* (New York: Columbia University Press, 1996).

13. Robert Southwell, in "His circumcision," from *Moeoniae* (London, 1595), anticipates Milton's diction while representing a more Catholic perspective on the event. Of Mary's grief at the sight of her son's circumcision, Southwell writes: "The knife that cut his flesh did pierce her heart." The first stanza of Wither's "The Circumcision, or New-yeares Day," from *The Hymnes and Songs of the Church* (London, 1623), establishes the figures that will structure many of the century's subsequent poems on the event:

This Day thy flesh, oh Christ, did bleed,
Mark't by the Circumcision knife:
Because the Law, for mans misdeed,

Requir'd that Earnest of thy life.
Those droppes deuin'd that showre of blood,
Which in thine Agonie beganne:
And that great showre foreshew'd the Flood,
       Which from thy Side the next day ranne.

Jim Ellis discusses the poems of Herrick, Quarles and Crashaw in "The Wit of Circumcision, the Circumcision of Wit," in *The Wit of Seventeenth Century Poetry*, ed. Claude J. Summers and Ted-Larry Pebworth (Columbia: University of Missouri Press, 1995), 62–77. Some post-Miltonic poetic treatments of Christ's circumcision, not mentioned by Ellis, include Martin Lluelyn (1618–1682), "Caroll, Sung to His Majesty on New-yeares day, being the Circumcision. 1643," in *Men-Miracles. With other Poems* (Oxford, 1646); Joseph Beaumont, "The Great Little One," canto 7 of *Psyche in XXIV. Canto's* (1648); William Cartwright (1611–1643), "On the Circumcision," in *Comedies, Tragi-comedies, With other Poems* (1651); Thomas Washbourne (1606–1687), "A Soliloquy upon the Circumcision, commonly called New-yeers-day," *Divine Poems* (London, 1654); and John Austin (1613–1669), whose "Hymn XXIX. Jesu, who from thy Fathers throne," *Devotions in the Ancient Way of Offices* (Paris, 1668), shows a particularly strong indebtedness to Milton's lyric.

14. A closely related tic interrupts the speaker's musings in *The Passion:* "Yet more; the stroke of death he must abide" (20–21). Nearly all of Milton's religious lyrics feature some version of this gesture, the speaker's alarmed, eleventh-hour recollection of the necessity of atonement. Each poem stages the surprised realization that the glorious end of Christian history must hinge on the brutal sacrifice of the Son of God. This trick, or surprise, may well be the strongest of the dramatic elements Milton brings to the seventeenth century religious lyric. But, at least in the context of Milton's early verse, it becomes perhaps one of the most predictable.

15. See, for example, A. B. Chambers, "'Upon the Circumcision': Backgrounds and Meanings," *Texas Studies in Literature and Language* 17 (1975): 687–97.

16. For Calvin, in the *Commentaries on the Epistle of Paul the Apostle to the Romans*, translated by Milton's contemporary, John Owen (Grand Rapids: Eerdmans, 1955), the dispute about the single rite of circumcision was "not about one rite, but that under one thing is included every work of the law; that is, every work to which reward can be due. Circumcision then was especially mentioned, because it was the basis of the righteousness of the law" (163). Nearly all Protestant theology followed Calvin's identification of circumcision with works. Milton, too, in the *De doctrina Christiana*, would write that "after the giving of the law circumcision seems to have been a symbol for the covenant of works," *The Complete Prose Works of John Milton*, 8 vols. in 10, gen.

ed. Don M. Wolfe et al. (New Haven: Yale University Press, 1953–82), 6.543; hereafter cited as YP in the text.

17. In an elaborate comparison of the Jewish Galatians with contemporary Catholics, Perkins, in his 1604 *Commentary on Galatians* (New York: Pilgrim Press, 1989), repeatedly turns to circumcision as a figure for the righteous action mistakenly believed to be a "meritorious cause of salvation" (332). John Owen would, throughout his career, elaborate Perkins's arguments with even more angry derision, aligning Jewish circumcisers with the Arminians and Socinian Antitrinitarians of his own day.

18. Shapiro, *Shakespeare and the Jews*, 115. See the discussion of the Transits, and other seventeenth century Christian Judaizers, in David S. Katz, *Philo-Semitism and the Readmission of the Jews to England, 1603–1655* (Oxford: Clarendon, 1982), 18–34.

19. John Locke, *The Reasonableness of Christianity as Delivered in the Scriptures*, ed. George W. Ewing (Washington, D.C.: Regnery Gateway, 1965), 7. The biblical foundation for the reading of moral righteousness as a claim to a legal right was explored in detail by the Socinian Antitrinitarian Johann Crell (1590–1633), whose commentary on the Epistle to the Galatians was translated into English in 1650. See Crell's philological discussion of the connection of "righteousness" and "right" in *The Justification of a Sinner: Being the Maine Argument of the Epistle to the Galatians* (London, 1650), 291–95.

20. Jason Rosenblatt, *Torah and Law in Paradise Lost* (Princeton: Princeton University Press, 1994), 32–33.

21. Rosenblatt, whose important book reveals the strong Hebraic sources for Milton's resistance to the theology of vicarious atonement, discusses this passage from *Tetrachordon* in *Torah and Law*, arguing that "Milton contends throughout the divorce tracts that the purpose of the entire Mosaic law is to remove sin entirely, not merely to limit it" (32).

22. Milton was preceded by John Donne in figuring the eradication of sin as a removal of excess, an action explicitly tied by Donne to the work of circumcision. For Donne, in *The Sermons of John Donne*, 10 vols., ed. Evelyn Simpson and George Potter (Berkeley and Los Angeles: University of California Press, 1954–62), 6:200, "In this Circumcision, we must cut the *root*, the *Mother-sinne*, that nourishes all our sinnes. . . . It is not the Circumcision of an *Excessive* use of that sinne, that will serve our turne, but such a circumcision, as amounts to an *Excession*, a cutting off the *root*, and *branch*, the *Sinne*, and the *fruits*, the *profits* of that sinne."

23. Moses Maimonides, *The Guide for the Perplexed*, trans. M. Friedländer (New York: Dover, 1956): "Circumcision simply counteracts excessive lust; for there is no doubt that circumcision weakens the power of sexual excitement, and sometimes lessens the natural enjoyment;

the organ necessarily becomes weak when it loses blood and is deprived of its covering from the beginning" (378).

24. Jean Baptiste van Helmont, *Ortus Medicinae* (London, 1648); translated as *Oriatrike, or Physick Refined* (London, 1662), 968.

25. Thomas Browne, "To the deceased Author, Upon the *Promiscuous* printing of his Poems, the *Looser sort*, with the *Religious*," in *The Poems of John Donne*, 372–73.

26. John Bulwer, *Anthropometamorphosis* (London, 1654), 366–68.

27. Thomas Fuller, *The Infants Advocate* (London, 1653), 2–3. But Milton's powerful evocation of God's love, his claim that love exceeds the other motives for the Atonement, differs crucially from Fuller's. For Fuller, as for all the Reformation theologians from Luther and Calvin on, it must be the *Father's* love that precipitates atonement; the human aspect of Christ must not be said to have contributed in any way to the redemption. But the more exceeding love that strikes Milton must, in the context of the discussion of the Son's sacrifice, be considered the Son's love. The beginnings of Milton's Antitrinitarianism might be discerned in this careful distinction between Father and Son; but in a poem designed, at least in part, to justify the Son's subjection to the twin torments of infant circumcision and adult Crucifixion, the unwillingness here to attribute love to the Father is striking.

28. Hugo Grotius, *De veritate religionis Christianae* (1627), translated as *True Religion Explained* (1694), book 5, sect. 11 ("Also of outward circumcision"), p. 81.

29. For Hanford, in "The Youth of Milton" (1925), in *John Milton Poet and Humanist: Essays by James Holly Hanford* (Cleveland: Case Western Reserve University Press, 1966), only here does Milton "achieve[s] real beauty of feeling and expression. . . . The succeeding lines show, to my judgment, a falling off of inspiration" (46).

30. See William Kerrigan, *The Prophetic Milton* (Charlottesville: University Press of Virginia, 1974), who notes that the narrator of Milton's *The Passion* "does not attribute his song to an agent of divine prompting. He never gives up his voice. Here the poem is 'my song,' 'my roving verse' . . . the narrator does not forfeit his voice to a heavenly creator" (200).

31. "I neither lend nor borrow / By taking nor by giving of excess," Antonio told Shylock in *The Merchant of Venice*, employing "excess" as an archaic term for interest. See the *Oxford English Dictionary*, "excess, *n.*," 6c.

32. George Sandys, *A relation of a journey begun An:Dom:1610. Fovre bookes* (London, 1615), 186.

33. Taking note of the difference between Sandys's original description of the rites of Moloch in Sandys and its reappearance in the Nativity ode, Warton articulates brilliantly what it is that Milton, "like a true poet," has omitted: "A new use is made of the cymbals of the disappointed priests. He does not say, 'Moloch's idol *was* removed, to which infants

were sacrificed; *while* their cries *were* suppressed by the sound of cymbals' . . . Milton, like a true poet, in describing the Syrian superstitions, selects such as were most susceptible of poetical enlargement; and which, from the wildness of their ceremonies, were most interesting to the fancy" (ibid.).

Notes to Chapter 9/Rumrich

1. William B. Hunter, "The Provenance of the *Christian Doctrine, Studies in English Literature* (hereafter, *SEL*) 32 (1992): 129–42. Responses by Barbara K. Lewalski and John T. Shawcross, as well as rebuttal by Hunter, follow Hunter's essay under the title "Forum: Milton's *Christian Doctrine,*" 143–66. Hunter added to his case with "The Provenance of the *Christian Doctrine*: Addenda from the Bishop of Salisbury," *SEL* 33 (1993): 191–207. Maurice Kelley and Christopher Hill responded to Hunter in, respectively, "The Provenance of John Milton's *Christian Doctrine:* A Reply to William B. Hunter," and "Professor William B. Hunter, Bishop Burgess, and John Milton," *SEL* 34 (1994): 153–63, 165–93. Hunter's reaction, "Animadversions upon the Remonstrants' Defenses against Burgess and Hunter," appears in the same issue, 195–203. Hereafter, these works will be cited parenthetically according to volume and page number in the text. Hunter's many publications on this topic are collected in *Visitation Unimplor'd: Milton and the Authorship of "De doctrina Christiana"* (Pittsburgh: Duquesne University Press, 1998).

2. Gordon Campbell, Thomas N. Corns, John K. Hale, David I. Holmes, and Fiona Tweedie, "The Provenance of *De doctrina Christiana,*" *Milton Quarterly* 31 (1997): 110. Subsequent references to this report (abbreviated as *MQ*) will appear parenthetically in the text.

3. Gordon Campbell, "*De doctrina Christiana*: Its Structural Principles and Its Unfinished State," *Milton Studies*, vol. 9, ed. James D. Simmonds (Pittsburgh: University of Pittsburgh Press, 1976), 243–60. Maurice Kelley exposed the shortcomings of Campbell's claims and seemed to have settled the dispute in "On the State of Milton's *De doctrina Christiana,*" *English Language Notes* 27 (1989): 43–48.

4. In addition to the introduction (1–20), two essays in *Milton and Heresy*, ed. Stephen B. Dobranski and John P. Rumrich, (Cambridge: Cambridge University Press, 1998), directly address the provenance controversy. See Stephen M. Fallon, "'Elect above the rest': Theology as Self-Representation in Milton," 93–116, and John P. Rumrich, "Milton's Arianism: Why it Matters," 75–92. Also see Fallon, "Milton's Arminianism and the Authorship of *De doctrina Christiana,*" *Texas Studies in Literature and Language* 41 (1999): 103–27. The section of the present essay devoted to the treatise's reception history depends on,

and occasionally repeats, what I wrote in *Milton and Heresy*. The section of this essay that assesses the committee's stylometric analysis of the treatise repeats arguments and wording that also appear in my "Stylometry and the Provenance of *De doctrina Christiana*," in *Milton and the Terms of Liberty*, ed. Graham Parry (Suffolk, England: Boydell & Brewer, 2002), 125–36. In sum, the present essay combines what I have previously written in several other places concerning the provenance controversy and thereby attempts to track its development in a single, coherent argument.

5. Fiona J. Tweedie, David I. Holmes and Thomas N. Corns, "The Provenance of *De doctrina Christiana*, Attributed to John Milton: A Statistical Investigation," *Literary and Linguistic Computing* 13 (1998): 86. Subsequent references to this article (abbreviated as *Computing*) will appear parenthetically in the text.

6. Kelley, *This Great Argument* (Princeton: Princeton University Press, 1941).

7. C. S. Lewis, *A Preface to "Paradise Lost"* (London: Oxford University Press, 1942), 92; C. A. Patrides, "Milton and the Arian Controversy," *Proceedings of the American Philosophical Society* 120 (1976): 245–52.

8. Regina Schwartz, *Remembering and Repeating: Biblical Creation in "Paradise Lost"* (Cambridge: Cambridge University Press, 1988), 13, 31; John Rogers, *The Matter of Revolution* (Ithaca, N.Y.: Cornell University Press, 1996), 130–37; John Leonard, introduction to *Paradise Lost* (London: Penguin, 2000), xix–xx. For a contrary view, see John Rumrich, "Milton's God and the Matter of Chaos," *PMLA* 110 (1995): 1035–46 and *Milton Unbound* (Cambridge: Cambridge University Press, 1996), 118–46.

9. John Milton, *The Complete Prose Works*, 8 vols., gen. ed. Don M. Wolfe (New Haven, Conn.: Yale University Press, 1953–82), 6:308; hereafter cited in the text as YP.

10. William Kerrigan, *The Sacred Complex* (Cambridge, Mass.: Harvard University Press, 1983), 193–262; Stephen M. Fallon, *Milton among the Philosophers: Poetry and Materialism in Seventeenth-Century England* (Ithaca, N.Y.: Cornell University Press), 79–110, 137–243.

11. William B. Hunter, C. A. Patrides and J. H. Adamson, *Bright Essence* (Salt Lake City: University of Utah Press, 1971), 10; Gordon Campbell, "The Son of God in *De doctrina Christiana* and *Paradise Lost*," *Modern Language Review* 75 (1980): 507–14. For rebuttal, see Michael E. Bauman, *Milton's Arianism* (Frankfurt: Peter Lang, 1987).

12. John P. Rumrich, "Milton's Arianism"; see note 4 above.

13. Gregory Chaplin of the University of Texas contributed this citation.

14. See Helen Darbishire, ed., *The Early Lives of Milton* (London: Constable & Co., 1932), 9–10, 29, 31, 45–47, 61, 192.

15. See Dobranski and Rumrich, introduction to *Milton and Heresy*, 1–12.

16. In the mid-eighteenth century, the indebtedness of *Paradise Lost* to previous authors became the basis for suggesting that Milton was no true author, but a plagiarist. See *An Essay upon Milton's Imitations of the Moderns, in His "Paradise Lost"* (London: Printed for J. Payne and J. Bouquet, 1750). The work has long been attributed to William Lauder, a gifted classicist and a forger who inserted into seventeenth century neo-Latin poems (by Masenius and Staphorstius) extracts from a Latin verse rendering of Milton's epic (by William Hog, 1690) so that he could then prove that Milton stole from Masenius and Staphorstius. John Douglas came to Milton's defense in *Milton Vindicated from the Charge of Plagiarism* (London: Printed for A. Millar, 1751). A few years later Lauder renewed his attack on Milton, accusing him of committing precisely Lauder's own fraud. That is, he alleged that Milton contrived to have Pamela's prayer from Sir Philip Sydney's *Arcadia* inserted into King Charles's *Eikon Basilike* so that Milton in *Eikonoklastes* could then accuse the king of plagiarism. See *King Charles I Vindicated from the Charge of Plagiarism Brought against Him by Milton, and Milton Himself Convicted of Forgery, and a Gross Imposition on the Publick* (London: Printed for W. Owen, 1754).

17. Michael Bauman, *A Scripture Index to John Milton's "De doctrina christiana"* (Binghamton, N.Y.: Medieval and Renaissance Texts and Studies, 1989), 9, 176–78.

18. William B. Hunter, "Responses," *MQ* 33 (1999): 34.

19. The draft version of the committee's report, entitled "Milton and *De doctrina Christiana*," was published electronically on October 5, 1996, on the home pages of *Milton Quarterly* and the English Department of the University of Wales, Bangor.

Notes to Chapter 10/Lieb

1. *Milton and Heresy*, ed. Stephen B. Dobranski and John Rumrich (Cambridge: Cambridge University Press, 1998), 1. I am deeply indebted to John T. Shawcross for his astute evaluation of this study and invaluable suggestions and recommendations. As a fellow of the Institute for the Humanities at the University of Illinois at Chicago during the 2000–2001 academic year, I also extend my thanks to the members of the institute, and especially to its director, Mary Beth Rose, for both their assistance and guidance in the writing of this essay.

2. See Christopher Hill, *Milton and the English Revolution* (New York: Viking Press, 1977).

3. Ibid., 285. Hill himself does not hesitate, of course, to argue on behalf of what he feels is Milton's implicit relationship to the under-

ground radical traditions (particularly those centered in the Muggle-tonians) of the seventeenth century.

4. Janel Mueller, "Milton on Heresy," in Dobranski and Rumrich, eds., *Milton and Heresy*, 22–25.

5. References to Milton's works in my text are as follows: References to the poetry are to the *Complete Poetry of John Milton*, ed. John T. Shawcross, 2d ed. rev. (Garden City, N.Y.: Doubleday, 1971). References to Milton's prose by volume and page number are to *The Complete Prose Works of John Milton*, 8 vols. in 10, ed. Don M. Wolfe et al. (New Haven: Yale University Press, 1953–1982), hereafter designated YP. Correspond-ing references to the original Latin (and on occasion to the English translations) are to *The Works of John Milton*, 18 vols. in 21, ed. Frank Allen Patterson et al. (New York: Columbia University Press, 1931–1938), hereafter designated CM.

6. According to Shawcross, ed., *Complete Poetry*, 212 n. 7, Milton in *On the Forcers of Conscience* refers to Thomas Edwards's *Gangraena; or, A Catalogue and Discovery of Many of the Errours, Heresies, Blasphemies and pernicious Practices of the Sectaries of this Time* (London, 1646), which includes Milton's *Doctrine and Discipline of Divorce* under error 154, among the 180 errors or heresies in its arsenal. Also pertinent in this regard is Ephraim Pagitt's *Heresiography; or, A description of the Hereticks and Sectaries of these latter times* (London, 1645). For excerpts on the "heretical Milton" from these and other works, see *Milton's Contemporary Reputation*, comp. William Riley Parker (1940; reprint, New York: Haskell House, 1971), esp. 75–77. For an exhaustive listing of works by and about Milton during the seventeenth century, see *Milton: A Bibliography for the Years 1624–1700*, comp. John T. Shawcross (Binghamton, N.Y.: Medieval and Renaissance Texts and Studies, 1984).

7. David Masson, *The Life of John Milton: Narrated in Connection with the Political, Ecclesiastical, and Literary History of His Time*, 6 vols. (1896; reprint Gloucester, Mass.: Peter Smith, 1965), 3:15. According to Shawcross, "the two earliest uses of *Miltonist* on record specifically refer to a follower of Milton in his views on divorce." See Shawcross's entry "Miltonian, Miltonic, Miltonist," in *A Milton Encyclopedia*, 9 vols., gen. ed. William B. Hunter Jr. (Lewisburg, Va.: Bucknell University Press, 1978–1983), 5:139–40.

8. Although Socinianism and Unitarianism are often viewed as interchangeable, differences between the two emerged in the evolution from the first movement to the second during the later seventeenth century and beyond. See H. John McLachlan, *Socinianism in Seventeenth-Century England* (London: Oxford University Press, 1951), 316–35. Among other studies of the subject, see Earl Morse Wilbur's two books *A History of Unitarianism: Socinianism and Its Antecedents* (Cambridge, Mass.: Harvard University Press, 1946), and *A History of*

Unitarianism: In Transylvania, England, and America (Cambridge, Mass.: Harvard University Press, 1952). The development of Unitarianism is tied to the passing of the Toleration Act (1689) and the publication of the Unitarian Tracts (1691–1703).

9. Hill, *Milton and the English Revolution*, p. 6; H. John McLachlan, *The Religious Opinions of Milton, Locke, and Newton* (Manchester: Manchester University Press, 1941).

10. Hugh MacCallum, *Milton and the Sons of God: The Divine Image in Milton's Epic Poetry* (Toronto: University of Toronto Press, 1986), 55, and passim. For an earlier reading in accord with the idea of associating Milton with the Socinians, see George Newton Conklin, *Biblical Criticism and Heresy in Milton* (New York: Columbia University Press, 1949), 37–40, and passim. Most recently, John Rogers has engaged the Socinian dimensions of Milton's theology. In this volume, see his essay, "Milton's Circumcision," which focuses on the Atonement. Also of significance is his "Delivering Redemption in *Samson Agonistes*" (paper presented at the annual meeting of the Modern Language Association, Chicago, December 1999, and at the meeting of the East Coast Milton Seminar, Princeton, April 2001).

11. McLachlan, *Socinianism in Seventeenth-Century England*, p. 3.

12. See "sozzamente," "sozzare," "sozzezza," "sozzo," "sozzume, sozzura," in *Cassell's Italian Dictionary*, comp. Piero Rebora (New York: Funk and Wagnalls, 1967), and corresponding references in *The Follett / Zanichelli Italian Dictionary*, comp. Giuseppi Ragazzini et al. (Chicago: Follett, 1968), 1716.

13. See the entry on "Socinians" in *A Milton Encyclopedia*, 8:12–13.

14. This summary is indebted to the entry on Socinianism by G. H. Williams in the *New Catholic Encyclopedia*, 16 vols., editorial staff of the Catholic University of America (New York: McGraw-Hill, 1967), 1:397–98.

15. Wilbur, *History of Unitarianism: Socinianism and Its Antecedents*, 39.

16. George Huntstan Williams, ed., *The Polish Brethren: Documentation of the History and Thought of Unitarianism in the Polish-Lithuanian Commonwealth and in the Diaspora, 1601–1685*, 2 vols. (Missoula, Mont.: Scholars Press, 1980), 1:184–85, 188 n. 7. Interestingly, the Polish Brethren (so-called "Socinians") were accused by their enemies of being Arians. The views of the Brethren were similar to those of Michael Servetus. See Piotr Wilczek, "Catholics and Heretics: Some Aspects of Religious Debates in the Old Polish-Lithuanian Commonwealth," available on the Internet at http://www.ruf.rice.edu/~sarmatia/ 499/wilczek.html. For the relationship between Michael Servetus's views and those of Milton, see M. A. Larsen, "Milton and Servetus: A Study in the Sources of Milton's Theology," *PMLA* 41 (1926): 891–934.

17. See, in this regard, George Huntston Williams, *The Radical Reformation* (Philadelphia: Westminster Press, 1962), 756–63.

Racovian Catechism, this doctrinal account is indebted to Wilbur, *History of Unitarianism: Socinianism and Its Antecedents*, 412–14; and Williams, *Radical Reformation*, 750–55.

19. According to *The Racovian Catechism*, with right reason "we could neither perceive with certainty the authority of the sacred writings, understand their contents, discriminate one thing from another, nor apply them to any practical purpose." Scripture is entirely "sufficient for our salvation" (15). References in my text are to *The Racovian Catechism*, trans. Thomas Rees (London: Longman, Hurst, Rees, Orme, and Brown, 1818), hereafter designated *RC*. This version replicates that of the 1652 translation ascribed to John Biddle. See McLachlan, *Socinianism in Seventeenth-Century England*, 187–88, 190–93.

20. "The principal thing is to guard against falling into the common error . . . that there is in God only ONE essence, but that he has three persons." The essence of God "cannot, in any way, contain a plurality of persons." We must always endorse the belief in one God and only one God, and we must ever disavow the belief in the Trinity, for such a belief is simply illogical (*RC*, 33, 44–45).

21. There are four things pertaining to the nature of God, the knowledge of which is necessary for salvation: "first, That God is; secondly, That he is one only; thirdly, That he is eternal; and fourthly, That he is perfectly just, wise, and powerful" (*RC*, 26).

22. For the notion of a preincarnate Son, *The Racovian Catechism* maintains that there is in Scripture no mention of an eternity in which the Son (or the Son of Man) is said to have existed (*RC*, 66, 69). "The Holy Spirit is never expressly called God in the Scriptures. Nor is it to be inferred that it is itself God, or a person of the divinity" (*RC*, 36, 287).

23. "Jesus Christ was truly a man." After his Resurrection, "he was constituted by God both Lord and Christ, made the head of the church, and appointed to be the judge of quick and dead." Christ by nature was "truly a man: a mortal man while he lived on earth, but now immortal." On earth, Christ was not a "mere man." "For being conceived of the Holy Spirit, and born of a virgin, without the intervention of any human being, he had properly no father besides God." At the same time, "he also had a mortal father, of whom Christ was the son" (*RC*, 46, 51–53).

24. On the question of the hypostatical union of divine and human in Christ, *The Racovian Catechism* says: "If by the terms divine nature or substance I am to understand the very essence of God, I do not acknowledge such a divine nature in Christ; for this were repugnant both to right reason and to the Holy Scriptures." As a man, Christ, moreover, possesses only limited knowledge; he is not aware, for example, of the day of judgment (*RC*, 55–56, 59).

25. Through the Resurrection, Christ was begotten "a second time." Once he has undergone Resurrection and Ascension, "he is made to resemble, or, indeed, to equal God" (*RC*, 54, 131).

26. The words "Christ died for us" (1 John 3:16) means not *pro quo* (for whom) but *propter quem* (for [or on account of] whom) (*RC*, 309–10). For *The Racovian Catechism* this distinction is absolutely crucial.

27. The notion of satisfaction is "false, erroneous, and exceedingly pernicious." One cannot conceive that Christ "suffered an equivalent punishment for our sins, and by the price of his obedience exactly compensated our disobedience." It is repugnant to Scripture and to right reason to single out the Crucifixion as the sign of satisfaction (*RC*, 303–6).

28. See the discourse on original sin in Faustus Socinus, *Praelectiones Theologiae Fausti Socini Senensis*, in *Fausti Socini Senensis Opera Omni in Duos Tomos distincta* (Irenopoli, 1656), 540.

29. McLachlan, *Socinianism in Seventeenth-Century England*, p. 31.

30. From Paul M. Zall's entry "Socinians" in *A Milton Encyclopedia*, 8:12–13.

31. Wilbur, *History of Unitarianism: In Transylvania, England, and America*, 184–87.

32. "An Ordinance for the punishing of Blasphemies and Heresies, with the several penalities therein expressed" (May 2, 1648), *Acts and Ordinances of the Interregnum, 1642–1660*, 2 vols., ed. C. H. Firth and R. S. Rait (London: Wyman and Sons, 1911), 1:1133–36. See also "An Act against several Atheistical, Blasphemous, and Execrable Opinions, derogatory to the honor of God, and destructive to humane Society" (August 9, 1650), in *Acts and Ordinances*, 2:409–12.

33. Although the act stipulates the possibility of death for repeat offenders, such extreme measures were not actually carried out.

34. In keeping with Socinian belief, the act interdicts the mortalist belief "that the soul of man dieth or sleepeth when the body is dead" (1:1135). For a fine discussion of Milton's own ambivalent response to the Blasphemy Act, as well as of the significance of his silences in the face of radical sectarian controversies that raged during his career as polemicist, see David Loewenstein, "Milton among the Religious Radicals and Sects: Polemical Engagements and Silences," in *Milton Studies*, vol. 40, ed. Albert C. Labriola (Pittsburgh: University of Pittsburgh Press, 2001).

35. See Francis Cheynell, *The Rise, Growth, and Danger of Socinianism* (London, 1643), and *The Divine Trinunity of the Father, Son, and Holy Spirit* (London, 1650); Pagitt, *Heresiography*; Edwards, *Gangraena*; John Owen, *A Brief Declaration and Vindication of the Doctrine of the Trinity* (London, 1676); Bernard Skelton, *Christus Deus, The Divinity of Our Saviour* (London, 1692); Francis Fullwood, *The Socinian Controversie* (London, 1693); Edward Stillingfleet, *A Discourse Concerning the*

Doctrine of Christ's Satisfaction (London, 1696); and John Tillotson, *A Seasonable Vindication of the B. Trinity* (London, 1693), among many others.

36. Cheynell, *The Rise, Growth, and Danger of Socinianism*, 24, and passim.

37. See Pagitt, *Heresiography*, 134–36, 152–54; and Thomas Edwards, *Gangraena*, 13.

38. McLachlan, *Socinianism in Seventeenth-Century England*, 128–29. See Owen's *Vindiciae evangelicae; or, The Mystery of the Gospel vindicated and Socinianism examined* (London, 1655).

39. Owen, *A Brief Declaration*, 87.

40. Skelton, *Christus Deus*, 7. Pelagius is invoked because Socinianism disavows original sin. For Photinus (as for Socinus), the Son does not exist until the human birth of Christ. Socinus declared that the Son of Mary was a man.

41. Ibid., 10. By the time Skelton was writing, "Socinian" and "Unitarian" had become interchangeable (8). See also Stillingfleet, *Discourse*, iv, xxvii.

42. John Biddle, *The Apostolical and True Opinion concerning the Holy Trinity, Revived and Asserted* (1653; reprint, London, 1691), 1.

43. In *A Brief History of the Unitarians, Called also Socinians, In Four Letters Written to a Friend* (London, 1687), Stephen Nye confirms the view. The whole Scripture "speaks of God as but one Person; and speaks of him and to him by singular Pronouns" (19). Nye ventures this observation in the context of disputing the Trinity. In so doing, he also refines the commonplace conflation of Arianism and Socinianism, both of which were looked upon as nascent forms of the "Judaizing" of godhead. Although both the Arians and the Socinians agree that God is only "one Person," Nye says, "they differ concerning their views of the Son and Holy Spirit. The Son, according to the *Arians*, was generated or created some time before the World, and in process of time. . . . The Holy Ghost (they say) is the Creature of the Son, and subservient to him in the Work of Creation. But the *Socinians* deny that the Son our Lord Christ had any Existence before he was born of Blessed *Mary*, being conceived in her by the holy Spirit of God" (33). According to Nye, both Socinians and Arians are nonetheless called Unitarians and look upon each other as true Christians, "because they agree in the principal Article, that there is but one God, or but one who is God" (34). McLachlan observes that the term "Unitarian" as employed by Nye is used generically for all who believe in the "Unipersonality of the Supreme Being." From that time forth, "Unitarian" was used as a term that embraced Antitrinitarians of various sorts, including Arians, Socinians and Sabellians. It is of some note that Nye's *Brief History* is the first book in which the term "Unitarian" appears on the title page (*Socinianism in Seventeenth-Century England*, 320).

44. References are to John Dryden, *The Poems of John Dryden*, ed. Paul Hammmond (London: Longman, 1995). Similar attitudes were expressed by Alexander Pope in *An Essay on Criticism* (1711), in *The Poems of Alexander Pope*, ed. John Butt (New Haven: Yale University Press, 1963). See especially lines 543–49.

45. McLachlan, *Socinianism in Seventeenth-Century England*, 326. According to McLachlan, the autograph catalog of Locke's library, as well as book lists of works in his possession, reveals how extensive is his collection of Sociniana. McLachlan enumerates the plethora of Socinian titles, both English and continental. These works were Locke's "tools, authorities, and sources for reference, as extracts from his commonplace books reveal" (326–30). See also Dewey D. Wallace Jr., "Socinianism, Justification by Faith, and the Sources of John Locke's *The Reasonableness of Christianity*," *Journal of the History of Ideas*, 45 (1984): 49–66.

46. Alexander Gordon, *Heads of English Unitarian History* (London: Philip Green, 1895), 31, cited by McLachlan, *Socinianism in Seventeenth-Century England*, 326.

47. Such an outlook, one might argue, is present in Locke's other works, such as *An Essay Concerning Human Understanding* (London, 1690) and *Reason and Religion* (London, 1694). John Locke, *The Reasonableness of Christianity, as Delivered in the Scriptures* (1695), in *The Works of John Locke*, 10 vols. (1823; reprint Aalen: Scientia Verlag, 1963). Unless otherwise noted, references to Locke are from this edition.

48. Robert Wallace, *Antitrinitarian Biography; or, Sketches of the Lives of Distinguished Antitrinitarians*, 3 vols. (London: E. T. Whitfield, 1850), 1:406.

49. John Edwards, *Socinianism Unmask'd: A Discourse Shewing the Unreasonableness of a Late Writer's Opinion* (London, 1696), 4, 28–29, and passim. For other contemporary views, see John Milner, *An Account of Mr. Locke's Religion, Out of His Own Writings, and in His Own Words* (London, 1700).

50. *A Second Vindication*, in *The Works of Locke*, 7:859.

51. Locke's first published work, the *Epistola de Tolerantia* (1689) was translated into English by William Popple (1689). This, in turn, was followed by *A Second Letter concerning Toleration* (1690) and *A Third Letter concerning Toleration* (1692). For Miltonic influence on Locke's Letters on Toleration, see John T. Shawcross, " 'Connivers and the Worst of Superstitions': Milton on Popery and Toleration," *Literature and History* 7 (1998): 51–69. Quotations from John Locke, *Epistola de Tolerantia* (1689), trans. J. W. Gough, ed. Raymond Klibansky (Oxford: Clarendon Press, 1968), 96–97, 143–45.

52. Frank E. Manuel, *The Religion of Isaac Newton* (Oxford: Clarendon Press, 1974), 12. As Manuel observes, "during Newton's lifetime nobody cast aspersions on his Anglican orthodoxy," nor did he

participate "in any public manifesto on matters of doctrine" (7). See also McLachlan, *Socinianism in Seventeenth-Century England*, 330–31. For McLachlan, those opinions are decidedly Socinian.

53. The work is entitled "A Historical Account of Two Notable Corruptions of Scripture," a copy of which Newton sent to John Locke. In his response to 1 Timothy 3:16 and 2 John 5:7, Locke argues that both texts are interpolations into later editions of the New Testament and calls into question the biblical authenticity of concept of the "three that bear witness in heaven."

54. Manuel, *Religion of Isaac Newton*, 11–13, 16–18. These manuscripts (and others) have since been published by H. John McLachlan, ed., *Sir Isaac Newton: Theological Manuscripts* (Liverpool: University Press, 1950). These documents (addressing variously the doctrine of the Trinity, the controversy between Arius and Athanasius, the question of the essence that constitutes Father and Son, the nature of Jesus, and the person of the Holy Spirit) are particularly revealing in what they disclose about Newton's theological views. For an early (but still engaging) discussion of much of this material, see Wallace, *Antitrinitarian Biography*, 1:428–68. The "Taskmaster" phrase is Manuel's (16). One assumes that Manuel alludes to Milton's *Sonnet 7*: "As ever in my great task-maisters eye."

55. The first edition of the *Philosophiae naturalis principia mathematica* appeared in 1687. In my treatment of the *Principia*, I refer to *Sir Isaac Newton's Mathematical Principles of Natural Philosophy and His System of the World*, trans. Andrew Motte (1729); rev. and ed. Florian Cajori (Berkeley and Los Angeles: University of California Press, 1946).

56. For an account of Bishop Berkeley's and Leibniz's respective criticisms, see the appendix to Cajori's edition of the *Principia*, 668–69. In his *Principles of Human Knowledge* (1710), Berkeley finds in Locke's treatise a "dangerous dilemma . . . of thinking either Real Space is God, or else that there is something besides God which is eternal, uncreated, infinite, indivisible, unmutable." Both of these notions "may justly be thought pernicious and absurd." In a letter of May 5, 1712, to one Hartsoeker (a Dutch physician at Dusseldorf), Leibniz, in turn, questions Newton's arguments on similar grounds.

57. *Principia*, 545–46. For additional statements on the nature of God, see Newton's *Opticks; or, A Treatise of the Reflections, Refractions, Inflections, and Colours of Light*, 4th ed. (London, 1730), passim. The issues raised in the Berkeley / Leibniz responses to the first edition of the *Principia* continued beyond the second edition. In that context, the issues were further developed in the exchange between Leibniz and Samuel Clarke. See *The Leibniz-Clarke Correspondence, Together with Extracts from Newton's "Principia" and "Opticks,"* ed. H. G. Alexander (New York: Philosophical Library, 1956). Especially interesting is Leibniz's charge that Sir Isaac Newton and his followers have a very "odd opinion

concerning the work of God." "According to their doctrine, God Almighty wants to wind up his watch from time to time: otherwise it would cease to move." For Leibniz, the Newtonians conceive God as a clockmaker "obliged to clean" and "mend" his mechanism now and then (11). This approaches Deism. See John Leland, *A View of the Principal Deistic Writers*, 3 vols. (London, 1757).

58. Manuel, *Religion of Isaac Newton*, 57–64.

59. McLachlan, *Socinianism in Seventeenth-Century England*, 330–31.

60. Maurice Kelley, introduction to *Christian Doctrine* in *YP* 6:68.

61. Zall, "Socinians," in *A Milton Encyclopedia*, 8:13.

62. The 1651 version is consistent with the earlier Latin versions. In the 1651 version, the place of publication is listed as Racovia but is in fact London. As indicated earlier, an English translation appeared as *The Racovian Catechism* in 1652. The translation has been attributed to John Biddle.

63. References are to John T. Shawcross's entries on William Dugard and *The Racovian Catechism*, in *A Milton Encyclopedia*, 2:183–84 and 7:88–89, respectively. For accounts of the affair, see Masson, *Life of John Milton*, 4:438–39; and William Riley Parker, *Milton: A Biography*, 2 vols., 2nd ed. and rev. by Gordon Campbell (Oxford: Clarendon Press, 1996), 1:395; 2:994. For pertinent documents, see J. Milton French, *The Life Records of John Milton*, 5 vols. (New Brunswick: Rutgers University Press, 1954), 3:157, 206.

64. Shawcross, entry on *The Racovian Catechism*, in *A Milton Encyclopedia*, 7:88. For a discussion of Aitzema, see Paul R. Sellin's entry on Lieuwe van Aitzema in *A Milton Encyclopedia*, 1:34–35. The Aitzema document, along with a translation, appears in French, *Life Records*, 3:206.

65. "Licensing Milton's heresy," in Dobranski and Rumrich, ed., *Milton and Heresy*, 139–58. Dobranski maintains that "with so little evidence corroborating Aitzema's report, we ought to hesitate before using the episode to judge Milton's activities as licenser." See Dobranski's treatment in *Milton, Authorship, and the Book Trade* (Cambridge: Cambridge University Press, 1999), pp. 125–53. Reproducing the report in *Life Records*, French notes that he has not seen the original manuscript, held in the Dutch Archives in The Hague, and admits that its authenticity "is not certain" (144).

66. Dobranski, "Licensing Milton's heresy," 143.

67. It has been conjectured that the Bodleian copy of the marginal notes to Paul Best's *Mysteries Discovered* (1647) are by Milton. The attribution was first made by the Unitarian R. Brook Aspland in *The Christian Reformer*, n.s. 9 (1853): 561–63; and in his *Paul Best, The Unitarian Reformer* (London, 1853), 13–15. Because of Best's Socinian leanings, the attribution (were it true) might go far to help establish even further Milton's ties to the Socinians. The notes to Best are printed in the CM

18:341–44 (along with editorial confirmation, 18:572), and the Miltonic authorship is asserted on various occasions, most importantly, in McLachlan, *Socinianism in Seventeenth-Century England*, 160–62. Had the Miltonic authorship been established, the substance of the notes would have confirmed a Socinian Milton, beyond the shadow of a doubt. But such was not to be. In his "Milton and the Notes on Paul Best," *Library*, 5th ser. 5 (1950): 49–51, Maurice Kelley establishes beyond a doubt that Milton is not the author of the notes.

68. The attribution is that of Arnold Williams, in his notes to his edition of *Tetrachordon* in YP 2:604 n.

69. See my discussion of this passage in "Milton and 'Arianism,'" *Religion and Literature* 32 (2000): 197–220.

70. In Parker, *Milton*, 1:628.

71. See Masson, *Life of John Milton*, 6:690–99; Parker, *Milton*, 1:622–29; Stavely, preface to *Of True Religion*, in YP 8:408–15; Henry, "Milton's Last Pamphlet: Theocracy and Intolerance," in *A Tribute to George Coffin Taylor*, ed. Arnold Williams (Chapel Hill: University of North Carolina Press, 1952), 197–210; and Henry's entry, "*Of True Religion*," in *A Milton Encyclopedia*, 6:22. See also Sanchez, "'Worst of Superstitions,'" *Prose Studies* 9 (1986): 21–38. More recently, see Sanchez, *Persona and Decorum in Milton's Prose* (Madison, N.J.: Fairleigh Dickinson University Press, 1997). My brief overview of the events that prompted the publication of Milton's *Of True Religion* is indebted to the foregoing.

72. The Apostles' Creed (which professes belief in God the Father, Jesus Christ the Son, and the Holy Spirit) is the statement of faith adopted not only by Roman Catholics but by Anglican and many Protestant churches as well. Although the creed was traditionally looked upon as a document composed by the 12 apostles, it is the product of the early church. It reached its final form in the late sixth or early seventh century. In his *Apology for Smectymnuus*, Milton counters the argument "that if we must forsake all that is Rome's, we must bid adieu to our Creed." In response, Milton declares: "I had thought that our Creed had been of the Apostles; for so it beares title." But if it must be abandoned in order to do away with the Catholic Church, "let her take it." For, he says, "we can want no Creed, so long as we want not the Scriptures" (YP 1:943). The Bible itself is the ultimate "creed."

73. The association would have been so automatic as to obviate the need for proof. In Milton's own works, see texts ranging from the "Attack on the Scholastic Philosophy" in the third *Prolusion* (YP 1:240–48) to the references in *Animadversions* to "doltish and monasticall School-men" (YP 1:718) and in the *Doctrine and Discipline of Divorce* to "those *decretals, and sumles sums*, which the *Pontifical Clerks* have doted on" ever since the birth of Catholic divines with their "scholastick Sophistry, whose overspreading *barbarism*" has corrupted the church (YP 2:350–51). The attitude is reflected throughout his career.

74. Among those who interpret the passage differently, the most

outspoken is William B. Hunter, *Visitation Unimplor'd: Milton and the Authorship of "De Doctrina Christiana"* (Pittsburgh: Duquesne University Press, 1998). Hunter adopts the passage from *Of True Religion* to argue on behalf of Milton's orthodox Trinitarianism. Approaching the passage from the perpective of "statement" and "response," Hunter argues that the phrase "a mystery indeed in their Sophistic Subtilties, but in Scripture, a plain Doctrin" is Milton's response to the Arian and Socinian position. According to Hunter, "such a division of the sentences shows clearly that Milton recognizes the position of the Arians and Socinians but flatly rejects 'their Sophistic Subtilties' to accept the 'plain Doctrin' of Trinitarian scripture" (103–4). I am convinced, however, that Hunter misreads.

75. See Hunter, *Visitation Unimplor'd*, which provides a detailed account of the issues that define the debate, one that continues unabated to this day. In this volume, see John Rumrich, "The Provenance of *De Doctrina Christiana*: A View of the Present State of the Controversy." For an astute reading of the very notion of Miltonic authorship, see Joseph Wittreich, "'Reading' Milton: The Death (and Survival) of the Author," in *Milton Studies*, vol. 38, *John Milton: The Writer in His Works*, ed. Albert C. Labriola and Michael Lieb (Pittsburgh: University of Pittsburgh Press, 2000), 40–42.

76. I have considered these matters in connection with my "Milton and 'Arianism.'" In my own thinking about the matter, I have moved beyond the almost dismissive gesture (common to essays that address matters of theology in Milton) of saying something like "For the sake of discussion, I shall assume that Milton authored *De Doctrina Christiana*." Such statements are no longer meaningful. In fact, in my discussion of *De doctrina Christiana*, I shall refer not to "Milton" but to the "author" of the tract. Even this is misleading, however, for, given the scribal changes that were incorporated into the tract, the work itself might well be considered of composite authorship. Dates of possible composition are conjectural. These include the following: before 1641, 1643–1645, 1655–1658, 1658–1660, and 1660 or later. For an excellent summary of some of the important issues, see John M. Steadman's entry on the *De doctrina Christiana*, in *A Milton Encyclopedia*, 2:111–19.

77. Compare the corresponding chapters in *The Racovian Catechism*, sec. 1, chaps. 1–3, devoted to the authenticity and authority of Scripture. Although *The Racovian Catechism* acknowledges the possibility that certain aspects of Scripture have been corrupted in transmission, none of these corruptions is sufficient to compromise the full meaning of the text (*RC*, 5).

78. Compare *The Racovian Catechism*: "Although some difficulties do certainly occur in them; nevertheless, those things which are necessary to salvation, as well as many others, are so plainly declared in different passages, that every one may understand them" (17). In *De*

doctrina Christiana, the discussion of "the right method of interpreting the Scriptures" (including knowledge of languages, consideration of intent, ability to distinguish between literal and figurative meaning, attention to context and willingness to compare one text with another) is iterated in a corresponding passage in *The Racovian Catechism* (18).

79. This runs contrary to the Socinian belief in the absolute power of reason. Without right reason, "we could neither perceive with certainty the authority of the sacred writings, understand their contents, discriminate one thing from another, nor apply them to any practical purpose" (*RC*, 15).

80. As has been noted before, the emphasis upon number is a significant characteristic of Milton's *Artis Logicae*, particularly in the association it advances between number and essence: "Things which differ in number also differ in essence . . . : *Here let the Theologians take notice [Evigilent hic Theologi]*" (YP 8:233; CM 11:58–59). The passage has been variously interpreted. See Hunter, *Visitation Unimplor'd*, 115–16.

81. In his note to this passage in YP, Maurice Kelley cites *The Racovian Catechism* for an analogous view (6:213 n. 32).

82. See Kelley's editorial note to this passage in YP 6:419–20 n. 18. Kelley cites the ancient Jewish-Christian sect of Ebionism as a source as well. William B. Hunter approaches Milton's views on the Incarnation from the perspective of Nestorianism. See Hunter's "Milton on the Incarnation," in *Bright Essence: Studies in Milton's Theology*, ed. William B. Hunter et al. (Salt Lake City: University of Utah Press, 1971), 131–48.

83. Another departure concerns the all-important matter of "satisfaction." Whereas the Socinians categorically dismissed the idea of Christ's satisfaction in the atonement for sins in the Crucifixion, the author of *De doctrina Christiana* endorses the doctrine of satisfaction without qualification. "SATISFACTION means that CHRIST AS THEANTHROPOS FULLY SATISFIED DIVINE JUSTICE BY FUL-FILLING THE LAW AND PAYING THE JUST PRICE ON BEHALF OF ALL MEN [PRO OMNIBUS]." The argument for the efficacy of "satisfaction" in *De doctrina Christiana* appears to be taking into account the precise argument against the efficacy of "satisfaction" among the Socinians, who argue, we recall, that the words "Christ died for us" (1 John 3:16) mean not "pro quo" (for whom) but "propter quem" (for [or on account of] whom). See the discussion in *De doctrina Christiana* (YP 6:443–46; CM 15: 314–15, 322–25). Milton endorses the doctrine of satisfaction throughout his poetry. See *Upon the Circumcision* (lines 20–21); *Paradise Lost* 3.209–12, 294–97; 12.415–35.

84. Introduction to John T. Shawcross, ed., *Milton: The Critical Heritage* (London: Routledge, 1970), 25.

85. In *The Early Lives of Milton*, ed. Helen Darbishire (1932; reprint, New York: Barnes and Noble, 1965), 188–92. See John T. Shawcross's entry on John Toland in *A Milton Encyclopedia*, 8:69–70. For the genesis

of the idea of a "System of Divinity" among Milton's early biographers, see Hunter's *Visitation Unimplor'd*, 19–33.

86. In *A Milton Encyclopedia*, 8:69–70. "Toland's first book *Christianity Not Mysterious*, finished while he was still a student at Oxford, was published in 1696 and plunged him into religious controversy, which raged the rest of his life. He espoused deism and Socinianism against the orthodox view, and brought his beliefs into his 'Life of Milton.'" In response to Toland's "Life," Reverend Offspring Blackall published *Remarks on the Life of Mr. Milton* (1699). Responding to Blackall, Toland, in turn, defended himself in *Amyntor: or, A Defense of Milton's Life* (1699). Other tracts followed; see *A Milton Encyclopedia*, 8:69.

87. See *Christianity not Mysterious; or, A Treatise Shewing, That there is nothing in the Gospel Contrary to Reason, Nor Above it: And that no Christian Doctrine can be properly call'd A MYSTERY* (London, 1696). Interestingly, this tract ventures statements that appear to be critical of Arianism and Socinianism: Neither the Arians nor the Socinians "can make their Notions of a *dignifi'd and Creature-God capable of Divine Worship,* appear more reasonable than the Extravagancies of other Sects touching the Article of the *Trinity*" (25). In response to Toland's tract, Thomas Beverly published *Christianity, the great mystery in answer to a late treatise: Christianity not mysterious, that is, not above, not contrary to reason* (London, 1696), as well as other tracts such as Jean Gailhard's *The blasphemous Socinian heresie disproved and confuted* (London, 1697). Among the Socinian works attributed to John Toland is *Socinianism truly Stated; Being An Example of fair Dealing in all Theological Controversys . . . Recommended by a Pantheist to an Orthodox Friend* (London, 1705). Providing an excellent overview of Socinian doctrine, this tract is supposed to represent the first instance of the use of the word "pantheist." In this regard, see Toland's *Pantheisticon* (New York: Garland, 1976).

88. John Dennis, "The Grounds of Criticism in Poetry" (1704), in *The Critical Works of John Dennis*, 2 vols., ed. Edward Niles Hooker (Baltimore: The Johns Hopkins Press, 1939), 1:344–45.

89. Jonathan Richardson, *Explanatory Notes and Remarks on Milton's "Paradise Lost." By J. Richardson, Father and Son. With the Life of the Author, and a Discourse on the Poem. By J. R. Sen.* (1734), in *Milton 1732–1801: The Critical Heritage*, ed. John T. Shawcross (London: Routledge, 1972), 84.

90. See the selections from the *Gentleman's Magazine* (1738) in Shawcross, ed., *Milton 1732–1801*, 93–98.

91. See Theophilus Lindsey, *The Apology of Theophilus Lindsey, M.A., on the Resigning the Vicarage of Catterick, Yorkshire* (Dublin, 1774).

92. References are to the entry on Theophilus Lindsey in *The Dictionary of National Biography*, 29 vols., ed. Sir Leslie Stephen and Sir Sidney Lee (London: Oxford University Press, 1917), 11:1196–97.

93. Theophilus Lindsey, *A Sequel to the Apology on Resigning the Vicarage of Catterick, Yorkshire* (London, 1776), 404–9. For further discussion of Lindsey's views of Milton, see Wallace, *Antitrinitarian Biography*, 1:331–33. See Thomas Newton's edition of *Paradise Lost*, 2 vols. (London, 1749). According to Shawcross, Newton "produced the most reprinted life of Milton and the texts generally employed for editions of Milton's poems during the last half of the eighteenth century" (*Milton 1732–1801*, 153). McLachlan notes that in later years Samuel Taylor Coleridge also found Socinianism in *Paradise Regained*. According to Coleridge, Milton had "represented Satan as a sceptical Socinian . . . as knowing the prophetic and Messianic character of Christ, but sceptical as to any higher claim." On the other hand, John Keats, whose brother George was a Unitarian, "failed to discern the heretical tendencies" in Milton. See McLachlan, *The Religious Opinions of Milton, Locke, and Newton*, 18–19). For the Romantic contexts of Milton's works, see *The Romantics on Milton: Formal Essays and Crtitical Asides*, ed. Joseph Wittreich (Cleveland: Case Western Reserve University Press, 1970).

94. *An Historical View*, xxi–xxii. Lindsey also produced *Two Dissertations: I. On the Preface to St. John's Gospel. II. On Praying to Jesus Christ* (London, 1778). In section 1 of *On Praying to Jesus Christ*, Lindsey invokes *Paradise Lost* 2.561: "And found no end, in wandring mazes lost" (66).

95. Charles R. Sumner, "Preliminary Observations," in *A Treatise of Christian Doctrine, Compiled from the Holy Scriptures Alone*, trans. Charles R. Sumner (Cambridge: Cambridge University Press, 1825), xxxiii–xxxv. Shortly after its discovery in 1823, the treatise was known as *De Dei Cultu*. See William B. Hunter, "*De Doctrina Christiana: Nunc Quo Vadis?*" *Milton Quarterly* 34 (October 2000): 98.

96. Francis E. Mineka, "The Critical Reception of Milton's *De Doctrina Christiana*," *University of Texas Studies in English* 22 (1943): 115–47. See also Maurice Kelley, "The Recovery, Printing, and Reception of Milton's *Christian Doctrine*," *Huntington Library Quarterly* 31 (1967): 35–41.

97. "Harrowing" quote from *Evangelical*, n.s. 3 (1825): 507, cited in Mineka, "Critical Reception," 119; "Socinians of Poland" quote from *Evangelical*, n.s. 4 (1826): 51, cited in Mineka, 121.

98. *Congregational Magazine* 8 (1825): 588, cited in ibid., 127.

99. *Gentleman's Magazine* 95 (1825): 344–45, cited in ibid., 141. In response to the publication of *De doctrina Christiana* and the review of it in the periodical literature, Samuel Taylor Coleridge, in *The Notebooks*, 4 vols., ed. Kathleen Coburn and Merton Christiansen, Bollingen Series L (Princeton: Princeton University Press, 1990), expressed astonishment at the views of God and the godhead reflected in the theological treatise. Alluding to the treatise in the context of earlier discussions of the Socinian movement, Coleridge maintains (May–November 1825) that

De doctrina Christiana prompts one to "exclude all Philosophy! Extinguish all Ideas! Hold in contempt all Church Tradition," and "in short, depose at once Reason & the Church from the Chair of Interpretation." As applied to "Absolute Being," Milton's words (for Coleridge) are "nonsense." The very idea of what such thoughts of godhead may lead to is "shriek of a Delirium!" According to Coleridge, Arians and, by implication, Socinians will "reap the harvest" of such an endeavor. The Deists, the Boehmenists, and the Swedenborgians, among others, fall into the same camp (vol. 4, items 4797, 5213, 5262). I am grateful to Mark Canuel for alerting me to this material.

100. Shawcross, introductions to *Milton: The Critical Heritage,* 25; and *Milton 1732–1801: The Critical Heritage,* 26, calls attention to Henry John Todd, Milton's important nineteenth century editor, whose revision of his fourth variorum edition in 1842 "registers shock and disbelief and acceptance and discomfort. Todd did not want to accept Arian influence on *Paradise Lost,* and yet he could not deny its tenets in *De doctrina Christiana.* The poem and its author had fallen irretrievably in his judgment." Of corresponding interest is the figure of Thomas Burgess, bishop of Salisbury, of whom Hunter provides interesting accounts in *Visitation Unimplor'd,* 4–7, and passim. Burgess, who disputed the notion of the Miltonic authorship of *De doctrina Christiana,* produced *Milton Not the Author of the Lately Discovered Arian Work "De Doctrina Christiana," Three Discourses, Delivered at the Anniversary Meetings of the Royal Society of Literature, in the Years 1826, 1827, and 1828, to which is Added Milton Contrasted with Milton and with the Scriptures* (London: Thomas Brettell, 1829). Of particular interest is the section entitled *Milton Contrasted with Milton and with the Scriptures,* which constructs two personas, that of the orthodox Trinitarian Milton of *Paradise Lost* and that of the heterodox Antitrinitarian (that is, Arian *and* Socinian or Unitarian) Milton of *De doctrina Christiana.* For Burgess, one is entirely incompatable with the other. Alluding to Samuel Johnson's observation in his *Life of Milton* (1779) that "Milton appears to have had full conviction of the truth of Christianity, and to have been untainted with any heretical peculiarity of opinion," Burgess remains steadfast in his adherence to the orthodox Milton (165–66). Even Burgess, however, is prompted to acknowledge the distinctly "*human* existence" of Jesus in *Paradise Regained,* an idea, Burgess suggests, apparently at odds with "the eternal Divinity of the Son of God" in *Paradise Lost.* For a brief moment, the persona of a Socinian Milton arises in Burgess's criticism, but the idea is entertained, only to be dismissed (171–72). For additional commentary, see James Ogden, "Bishop Burgess and John Milton," *Bibliographical and Contextual Studies,* nos. 29 and 30 (1997), 79–98.

101. Mineka, "Critical Reception," 130–33.

102. *Monthly Repository,* 20 (1825): 692, cited in ibid., 131.

103. References are to the entry on William Ellery Channing in *Ame-*

rican National Biography, 24 vols., gen. eds. John A. Garraty and Mark C. Carnes (New York: Oxford University Press, 1999), 4:680–81. The estimate of Channing as "the single most important figure in the history of American Unitarianism" is from David Robinson, *The Unitarians and the Universalists* (Westport, Conn.: Greenwood Press, 1985), 229.

104. *American National Biography*, 4:681.

105. References to Channing's *Remarks on the Character and Writings of John Milton* are to the third edition (Boston: Benjamin Perkins, 1828), hereafter cited in the text by page number. The work was originally issued in *The Christian Examiner* (1826). For an extended study of Channing's treatment of Milton's *De doctrina Christiana*, among his other works, see Kevin P. van Anglen, *The New England Milton: Literary Reception and Cultural Authority in the Early Republic* (University Park, Pa.: The Pennsylvania State University Press, 1993), 81–108. According to van Anglen, Channing's *Remarks* is "the most important treatment of Milton by any Unitarian" (82). During Channing's lifetime, his essay came under attack on the Trinitarian front by the Reverend Frederick Beasley of New Jersey in a pamphlet that questioned the theological arguments of *De doctrina Christiana* and emphasized those aspects of *Paradise Lost* that bore an anti-Unitarian imprint (105). Van Anglen also explores what he calls "The Unitarian Milton," that is, the reception of Milton among the New England Unitarian community (40–79). Important to the Unitarian reception of Milton's works, including *De doctrina Christiana*, is Robin Grey, *The Complicity of Imagination: The American Renaissance, Contests of Authority and Seventeenth Century English Culture* (Cambridge: Cambridge University Press, 1997), esp. 38–45. See also Keith W. F. Stavely, *Puritan Legacies: "Paradise Lost" and the New England Tradition, 1630–1890* (Ithaca, N.Y.: Cornell University Press, 1987).

106. Along with Milton's "Antitrinitarianism," Channing is determined to see in *De doctrina Christiana* a lack of conviction in the author's treatment of the doctrine of satisfaction: "With respect to Christ's mediation, he [Milton] supposes, that Christ saves us by bearing our punishment, and in this way satisfying God's justice. His views indeed are not expressed with much precision, and seem to have been formed without much investigation" (94).

107. It is interesting that by the time Ralph Waldo Emerson produced his lecture "John Milton" (1835), in *The Early Lectures of Ralph Waldo Emerson*, 3 vols., ed. Stephen E. Wicher et al. (Cambridge: Harvard University Press, 1959–72), Emerson is able to dismiss the discovery of *De doctrina Christiana* in 1823 as an event of only passing interest: "But the new-found book having, in itself, less attraction than any other work of Milton, the curiosity of the public as quickly subsided, and left the poet to the enjoyment of his permanent fame" (p. 145). For a discussion of the influence of Canning's review on Emerson's essay, see van Anglen, *New England Milton*, 109–37.

Select Publications of Joseph Wittreich

Books

Angel of Apocalypse: Blake's Idea of Milton. Madison: University of Wisconsin Press, 1975.

Visionary Poetics: Milton's Tradition and His Legacy. San Marino, Calif.: Huntington Library, 1979.

"Image of that Horror": History, Prophecy, and Apocalypse in "King Lear." San Marino, Calif.: Huntington Library, 1984.

Interpreting "Samson Agonistes." Princeton: Princeton University Press, 1986. Winner of the James Holly Hanford Award presented by the Milton Society of America, 1987.

Feminist Milton. Ithaca, N.Y.: Cornell University Press, 1987.

Shifting Contexts: Reinterpreting "Samson Agonistes." Pittsburgh: Duquesne University Press, 2002.

Editions

The Romantics on Milton: Formal Essays and Critical Asides. Cleveland: Press of Case Western Reserve University, 1970.

Calm of Mind: Tercentenary Essays on "Paradise Regained" and "Samson Agonistes." Cleveland: Press of Case Western Reserve University, 1971.

Blake's Sublime Allegory: Essays on The Four Zoas, Milton, and Jerusalem. Edited with Stuart Curran. Madison: University of Wisconsin Press, 1973.

Milton and the Line of Vision. Madison: University of Wisconsin Press, 1975.

Composite Orders: The Genres of Milton's Last Poems. Edited with Richard Ide. A special issue of *Milton Studies*, vol. 17. Pittsburgh: University of Pittsburgh Press, 1983.

The Apocalypse in English Renaissance Thought and Literature. Edited with C. A. Patrides. Ithaca, N.Y.: Cornell University Press, 1984.

Soundings of Things Done: Essays on Early Modern Literature in Honor of S. K. Heninger Jr. Edited with Peter Medine. Newark: University of Delaware Press, 1997.

Altering Eyes: New Perspectives on "Samson Agonistes." Edited with Mark R. Kelley. Newark: University of Delaware Press, 2002.

Pamphlets

William Blake's Illustrations for John Milton's "Paradise Regained." Cleveland: Rowfant Club Publication, 1971.

Monographs

"William Blake: Illustrator-Interpreter of *Paradise Regained*," 93–132; "Milton's Illustrators and Their Subjects, 1713–1816," 309–29; and "A Catalogue of Blake's Illustrations to Milton," 331–42. In *Calm of Mind*.

"Opening the Seals: Blake's Epics and the Milton Tradition." In *Blake's Sublime Allegory*, 23–58.

"'The Crown of Eloquence': The Figure of the Orator in Milton's Prose Works." In *Achievements of the Left Hand: Essays on Milton's Prose Works*, ed. Michael Lieb and John T. Shawcross, 3–54. Amherst: University of Massachusetts Press, 1974.

"'A Poet Among Poets': Milton and the Tradition of Prophecy." In *Milton and the Line of Vision*, 92–142.

"Milton's Illustrators, 1645–1954." In *A Milton Encyclopedia*, vol. 4. Edited by William B. Hunter Jr. et al., 55–78. Lewisburg, Pa.: Bucknell University Press, 1978.

"The Apocalypse: A Bibliography." In *The Apocalypse in English Renaissance Thought and Literature*, 369–440.

"'John, John, I Blush for Thee!': Mapping Gender Discourses in *Paradise Lost*." In *Out of Bounds: Male Writers and Gender Criticism*. Edited by Laura Claridge and Elizabeth Langland, 22–54. Amherst: University of Massachusetts Press, 1990.

"'Inspir'd with Contradiction': Mapping Gender Discourses in *Paradise Lost*." In *Literary Milton: Text, Pretext, Context*. Edited by Diana Treviño Benet and Michael Lieb, 132–59. Pittsburgh: Duquesne University Press, 1994.

"'Under the Seal of Silence': Repressions, Receptions, and the Politics of *Paradise Lost*." In *Soundings of Things Done*, 293–323.

"'Reading' Milton: The Death (and Survival) of the Author." In *John*

Milton: The Writer in His Works. Edited by Albert C. Labriola and Michael Lieb, 10–46. Pittsburgh: University of Pittsburgh Press, 2000. A special issue of *Milton Studies*, vol. 38.

"*Samson Agonistes:* Thought Colliding with Thought." In *Altering Eyes: New Perspectives on "Samson Agonistes."*

Articles

"Milton, Man and Thinker: Apotheosis in Romantic Criticism." *Bucknell Review* 16 (1968): 64–84.

"The 'Satanism' of Blake and Shelley Reconsidered." *Studies in Philology* 65 (1968): 816–33.

"Milton's 'Destin'd Urn': The Art of *Lycidas.*" *PMLA* 84 (1969): 60–70.

"Domes of Mental Pleasure: Blake's Epics and Hayley's Epic Theory." *Studies in Philology* 69 (1972): 201–29.

"'Sublime Allegory': Blake's Epic Manifesto and the Milton Tradition." *Blake Studies* 4 (1972): 15–44.

"Milton's *Areopagitica:* Its Isocratic and Ironic Contexts." In *Milton Studies*, vol. 4. Edited by James D. Simmonds, 101–15. Pittsburgh: University of Pittsburgh Press, 1972.

"The Dating of Shelley's 'On the Devil, and Devils.'" *Keats-Shelley Journal* 22 (1973): 80–102 (written with Stuart Curran).

"'Divine Countenance': Blake's Portrait and Portrayals of Milton." *Huntington Library Quarterly* 38 (1975): 125–60.

"Blake's Milton: 'To Immortals, . . . A Mighty Angel.'" In *The Presence of Milton.* Edited by Balachandra Rajan, 51–82. Pittsburgh: University of Pittsburgh Press, 1978. A special issue of *Milton Studies*, vol. 11.

"Perplexing the Explanation: Marvell's 'On Mr. Milton's *Paradise Lost.*'" In *Approaches to Andrew Marvell: York Tercentenary Lectures.* Edited by C. A. Patrides, 280–305. London: Routledge & Kegan Paul, 1978.

"Painted Prophecies: The Tradition of Blake's Illuminated Books." In *Blake in His Time.* Edited by Robert N. Essick and Donald Pearce, 101–15. Bloomington: Indiana University Press, 1978.

"Beelzebub." In *Milton Encyclopedia*, 1:133–38.

"Portraits of Milton." In *Milton Encyclopedia*, 6:202–9.

"From Pastoral to Prophecy: The Genres of *Lycidas.*" In *Milton Studies*, vol. 13. Edited by James D. Simmonds, 59–80. Pittsburgh: University of Pittsburgh Press, 1979.

"'The Illustrious Dead': Milton's Legacy and Romantic Poetry." *Milton and the Romantics* 4 (1980): 17–32.

"'All Angelic Natures Joined in One': The Council Scenes in *Paradise Lost.*" In *Composite Orders: The Genres of Milton's Last Poems*, 43–74.

"'Image of that Horror': The Apocalypse in *King Lear.*" In *The Apocalypse in English Renaissance Thought and Literature*, 175–206.

"'The Poetry of the Rainbow': Milton and Newton Among the Prophets." In *Poetic Prophecy in Western Literature*. Edited by Jan Wojcik and Raymond-Jean Frontain, 94–105, 202–3. Madison, N.J.: Fairleigh Dickinson University Press, 1984.

"'Strange Text!': PARADISE REGAIN'D . . . To Which Is Added *Samson Agonistes.*" In *Poems in Their Place: The Intertextuality and Order of Poetic Collections*. Edited by Neil Fraistat, 164–94. Chapel Hill: University of North Carolina Press, 1986.

"'In Copious Legend, or Sweet Lyric Song': Typology and the Perils of the Religious Lyric." In *Bright Shootes of Everlastingnesse: The Seventeenth-Century Religious Lyric*. Edited by Ted-Larry Pebworth and Claude J. Summers, 192–215. Columbia: University of Missouri Press, 1987.

"'The Work of Man's Redemption': Prophecy and Apocalypse in Romantic Poetry." In *The Age of William Wordsworth: Critical Essays on the Romantic Tradition*. Edited by Kenneth R. Johnston and Gene M. Ruoff, 39–61, 347–48. New Brunswick, N.J.: Rutgers University Press, 1987.

"Apocalypse." In *A Spenser Encyclopedia*. Edited by A. C. Hamilton et al., 89–93. Toronto: University of Toronto Press, 1989.

"'He Ever Was a Dissenter': Milton's Transgressive Maneuvers in *Paradise Lost.*" In *Arenas of Conflict: Milton and the Unfettered Mind*. Edited by Charles W. Durham and Kristin P. McColgan, 21–40. Selinsgrove, Pa.: Susquehanna University Press, 1997.

"Laboring into Futurity." In *Blake, Politics, and History*. Edited by Jackie DiSalvo, Christopher Z. Hobson and G. A. Rosso, 136–43. New York: Garland Press, 1998.

"Milton's Trangressive Maneuvers: Receptions (Then and Now) and the Sexual Politics of *Paradise Lost.*" In *Milton and Heresy*. Edited by John P. Rumrich and Stephen B. Dobranski, 244–66. Cambridge: Cambridge University Press, 1998.

About the Contributors

SHARON ACHINSTEIN is a University Lecturer and Fellow at St. Edmund Hall, Oxford, having recently taught at the University of Maryland. Her *Literature and Dissent in Milton's England* is forthcoming from Cambridge University Press.

LYNNE GREENBERG received her Ph.D. from The City University of New York in June 2001, and is now an Assistant Professor at Hunter College, CUNY. She has a J.D. from the University of Chicago Law School. She has published essays on Milton, English legal history and First Amendment and copyright law.

MARK R. KELLEY has presented papers on the relationships between Milton's work and Euripides', a copy of whose plays include Milton's annotations. With Joseph Wittreich he co-edited *Altering Eyes: New Perspectives on 'Samson Agonistes'* (Newark, Del.: University of Delaware Press, 2002).

MICHAEL LIEB is Professor of English and Research Professor of Humanities at the University of Illinois at Chicago. His most recent books include *Children of Ezekiel: Aliens, UFOs, the Crisis of Race, and the Advent of End Time* (Durham: Duke University Press, 1998); *Milton and the Culture of Violence* (Ithaca, N.Y.: Cornell University Press, 1994); and *The*

Visionary Mode: Biblical Prophecy, Hermeneutics, and Cultural Change (Ithaca, N.Y.: Cornell University Press, 1991), as well as other books and collections of essays on Milton. The recipient of fellowships from the Guggenheim, ACLS and NEH, Lieb is currently writing a book on Milton's theology and doctrine of godhead.

PETER E. MEDINE is Professor of English at the University of Arizona. He received his B.A. from Northwestern University and his M.A. and Ph.D. from the University of Wisconsin at Madison, and has held research fellowships at the Folger Shakespeare Library and the Huntington Library. He is author or editor of five books and various articles. His critical edition of Roger Ascham's *Toxophilus* was published in 2003.

DAVID NORBROOK is Merton Professor of English Literature at the University of Oxford. Among his publications are *Writing the English Republic: Poetry, Rhetoric, and Politics, 1627– 1660* (Cambridge: Cambridge University Press, 1999), presented with the James Holly Hanford Award of the Milton Society of America for 1999, and an edition of Lucy Hutchinson's *Order and Disorder* (Oxford: Blackwell, 2001).

ANNABEL PATTERSON is the Sterling Professor of English at Yale University. A recent book is *Early Modern Liberalism* (Cambridge: Cambridge University Press, 1997); more recent is *Nobody's Perfect: A New Whig Interpretation of History* (2002).

JOHN ROGERS, Professor of English and Master of Berkeley College at Yale University, is the author of *The Matter of Revolution: Science, Poetry, and Politics in the Age of Milton*, as well as articles on seventeenth century literature and culture. He is currently at work on a book, *Milton's Passion*, which examines Milton's failure to write about the Crucifixion in the context of early modern Antitrinitarianism.

JOHN P. RUMRICH is Thamen Professor of English at the University of Texas, Austin, and editor of *Texas Studies in Literature and Language.* His publications on Milton include *Matter of Glory: A New Preface to "Paradise Lost"* (Pittsburgh: University of Pittsburgh Press, 1987); *Milton Unbound* (Cambridge: Cambridge University Press, 1996); and *Milton and Heresy* (Cambridge: Cambridge University Press, 1998), edited with Stephen B. Dobranski.

JOHN T. SHAWCROSS, Professor of English, Emeritus, University of Kentucky, is author of *John Milton: The Self and the World* (Lexington: University Press of Kentucky, 1993), *The Uncertain World of "Samson Agonistes"* (Cambridge: D. S. Brewer, 2001), and the forthcoming *Milton: A Bibliography for the Years 1624–1700: Revised and for the Years 1701–1799* (Tempe, Ariz.: Medieval and Renaissance Texts and Studies).

SUSANNE WOODS is Provost and Professor of English at Wheaton College, Massachusetts, and Adjunct Professor of English at Brown University, where she taught for many years and was founding director of the Women Writers Project. She has edited *The Poems of Aemilia Lanyer* (New York: Oxford University Press, 1993), and written the critical study *Lanyer: A Renaissance Woman Poet* (New York: Oxford University Press, 1999), and with Margaret P. Hannay, *Teaching Tudor and Stuart Women Writers* (New York: Modern Language Association, 2000). In addition to numerous articles on Milton and on Renaissance poetry, she published a book on the development of English verse, *Natural Emphasis: English Versification from Chaucer to Dryden* (San Marino, Calif.: Huntington Library Press, 1985).

Index